Ethics in Practice

ETHICS *in* PRACTICE

Lawyers' Roles, Responsibilities, and Regulation

Edited by

D E B O R A H L . R H O D E

OXFORD
UNIVERSITY PRESS

OXFORD
UNIVERSITY PRESS

Oxford   New York
Auckland   Bangkok   Buenos Aires   Cape Town   Chennai
Dar es Salaam   Delhi   Hong Kong   Istanbul   Karachi   Kolkata
Kuala Lumpur   Madrid   Melbourne   Mexico City   Mumbai   Nairobi
São Paulo   Shanghai   Singapore   Taipei   Toyko   Toronto

Copyright © 2000 by Oxford University Press, Inc.

First published in 2000 by Oxford University Press, Inc.
198 Madison Avenue, New York, New York 10016

First issued as an Oxford University Press paperback, 2003

Oxford is a registered trademark of Oxford University Press

Library of Congress Cataloging-in-Publication Data
Ethics in practice: Lawyers' roles, responsibilities, and regulation
/ edited by Deborah L. Rhode.
p. cm.
Includes bibliographical references.
ISBN 978-0-19-516767-2
1. Legal ethics—United States. I. Rhode, Deborah L.
KF306 .E844 2000
174'.3'0973—dc21   99-058064

Printed in the United States of America
on acid-free paper

For Thomas LeBien and Mary Tye

Preface

Lawyers' ethics have been condemned for centuries, but only in the last few decades have they been the subject of significant education and research. *Ethics in Practice* brings together leaders of this emerging field to explore longstanding problems of professonalism. Those problems are a matter of public as well as professional concern. Attorneys play a central role in the structure of legal, economic, and political institutions. The principles that guide professional practice have crucial social consequences.

Those principles are the subject of the essays that follow. The contributors to this volume bring diverse perspectives but share common concerns. They come from different disciplinary backgrounds and draw on varied frameworks in addition to law, including philosophy, psychology, economics, sociology, history, political science, management, and organizational behavior. Yet these authors also are united in their conviction that lawyers have public obligations that have not been adequately institutionalized in practice. Despite a growing cottage industry of commissions, conferences, and committees on professionalism, many dilemmas of professional responsibility remain unsolved. This collection provides a better understanding of what stands in the way. In the process, it identifies strategies that may narrow the gap between the ideals and institutions of legal practice.

To that end, the volume begins with an overview of the central ethical challenges facing the profession. "Ethics in Practice" explores the complex relationships between incentives, institutions, and ideologies that give rise to problems of professionalism. Its focus includes the economic and organizational structures of practice, the constraints of an adversarial system, the social context of workplace inequalities, and the limitations of ethical rules and enforcement strategies. Unless the bar becomes more willing to address the underlying forces that erode professional values, a sharp disjuncture will persist between lawyers' rhetorical commitments and daily practices.

The essays in Part I take up that challenge. Anthony Kronman identifies the core features of "The Law as a Profession" and the social responsibilities that they imply. His basic premise is that lawyers play a central role as stewards of our private affairs and public institutions. That role imposes a "duty to the common good and integrity of the [legal] system." Law is "a generalist's craft that engages the whole personality of the practitioner" and links him to a tradition of crucial cultural importance. Law as a "public calling" supplies a counterweight to private concerns, and lawyers serve as essential mediators between individual interests and social values.

Robert Gordon makes a similar claim in explaining "Why Lawyers Can't Just Be Hired Guns." Although the bar has "fallen out of the habit" of discussing its social responsibilities except on ceremonial occasions, those responsibilities need to be central constituents of daily practice. The legal system is a common good that cannot survive if participants pursue purely self-regarding objectives. Law presents ample opportunities for delay, deception, and harassment. Neither the justice system, nor the democratic market structures that it sustains, can function effectively in the face of unrestrained self-interest. As trustees of that system, attorneys have obligations to maintain the procedural frameworks and cultural values on which the rule of law depends. Adherence to basic principles such as honesty, fairness, and good faith is necessary to preserve a structure that serves the long-term interest of both lawyers and clients. Professionalism needs to be seen not simply as a ceremonial ideal but as a practical necessity in legal culture.

Part II explores the role of ethical theory and ethical rules in fostering that sense of professionalism. Lynn Sharp Paine, drawing on her background both in law and business ethics, makes the case for "Moral Thinking in Management." Like Gordon and Kronman, she sees social responsibility as an essential capacity in legal counseling. To achieve sustained profitability over time, businesses must pursue profits in ways that are morally acceptable. Corporate managers need advisers who engage in "principled consequentialist" analysis—who evaluate options within a "framework of general principles to advance the well-being of corporate stakeholders."

By contrast, Geoffrey Hazard questions the effectiveness of such frameworks in resolving concrete ethical dilemmas. Although he does not disagree with the appropriateness of moral analysis or with approaches like the one Paine proposes, he is skeptical about the capacity of abstract principles to illumine the "limits of justifiable conduct or the meaning of justification." In the practice of law, "viewed unromantically," virtues of autonomy, truth, and impartiality cannot be fully realized. To make appropriate tradeoffs in particular circumstances requires situational judgments. Moral philosophy has its limits in identifying the bounds of partisanship or coping with inequalities in the distribution of legal services.

David Luban's essay on "Wrongful Obedience" points up further limitations of ethical theory in guiding ethical conduct. Luban takes as his starting point Stanley

Milgram's famous obedience studies. Almost all of Milgram's subjects complied with instructions to deliver what they believed were painful electrical shocks, although almost no survey participants expected that they personally would do so, or believed that compliance would be morally acceptable. Luban attributes this result to a "corruption of judgment." Subjects initially agreed to deliver what seemed to be painless shocks and were directed to escalate in degrees. Rather than admit that their prior compliance was morally problematic, most individuals continued to follow instructions as the voltage edged into the danger zone. Luban suggests that a similar dynamic may explain certain common pathologies of legal practice. For example, when lawyers yield to pressure from colleagues or clients to engage in abusive discovery tactics, they often develop rationalizations that distort their assessments of what constitutes abuse. Evasion, obfuscation, and delay are condemned in principle but normalized in practice. There are no simple correctives, but promising options include reducing situational pressures and increasing lawyers' understanding of the processes likely to skew judgment.

The essays in Part III suggest further explanations and stategies for the pathologies of practice. Carrie Menkel-Meadow's survey of the "The Limits of Adversarial Ethics" identifies chronic problems that arise in competitive, combative approaches to dispute resolution. Self-interested presentations by partisan advocates with unequal information and resources can distort outcomes. For some controversies, the adversary system's reliance on oppositional frameworks and win/lose outcomes may produce less effective resolutions than problem-solving approaches that incorporate more party participation and remedial flexibility. Our legal needs would be better served by greater choice among "appropriate dispute resolution procedures." If lawyers saw their role "less as zealously representing clients' interests and more as solving clients'—as well as society's—problems," then changes in legal ethics would also be necessary and desirable. Attorneys should have obligations to inform clients about all possible methods of meeting their legal needs. In the course of representation, attorneys should not conceal relevant facts, deceive third parties, or participate in outcomes that they have reason to know would cause substantial injustice. In essance, lawyers " should do no harm" and should "treat all parties to a legal matter as they would wish to be treated themselves."

Such rules of conduct would help address the problems that Austin Sarat identifies in "Ethics in Litigation." However, his analysis also reveals the barriers to obtaining and enforcing more ethically demanding norms. The economic structures of practice reward adversarial excesses. Many clients want a "take no prisoners" approach and law firms' hourly billing systems make it profitable to satisfy those desires. Although surveyed lawyers and judges are critical of the incivility, deception, and delay that often accompany litigation practice, they tend to put blame anywhere and everywhere else. Judges fault lawyers who see discovery as a cash cow and professionalism as symbolic window dressing. Lawyers fault judges who see little to gain from sanctioning attorney misconduct. In-house counsel condemn firms for maxi-

mizing fees, not results. Defense lawyers blame plaintiffs' lawyers for bringing frivolous claims, and plaintiffs' lawyers blame defense lawyers for withholding evidence
and waging wars of attrition. All too often, ethical problems are treated as "someone
else's problems," and those with greatest power in the profession see themselves as
powerless to develop solutions. Given such attitudes, Sarat does not underestimate
the obstacles to reform, but he does propose some promising directions for it to take.
The judicial system should provide more resources and support for monitoring discovery abuse. Sanctions for misconduct should be more frequent and severe, and
should target law firms as well as individual practitioners. Firms should make ethical
behavior a priority in training, mentoring, and evaluation. In effect, the bar needs
structural incentives that are more consistent with professional aspirations.

While many adversarial pathologies involve overly zealous representation of
client interests, other ethical problems arise from underrepresentation of those interests or difficulties in identifying what those interests are. Part IV addresses these issues. William Simon's essay on "Lawyer Advice and Client Autonomy" explores the
inadequacy of conventional ethical norms in dealing with these concerns. The traditional assumption has been that attorneys' central responsibility is to pursue clients'
objectives zealously within the bounds of the law. But "any plausible conception of
good practice requires lawyers to make judgments about the client's interests and to
influence clients to accept those judgments." The point is not that lawyers should act
paternalistically, by substituting their conception of the client's well-being for that of
the client. Rather, the point is that in most legal representation, autonomous client
decision making is impossible. Attorneys inevitably will exert influence through their
selection, presentation, and evaluation of information. Drawing on one of his own
cases from practice, Simon demonstrates how two attorneys' contrasting descriptions of the same plea bargain dramatically shifted a client's preferences. The assumption that lawyers should simply respect autonomous client choices has per-
sisted less because it is an accurate description of the counseling relationship than
because it absolves lawyers of awkward responsibilities. If clients can independently
judge their own interests, then attorneys are relieved of that burden. This is especially
convenient in contexts like criminal defense, legal services, or public interest representation, where lawyers are underfunded and overextended and clients cannot afford to educate counsel fully about their goals and values. Yet if, as Simon suggests,
totally autonomous decisions are impossible, then lawyers cannot escape the ethical
responsibilities of "connection." They have an obligation to learn enough about their
clients to provide assistance that serves those individuals' interests in fact as well as
form.

Susan Koniak and George Cohen advocate similar responsibilities when the
client is an entity. "In Hell There Will Be Lawyers Without Client or Law" chronicles
the ethical problems that arise in class action representation. For such contexts, neither procedural rules nor bar disciplinary requirements impose sufficient obligations. In theory, lawyers must "adequately represent" the class. In practice, no con-

stituency often has sufficient incentives to police that requirement. Opponents use issues of class representation strategically, or collusively, to extract concessions in settlement negotiations, not to prevent overreaching by opposing counsel. Individual class members generally lack enough information or stake in the outcome to second guess their attorney's performance. Overburdened trial judges are reluctant to raise problems that will prolong not resolve the controversy. The resulting lack of oversight creates obvious risks of abuse, given the common misalignment of lawyers' and clients' interests. Outside public interest contexts, class counsel generally are most concerned with maximizing fees; class members typically are most concerned with maximizing recoveries. The problems are compounded when different subgroups of the class have competing interests and lawyers can trade some members' remedial opportunities in exchange for generous fees. Here again, effective responses will require structural reforms. More concrete obligations to class members need to be established and enforced. The central challenge, however, lies in finding some constituency with sufficient influence and incentives to institutionalize such reforms.

Part V of the volume addresses lawyers' personal identities and professional values, and the obligations that they impose in practice. In "Beyond 'Bleached Out' Professionalism," David Wilkins explores the role that race, gender, and ethnicity should play in lawyers' choices about clients to represent or strategies to pursue. For example, should a black lawyer defend a Grand Dragon of the Ku Klux Klan if the First Amendment rights at issue are important to civil rights organizations? Should lawyers ever consider race in assigning lawyers to particular cases, or in deciding where to hold a trial? Is it legally permissible or ethically appropriate for a female attorney to accept only female clients in divorce cases? Wilkins's answer is that the legitimacy of invoking race or gender depends on the context. The legal system has a strong stake in affirming equal rights before the law. And in some circumstances, such as selection of clients, no countervailing concerns are sufficient to justify discrimination based solely on race, gender, or similar characteristics. But in other settings, ignoring racial and gender differences will simply perpetuate them. Prosecuting racially freighted cases in counties likely to produce an all-white jury would not, in Wilkins's view, enhance either the fact or appearance of justice. Group treatment is a pervasive feature of America's social and legal landscape, and neutrality in formal principles will not necessarily correct for biases in cultural practices. Identity matters in law as in life, and lawyers have a professional responsibility to consider both the short- and long-term consequences of race and gender consciousness in particular factual contexts.

Lawyers as a group have similar responsibilities. In "Contested Identities: The Bias Task Forces and the Obligations of the legal Profession," Deborah Hensler and Judith Resnik trace the bar's efforts to live up to that responsibility. Almost sixty state and federal courts have commissioned reports on gender and/or racial bias. Like other initiatives that involve identity politics, their results have been condemned as too radical and not radical enough. Critics from the right have dismissed findings of bias as insignificant or unrepresentative, while critics from the left have objected to the "sugar coated" tone in which serious problems have been presented. Navigating these political minefields has been no small challenge. As Hensler and Resnik note, the task-force movement has made a major contribution to social justice by making bias visible and placing it on the professional agenda. But the greatest challenge remains: building the support necessary for effective reforms.

My own final essay in the collection explores a similar challenge in institutionalizing other professional values. "Cultures of Commitment: Pro Bono for Lawyers and Law Students" describes the gap between the rhetoric and reality of the bar's involvement in public service. Although ethical codes present pro bono assistance to underrepresented groups as a professional obligation, a majority of lawyers provide no such aid, and the average for the profession as a whole is under a half an hour a week. So too, despite accreditation requirements that law schools offer opportunities and encouragement for pro bono activities, most students graduate without pro bono experience. The bar's failure to secure broader participation in public service is all the more disappointing when measured against the extraordinary successes that such work has yeilded. Many of the nation's landmark public interest cases have grown out of lawyers' voluntary contributions, and such work has given purpose and meaning to lawyers' professional lives. Drawing on a broad array of interdisciplinary research, this final essay explores strategies that could foster broader cultures of commitment to public service within legal education and the legal profession.

This collection offers no easy answers to the core ethical dilemmas of legal practice. But the contributions taken as a whole identify the crucial questions and the most promising responses. Of all the responsibilities of professionals, none is more important than continuing scrutiny of what those responsibilities require in practice.

Contents

Contributors

GEORGE M. COHEN is Professor of Law and Edward F. Howrey Research Professor at the University of Virginia. His scholarly interests include economic analysis of lawyering and professional responsibility.

ROBERT W. GORDON is the Fred A. Johnson Professor of Law at Yale University. His work focuses on the history and contemporary responsibilities of the legal profession.

GEOFFREY C. HAZARD JR. is the former Director of the American Law Institute in Philadelphia, and Emeritus Trustee Professor of Law, University of Pennsylvania. His writings include *The Law of Lawyering* with William Hodes (1997) and *The Law and Ethics of Lawyering* with Susan Koniak and Roger Cramton (1994).

DEBORAH R. HENSLER is the John W. Ford Professor of Dispute Resolution at Stanford Law School. She is the author of *A Glass Half Full: A Glass Half Empty* (1995).

SUSAN P. KONIAK is a Professor of Law at Boston University. Her writings include *The Law and Ethics of Lawyering* (3rd ed. 1994) with Geoffrey C. Hazard Jr. and Roger C. Cramton, and numerous articles on legal ethics and class action practice.

ANTHONY T. KRONMAN is the Dean and Edward J. Phelps Professor of Law at Yale University. He published *The Lost Lawyer* in 1995.

DAVID J. LUBAN is the Frederick J. Haas Professor of Law and Philosophy at the Georgetown University Law Center in Washington, D.C. He is the author of *Lawyers and Justice* (1998) and coauthor of *Legal Ethics* (1995) with Deborah L. Rhode.

CARRIE MENKEL-MEADOW is a Professor of Law at the Georgetown University Law Center in Washington, D.C., and Chair of the Georgetown-CPR Institute of Dispute Resolution Commission on Ethics and Standards in ADR. She has written extensively on professional responsibilities in the legal profession and on alternative dispute resolution.

LYNN SHARP PAINE is a Professor at the Graduate School of Business Administration, Harvard University, and author of the book *Cases in Leadership, Ethics, and Organizational Integrity: A Strategic Perspective* (1996).

JUDITH RESNIK is the Arthur Liman Professor at Yale Law School, where she teaches and writes about federalism, procedure, large-scale litigation, and feminism. Her recent essays include *Trial as Error, Jurisdiction as Injury: Transforming the Meaning of Article III*, published in 113 *Harvard Law Review* 924 (2000), and *Asking About Gender in Courts* in 21 *Signs: Journal of Women in Culture and Society* 952 (Summer 1996).

DEBORAH L. RHODE is the Earnest W. McFarland Professor of Law at Stanford Law School and Director of the Keck Center on Legal Ethics and the Legal Profession. Her publications include *Professional Responsibility: Ethics by the Pervasive Method* (1998) and *Legal Ethics* (1995) with David Luban.

AUSTIN SARAT is the William Nelson Cromwell Professor of Jurisprudence and Political Science at Amherst College. He is the author of *Cause Lawyering* with Stuart Scheingold (1998), *Justice and Power in Sociolegal Studies* with Bryant G. Garth (1998), and *Everyday Practices and Trouble Cases* with Marianne Constable and David Engel (1998).

WILLIAM SIMON is the William and Gertrude Saunders Professor of Law at Stanford Law School and the author of *The Practice of Justice* (1998).

DAVID B. WILKINS is the Kirkland and Ellis Professor at Harvard Law School. His scholarship focuses both on professional responsibility and racial identity. His publications include "Race, Ethics, and the First Amendment: Should a Black Lawyer Represent the Ku Klux Klan?" (1995).

Ethics in Practice

1

Ethics in Practice

DEBORAH L. RHODE

Law, as Reinhold Niebuhr once noted, is a "compromise between moral ideas and practical possibilities."[1] The same is true of legal ethics. How lawyers reconcile the tension between moral aspirations and pragmatic constraints is important not just for the profession but also for the public. Lawyers play a crucial role in the structure of our private affairs and social institutions. This role carries multiple, sometimes competing responsibilities to clients, courts, and society generally. Lawyers also face conflicts between their professional obligations and personal interests. A central challenge of legal practice is how to live a life of integrity in the tension between these competing demands.[2]

This essay, like the collection that it introduces, provides an overview of ethics in practice. Most issues are matters of long-standing concern: Plato's condemnation of advocates' "small unrighteous souls" has echoed for centuries.[3] But while lawyers' ethics have never lacked for critics, only recently have they become a subject of formal rules and significant study. Not until 1969 did the American Bar Association (ABA) adopt a Model Code of Professional Responsibility with binding disciplinary rules. And not until 1974 did the ABA require law schools to offer instruction in legal ethics. Yet the decades that followed have witnessed an outpouring of codification, commentary, and curricular initiatives on professional responsibility. In the mid-1980s, the ABA adopted a revised set of standards, the Model Rules of Professional Conduct, and national, state, and local bar organizations launched a wide range of professionalism efforts: commissions, courses, centers, conferences, and codes.[4]

Despite this cottage industry, chronic ethical dilemmas remain unresolved. Part of the problem involves a lack of consensus about what the problems are, and what values should be most central to professional life. But at least some aspirations are broadly shared. The public deserves reasonable access to legal assistance and to

3

legal processes that satisfy minimum standards of fairness, effectiveness, and integrity. And the profession deserves conditions of practice that reinforce such standards in the service of social justice.

Such values, however self-evident in theory, have proven difficult to realize in practice. Much of the difficulty involves the bar's failure to address the institutional and ideological structures that compromise moral commitments. The discussion that follows focuses on these structures: the economic conditions, adversarial premises, and regulatory frameworks that shape ethics in practice. Until the bar addresses the underlying forces that drive professional choices, a wide gap will persist between the ideals and institutions of lawyers' working lives.

The Economic Structures of Practice

In some respects, the bar is a victim of its own success. No occupation offers a surer path to affluence and influence. Law is the second highest paying profession, and lawyers play leading roles in the nation's political and economic life.[5] Yet the expectation of doing well *and* doing good has proven increasingly difficult to realize, at least at the level that most practitioners hope to achieve. The last half century has brought fundamental changes in the structure of professional practice that are at odds with professional values. Competition and commercialism are increasing; collegiality and civility are headed in the opposite direction. Most practitioners agree that those trends will continue.[6] There is little corresponding consensus about what, if anything, to do about it.

Legal practice has become increasingly competitive along multiple dimensions. Over the past three decades, the legal profession has more than doubled in size. The growing number of lawyers has intensified competition and diminished the informal reputational sanctions once available in smaller professional communities. Heightened price consciousness among corporate clients, together with the erosion of anti-competitive restraints, also has forced closer attention to the bottom line. These pressures have led to more instability in client and collegial relationships and more constraints on professional independence. Sophisticated purchasers are increasingly likely to shop for representation on particular matters, rather than to build long-term relationships with a single lawyer or law firm.

Such trends have yielded some benefits in terms of increased efficiency and responsiveness to client concerns. But they have come at a considerable cost. As private practice becomes more competitive and transactional, lawyers face greater pressure to accept troubling cases or to satisfy clients' short-term desires at the expense of other values. Without a stable relationship of trust, it is risky for counsel to protest unreasonable demands or to deliver unwelcome messages about what legal rules or legal ethics require. In the study of litigation abuse described in Austin Sarat's essay, one participant put it bluntly: there is "no market for ethics."[7] If clients want to play hard ball, lawyers may come to see it as the only game in town.

Increases in the size and competitiveness of legal workplaces have had other unwelcome effects. As organizations grow larger, collegiality and collective responsibility become more difficult to sustain. So too, as partnership becomes harder to achieve and less likely to insure job security, fewer lawyers feel long-term institutional loyalty. Such environments offer inadequate incentives for mentoring junior attorneys and monitoring collegial conduct. It is, in short, a culture of increasing competition and declining commitment; clients are less committed to lawyers, lawyers are less committed to firms, and partners are less committed to associates.

Preoccupation with the bottom line has compromised other commitments as well, and one obvious casualty is pro bono work. Few lawyers come close to satisfying the ABA's Model Rules of Professional Conduct, which provide that "a lawyer should aspire to render at least 50 hours of pro bono publico legal services per year," primarily to persons of limited means or to organizations assisting such persons.[8] In fact, most attorneys offer little such assistance; the average for the profession as a whole is less than one half hour a week.[9] Part of the reason involves firm policies that fail to count pro bono activity toward billable-hour requirements or to value it in promotion and compensation decisions.[10]

Such policies undermine lawyers' personal and professional values. Pro bono contributions play an important, however partial, role in meeting the bar's unrealized commitment to equal access under law. Such work also has been crucial in giving purpose and meaning to professional life. Practitioners who lack the time or support for such experiences often feel short-changed. Indeed, the greatest source of disappointment among surveyed lawyers is the sense that they are not "contributing to the social good."[11] The bar's failure to provide more support for pro bono activities represents a significant lost opportunity for the profession as well as the public.

Another troubling byproduct of the preoccupation with profit has been the escalation of working hours. Over the last half century, lawyers' average billable hours have increased from between 1,200 and 1,500 hours per year to between 1,800 and 2,000. What has not changed are the number of hours in a day. To charge honestly at current levels, given average amounts of nonbillable office time, requires 60-hour weeks.[12] Expectations at most large firms are even greater. Such sweatshop schedules have compromised professional values in several respects. It has become increasingly difficult to insure equal opportunity for lawyers with substantial family and community commitments. Excessive workloads also create pressures to inflate hours and contribute to psychological difficulties that impair performance.

Working schedules are a major cause of the continued glass ceiling for women in the legal profession. Although 45 percent of new entrants to the bar are women, they fail to advance as far or as fast as men with similar credentials and experience.[13] As is clear from the gender bias task forces reviewed in Deborah Hensler and Judith Resnik's essay below, women remain significantly underrepresented in positions carrying greatest power, status, and economic rewards. Part of the explanation lies in female attorneys' disproportionate share of family obligations and the unwillingness of legal employers to make appropriate accommodations. Most law firms are what sociologists label "greedy institutions."[14] They preach an ethic of total availability and equate reduced schedules with reduced commitment. Lawyers with competing values generally end up with second-class status. Many drop off partnership and leadership tracks, leaving behind a decision-making structure insulated from their concerns.

That process takes a toll, not just on those with family commitments but on the profession as a whole. Lawyers have fewer opportunities for the community involvement, public service, and personal enrichment that build professional judgment and sustain a socially responsible culture. Even when measured in more narrow economic terms, current workplace priorities yield short-term profits at the expense of long-term gains. Employers who allow flexible and reduced schedules typically find increases in efficiency, morale, recruitment, and retention.[15] The inadequacy of such opportunities in legal practice, together with the escalation of "normal" working hours, also carries a substantial cost. Overwork is a leading cause of lawyers' job dissatisfaction, and their exceptionally high rates of stress, depression, and substance abuse.[16] Such personal problems are, in turn, a primary cause of neglect, incompetence, and related performance problems.[17]

The preoccupation with profit and billable hours contributes to other troubling conduct, particularly on matters involving legal fees. As Chief Justice Rehnquist has observed, if practitioners are expected to meet current billing requirements, "there are bound to be temptations to exaggerate the hours put in."[18] These temptations have fostered a range of abuses, reflecting everything from flagrant fraud and "creative timekeeping" to intentional inefficiency. The frequency of such abuses is difficult to gauge and police because it is often impossible to verify whether certain tasks are necessary and whether they require, or actually consume, the time charged for completing them. However, 40 percent of surveyed lawyers acknowledge that some of their work is influenced by a desire to bill additional hours, and auditors find questionable practices in about a quarter to a third of the bills that they review.[19] Such practices include inflating hours, overstaffing cases, performing unnecessary work, or double billing multiple clients for the same task. Under an hourly billing system, the temptation is to leave no stone unturned as long as lawyers can charge by the stone. In a few egregious cases, personal expenditures have been recast as litigation expenses: dry cleaning for a toupee, or running shoes labeled "ground transportation."[20] Such examples, together with the high cost of routine legal services, have fueled public skepticism about the fairness of lawyers' fees. Fewer than 5 percent of Americans believe that they get good value for the price of legal services.[21]

Although corporate clients have become more adept at monitoring and comparing prices, some abuses remain difficult to detect. Unsophisticated one-shot purchasers are especially vulnerable. Many of these individuals lack adequate information to assess the reasonableness of charges for nonroutine services. And in most class action litigation, no individual plaintiff will have sufficient incentives to challenge attorneys' fees. Nor will any one else. As Susan Koniak's and George Cohen's essay in this volume makes clear, opposing parties may agree to unduly generous compensation for counsel if it substantially reduces remedies for the class.[22] Overburdened trial courts often are reluctant to second guess such settlement provisions if the effect will be to prolong time-consuming litigation.

This absence of oversight creates obvious potential for abuse, particularly in contingent fee cases. For middle- and lower-income clients, the only way to finance litigation is generally through contingency agreements. These arrangements give counsel a share of any recovery, and no payment if the case is unsuccessful. Although such fee agreements are a crucial means of providing access to legal assistance, they often present conflicts of interest. Attorneys generally would like the highest possible return on their work; clients would like the highest possible recovery. For most claims of low or modest value, lawyers want a quick settlement. It frequently does not pay to prepare a case thoroughly and hold out for the best terms available for the client. Conversely, in high-stakes cases, once lawyers have invested substantial time, they may have more to gain from gambling for a large recovery than clients with inadequate incomes and immediate needs.[23]

A related problem is that a lawyer's return bears no necessary relationship to the amount of work performed or to the risk actually assumed. In many cases where liability is clear and damages are substantial, the standard one-third recovery will provide a windfall for the attorney. If defendants make an early settlement offer, plaintiffs' lawyers can end up with huge fees for minimal services. In some widely publicized cases, the amount of work actually done was so insignificant that it would amount to an hourly rate between $20,000 and $35,000.[24] In theory, clients can challenge contingency arrangements that yield unreasonable fees. In practice, few individuals do so because litigation is expensive and judges have been unreceptive. Courts lack the capacity to monitor even a small fraction of the approximately one million new contingent-fee cases filed each year.[25]

Trial judges also lack the ability or inclination to insure effective representation in other contexts, particularly in criminal cases involving appointed counsel for indigent defendants.[26] Yet the economic conditions of practice for these lawyers work against adequate trial preparation. Most cases are handled either by grossly understaffed public defenders or by private practitioners who receive minimal flat fees or low hourly rates. Compensation generally is capped at wholly unrealistic levels, often a $1,000 or under for felony cases. Thorough preparation is a quick route to financial ruin.[27] Defendants who hire their own counsel do not necessarily fare better. Most of these individuals have incomes just over the poverty line and cannot afford substantial legal expenses. Their lawyers typically charge a flat fee, payable in advance, which creates obvious disincentives for extensive work. These economic conditions help account for the high frequency of plea bargains in indigent criminal defense. About 90 percent of defendants plead guilty, and in the large majority of these cases counsel have interviewed no prosecution witnesses and filed no defense motions.[28]

These are not, however, the cases that attract media attention. The result is a wide gap between public perception and daily practice. Most Americans believe that the justice system coddles criminals and that lawyers routinely get their clients off on technicalities. In the courtrooms that the public sees, zealous advocacy is the norm. O. J. Simpson's lawyers left no angle unexplored. But their reputations were on view and their client could afford to pay. Neither is true in the vast majority of criminal cases. For many defendants, it is better to be rich and guilty than poor and innocent.

Yet seldom are judges with already unmanageable caseloads willing to oversee counsels' performance. In one representative survey, courts rejected 99 percent of claims alleging ineffective assistance of counsel.[29] The extent of judicial tolerance is well illustrated by a Texas murder case, in which a defense lawyer fell asleep several times during witnesses' testimony and spent only five to seven hours preparing for trial. In rejecting claims of ineffective representation, the judge declared that "[t]he Constitution says that everyone is entitled to an attorney of their choice. But the Constitution does not say that the lawyer has to be awake."[30]

Nor does the Constitution say that the poor are entitled to any legal assistance for civil matters. In the absence of explicit guarantees, or adequate government funding for poverty law programs, over four-fifths of the legal needs of the poor remain unmet.[31] Many middle-income Americans also are priced out of the market for services. An estimated one-third of their personal legal problems are not addressed and many collective concerns go unremedied.[32] Less than one percent of the nation's lawyers are engaged in full-time public interest practice, and the resources to pursue legal issues of broad social importance fall far short.[33] Not only do a vast array of needs lack any representation, but others are ineffectively addressed because the parties cannot afford the necessary assistance. Equal access to justice is what we enshrine on courthouse doors, not what we institutionalize in practice.

These inadequacies in legal services pose ethical issues for lawyers on both an individual and collective level. What are lawyers' responsibilities when they personally confront situations in which important interests are inadequately represented? And what are lawyers' responsibilities when they design rules for the profession in a world of unequal representation? Prevailing adversarial structures have worked against ethically satisfying responses. A system that presupposes equal, zealous representation of opposing interests copes poorly in a world of unequal resources, information, and incentives.

The Structure of an Adversarial System

The central premise of the American legal system is adversarial; it assumes that the pursuit of truth and protection of rights are best achieved through partisan presentations of competing interests. Under this framework, the basic obligation of American lawyers is to advance their clients' objectives "zealously within the bounds of the law."[34] According to the Preamble of the Model Rules of Professional Conduct, "when an opposing party is well represented, a lawyer can be a zealous advocate on behalf of a client and at the same time assume that justice is being done."[35]

There are a number of difficulties with this assumption. The first is that it equates procedural and substantive justice. Whatever emerges from the clash of partisan adversaries is presumed to be just. But even if both parties are well represented, the result may be inequitable because the underlying law or process is flawed. Wealth, power, and prejudice can skew legislative and legal outcomes. Decision makers may lack access to relevant information; single-interest groups may exercise undue influence over governing laws; unconscious race or gender bias may compromise trial judgments; and formal rules may be under- or overinclusive because the costs of fine tuning are too great. Moreover, the assumption that lawyers' role is simply to advance their clients' interests misdescribes a central aspect of the professional relationship. As William Simon's essay in this volume makes clear, attorneys' presentation of information and options inevitably helps shape clients' objectives.

Other defenses of zealous advocacy rest on equally questionable assumptions. The claim that adversarial clashes are the best means of determining truth is not self-evident or supported by any empirical evidence. Why should we suppose that the fairest possible outcomes will emerge from two adversaries arguing as unfairly as possible from opposing sides? It is not intuitively obvious that self-interested advocacy will yield more accurate accounts than disinterested exploration, particularly when the advocates have unequal information and resources. The vast majority of countries do not have an adversarial structure; they rely primarily on judges or investigating magistrates, not partisan advocates, to develop a case.[36] Nor do lawyers generally rely on adversarial methods outside of the courtroom; they do not hire competitive investigators.

An equally fundamental difficulty follows from a qualification that bar ethical codes acknowledge but do not adequately address. For situations when an opposing party is not "well represented," the Model Rules Preamble offers neither guidance nor reassurance. Yet, as noted above, unequal access to justice is the rule not the exception in the American legal system. In a society that tolerates vast inequalities in wealth and costly litigation procedures, it is likely that in law, as in life, the "haves come out ahead."[37] Among bar leaders, the usual "solution to this problem is not to impose on counsel the burden of representing interests other than those of his client, but rather to take appropriate steps to insure that all interests are effectively represented."[38] How that representation can realistically be achieved and financed is a matter conveniently overlooked.

Prevailing ethical rules also fail adequately to address the structural incentives and strategic opportunities that undermine the search for truth. Although bar rhetoric casts lawyers as "officers of the court" with a "special responsibility for the quality of justice," that role in practice is highly limited.[39] Apart from prohibitions on misconduct such as fraud, perjury, and knowing use of false testimony, which are applicable to all citizens, ethical codes impose few concrete obligations concerning the pursuit of truth. For example, attorneys may present evidence that they reasonably believe (but do not know) is false; they may withhold material information; they may pursue strategies primarily designed to impose expense and delay as long as that is not their only purpose; and they may mislead opponents or decision makers through selective presentation of facts and artful coaching of witnesses.[40] As Geoffrey Hazard notes, the adversary system in practice is less a search for truth than an exercise in theater, in which lawyers present clients in their "forensic best," and victory, not veracity, is the ultimate goal.[41]

Similar problems arise with the bar's traditional rights-based justifications for zealous advocacy. Such justifications implicitly assume that *any* legal interest deserves protection. This assumption confuses legal and moral rights. Some conduct that is socially indefensible is technically legal, either because it is too costly or difficult to prohibit, or because decision-making bodies are uninformed or compromised by special interests. An ethic of undivided client loyalty has encouraged lawyers' assistance in some of the most socially costly enterprises in recent memory: the distribution of asbestos and Dalkon Shields; the suppression of health information about cigarettes; and the financially irresponsible ventures of savings and loan associations.[42]

To justify zealous advocacy in such contexts requires selective suspension of the moral principle at issue. If protecting individual rights is the preeminent value, why should the rights of clients trump everyone else's? Yet under bar ethical codes and prevailing practices, the interests of third parties barely figure. As a practical matter, this difference in treatment makes perfect sense. Clients are, after all, the ones footing the bill for advocates' services. But from a moral standpoint, such selective concern often is impossible to justify, particularly when the client is an organization. A corporation's "right" to maximize profits through unsafe but imperfectly regulated methods can hardly take ethical precedence over a consumer's or employee's right to be free from reasonably avoidable risks. Moreover, an attorney's refusal to assist legal but morally dubious conduct does not necessarily compromise individual rights. Unless the lawyer is the last in town, his or her refusal to provide representation will not foreclose client choices. It may simply prompt clients to rethink the ethical consequences of their conduct or incur the costs of finding alternative counsel.

The over-valuation of client interests is especially unsettling on issues of confidentiality. The ABA's Model Rules, like its earlier Model Code, prohibit lawyers from revealing confidential information except under highly limited circumstances. The Model Rules do not *require* disclosure of confidential information except where necessary to prevent fraud on a tribunal. Nor do the Rules even *permit* such disclosure to prevent noncriminal but life-threatening acts or to avert massive economic injuries.[43] Although a growing number of states have expanded the circumstances in which disclosure is permissible, few have adopted any broad mandatory provisions.

It bears note that the most widespread and longstanding exception to confidentiality obligations is for lawyers attempting to defend their own conduct or to collect unpaid fees.[44]

From the profession's perspective, these rules make sense. They give lawyers maximum scope to protect their own interests and those of paying clients. From the public's perspective, however, it is not self-evident why attorneys have the right to reveal anything to collect a bill but not the responsibility to prevent far more significant injuries. Bar ethical rules have, for example, authorized withholding information that would exonerate a wrongfully convicted defendant facing execution or that would reveal substantial health or product safety risks.[45] Nothing in the bar's traditional defense of confidentiality offers adequate justification for such practices.

The most common rationale for confidentiality protections parallels the most common rationale for the adversary system. The argument is that legal representation is essential to protect individual rights, and that effective representation depends on clients' willingness to trust their lawyers with confidential information. This claim is not without force, but it fails to justify the scope of current confidentiality protections. Concerns about individual rights cannot explain why confidentiality principles should shield organizational misconduct. Nor do such concerns explain why the rights of clients should always take precedence over the rights of innocent third parties, particularly where health, safety, or financial livelihood are at risk. The exceptions to current confidentiality obligations are equally hard to justify. If less self-interested decision makers were responsible for formulating the rules, it seems highly unlikely we would end up with the current version. Would any group other than judges require disclosure to prevent a fraud on a court but not to save a life? Would anyone outside the bar permit disclosures to help lawyers collect a modest fee but not to prevent a massive health or financial disaster? Indeed, in one of the only comparative surveys on point, over four-fifths of nonlawyers believed that lawyers should disclose confidential product safety information, while three-quarters of lawyers indicated they would not make such disclosures under current rules.[46]

Attorneys generally claim that unless they can promise confidentiality, clients would withhold relevant information. But current rules are riddled with exceptions and indeterminacies that few clients comprehend. It is by no means clear that adding some further limitations would frequently foreclose attorneys' access to crucial facts. In one New York study, about two-thirds of clients reported giving information to their lawyers that they would still have given without a guarantee of confidentiality.[47] Even individuals who might want to withhold compromising information may be unable to do so either because their lawyer will have other sources for the information, or because their need for informed legal assistance will outweigh the risks of disclosure. Historical, cross-cultural, and cross-professional data make clear that practitioners have long provided assistance on confidential matters without the sweeping freedom from disclosure obligations that the American bar has now obtained. Businesses routinely channeled compromising information to attorneys before courts recognized a corporate privilege. And many individuals are reasonably candid with accountants, financial advisers, private investigators, and similar practitioners who cannot promise protection from disclosure obligations.[48]

Both in theory and in practice, the bar's traditional defenses of adversarial practices fall far short. The premium placed on client interests, however economically convenient for the profession, poses substantial costs for society. Current norms offer ample opportunities to evade, exhaust, and exploit opponents. The result is a justice system that too often fails to deliver justice as most participants perceive it. Three-quarters of Americans believe that litigation costs too much and takes too long; 90 percent believe that wealthy litigants have unfair advantages.[49] The problems are especially pronounced in large cases, where pretrial discovery abuses remain common.[50] All too often, the pursuit of truth is waylaid by the "antics with semantics" that current rules have failed to control.[51]

In the long run, the profession as well as the public pays a price for such conduct. As Robert Gordon's essay makes clear, the legal system is a common good that cannot function effectively in the face of unrestrained partisanship. Failure to observe basic principles of honesty and fairness erodes the procedural frameworks and cultural values on which the justice system depends.[52] Excessively adversarial ideologies and institutions also have constrained the profession's capacities in problem solving. Carrie Menkel-Meadow's essay identifies the inadequacies of partisan principles in preserving relationships, providing remedial flexibility, expressing community values, and enabling party participation.[53]

Yet these inadequacies are readily overlooked by a profession that has come to see adversarial advocacy as an end in itself. The result is what David Luban describes as a "corruption of judgment."[54] Lawyers' rationalizations for minor abuses and injustices create a climate in which serious ethical lapses no longer appear serious. Over time, deception and delay, inequalities in access and outcomes, come to seem like inevitable byproducts of adversarial processes. If they are a problem, they are someone else's problem. Judges and clients blame lawyers; lawyers blame clients, judges, and other lawyers. A constant refrain in studies of adversarial misconduct is that it is always "the other fella's fault."[55]

G. K. Chesterton observed that abuses in the legal system arose not because individuals were "wicked" or "stupid," but rather because they had "gotten used to it."[56] The problem is compounded when those same individuals are responsible for their own regulation.

The Structure of Professional Regulation

Leaders of the organized bar have long asserted that their organization is not, after all, "the same sort of thing as a retail grocers' association."[57] If they are right, it is for the wrong reasons. Lawyers no less than grocers are motivated by parochial concerns. What distinguishes professionals is their ability to repackage occupational interests as societal imperatives. The American bar retains far more control over its own regulation than any other occupational group. This freedom from external oversight too often serves the profession's interests at the expense of the public's.

The self-regarding tendencies of self-regulating processes are, however, matters that the bar discretely overlooks. Rather, the profession has long insisted that its regulation should remain under professional control. Courts have asserted inherent authority to regulate the practice of law and have delegated much of that power to the organized bar. According to the Preamble of the ABA's Model Rules, self-regulation "helps maintain the profession's independence from government domination. An independent legal profession is an important force in preserving government under law, for abuse of legal authority is more readily challenged by a profession whose members are not dependent on government for the right to practice."[58] Although this argument has considerable force, it cannot justify current regulatory structures. Protecting the bar from state control serves important values, but total professional autonomy and government domination are not the only alternatives. Many countries with an independent bar have more public accountability than the American legal profession and have involved more nonlawyers in the oversight process. Unlike regulatory bodies in these countries, the ABA Commissions that drafted the Code and the Model Rules, as well as the "Ethics 2000" Commission considering revisions, have been composed almost exclusively of lawyers.[59]

This bias in the drafting phase is exacerbated by a ratification process in which only the bar is entitled to vote. Although final approval rests with state supreme court judges, they are, by training and temperament, members of the profession, sympathetic to its interests, and often dependent on its good will for their reputation and support. Such a decision-making framework is hardly conducive to a disinterested accommodation of the interests at stake. Nothing in the history of the bar's own self-regulation suggests that lawyers are exempt from the natural human tendency to prefer private over public ends and to lose sensitivity to interests at odds with their own.

Part of the problem is tunnel vision. Without doubt, most lawyers and judges involved in bar regulation are committed to improving the system in which they work. What is open to doubt is whether a body of rules drafted, approved, and administered solely by the profession is the most effective way of realizing that commitment. No matter how well intentioned, lawyers regulating lawyers cannot escape the economic, psychological, and political constraints of their position. Those constraints compromise both the content and enforcement of ethical standards.

Bar leaders have long proclaimed that the primary purpose of regulation is to protect the public. In fact, the debates over ethical standards make clear that on many issues the overriding purpose has been to protect the profession *from* the public. Lawyers' concerns about liability to clients and third parties have dominated debates over advocacy, confidentiality, competence, and fees. The result has been to codify the minimum requirements that a highly self-interested constituency is prepared to see enforced in disciplinary or malpractice proceedings. In response to practitioners' objections, the Model Rules drafting commission dropped provisions requiring disclosure of material facts or information necessary to prevent imminent risks of life or substantial bodily harm. Also deleted were provisions mandating written fee agreements, cost-effective services, and fairness and candor in negotiating behavior, as well as prohibitions on drafting unconscionable clauses and procuring unconscionable results.[60]

The bar similarly has resisted proposals, including some from its own expert commissions, designed to increase public access to legal services. Opposition from lawyers has repeatedly blocked proposed requirements of even minimal contributions of pro bono services.[61] Bar objections also prompted ABA leadership to bury a report by its Commission on Nonlawyer Practice. The report's hardly radical recommendation was that states reconsider their sweeping prohibitions on lay competition in light of consumers' interest in obtaining affordable services as well as protection from unqualified or unethical providers.[62] Despite the vast range of unmet legal needs among low- and middle-income consumers, the organized bar has resisted such recommendations. It has also blocked proposals to license nonlawyer specialists, to permit greater competition from already licensed groups like accountants or real estate brokers, and to provide substantial courthouse assistance to pro se litigants.[63] Although the profession has long insisted that its concern is consumer protection and that the "fight to stop [nonlawyer practice] is the public's fight," the public itself has remained notably unsupportive of the campaign.[64] On the rare occasions when their views have been solicited, Americans have rated the performance of lay providers of routine services higher than lawyers and have overwhelmingly agreed that many legal tasks could be completed as effectively and less expensively by nonlawyer specialists.[65] Evidence concerning the performance of such specialists here and abroad similarly suggests that consumers would benefit from less restrictive rules on lay practice.[66]

They would also benefit from more adequate disciplinary and malpractice structures. "Too slow, too secret, too soft, and too self regulated"—that is how the public views the discipline system, according to a prominent 1992 ABA commission report. As the commission also acknowledged, much of this popular criticism is "justified and accurate."[67] Similar acknowledgments have surfaced in virtually every major study that the bar has undertaken. Yet all of those studies have recommended that the profession retain control over the regulatory process. In one particularly striking survey, only 20 percent of lawyers believed that the disciplinary system did a good job, but some 90 percent believed that the bar should continue to conduct disciplinary activities.[68]

In justifying this continued authority, bar leaders have emphasized the importance of insuring that "those individuals . . . who pass judgment on attorney conduct be knowledgeable regarding the practice of law."[69] But in fact, the disciplinary complaint processes proceed on precisely the opposite basis. They rely almost exclusively on clients as a source of information about ethical violations. Those with the most knowledge concerning practice standards—lawyers and judges—rarely report misconduct. And ethical rules requiring attorneys to make such reports are almost never enforced.[70]

This failure to disclose misconduct reflects a combination of social, psychological, and economic factors. Part of the problem involves the difficulty that Geoffrey Hazard's essay describes: many legal-ethics standards, like other ethical principles, are formulated in broad abstract terms. How they apply in particular cases is often difficult to determine. What constitutes an "incompetent" performance or "unreasonable" fee are highly fact-specific questions, and lawyers usually have no incentive to acquire the relevant information. Disciplinary structures reflect what economists view as classic free-rider/common action-problems. Attorneys who report misconduct benefit society and the profession as a whole, but seldom gain any personal advantage.

As a consequence, bar agencies depend almost exclusively on complaints from clients, along with felony convictions, as a basis for discipline. These sources are highly inadequate. Clients frequently lack sufficient information or incentives to file grievances. Some forms of attorney misconduct, such as discovery abuse, benefit clients; other violations are difficult to detect or prove. Bar disciplinary agencies dismiss about 90 percent of complaints without investigation because the facts alleged do not establish probable cause or fall outside agency jurisdiction.[71] Grievances involving neglect, "mere" negligence, or fee disputes generally are excluded on the ground that disciplinary agencies lack adequate resources and other remedies are available through malpractice suits or alternative bar-sponsored arbitration processes.[72] However, malpractice litigation is too expensive for most of these matters. Seldom does it make sense to sue unless the conduct is egregious, the damages are substantial, and the lawyer has malpractice insurance. Over a third of the bar does not. Nor do most states offer alternative dispute-resolution programs to resolve minor grievances. The programs that are available almost always are voluntary, and clients most in need of assistance seldom find their attorneys willing to cooperate.[73]

A further problem involves the inadequacy of sanctions. Less than 2 percent of complaints result in public discipline such as reprimands, suspensions, or disbarment.[74] Although some grievances clearly are without basis, and reflect dissatisfaction with outcomes rather than deficiencies in attorney performance, the infrequency of significant sanctions also reflects fundamental problems in the regulatory process. Most disciplinary agencies are underfunded and understaffed.[75] To varying degrees, these agencies depend on good relations with the profession, which controls their budget and monitors their performance. Many of the judges and bar leaders who regulate the regulators have a "there but for the grace of God go I" attitude toward all but the most serious misconduct.

Similar problems arise with malpractice litigation as a remedy for incompetent or unethical conduct. Despite the recent growth in claims, a large number of valid grievances are never filed because the stakes are insufficient or the attorney has no malpractice insurance and it is seldom worthwhile to sue uninsured lawyers. About half of the claims that are filed fail to satisfy the profession's highly demanding standards of proof.[76] To obtain any remedy, plaintiffs must show not only that their lawyers' performance fell below prevailing practices, but also that it was the sole cause of quantifiable damages. That burden generally requires a trial within a trial; claimants need to establish that but for the lawyer's malpractice, they would have been successful in the matter on which they sought legal assistance. For criminal matters, barriers to recovery are even higher and usually insurmountable: clients must prove that they actually were innocent of the crime charged and that their attorney's inadequate performance was responsible for their conviction.[77] In many jurisdictions, not even violations of bar ethical rules are sufficient to establish malpractice. The rules themselves emphasize that they are not intended to define standards for civil liability, and some courts have excluded evidence of noncompliance.[78]

Malpractice case law also imposes undue limits on who can recover for violations of professional standards. The bar has long resisted extending liability to nonclients, and courts have usually agreed. Litigants typically cannot recover for dishonest or abusive conduct by their opponents' lawyer on the theory that concern about such remedies might interfere with zealous advocacy. Similar reasoning in some jurisdictions has served to deny third-party claims by buyers or investors who reasonably relied on attorneys' negligent misrepresentations. These decisions hold lawyers to lower standards than used-car dealers.[79]

Long-standing inadequacies in bar regulatory frameworks argue for a more accountable alternative. If, as the profession insists, its ultimate objective is protecting the public, then the public should have a greater role in the process. No occupational group can make unbiased judgments on matters where its own status and livelihood are so directly at issue.

Alternative Frameworks

Bar discussions of the "crisis of professionalism" generally vacillate between sweeping descriptions of the problem and dispiritingly ineffectual proposals to address it. That mismatch is not entirely surprising. Lawyers as a group are diverse, divided, and anything but disinterested on matters affecting self-regulation. The politics of professional reform make it easier to lament lost ideals than to invite the cost and conflict involved in institutionalizing them. But more could be accomplished if a greater number of lawyers, individually and collectively, addressed the structural sources of the ethical problems they confront.

An obvious place to start is the economic conditions of practice. The tension between profit and professionalism is too self-evident to overlook, but also too uncomfortable to acknowledge fully. The result has been various strategies of confession and avoidance. So, for example, the ABA's Commission on Professionalism framed the central question: "Has our profession abandoned principle for profit, professionalism for commercialism?" The answer, it turned out, "cannot be a simple yes or no."[80] The commission's report acknowledged that economic pressures were compromising ethical values. But, like other professionalism initiatives, its impact has been largely symbolic and its efforts to "rekindle" a sense of social responsibility through education and exhortation have fallen far short.

Significant progress will require more fundamental changes in the conditions of practice. Most of the necessary reforms follow directly from the diagnosis set forth above. Lawyers' working environments should aim to foster a decent quality of life, a basic equality of opportunity, and a commitment to social justice. Such environments will require realistic billable-hour requirements and adequate accommodations for those with significant family and pro bono commitments. Part-time schedules should be plausible options, and public service should be rewarded in practice as well as principle. Although such reforms are not without short-term costs, the long-term gains are likely to be considerably greater. More humane and flexible schedules yield improvements in job satisfaction, morale, recruitment, retention, and efficiency.[81] And pro bono service provides opportunities not only for personal fulfillment but also for valuable training, contacts, and recognition.[82]

If these benefits are as substantial as recent research suggests, the question then becomes why so many legal workplaces have failed to respond. Why have lawyers so often opted for short-term profits at the expense of broader values? At least part of the explanation may lie in the widespread tendency to overvalue money in comparison with other workplace characteristics that are in fact more likely to yield enduring satisfaction. People generally believe that 25 percent more income would significantly increase their happiness and that more money is the change in circumstance that would most improve the quality of their lives.[83] They are generally wrong. As a wide array of research makes clear, people quickly adjust to higher earnings and their expectations and desires increase accordingly.[84] At attorneys' income levels, the cliche is correct: money does not buy happiness. The priority that many lawyers and law firms attach to salaries compromises other goals that are more central to fulfillment, such as time for families and friends, and choice of work that is morally and intellectually satisfying.

A related problem is that individuals who fail to find such meaning in their legal practice often feel a sense of deprivation that fuels heightened financial demands. Attorneys working too hard on matters they care too little about have greater needs to live well outside work. Patterns of compensatory consumption can then become self-perpetuating. As lawyers become accustomed to high incomes, luxuries become necessities and relative salaries become ways of keeping score. The problem is compounded by surveys that rank law firms based only on profit, and by the difficulties of gaining consensus within any particular firm about the relative importance of other values. Since almost everyone gives high priority to money, it can displace goals on which preferences are more divided.

Changing these priorities is no easy task, but some modest progress may be possible through better information. Few law school curricula or continuing legal education programs address issues of workplace structure and career satisfaction, and few efforts have been made to rate employers on values other than profitability. If more comparative data were available on quality of life and pro bono issues, it might provide significant leverage for reform.

Lawyers and legal employers could also be rated along other ethical dimensions. For example, information could be centrally compiled and published on matters such as disciplinary violations, malpractice judgments, and judicial sanctions for discovery abuse. Bar leaders and regulatory bodies could work together to develop best practice standards on ethical issues and procedures for certifying compliance. These standards could include educational programs, practice guidelines, oversight committees, mentoring strategies, and reporting channels. Voluntary bar associations in particular substantive fields could also adopt heightened ethical requirements. Organizations such as the American Academy of Matrimonial Lawyers, and the ABA Tax Section already have developed more specific and morally demanding codes than the prevailing Model Rules.[85] Lawyers' willingness to comply with such codes and to meet best practice standards could serve as a reputational signal for clients, courts, and colleagues. Analogous approaches have had modest positive effects in other contexts where organizations have been evaluated on ethical dimensions, such as compliance with environmental standards or international bribery and sweatshop prohibitions. Developing reputational rewards and sanctions for the legal profession could push in similar, socially responsible directions.

A further set of reforms should focus on adversarial institutions and ideologies. A more ethically satisfying framework would build on one central premise: lawyers should accept personal moral responsibility for the consequences of their professional actions. Attorneys' conduct should be justifiable under consistent, disinterested, and generalizable ethical principles. These principles can, of course, recognize the distinctive needs of lawyers' occupational role. Morally responsible decision making always takes into account the context in which a person acts. The extent of attorneys' responsibilities for client conduct would depend on their knowledge, involvement, and influence, as well as on the significance of values at stake. So, for example, the importance of protecting free speech for unpopular causes or fair trials for criminal defendants may justify zealous representation despite other costs. But such cases should not set the standard for partisanship in cases where no such principles are at stake.

Unlike the bar's prevailing approach, this alternative framework would require lawyers to assess their conduct in light of all the societal interests at issue in particular practice contexts. An advocate could not simply retreat into some fixed conception of role that denies personal accountability for public consequences or that unduly privileges the interests of lawyers and clients. Nor should attorneys invoke some idealized model of adversarial and legislative processes to justify zealous advocacy. Rather, they must assess their actions against a realistic backdrop in which wealth, power, and information are unequally distributed, not all interests are adequately represented, and most matters never will reach a neutral tribunal. Client trust and confidentiality are entitled to weight, but they must be balanced against other equally important concerns. Lawyers also have responsibility to prevent unnecessary harm to third parties, to promote a just and effective legal system, and to respect core values such as honesty, fairness, and good faith on which that system depends. "What if everyone did that?" should become a common check on adversarial excesses. Attorneys need to consider the cumulative impact of their individual decisions on the effectiveness of legal processes.

Bar leaders often object that these responsibilities are too vague to serve as the basis for an ethical code, or that lawyers have no special right or expertise to determine what justice requires. But these objections are highly selective. We routinely ask judges, juries, and prosecutors to pursue "justice" or to determine "fairness," and we impose significant penalties on businesses for not acting in "good faith." Lawyers charge substantial fees for interpreting such requirements. The interpretative process is no different when lawyers' own actions are involved. Attorneys should consider the justice of their actions, not because they have special moral expertise, but because they deserve no special moral exemption.

Under this alternative framework, lawyers' ethical responsibilities should extend not only to the cases that they accept and the strategies that they pursue, but also to the structure of the justice system. As architects of ethical codes and legal procedures, lawyers should help to develop a range of "appropriate dispute resolution processes" that can respond to the particular individual and societal interests at stake.[86] For many controversies, it may be possible to craft structures in which money matters less and the merits matter more than is currently the case. The adversary system is not an end in itself and the bar should take a leadership role in developing more cost-effective alternatives.

A final cluster of reforms should focus on bar regulatory structures. Increasing the public accountability of professional oversight should be a key priority. The design of an adequate system does, however, present special challenges. Political control of regulatory processes does not guarantee public protection. Legislatively created oversight agencies often suffer from the same problems of understaffing, underfunding, delays, and capture by regulated groups as bar authorities.[87] And governmental control of regulatory structures pose risks of retaliation against lawyers representing unpopular causes. Yet some progress is likely through frameworks that balance concerns for both public accountability and professional independence. One promising proposal by a California task force would have created a regulatory commission subject to state supreme court control but independent of the organized bar. That commission would have included both lawyers and nonlawyers with expertise in consumer protection; some members would have been chosen by the legislature, some by the governor, and others by the judiciary.[88] Such structural reforms could produce a more responsive system than the prevailing one.

However these accountability issues are resolved, fundamental changes are essential on other fronts. First, disciplinary agencies need more information about misconduct. One obvious strategy is to enforce rules requiring lawyers to report ethical violations by other lawyers. Illinois, the only state that has attempted to do so, has seen a dramatic increase in such reports after its supreme court suspended an attorney for failing to disclose fraud by his client's previous lawyer.[89] Bar agencies also could take more proactive steps to identify disciplinary violations. For example, enforcement officials should initiate investigations based on judicial findings of malpractice, overcharging, and discovery abuse.[90] Disciplinary agencies could also encourage reports from clients by publicizing complaint processes, helping parties file grievances, and requiring attorneys to distribute a "consumer bill of rights" including information about remedial options.

A related set of reforms should focus on improving responses to reported misconduct. Bar disciplinary systems need significantly more professional staff, investigatory resources, and remedial options. Only a few jurisdictions allow permanent disbarment, no matter how serious the offense, or authorize discipline for law firms as well as individual lawyers. Such sanctions should be universally available. Firms should be liable where responsibility for misconduct is broadly shared and reflects failures to provide adequate education, supervision, reporting channels, or remedial responses.[91] Malpractice standards also should be strengthened and all attorneys should be required to carry liability insurance. Remedies should be available for violations of bar ethical rules and for performance that does not conform to reasonable persons' expectations.[92]

Courts and administrative agencies also should become more involved in enforcing ethical standards. The judiciary should have expanded responsibilities and resources to monitor the litigation misconduct, fee-related abuses, and ineffective representation noted earlier. Government agencies should play a more active role as employers, purchasers, and regulators. Agencies can demand a higher standard of conduct than bar disciplinary rules require, both for their own employees and for private practitioners who provide government-subsidized legal services. Further efforts should also be made along the lines developed by the Securities and Exchange Commission and the Office of Thrift Supervision to hold lawyers accountable for facilitating client fraud.[93]

Finally, more attention should focus on increasing access to justice. Obvious strategies include more procedural simplifications, additional pro bono and government-subsidized services, and greater reliance on qualified nonlawyer providers. Although the organized bar needs to play a central role in these reform efforts, decisions about lay competition should not rest with those whose status and income is so directly at risk.

This is not a modest agenda, and significant progress will require sustained efforts on the part of both the profession and the public. These efforts should start with law schools. Although ABA accreditation standards require schools to offer instruction in professional responsibility, the vast majority satisfy their obligation with a single mandatory course that focuses on bar disciplinary codes. Too often, the result is "legal ethics without the ethics."[94] Students learn what the codes require but lack foundations for critical analysis. Topics like access to justice, the quality of professional life, or the limits of bar regulation generally receive inadequate attention. Most students get too little theory and too little practice; classroom discussions are too far removed from real life contexts and too uninformed by insights from other disciplines, other professions, and other cultures. Few schools require pro bono service or make systematic efforts to integrate legal ethics into the core curricula. This minimalist approach to professional responsibility marginalizes its significance. Educational priorities are apparent in subtexts as well as texts. What the core curriculum leaves unsaid sends a powerful message that no single course can counteract.

Research on ethics in practice has been similarly neglected. On many key issues, our knowledge base is embarrassingly thin. We know too little about strategies that might prevent misconduct or improve regulatory processes. Despite an enormous expenditure of effort on drafting and redrafting ethical rules, little attention has focused on how those rules play out in practice. Do differences in state confidentiality rules significantly affect lawyer-client communication or protections for third parties? What efforts by courts and disciplinary agencies have been most effective in controlling discovery abuse? We also know too little about how to educate and enlist the public on a plausible reform strategy. Lawyer bashing is in ample supply but thoughtful critiques and constructive proposals are not.

Any adequate reform agenda will require a clearer understanding of lawyers' ethical problems and the tradeoffs involved in addressing them. Professional responsibility is an evolving ideal in which both the profession and the public have a common stake. The challenge is for these constituencies to work together toward standards that can be justified in principle and reinforced in practice. That agenda does not seem unduly idealistic. On matters of public interest not involving their own regulation, lawyers have been crucial in bridging the gap between ideals and institutions. By turning similar energies inward, the bar may narrow the distance between ethical aspirations and daily practices.

Notes

1. Reinhold Niebuhr, *The Nature and Destiny of Man* (New York: Charles Scribner's Sons, 1941), 2: 302.
2. See Anthony Kronman, quoted in "On Making Lawyers Truly Officers of the Court," *The Responsive Community*, Fall 1996, 44.
3. Plato, *The Dialogues of Plato,* trans. B. Jowitt (New York: Random House, 1937), 175.
4. Working Group on Lawyer Conduct and Professionalism, *A National Action Plan on*

Lawyer Conduct and Professionalism: Report to the Conference of Chief Justices Committee on Professionalism and Lawyer Competence (August 13, 1998); American Bar Association (hereafter cited as ABA), *Promoting Professionalism: ABA Programs, Plans, and Strategies* (Chicago: ABA, 1998).

5. Peter Passell, "Earning It: Royal Blue Collars," *New York Times*, March 22, 1998, E1.

6. Nancy McCarthy, "Pessimism for the Future," *California Business Journal*, November, 1994, 1.

7. Austin Sarat, "Ethics in Litigation: Rhetoric of Crisis, Realities of Practice," infra.

8. ABA, *Model Rules of Professional Conduct* (Chicago: ABA, 1998, Rule 6).

9. Deborah L. Rhode, "Cultures of Commitment: Pro Bono Service as a Professional Obligation," infra.

10. ABA, Model Rules, Rule 6.1; Carroll Seron, *The Business of Practicing Law* (Philadelphia: Temple University Press, 1996), 129–35; sources cited in Rhode, "Cultures of Commitment," infra.

11. Donald W. Hoagland, "Community Service Makes Better Lawyers," in *The Law Firm and the Public Good*, ed. Robert A. Katzmann (Washington, D.C.: Brookings Institution, 1995), 104, 109; ABA, Young Lawyers Division Survey, *Career Satisfaction* (Chicago: ABA, 1995), 11.

12. See studies cited in Patrick Schultz, "On Being a Healthy and Ethical Member of an Unhealthy and Unethical Profession," 52 *Vanderbilt Law Review* 871 (1999); and Deborah L. Rhode, "The Professionalism Problem," 39 *William and Mary Law Review* 283, 300 (1998).

13. Deborah L. Rhode, "Myths of Meritocracy," 65 *Fordham Law Review* 585, 587 (1996); Cynthia Epstein et al., "Glass Ceilings and Open Doors: Women's Advancement in the Legal Profession," 64 *Fordham Law Review* 291 (1995); ABA, Commission on the Status of Women, *Unfinished Business: Overcoming the Sisyphus Factor* (Chicago: ABA, 1995).

14. Lewis A. Coser, *Greedy Institutions: Patterns of Undivided Commitment* (New York: Free Press, 1974); Cynthia Fuchs Epstein, Carroll Seron, Bonnie Oglensky, and Robert Saute, *The Part Time Paradox: Time Norms, Professional Life, Family, and Gender* (New York: Routledge, 1999).

15. Juliet B. Schor, *The Overworked American: The Unexpected Decline of Leisure* (New York: BasicBooks, 1991), 10–12; Carrie Menkel-Meadow, "Culture Clash in the Quality of Life in the Law: Changes in the Economic Diversification and Organization of Lawyering," 44 *Case Western Reserve Law Review* 621, 658–59 (1994).

16. For dissatisfaction rates, see Shultz, "Unhealthy Profession"; and Rhode, "Professionalism Problem," 296–97. Attorneys are four times as likely to be depressed than the population and twice as likely to have substance-abuse problems (297). Michael J. Sweeny, "The Devastations of Depression," *Bar-Leader*, March–April 1998, 11; Laura Gatland, "Dangerous Dedication," *ABA Journal*, December 1997, 28. Lynn Preengenza, "Substance Abuse in the Legal Profession: A Symptom of Malaise," 7 *Notre Dame Journal of Law and Ethics* 305, 306 (1993).

17. See Deborah L. Rhode and David Luban, *Legal Ethics* (St. Paul: Foundation Press, 1995), 876–77.

18. William H. Rehnquist, "The Legal Profession Today," 62 *Indiana Law Journal* 151, 153 (1987).

19. Ralph Nader and Wesley J. Smith, *No Contest* (New York: Random House, 1996), 233–42; William G. Ross, *The Honest Hour: The Ethics of Time-Based Billing by Attorneys* (Durham, N.C.: Carolina Academic Press, 1996), 27–30.

20. Macklin Fleming, *Lawyers, Money, and Success* (Westport, Conn.: Quorum Books, 1997), 38-39; Lisa Lerman, "Gross Profits: Questions about Lawyer Billing Practices," 22 *Hofstra Law Review* 645, 649 (1994); John J. Marquess, "Legal Audits and Dishonest Legal Bills," 22

Hofstra Law Review 637, 643–44 (1994); Lisa Lerman, "Regulation of Unethical Billing" (unpublished manuscript, 1998); Darlene Richter, "Greed, Ignorance, and Overbilling," *ABA Journal*, August 1994, 64–66.

21. Marc Galanter, "Anyone Can Fall Down a Manhole: The Contingency Fee and Its Discontents,"42 *Depaul Law Review* 457, 459 (1994).

22. See George Cohen and Susan Koniak, "In Hell There Will Be Lawyers Without Clients or Law," infra; and John C. Coffee Jr., "The Corruption of the Class Action: The New Technology of Collusion," 80 *Cornell Law Review* 851 (1995).

23. Deborah L. Rhode, *Professional Responsibility, Ethics by the Pervasive Method* (Boston: Aspen, 1998), 799–804; Lester A. Brickman, "Contingency Fee Abuses, Ethical Mandates and the Disciplinary System: The Case Against Case-by-Case Enforcement," 53 *Washington and Lee Law Review* 1339 (1996).

24. Brickman, "Contingency Fee Abuses, 1345 n. 22.

25. Ibid., 1349; Lester Brickman, "ABA Regulation of Contingency Fees: Money Talks, Ethics Walks," 65 *Fordham Law Review* 247, 305–8 (1996); Michael Hytha, "'People's Lawyer' Gets Mild Penalty from State Bar," *San Francisco Chronicle*, August 8, 1997, A19 (describing private reproval for lawyer charging up to 46 percent on simple insurance claims).

26. Steven K. Smith and Carol J. DeFrancis, "Indigent Defense," United States Department of Justice, Bureau of Justice Statistics, Selected Findings, February 1996, 3 (Table 4).

27. Marcia Coyle, "Hoping for $75/Hour," *National Law Journal*, June 7, 1999, A1; Ronald Smothers, "Court-Appointed Defense Offers the Poor a Lawyer, But the Cost May Be High," *New York Times*, February 14, 1994, A12.

28. Mike McConville and Chester Mirsky, "Guilty Plea Courts: A Social Disciplinary Model of Criminal Justice," 42 *Social Problems* 216 (1995); Stephen J. Schulhofer, "Plea Bargaining as Disaster," 101 *Yale Law Journal* 1979, 1988 (1992); Kenneth B. Mann, "The Trial as Text: Allegory, Myth, and Symbol in the Adversarial Criminal Process–A Critique of the Role of Public Defender and a Proposal for Reform," 32 *American Criminal Law Review* 743, 803–12 (1995).

29. Victor E. Flango and Patricia McKenna, "Federal Habeas Corpus Review of State Court Convictions," 31 *California Western Law Review* 237, 259–60 (1995).

30. Bruce Shapiro, "Sleeping Lawyer Syndrome," *The Nation*, April 7, 1997, 27–29 (quoting Judge Doug Shaver).

31. Offices of Legal Services, State Bar of California, *And Justice for All: Fulfilling the Promise of Access to Justice in California* (San Francisco: State Bar of California, 1996), 17; Albert H. Cantrill, *Agenda for Access: The American People and Civil Justice* (Chicago: ABA, 1996), 26–27.

32. Cantrill, *Agenda for Access*, 26–27.

33. Rhode and Luban, *Legal Ethics*, 749–50; Pam Sturner, "At Stanford, a Forum for Public Interest Law," *San Jose Post Record*, March 17, 1999, 1.

34. ABA, Model Code of Professional Responsibility (Chicago: ABA, 1980), Ethical Consideration 7-1.

35. ABA, Model Rules, Preamble.

36. Rhode and Luban, *Legal Ethics*; David Luban, "The Adversary System Excuse," in *The Good Lawyer*, ed. David Luban (Rowman & Allanheld, 1984), 83.

37. Marc Galanter, "Why the Haves Come Out Ahead: Speculations on the Limits of Legal Change," 9 *Law and Society Review* 95 (1974).

38. Abe Krash, "Professional Responsibility to Clients and the Public Interest: Is There a Conflict?," 55 *Chicago Bar Record* 31, 37 (1974).

39. ABA, Model Rules, Preamble.

40. See ABA, Model Rules, Rules 3.3, 4.1.

41. Geoffrey Hazard Jr., "Law Practice and the Limits of Moral Philosophy," infra.

42. See Paul Brodeur, *Outrageous Misconduct: The Asbestos Industry on Trial* (New York: Pantheon, 1985); Susan Perry and Jim Dawson, *Nightmare: Women and the Dalkon Shield* (New York: Macmillan, 1985), 208; David Margolick, " 'Tobacco' Its Middle Name, Law Firm Thrives, for Now," *New York Times*, November 20, 1992, A1; *Lincoln Savings and Loan Association v. Wall*, 743 F. Supp. 901 (D.D.C. 1990).

43. ABA, Model Rules, Rules 3.1, 1.6.

44. ABA, Model Rules, Rule 1.6.

45. See, for example, Arthur Powell, "Privilege of Counsel and Confidential Communications," 6 *Georgia Bar Journal* 334, 335 (1964) David Kaplan, "Death Row Dilemma," *National Law Journal*, January 25, 1988, 35; *Spaulding v. Zimmerman*, 116 N.W.2d 704 (Minn. 1962); *Balla v. Gambo Inc.*, 584 N.E.2d 104 (Ill. Sup. Ct., 1991).

46. Fred C. Zacharias, "Rethinking Confidentiality," 74 *Iowa Law Review* 351, 382–83 (1989).

47. Ibid.

48. Deborah L. Rhode, "Ethical Perspectives on Legal Practice," 37 *Stanford Law Review* 589, 614 (1985); Steven Lubet and Cathryn Stewart, "A 'Public Assets' Theory of Lawyers' Pro Bono Obligations,"145 *University of Pennsylvania Law Review* 1245, 1280–81 (1997).

49. ABA, *Perceptions of the U.S. Justice System* 59 (Chicago: ABA, 1999), 59.

50. See Symposium, "Conference on Discovery," 39 *Boston College Review* 517–840 (1998); and Litigation Ethics in "Ethics: Beyond the Rules," 67 *Fordham Law Review* 691–896 (1998).

51. Sarat, "Ethics in Litigation," infra. See also Working Group on Lawyer Conduct and Professionalism, *A National Action Plan*, 29, 50; and Rhode, *Professional Responsibility*, 187–88.

52. Robert Gordon, "Why Lawyers Can't Just Be Hired Guns," infra.

53. Carrie Menkel-Meadow, "The Limits of Adversarial Ethics," infra.

54. David Luban, "Wrongful Obedience: Bad Judgments and Warranted Excuses," infra.

55. Sarat, "Ethics in Litigation," infra; Douglas N. Frenkel, Robert L. Nelson, and Austin Sarat, "Introduction: Bringing Legal Realism to the Study of Ethics and Professionalism," 67 *Fordham Law Review* 697, 703 (1998).

56. G. K. Chesterton, "The Twelve Men," in *Tremendous Trifles* (New York: Dodd, Mead and Co., 1929), 57–58.

57. Roscoe Pound, *The Lawyer from Antiquity to Modern Times* (St. Paul: West Publishing Co., 1953), 7.

58. ABA, Model Rules, Preamble.

59. The Model Rules Commission and Ethics 2000 each had one lay member; the Code had none. See Rhode, *Professional Responsibility*, 48.

60. See Deborah L. Rhode, "Ethical Perspectives on Legal Practice," 37 *Stanford Law Review* 589, 611 (1985); ABA, Model Rules of Professional Conduct, Discussion Draft.

61. See Rhode, "Cultures of Commitment," infra.

62. ABA Commission on Nonlawyer Practice, *Nonlawyer Activity in Law-Related Situation: A Report with Recommendations*, 3–8 (Chicago: ABA, 1995).

63. Deborah L. Rhode, "Professionalism in Perspective: Alternative Approaches to Nonlawyer Practice," 22 *New York Review of Law and Social Change*, 701 (1996).

64. ABA, *Committee on Evaluation of the National Conference on the Unauthorized Practice of Law* (1962), 153 (quoting former ABA president John Sattefield).

65. See surveys cited in Rhode, "Professionalism in Perspective," 709; Deborah L. Rhode, "Policing the Professional Monopoly: A Constitutional and Empirical Analysis of Unauthorized Practice Prohibitions," 34 *Stanford Law Review* 1 (1981).

66. See the evidence summarized in Rhode, "Professionalism in Perspective," and "Policing the Unauthorized Practice."

67. ABA Commission on Evaluation of Disciplinary Enforcement, *Lawyer Regulation for a New Century* (Chicago: ABA, 1992), xx; Paula Hannaford, "What Complainants *Really* Expect of Lawyers' Disciplinary Agencies," 7 *Professional Lawyer* 4 (May 1996) (finding majority of complainants rated Virginia's system as poor or very poor).

68. Deborah Hensler and Marissa E. Reddy, *California Lawyers View the Future* (Santa Monica: Rand, 1994), 18.

69. Commission on the Future of the Legal Profession and the State Bar of California, *The Future of the California Bar* (San Francisco: State Bar of California, 1995), 103.

70. Darryl Van Duch, "Best Snitches: Illinois Lawyers," *National Law Journal*, January 26, 1997, A1; Laura Gatland, "The Himmel Effect," *ABA Journal*, April 1997, 24–28. See ABA, Model Rules, Rule 8.3, and Model Code, DR 1–103.

71. New York Bar Committee on the Profession and the Courts, *Final Report to the Chief Judge* (November 1995), 44; ABA Commission, *Lawyer Regulation*, xv.

72. Geoffrey Hazard Jr., Susan P. Koniak, and Roger Cramton, *The Law and Ethics of Lawyering* (Westbury, N.Y.: Foundation Press, 1994), 172.

73. "ABA Committee Proposes Rules for Lawyer-Client Mediation," 13 *ABA/BNA Lawyers Manual on Professional Conduct* 398 (Dec. 24, 1997); ABA Commission, *Lawyer Regulation*, 129.

74. Rhode, *Professional Responsibility*, 72; Beth M. Daley, "Is the Illinois Disciplinary System Working?," *Legal Reformer*, Spring 1998, 3.

75. Nader and Smith, *No Contest*, 132; Rhode, *Professional Responsibility*, 70–72.

76. ABA Standing Committee on Lawyers' Professional Liability, *Legal Malpractice Claims in the 1990s*, 12, 16 (ABA: Chicago, 1996); John Gibeaut, "Good News, Bad News in Malpractice," *ABA Journal*, March 1997, 101; Manual Ramos, "Malpractice: Reforming Lawyers," 70 *Tulane Law Review* 2583, 2603, 2612 (1996).

77. Charles Wolfram, *Modern Legal Ethics* (St. Paul: West Publishing Co., 1986), 218–22; *Wiley v. San Diego County*, 966 P.2d 983 (Cal. 1998).

78. ABA, Model Rules, Scope; ABA, Model Code, Prefatory Note; Wolfram, *Modern Legal Ethics*, 207–15; Gary A. Munneke and Anthony E. Davis, "The Standard of Care in Legal Malpractice: Do the Model Rules of Professional Conduct Define It?," 22 *Journal of the Legal Profession* 33, 62–25 (1998).

79. *Goodman v. Kennedy*, 556 P.2d 737 (Cal. 1976); *Shatz v. Rosenberg*, 943 F.2d 485 (4th Cir.1991), cert. denied, 503 U.S. 936 (1992); John Leubsdorf, "Legal Malpractice and Professional Responsibility," 48 *Rutgers Law Review* 101, 111, 130–35 (1995); Bowman, "Lawyer Liability to Non-Clients," 97 *Dickinson Law Review* 267–76 (1993).

80. ABA, Commission on Professionalism, *In the Spirit of a Public Service* (Chicago: ABA Commission on Professionalism, 1986), 1.

81. Schor, *Overworked American*, 10–12; Menkel-Meadow, "Culture Clash," 658–59.

82. See sources cited in Rhode, "Cultures of Commitment," infra.

83. Robert Lane, "Does Money Buy Happiness?," *Public Interest*, Fall 1993, 56, 61; Robert Frank, "Luxury Fever" (unpublished manuscript, 1998).

84. David G. Myers, *The Pursuit of Happiness* (New York: William Morrow, 1992), 51–58; Lane, "Happiness," 61; Frank, "Luxury Fever," Chap. 8.

85. See American Academy of Matrimonial Lawyers, *Standards of Conduct* (Chicago:

ABA, 1992); Frederick G. Cornell, "Guidelines to Tax Practice Second," 43 *Tax Lawyer* 297 (1990).

86. Menkel-Meadow, "The Limits of Adversarial Ethics," infra.

87. ABA Commission, *Lawyer Regulation*, 4; David Wilkins, "Who Should Regulate Lawyers?," 105 *Harvard Law Review* 801, 817 (1992).

88. See Rhode and Luban, *Legal Ethics*, 953–54. For a similar proposal, see Robert Fellmeth, "Lessons of the Dues Debacle," *California Bar Journal*, June 1998, 8.

89. *In re Himmel,* 533 N.E.2d 790 (Ill. 1988); Gatland, "The Himmel Effect," 24.

90. Michael Higgins, "Getting Out the Word," *ABA Journal*, September 1998, 22.

91. Committee on Professional Responsibility, "Discipline of Law Firms," 48 *Record of the Association of the Bar of the City of New York* 628, 631 (1993); Ted Schneyer, "Professional Discipline for Law Firms," 77 *Cornell Law Review* 1 (1991).

92. Leubsdorf, "Legal Malpractice," 111–19, 149; William Simon, *The Practice of Justice* (Cambridge, Mass.: Harvard University Press), 5-7, 166–69.

93. See Wilkins, "Who Should Regulate Lawyers?," 868.

94. William Simon, "The Trouble with Legal Ethics," 41 *Journal of Legal Education* 65, 66 (1991).

PART I

Public Responsibilities in Professional Practice

2

The Law as a Profession

ANTHONY T. KRONMAN

I.

The field of legal ethics, or professional responsibility as it is often called, appears to consist of an immense accumulation of rules. This is how the subject looks to students when they first approach it, and the manner in which it is taught, and then later tested on bar examinations, tends to confirm this impression.

In this century, legal ethics has indeed become an increasingly rule-bound discipline. The number of rules governing the ethical conduct of lawyers has grown enormously, and the rules themselves have become more and more detailed. The Canon of Legal Ethics, which was promulgated by the American Bar Association in 1909, consisted of a few hortatory injunctions. By contrast, the Model Rules of Professional Conduct, adopted by the ABA in 1983, has the appearance of a full-blown code. It is tempting to assume that one becomes an ethical lawyer by mastering the complex body of rules that govern a lawyer's relations with clients, adversaries, officials, and other third parties, and to infer that these rules define, perhaps exhaust, the subject of professional responsibility.

But that is too narrow a view. One becomes a professionally responsible lawyer by entering the profession, a process that includes the mastery of certain rules, but which taken as a whole is better conceived as the process of acquiring the habits of a culture. This culture provides the setting for the rules of legal ethics, and the meaning of these rules cannot be grasped, nor conflicts among them meaningfully argued, apart from the culture in which they are set. Every education in legal ethics must in this sense be an induction into a culture, into a distinctive way of life, into the profession of law—a concept that cannot be reduced to the rules of legal ethics, but rather is indispensable to their understanding and application.

The way in which lawyers acquire a sense of professional responsibility resembles the process by which we learn to speak any natural language, like English or Arabic or Italian. Every language has its rules of grammar, and these must be studied at some point in the process of learning to speak it, if one aspires to speak the language in a formally correct manner. But fluency can never be achieved by studying these rules alone. That requires something more. It requires the speaker to be at home in the habits of the language, to have acquired these habits himself, to be a participant in what Wittgenstein called the "form of life" that every language represents.[1] The legal profession is also a form of life, and a lawyer's sense of professional responsibility can no more be reduced to a knowledge of the rules of legal ethics than command of English can be reduced to a knowledge of the rules of English grammar.

But a form of life can be strong or weak. It can grow, acquiring new vitality and incorporating additional areas of human experience within its range. Or it can shrink, losing potency and territory, and eventually wither and die. Today, for example, the form of life which the language of Homeric Greek once vividly expressed has disappeared, and only the grammar of the language remains—only the rules of its construction, its semantics and syntax, from which we must attempt to reconstruct, artificially and incompletely, some notion of the vanished form of life that formed the setting of the language—that formed the language—a world now irrecoverably lost.

Among American lawyers at the end of the twentieth century, there is a growing fear that something like this may be happening to the culture of professionalism that formed the setting within which the rules of legal ethics have evolved. These rules are today vastly more numerous and detailed than they were a hundred years ago, but the culture in which they are set, and are meant to express, is thought by many lawyers to be weakened and in danger of collapse. There is a widespread anxiety, within the legal profession, that professionalism itself has lost much of its vitality and meaning for lawyers, and like a language that is falling out of use but whose formal rules of grammar survive, may soon become a dead culture whose outlines can still be seen in the now-inert rules of legal ethics to which the culture of legal professionalism once gave meaning and life. Judging by the frequency with which it is discussed at bar association meetings, and other informal gatherings of lawyers, and by the number of books and articles devoted to it, no topic possesses a greater urgency for lawyers at century's end than the death of legal professionalism.[2] The demise of professionalism in other fields—in medicine, for example—has of course been a subject of anxious discussion, too.[3] But the amount of time that lawyers have devoted to the subject, and the intensity of the concerns they have expressed about it, reflect a particularly acute disturbance in the self-understanding and self-confidence of the legal profession, whatever the situation may be in other fields, and whether or not the present crisis of legal professionalism—for *crisis* is the right word to describe the cultural anxieties that lawyers are now experiencing—is part of a wider crisis of professionalism generally.

Despite the breadth and seriousness of this crisis, however, the concept of legal professionalism itself has not been well examined. Many have complained, with justification, about its demise, but few have attempted to say what it is, and even fewer have tried to explain why anyone outside the profession should be at all concerned about its continuing vitality.[4] This is what I hope to do in my brief introduction to this collection of essays.

I seek, first, to identify those features of law practice that make it a profession as distinct from a business or trade, and that explain the "status pride" of lawyers—the high self-regard they experience as the members of a profession.[5] Second, I aim to describe the contribution that legal professionalism makes to the wider social order in which lawyers work, a contribution of importance to those outside the profession as well as those within it. In a concluding section I shall quickly survey the forces that today put the culture of legal professionalism under such stress, and that together have provoked the anxieties that so many lawyers, in every branch of the profession, now share.

II

Every profession is a job. Every professional makes a living by doing what he does. But not every job is a profession. Not every job is a way of life. The word *profession* suggests a certain stature and prestige. It implies that the activity to which it is attached possesses a special dignity that other, nonprofessional jobs do not. For centuries, the practice of law has been considered a profession, both by lawyers and laypeople, and legal education has always been thought of as a form of professional, and not merely vocational, training. What lies behind these ancient assumptions? What makes the law a profession?

My answer to this question has four parts. The practice of law has four characteristic features that make it a profession and entitle those engaged in it to the special respect this word implies.

The first characteristic is that the law is a public calling which entails a duty to serve the good of the community as a whole, and not just one's own good or that of one's clients. In the second chapter of *The Wealth of Nations*, Adam Smith makes the famous observation that "it is not from the benevolence of the butcher, the brewer, or the baker, that we expect our dinner, but from their regard to their own interest."[6] Smith goes on to explain how each of these, pursuing his business with an eye solely to his own advantage, produces by means of an invisible hand an addition to the public good. With lawyers, it is different. Like the butcher, the brewer, or the baker, the lawyer also expects an income from his work. Like them, the lawyer generally is not motivated by benevolence to do what he does. But, in contrast to Smith's tradesmen, it *is* a part of the lawyer's job to be directly concerned with the public good— with the integrity of the legal system, with the fairness of its rules and their administration, with the health and well-being of the community that the laws in part establish and in part aspire to create. We say that every lawyer is "an officer of the court."[7] What we mean is that lawyers, like judges, are bound by their position to look after the soundness of the legal system and must take steps to insure its justice—conscious, direct, and deliberate steps, not those indirect and unanticipated ones that lead the butcher and his friends from a preoccupation with their own advantage to the surprising and wholly unintended production of a public good.

This is not to say that lawyers are exclusively concerned with the public good. Of course they are not. Lawyers represent clients and causes whose partisan interests often contribute nothing to the public good and sometimes conflict with it. But a lawyer must always keep at least one eye on the public good, and make sure it is well-protected against the assaults of private interest, including those of his own clients. And a lawyer must do this not just occasionally, not just in the fraction of time he devotes to pro bono activities, but constantly and consistently, in every moment he is practicing law. A lawyer who is doing his job well dwells in the tension between private interest and public good, and never overcomes it. He struggles constantly between the duty to serve his client and the equally powerful obligation to serve the good of the law as a whole. Adam Smith's tradesmen do the latter automatically and unthinkingly by doing the former, and so never experience a tension between the two. The lawyer does because, unlike the butcher, brewer, and baker, he is charged with a conscious trusteeship of the public good that cannot be discharged by any mechanism other than his own direct intervention. This is what is implied by the claim that every lawyer is an officer of the court, and the law a public calling, the first of the four features of law practice that explains its standing as a profession.

The second is the nonspecialized nature of law practice. The legal profession remains, to a surprising degree, a generalist's craft, whose possessor can move from one field to another—from criminal law to bankruptcy to civil rights—with only modest readjustments. The law is not a form of technical expertise but a loose ensemble of methods and habits easily transported across doctrinal lines, and a lawyer is not a technician, trained to do one thing well, but a jack (or jill) of all trades. Here again, the practice of law differs from the other activities that Adam Smith takes as his paradigm of modern economic life: pinmaking, for example, a process marked, he says, by the division of tasks into ever finer parts, each the province of a specialist with a tremendously developed but excruciatingly narrow expertise.[8] Lawyers, by contrast, perform a range of different tasks—counseling clients, drafting documents for them, negotiating and litigating on their behalf, touching, in the process, on a dozen different areas of law—and move about among these tasks with a flexibility unthinkable in Adam Smith's pinmaking factory.

The education that lawyers receive reflects this. The purpose of a legal education is not to produce experts, as many nonlawyers wrongly believe. It is to train students, as the saying goes, to think like lawyers, which means: to be attentive to the facts and to know which ones, in any given situation, are important; to be able to tell a story with the facts, to master the power of narration; to recognize what others hope to achieve, even—or especially—when they have a hard time defining their own ambitions; and to appreciate, empathically, a range of purposes and values and ideals wider than one's own. The man or woman who lacks these qualities will never think like a lawyer, no matter how much doctrinal knowledge he or she possesses. By contrast, the man or woman who possesses these qualities need have only the most elementary knowledge of legal rules and procedures to be well-prepared for the practice of law, to have the kind of preparation that the best law schools provide. From the standpoint of the pin factory and all the other modern forms of enterprise whose success depends upon the division of labor and the cultivation of a deep but narrow expertise, the fact that the law remains a generalist's craft can only be interpreted as a sign of its dilettantism and amateurish backwardness. But viewed in another light, with pride and not embarrassment, the nontechnical nature of his work constitutes a second enduring source of the lawyer's claim to be a professional with a freedom and range of activity that specialization destroys.

A third source of the lawyer's professionalism—related to this second one—is the capacity for judgment. I said that the goal of legal education is not to impart a body of technical knowledge but to develop certain general aptitudes or abilities: the ability, for example, to see facts clearly, and to grasp the appeal of points of view one doesn't embrace. To do this requires more than intellectual skill. It also requires the development of perceptual and emotional powers, and hence necessarily engages parts of one's personality other than the cognitive or thinking part. A good legal education is a process of general maturation in which the seeing, thinking, and feeling parts of the soul are reciprocally engaged. It is a bad mistake to think that legal training sharpens the mind alone. The clever lawyer, who possesses a huge stockpile of technical information about the law and is adept at its manipulation, but who lacks the ability to distinguish between what is important and what is not and cannot sympathetically imagine how things look and feel from his adversary's point of view, is not a good lawyer. He is, in fact, a rather poor lawyer, who is more likely to do his clients harm than good. The good lawyer—the one who is really skilled at his job—is the lawyer who possesses the full complement of emotional and perceptual and intellectual powers that are needed for good judgment, a lawyer's most important and valuable trait.[9] And because of this, the process of training to become a lawyer, and the subsequent experience of being one, gather the soul's powers in a way that confirms one's sense of wholeness as a person and the sense of being wholly engaged by one's work—in contrast to all activities that can be mastered by the mind alone, which often produce, among the technicians who perform them, a sense of partial engagement only. The good lawyer knows that he needs all his human powers to do his job well, and the knowledge that he does gives his work a dignity no expertise, however demanding intellectually, can ever possess. This is the third feature of law practice that entitles us to call it a profession.

The fourth, and last, concerns time, and the location of law within it. Every activity has a past. Every activity therefore has a history, which can be studied and written down in books. I am sure that even pinmaking has been studied by historians. But the law has a special relation to the past. The law's past is not only something that can be observed from the outside; it also possesses value and prestige within the law itself. In pinmaking, the fact that pins were made a certain way before is no argument at all for continuing to make them this way now. We may do so, out of habit, but prior practice has no normative force in pinmaking, or computer chipmaking, or any other line of manufacture. Put differently, precedent is not a value in these activities; at most, it is a fact. By contrast, precedent *is* a value in the law: not always the final or weightiest value, but a value that must always be taken into account. The fact that a law has been in existence for some time is always a reason for continuing to respect it, and this reason must be considered and weighed even when we reject it.

The law is internally connected to its past—connected by its own defining norms and values—and not just externally connected, as every enterprise is, through the story an observer might tell about its development over time. To enter the legal profession is therefore to come into an activity with self-conscious historical depth, to feel that one is entering an activity that has long been under way, and whose fulfillment requires a collaboration among many generations. It is to know that one belongs to a tradition. By contrast, in many lines of work—even those with a long history—all that matters is what is happening now, and the temporal horizon of one's own engagement in the work shrinks down to the point of the present. I imagine the experience of those in the computer industry, which seems to undergo a revolution every two years, to be like this, though I am only guessing. What I do know, from my own experience and from the experience of my students, is that the work of lawyers joins them in a self-conscious colleagueship with the dead and the unborn,[10] and that this widening of temporal outlook is part of what lawyers mean when they describe their work as a profession.

I have now identified the four features of law practice that make it a profession. The practice of law is a public calling and a generalist's craft that engages the whole personality of the practitioner and which links him to a tradition that joins the generations in a partnership of historical proportions. Together, these four features give the practice of law a dignity that is the source of the lawyer's professional pride, of his belief that what he does for a living constitutes a way of life with special worth. They form the basis of the culture of professionalism in which this approving self-image is anchored and through which it is transmitted from one generation of lawyers to the next. It is therefore easy to understand why the weakening of this culture must be of great concern to lawyers, for their own high self-regard—the special value they assign their work and hence themselves—is rendered less secure by the enfeeblement of the culture of professionalism that supports and affirms it.

III

But why should anyone else care whether legal professionalism is alive or dead? That is a harder question to answer.

It is appropriate to begin by recalling how large a role lawyers play in American life. Despite the fact that we have always viewed our lawyers with a measure of distrust—-inevitable, even salutary, in a democracy in which lawyers possess the keys to the house of the law and, with that, a disproportionate share of power—we have also assigned them a leading role in arranging our affairs, both public and private. Fearing and even occasionally loathing lawyers, we have nevertheless entrusted them with great powers and responsibilities, and made them, to a remarkable degree, the stewards of our republic. Behind all the cynicism and fashionable disgust, behind all the complaints—many of them justified—about the excesses of the adversary system and the partisan exploitation of loopholes and technicalities, lies this basic fact of trust, the huge trust we have placed in our lawyers. We have trusted our lawyers to play a central role in the design and management of our society, and if one asks why, a partial answer would be that we have done so because the same four features of legal professionalism that constitute the basis of their status pride also equip them to play a leading role in the government of society, a role that lawyers become less able to perform in proportion to the weakening of their professional culture. Let me explain.

We live today in a sprawling, heterogeneous, and highly interdependent society, the most complex society the world has ever known. The great nineteenth-century European sociologists who observed the development and growth of this novel social order were struck by its economic and cultural connections and by the assimilative powers linking its many parts, powers that have increased in strength with the spread of democratic institutions and, above all, with the expansion of the capitalist system of production. But these same observers were also impressed by the disintegrative forces at work within our modern world, and by the need to find a counterweight that might resist them.

The forces of disintegration they identified were four. The first was privatization, the tendency in a large free-enterprise economy for individuals to concern themselves exclusively with their own private welfare, and to neglect or forget entirely the claims of public life, which the Greeks and Romans, and their humanist successors, had pursued with such memorable passion.[11] The second was specialization, whose inexorable tendency is to separate those in different lines of work and to reduce their fund of shared experience, the common world of similar endeavors.[12] The third was alienation, the sense of detachment from one's work, and secondarily from other human beings, the experience of being only partially engaged by—and hence only partially revealed through—the activities that constitute one's living.[13] And the fourth disintegrative force that Tocqueville, Marx, Durkheim, Maine, and Weber identified as a threat to the farflung interdependencies of modern social life was forgetfulness, the loss of a sense of historical depth, and the consequent disconnection of the present moment—characterized by the idiocy of material comfort—from all that went before or is to follow, from the pain of the past and the calling of the future.[14] We are witnessing, these thinkers said, the evolution of a form of life more complex and interconnected than any seen before, but in the heart of this new order lurk forces of disintegration powerful enough to nullify its achievements: the forces of privatization, specialization, alienation, and forgetfulness, the loss of one's sense of location in time.

To each of these four forces of disintegration, one of the four elements of legal professionalism may be paired as a remedy of sorts. Thus, for example, the lawyer's obligation to promote the public good—the public nature of his calling—may be thought of as a counterweight against the strictly private concerns of his clients, who for the most part want only to succeed within the framework of the law but take no interest in the well-being of the law itself. Lawyers serve the private interests of their clients, but they also care about the integrity and justice of the legal system that defines the public order within which these interests are pursued. In this way, they provide a link between the realms of public and private life, helping to rejoin what the forces of privatization are constantly pulling apart.[15]

To the disintegrative effects of specialization, the generalist nature of law practice offers valuable resistance. Because they represent clients of many sorts, in many different lines of work, lawyers are in a position to evaluate the social order from a broader point of view unrestricted by the narrowing assumptions and experience of any single expertise, and to provide a kind of connective tissue among different forms of enterprise, which lawyers are often called upon to join, through a sort of shuttle diplomacy and the transactional schemes they design. If their commitment to the ideal of justice prepares them to provide a horizontal linkage upward from the realm of private concerns to that of public values, the fact that theirs is a generalist's craft equips lawyers to provide vertical linkages across the increasingly specialized world of work.

So far as alienation is concerned, it would of course be foolish to suggest that lawyers can combat its spread or soften its effects. We have all experienced, to one degree or another, the sense of separation from the world which the word *alienation* implies, and have known the loneliness associated with it, and there is little that lawyers, or anyone else, can do to change this basic fact of modern life. But to the extent the law remains a profession that engages the whole person, that calls upon all the powers of the soul—perceptual and emotional as well as intellectual—it offers those who enter it the hope of a complete engagement in their work, an engagement that is the antithesis of alienation, and which provides an image, at least, of what un-alienated work can be.

And, finally, the historical traditions of the law, which give the lawyers who work in it a self-conscious sense of their location in a continuing adventure with a past and future as well as a present, are a counterweight against the forgetfulness, the obliviousness to time, that characterizes our life today, with its rush of transient moments, each disconnected from the rest, in a contented but timeless present where the partnership among the generations—"the great primaeval contract of eternal society," as Burke called it[16]—is literally disintegrated, and forgotten. Much of the shallowness of our life—our fickle fascination with celebrities, for example, and the brevity of their fame—is the result of this loss of a sense of location in time. All those forms of work for which a sense of historical depth continues to be needed should be valued for the resistence they offer to the temporal flattening of experience. Among these forms of work, the practice of law remains especially important.

The four features of law practice that make it a profession are significant, therefore, not only because they justify the status pride of lawyers (which others often find grating), but also because each in a different way helps to ameliorate one of the four disintegrating forces which the very developments that have produced our wealthy and complex world have themselves unchained. The legal profession is an integrative force in a world of disintegrating powers, and this is one reason why, despite the natural suspicion that lawyers arouse in a democratic society like our own, they have been entrusted with such large responsibilities in matters of governance. It is also why everyone—and not just lawyers—should be concerned by a threat to the culture of legal professionalism. For the values that define this culture are the key to the work that lawyers do in bridging the divisions of our world, divisions whose disintegrative effects are at once the most familiar and most dangerous features of modern life.

IV

But are these values threatened today? Can we be confident that the culture of legal professionalism will survive? Is the self-esteem of lawyers secure? Will they continue to be able to play the same socially valuable role they have played in the past? I am troubled by doubts. I fear that things are changing rapidly, and for the worse. I am worried that legal professionalism is in danger—deep danger—and I want to conclude by briefly explaining why.

In the last quarter-century, the American legal profession has been transformed by a series of sweeping changes that have compromised each of the four features of law practice that justify its claim to be a profession. In the first place, the commercialization of law practice, especially in its upper reaches, at the country's largest and most prestigious firms, has introduced an element of competitiveness that has caused many lawyers in these firms to view their public responsibilities as a luxury they can no longer afford in the frantic scramble to attract business by appealing to the self-interest of clients.[17] This tendency has been exacerbated, I am bound to say, by the official pronouncements on legal ethics made by the American Bar Association and other organized groups, which increasingly endorse the view that lawyers serve the public best by serving the private interests of their clients with maximum zeal, in effect treating lawyers like Adam Smith's tradesmen, who count on an invisible hand to transmute their pursuit of private advantage into a benefit for the community as a whole.[18]

At the same time, the pressure for increased specialization in law practice has been growing, and it is uncertain how much longer this pressure can be resisted. In part, the demand for specialization reflects a change in the relationship of lawyers to clients, who today increasingly expect their lawyers to supply highly specialized instructions for a narrowly defined range of problems, and not the general, all-purpose advice that legal counselors a generation ago were often asked to provide. The sheer increase in the number and complexity of legal rules to which we are subject today has also increased the pressure for specialization. Vast quantities of new laws are enacted each year, and countless courts issue innumerable opinions construing them. In the expanding world of law, it seems increasingly unrealistic to expect any one lawyer ever to master more than a small portion of it, and so the demand for specialization grows, and with it, the demand for a more specialized law school curriculum.

Today, a higher percentage of lawyers work in large institutions—law firms of fifty or more—than ever before. This shift has meant, inevitably, an increase in bureaucracy and management, something every large organization requires. The result has been the development of a culture—again, most visible in the country's leading firms—marked by the managerial delimitation of assignments and responsibilities, by the substitution of teams for individuals, and by the emergence of relatively inflexible hierarchies of command in place of the older collegial arrangements that existed even in the largest firms two decades ago. Is it any surprise that many lawyers in these firms—the young lawyers especially—report a growing sense of detachment from their institutions, and from the work they do within them? Is it any surprise they complain, as workers in bureaucracies often do, about their diminished feeling of personal fulfillment and growing sense of alienation?[19]

And finally, like everything else in our world, the practice of law is today in danger of losing its temporal range and shrinking down to a series of disconnected points. The growing volume of law and the multiplication of decisions interpreting it has weakened the precedential value of each single judgment—since one can now often find many conflicting answers to the very same question—and this weakening of precedent has cut the practice of law off from its normative base in the past.[20] Technology has also, in a different way, foreshortened the temporal horizon of lawyers. The phone (now portable), the fax (now ubiquitous) and the computer (now able to generate documents and changes in documents at the speed of light) have together had the effect of accelerating the practice of law to the point where many lawyers today complain that their clients expect an instantaneous reply to every question and give them no time to think. The result is a fragmentation of experience, and the narrowing of one's temporal frame of reference, an inward state of mind that is outwardly reflected in the growing tendency of lawyers to move from one firm to the next with dizzying speed (a pattern that suggests the weakening of interest in, and attachment to, any institution that outlasts oneself).

In short, lawyers are today less public spirited and connected to their past, and more specialized and alienated from their work, than they were a quarter-century ago. Each of the four pillars of legal professionalism is today under assault. No one will deny that the legal profession has made dramatic gains during this same period, most notably by opening its doors (part way at least) to groups that had been barred from the profession by a prejudice unworthy of lawyers. But the profession to which these groups have with such justice been admitted is now in danger of losing all of the characteristic features that make it a profession and not just a job. If this happens, it will be a terrible irony for the profession's newest recruits and a blow to the self-esteem of all lawyers. But more important, it will be a blow to America, for the features of legal professionalism that are under such strain today have been a vital integrating force in the construction of our country and our way of life. If the pillars of legal professionalism crumble, we will all be hurt. The disintegrating tendencies of modern life will all meet with less resistance. The common ground on which we all depend will shrink and become less stable. The collapse of the culture of legal professionalism is something none of us can afford, and the challenge it presents, which transcends the field of legal ethics narrowly conceived, is one that lawyers and non-lawyers alike have a stake in meeting.

Notes

This essay was previously published, in a slightly altered form, as Anthony T. Kronman, *Chapman University School of Law Groundbreaking Ceremony, Chapman L. Rev.* 1 (1998).

    1. Ludwig Wittgenstein, *Philosophical Investigations* ¶ 19, at 8e (G.E.M. Anscombe trans., Macmillan 2d ed. 1967) (1953).

    2. See, e.g., Mary Ann Glendon, A Nation Under Lawyers: How the Crisis in the Legal Profession is Transforming American Society (1994) (documenting the current "crisis" in legal professionalism); Arlin M. Adams, "The Legal Profession: A Critical Evaluation, Remarks at the Tresolini Lecture at Lehigh University" (Nov. 10, 1988) in Dick. L. Rev. 643 (1989) (observing how rising commercialism has eroded legal professionalism); Norman Bowie, The Law: From a Profession to a Business, 41 Vand. L. Rev. 741 (1988) (describing the shift from law as a profession to law as a business); Chief Justice Warren E. Burger, The Decline of Professionalism, 63 Fordham L. Rev. 949 (1995) (observing that "the decline of [legal] professionalism has taken on epidemic proportions"). See also ABA Commission on Professionalism, "In the Spirit of Public Service: A Blueprint for the Rekindling of Lawyer Professionalism," reprinted in 112 F.R.D. 243, 251, 254 (1986) (asking, "[h]as our profession abandoned principle for profit, professionalism for commercialism" and "what, if anything, can be done to improve both the reality and perception of lawyer professionalism"); and Colin Croft, Note, "Reconceptualizing American Legal Professionalism: A Proposal for Deliberative Moral Community," 67 N.Y.U. L. Rev. 1256 (1992) (tracing the history of legal professionalism and its decline and suggesting a model structured on a deliberative moral community). See generally Jonathan Harr, A Civil Action (1995) (chronicling an environmental lawsuit wherein leukemia-stricken families find themselves at the mercy of greedy and frequently unprincipled lawyers); Sol M. Linowitz & Martin Mayer, The Betrayed Profession: Lawyering at the End of the Twentieth Century (1994) (exploring the conflict between lawyers' role as advocates and their status as independent professionals); Lincoln Caplan, "The Lawyers' Race to the Bottom," N.Y. Times, Aug. 6, 1993, A29 (arguing that "the practice of law has become hollow at its core").

    3. Even more so than in law, the decline in medical professionalism has been linked to rising commercialism (and the growing prevalence of health management organizations). See,

e.g., John H. McArthur and Francis D. Moore, "The Two Cultures and the Health Care Revolution: Commerce and Professionalism in Medical Care," 277 *JAMA* 985–87 (1997) (arguing that commerce's "invasion" of medical care has eroded medicine's professional tradition); Linda Emanuel, "Bringing Market Medicine to Professional Account," 277 *JAMA* 1004–5 (1997) (arguing that doctors must impose limits on profit-seeking behaviors to protect medical professionalism); Richard Gunderman, "Medicine and the Pursuit of Wealth," 28 *Hastings Center Rep.* 8–11 (decrying rising greed in the medical profession and physicians' consequent abandonment of their nobler aims); and George D. Lundberg, "The Business and Professionalism of Medicine," 278 *JAMA* 17803–4 (1997) (noting that while medicine has always been a balance between a business and a profession, the scales have tipped dangerously toward the business end during the 1990s).

4. A variety of scholars and professional organizations have noted the general lack of clarity about the nature of legal professionalism. See, e.g., ABA Commission on Professionalism, 261 (declaring that "[p]rofessionalism is an elastic concept the meaning and application of which are hard to pin down"); and Commission on Lawyer Professionalism, Florida Bar, Professionalism: A Recommitment of the Bench, the Bar, and the Law Schools of Florida 11 (1989) (acknowledging that "there is no universally accepted definition of 'professionalism'").

Available definitions of legal professionalism are frequently highly controversial. See Richard A. Posner, "Professionalism," 40 *Ariz. L. Rev.* 1, 15, 17–19 (1998) (arguing that the "final end" of legal professionalism should be "the transformation of law into a goal-oriented policy science consecrated to the perfection of instrumental reasoning"); and Richard L. Abel, "A Critique of Torts," 37 *UCLA L. Rev.* 785, 790–91 (1990) (interpreting legal professionalism as an artifice devised by lawyers to "separate[] tort victims from the means of redress" and thus "expropriate[] a fourth to a half of . . . victim[s'] recovery"). Rob Atkinson documents several competing views of legal professionalism in "A Dissenter's Commentary on the Professionalism Crusade," 74 *Tex. L. Rev.* 259, 271–76 (1995) (arguing that protagonists in the contemporary "professionalism crusade" "use the terms 'profession' and 'professionalism' in four overlapping but distinct senses": " 'Professionalism' as Description[,] . . . 'Professionalism' as Explanation[,] . . . 'Professionalism' as Locus of Regulation [and] . . . 'Professionalism' as Focus of Aspiration").

5. Max Weber, *Economy and Society* 1307 (1914; Guenther Roth and Claus Wittich, eds., Ephraim Fischoff et al., trans., Bedminster Press, 1968).

6. Adam Smith, *An Inquiry into the Nature and Causes of the Wealth of Nations* 14 (1776; Edwin Cannan, ed., Random House, 1937).

7. See Model Rules of Professional Conduct: Preamble ¶ 1 (1995) ("A lawyer is . . . an officer of the legal system"); Burger, *Decline*, 949 ("The bedrock of our profession from Blackstone's day has been the professional ideal: the lawyer as an officer of the court").

8. Smith, *Inquiry*, 4–5.

9. I have described at greater length the all-important, but mysterious, faculty we call judgment in Anthony T. Kronman, *The Lost Lawyer*, 16, 56–101 (1993).

10. See Edmund Burke, *Reflections on the Revolution in France*, 85 (1790; J. G. A., Pocock ed., Hackett 1987).

11. See Alexis de Tocqueville, *Democracy in America*, 540-41 (13th ed., 1850; J. P. Mayer, ed., George Lawrence, trans., HarperCollins, 1969).

12. See Emile Durkheim, *The Division of Labor in Society*, 294–95 (1893; W. D. Halls, trans., Free Press, 1984).

13. Karl Marx and Frederick Engels, *The German Ideology*, 53–56 (1846; C. J. Arthur, ed., Lawrence & Wishart, trans., International Publishers, 1970).

14. For an imaginative exploration of the struggle to retain historical depth in the face of

a government campaign to induce mass forgetting, see Milan Kundera, *The Book of Laughter and Forgetting* (1978; Michael Henry Heim, trans., Alfred A. Knopf, 1980). Hannah Arendt provides an equally inspired meditation on the roles of memory and forgetfulness in her essay on "The Gap Between Past and Future"; see especially Hannah Arendt, *Between Past and Future*, 6 (1954; Penguin Books, 1977).

15. See Robert W. Gordon, "Corporate Law Practice as a Public Calling," 49 *Md. L. Rev.* 255 *passim* (1990); Robert W. Gordon, "The Independence of Lawyers," 68 *B.U. L. Rev.* 1, 11, 13 (1988).

16. See Burke, *Reflections*, 85.

17. See Gordon, "Corporate Law Practice," 257.

18. See Model Rules of Professional Conduct: Preamble ¶ 7 (1995) ("when an opposing party is well represented, a lawyer can be a zealous advocate on behalf of a client and at the same time assume that justice is being done"). As Robert Gordon observes:

> Even the ABA's Model Rules of Professional Conduct were drafted (largely upon the insistence of the trial bar) to give primacy to the advocate's role and to reduce dissonance between pursuit of law-embodied norms and the client's immediate interests in favor of acquiescence to the client. *See id.* Under these rules, for example, lawyers are not to counsel or assist clients to engage in criminal or fraudulent conduct, *see id.* Rule 1.2, but have no positive duty to urge compliance or to go beyond "purely technical" advice, *see id.* Rule 2.1 cmt., if that is all the client wants; *see id.* Rule 1.2, and have virtually no formal leverage over clients who persist in illegal conduct, since they may disclose misconduct to outsiders only in extreme situations, *see id.* Rule 1.6, and may not even resign unless the company's highest authority resolves to proceed with a "clear" violation of law likely to result in "substantial injury" to the organization, *Id.* Rule 1.13. The lawyer who cannot count upon factual uncertainty, legal ambiguity, and vaguely worded client assurances that it will clean up its act, to relieve her of any pressure to invoke these (in any case nonobligatory) sanctions is sadly deficient in the casuistical and rationalizing defense-mechanisms of her profession.

Gordon, "Corporate Law Practice," 279.

Meanwhile, the codes of professional responsibility prepared by some state bar associations imply that lawyers' role as officers of the court is subsumed in their role as zealous advocates. See, e.g., New York State Bar Association Code of Professional Responsibility EC-7-1 (1996) (describing the lawyer's duty to the legal system as consisting of zealous representation within the bounds of the law).

19. See, e.g., Boston Bar Association Task Force on Professional Fulfillment, *Expectations, Reality and Recommendations for Change*, vi–vii, 7–11 (1997), describing the "growing sense of isolation and alienation expressed by many attorneys," in particular, young associates at large firms; and Chief Judge Carl Horn, "Restoring the Foundations: Twelve Steps Toward Personal Fulfillment in the Practice of Law" 10 *S.C. Law.* 32, 35 (1998): "The survey data and anecdotal evidence [show] . . . that many lawyers are working harder but enjoying it much less."

20. See Grant Gilmore, *The Ages of American Law*, 70–71, 80–81 (1977).

3

Why Lawyers Can't Just
Be Hired Guns

ROBERT W. GORDON

My theme in this essay is the public responsibilities of lawyers—their obligations to help maintain and improve the legal system: the framework of laws, procedures, and institutions that structures their roles and work.

Ordinarily this is a theme for ceremonial occasions, like Law Day sermons or bar association dinners or memorial eulogies—when we are given license to rise on the wings of rhetorical inspiration far above the realities of day-to-day practice. I want to try to approach the subject in a different spirit, as a workaday practical necessity for the legal profession. My argument is simple: that lawyers' work on behalf of clients positively requires—both for its justification and its successful functioning for the benefit of those same clients in the long run—that lawyers also help maintain and re-fresh the public sphere, the infrastructure of law and cultural convention that consti-tutes the cement of society.

The way we usually discuss the subject of lawyers' public obligations—outside ceremonial rhetoric—is as a problem in legal "ethics." We often hear things like, "Lawyers must be zealous advocates for their clients, but of course lawyers are also 'officers of the court'; and sometimes the duties mandated by these different roles come into conflict and must be appropriately balanced." And indeed some of the most contentious disputes about "ethics" in the legal profession concern such con-flicts between the "private" interests of lawyers and clients and their "public" obliga-tions to adversaries, third parties, and the justice system itself—issues like: When, if ever, should lawyers have to disclose client fraud or wrongdoing or withdraw from representing clients who persist in it? When, if ever, should they refuse to pursue client claims they believe legally frivolous? Or act to prevent clients or their witnesses from giving perjured or seriously misleading testimony or responses to discovery requests?

These are important issues, no doubt about it, but in this essay I want to look at them in a larger and slightly different perspective than we can usually get from the "legal-ethics" debates. For one thing, "ethics" isn't quite what I want to talk about. I suspect that most lawyers, when they hear "ethics," think, first, that something cosmically boring is about to be said, which one would only listen to in order to satisfy a bar admission or continuing legal education requirement; or else that they are about to hear some unwelcome news about a conflict of interest disqualifying them from taking on a client. "Ethics" has come to mean either: (1) the detailed technical rules in the professional-ethical codes; or, alternatively, (2) a strictly personal morality, the morality of individual conscience, an aspect of personal character which people just have or don't have, and if they have it, acquired it, if not in kindergarten, at least well before they became lawyers. The responsibilities of lawyers I'm talking about in this essay are of a different order; and I'll call them "public responsibilities" instead of ethics, to emphasize that they are responsibilities that attach to lawyers both in their functions as lawyers and as "citizens" who benefit, and whose clients benefit, from participation in the political, legal, social, and cultural order of a capitalist constitutional democracy, and who thereby owe that order some obligations to respect and help maintain its basic ground rules.

The order is *capitalist:* that is, constituted by the basic ground rules of a system of private property and market exchange. This is not, contrary to the antigovernment rhetoric we hear a lot of these days, a state of nature, but an order created and maintained by both coercive and facilitative government actions—the enforcement of rules of property, contract, tort, commercial law, employment law, and unfair competition; the facilitation of collective action through corporations, cooperatives, partnerships, and collective bargaining.

The order is also *democratic:* meaning that the ground rules that constitute the "private" economy and society are subject to revision and modification by democratically elected representative institutions and by the administrative bureaucracies that these legislatures create to carry out legislation.

Finally, the order is *constitutional:* in that its exercises of collective power are supposed to be limited by a set of fundamental substantive and procedural constraints—enforced in our system in the last instance by courts but supposedly respected by all power-wielding bodies, private as well as public.

The general premise of a liberal polity in short is that freely chosen goals (or "self-interest," if one prefers that reductive way of speaking) are to be pursued within a framework of constraints—established by norms, customary practices, rules, institutions, and procedures and maintained by systems of culture and morals backed by social sanctions and, selectively, by law.

Let's focus first on capitalism. Even the most libertarian theorists of capitalism, like Milton Friedman, for example, would stipulate that capitalism works only if there are strong conventions maintaining the framework of order within which, supposedly, self-interested behavior will add up to the general welfare. If individual players resort to theft, trespass, corruption, force, fraud, and monopoly; if they regularly inflict uncompensated harms upon others, and consistently get away with it, the order will collapse. The order of law, it has come to be pretty clear, is not enough in itself to sustain a market economy: a capitalist system also requires what might be called an order of custom—a cultural infrastructure of norms, learned dispositions to respect property and keep promises and pay taxes and refrain from private violence to settle disputes, and of a certain degree of mutual trust — confidence that others will, within limits, for the most part, also respect the norms. The law without the custom supporting it doesn't work, because no legal system can maintain order against persistent and pervasive violations or evasions. Without social conventions in place to maintain the framework, no state can be legitimate or strong enough to supply one. There will be no reliable system of contract enforcement, no effective safeguards against theft, fraud, and violence, no protection of consumers or labor against being cheated or abused, no effective protection of the environment, no way of extracting taxes to pay for public goods like law enforcement. Yet custom also needs the support of law. Norms of cooperation and mutual trust create openings for opportunists and free riders to abuse them, and outside of close-knit communities nonlegal social sanctions will not adequately police against such abuses. Although compliance with the framework norms has to be largely voluntary, you need coercive law to demonstrate the costs of abuse and also to reaffirm the norms against the moral "outsiders," the amoral calculators who would otherwise profit from everyone else's trusting law-abidingness.

Readers will recognize here an exaggerated—but only slightly exaggerated—description of the current Russian scene. The Russians are trying to run a market economy with no customs or traditions supporting a private framework of constraints on opportunistic behavior in those markets; and also without the legitimacy and support for the state authority to supplement and supply the deficiencies of the private framework. Framework functions that we take for granted—like routine security for personal safety and business assets, and routine contract enforcement—since they are not being supplied by custom or law enforcement, are hired out instead to private purveyors of violence, Mafiosi or ex-KGB thugs.

Let us return now to the developed capitalist economies such as ours. Such an economy in short depends as much on common agreement to abide by its ground rules as it does on competition and innovation, on the substructures of trust, cooperation, and law that maintain that agreement. These frameworks are public goods or common property; they are like the air we breathe.

Now where do lawyers come into the picture? Lawyers have a dual role. They are agents of clients, and in that role help clients to pursue their self-interest—to manipulate the rules and procedures of the legal system on their behalf, to negotiate through bureaucratic labyrinths, to repel assaults on persons or property or liberty.

But lawyers must also be agents of the common framework of institutions, customs, and norms within which their clients' interests must be pursued if the premises underlying all these individual exercises of freedom are to be made good. Let me try to develop this argument for the "public" side of lawyers' obligations.

The dominant ideology of the legal profession, the norm of zealous advocacy or adversary ideal, tends to obscure the public side of the ledger. But that side is always present, and is not adequately described by the ritualistic phrase "officer of the court." Much of the lawyer's role that is usually thought of as simply zealous representation is actually also designed to carry out the public framework-regarding aims of the legal system. The obvious example is criminal defense. Our own painful history and the experience of most other nations today teach that the criminal justice system is prone to systematic abuses. Police will break down doors at night, detain suspects in secret, and coerce confessions; prosecutors will fabricate evidence or suborn perjury of witnesses. Against such abuses, legal reformers over time have enacted both substantive and procedural safeguards. The defense counsel's primary role is to act as the outside monitor; he is the gadfly who keeps the system honest, and ensures that the police and prosecution go by the book in their treatment of suspects and collection of evidence. In this sense defense counsel is a public agent of the framework.

So, too, in the civil justice system. Lawyers serve as public agents in helping clients to vindicate claims given by the substantive law; and in preventing government agents or adversaries from abusing the law, or from gaining advantages that are not permitted by law. In short, the lawyer's role is part of the foundation of a capitalist democratic system.

The term *ethics* doesn't really capture these public functions of the lawyer. These are functions of *citizenship* in the broad sense, of obligations to the framework of law and custom that makes the overall social system—a market economy within the rule of law—work.

Well, what obligations can be derived from the role? At minimum, one would think, a set of negative obligations: in the words of the Hippocratic oath, "First, do no harm." Meaning, in this context, what the philosopher Jon Elster calls "everyday Kantianism"—refrain from actions which if multiplied and generalized would weaken or erode the essential framework of norms and customs.[1] Why are these specially obligations of lawyers? In part of course they are not, they are obligations on all citizens. (By citizens, incidentally, I don't mean technically born or naturalized citizens, but all people who benefit from participation in the framework; so a foreign company doing business in the United States or a lawyer for that company would be a citizen in this expanded sense.) But lawyers do have special obligations: they are in a unique position to safeguard framework arrangements, because they are also in a unique position both to ensure that those arrangements are carried into effect and to sabotage them. All procedures that exist to vindicate claims given by the substantive law, especially complex and expensive ones like litigation or administrative rule making, also deliver resources for strategic behavior—delay, obstruction, confusion of the record, raising costs to adversaries. The resources of law, in unscrupulous hands, can be used to nullify law. This is why we are told that outlaw organizations like the Mafia reportedly offer a key role to the *consigliere*—the lawyer who keeps the law at bay, so that the organization can operate outside the law.

But let us take a less extreme example. Suppose that the lawyer does not represent a persistently outlaw client—the enterprise that lurks at the margins of organized society, taking advantage of its rules and customs to rip off a surplus for itself—but the more usual client, like the ordinary business firm, whose interest is sometimes in vindicating, but also sometimes in avoiding, requirements of the substantive law: in enforcing some contracts but evading obligations under others, in protecting itself against employee theft or sabotage but in circumventing labor law to forestall union organizing campaigns, in seeking compensation for torts committed against it but immunity for its own torts. If lawyers employ every strategy to defeat the claims they don't like, they will erode the process's value for its good uses as well as its bad ones. Outcomes become expensive, time-consuming, and arbitrary. They reward wealth and cunning, and bear less and less relationship to judgment on the merits. Without controls, the system can rapidly deteriorate to a tool of oppression and extortion. By raising the enforcement costs of regulation, lawyers can encourage defiance of regulation by their competitors as well as themselves, and begin a race for the bottom in which nice guys finish last, the law-observing client is an innocent simpleton, a loser in the Darwinian struggle.

The legal-social framework is a common good, and self-interested individual behavior can destroy its value for everyone. Extreme adversariness in litigation or regulatory compliance settings is problematic not just because it is incredibly unpleasant and full of posturing and bad manners, but because it erodes the conditions of the economy and social order. Repeated lying in negotiations can destroy fragile networks of trust and cooperation that alone make negotiation—especially between relative strangers—possible. Strategic contract-breaking reduces the value of all contracts everywhere that are not already backed by strong customary sanctions.

Many lawyers at this point are tempted to say: We admit all this, but enforcing the framework norms isn't our business; it's the specialized role of public enforcement agents—judges, prosecutors, agency bureaucrats, and other officials. But if you accept any of the argument so far, this just has to be wrong. A legal system, like a social system, depends largely on voluntary compliance with its norms. When compliance is replaced by underground resistance—or only nominal compliance—when drivers stop at the red lights only when they think a cop is looking, or are prepared to exhaust the traffic court's limited resources by arguing the light was green—the system has broken down. Suppose that, as happens in many of the world's societies, individuals and businesses began serious cheating on their taxes. In a world in which there are resources to audit only 1 per cent of returns, the result is total system breakdown. Taxes that depend on self-reporting can no longer be collected. Some people are not very frightened by this particular prospect; but they might be if other enforcement mechanisms broke down—if, for instance, gangs of the physically strong, financed by the wealthy, started preying on their families and businesses, and counted on lawyers to stall enforcement of the legal controls on their predation.

In any case, lawyers, especially lawyers for powerful clients, are rarely just passive law-takers: they are active law-makers, designers of contractual and associational arrangements that create or limit rights and duties and dispute-settlement modes, and that are binding on trading partners, employees, suppliers, or customers. The employment lawyers who draft contracts requiring employees to waive rights given by state labor law and submit all disputes to arbitrators chosen by the employer; the HMO lawyers who draft clauses forbidding doctors under contract to the organization from disclosing to patients that the organization policies will not authorize certain treatments—these attorneys are engaged in what the "legal process" scholars Hart and Sacks called "private legislation".[2]

Lawyers have to help preserve the commons—to help clients comply with the letter and purpose of the frameworks of law and custom that sustain them all; and their obligation is clearly strongest where there is no adversary with access to the same body of facts to keep them honest, and no umpire or monitor to ensure conformity to legal norms and adequate protection of the interests of third parties and the integrity of the legal system.

Of course I realize that the view that I'm putting forward, a view which assigns to lawyers a major role as curators of the public frameworks that sustain our common existence, is drastically at odds with a view that is widespread if not dominant in the legal profession. This view, which I'll call the libertarian-positivist view, holds that the lawyer owes only the most minimal duties to the legal framework—the duties not to violate plain unambiguous commands of law, procedure, or ethics, not to tell plain lies to magistrates, and perhaps also not to offer such outrageously strained interpretations of facts or law to tribunals as to amount to outright misrepresentations—and owes no duties to the social framework at all, if performing them would conflict with his client's immediate interests. In this view the lawyer and client are alone together in a world where there are some positive rules: the lawyer's job is to help the client get what he wants without breaking the rules—or at least without breaking them when anyone's likely to notice—though it's all right to bend them.[3]

The problem I have with using the libertarian-positivist starting point is that in a democratic society it seems wrong to conceive of the law and the state wholly as adversaries, the "other," a bureaucratic maze to be adroitly negotiated on behalf of one's clients—and especially wrong if one's clients are members of groups who do in fact have some access to political power. We are after all members of a common political community, with agreed-upon procedures for establishing and changing its common frameworks. I would argue for the lawyer's starting from an opposite presumption from the libertarian one—though also rebuttable in particular contexts—a presumption that the law very imperfectly sets forth an approximately agreed-upon minimal framework of common purposes, a social contract. I don't mean a framework of "thick" moral norms such as a communitarian or civic republican would

imagine, but neither do I mean just a "thin" obligation to obey only the plainest unambiguous commands in circumstances where violations are likely to be detected.
The domain of these obligations lies somewhere between morality and resentful
minimal compliance with rules. The metaphor I'd suggest is that of a relational contract—the long-term contract calling for repeated occasions for performance, a contract structured by norms of trust, reciprocity, and fair dealing. A contract partner is
not expected to sacrifice her self-interest to the other party's, but does have a duty of
good-faith observance of the principles and purposes of the contractual framework
that has been set up to serve their mutual advantage. With most clients, including
business clients, the lawyer could start with the presumption that many good lawyers
do indeed begin with—that the client is not out to get away with anything he can in
pursuit of his objectives, but wants to abide by the spirit of the framework and be a
good citizen—and face the more difficult dilemma of whether to advise him how to
get around the rules only if he makes the intention to evade them manifest, after
being advised to comply.

I readily acknowledge that there's nothing simple or straightforward about complying with framework norms in the modern regulatory state—often just figuring
out what they are is a considerable undertaking. Regulatory regimes tend to be
appallingly complex and technical, crammed with loopholes and ambiguities,
sometimes put there by regulated interests, often inadvertent. Regulatory statutes are
often utopian; full compliance is impossible. They are often in part only symbolic—
sweeping commands considerably qualified or even retracted in practice by a large
discretion or ridiculously low budget for enforcement. Nonetheless, I think in most
contexts lawyers can fairly readily tell the difference between making good-faith efforts to comply with a plausible interpretation of the purposes of a legal regime, and
using every ingenuity of his or her trade to resist or evade compliance.

And just as clearly, I'd maintain, lawyers have another obligation as well—
though this is an obligation that they can discharge through collective action,
through organizations, surrogates, or representatives as well as personally: and that is
the obligation to work outside the context of representing clients to improve, reform,
and maintain the framework of justice. One thing this obligation unmistakably calls
for is helping to remedy the maldistribution—really nondistribution—of legal services to people with serious legal problems but without much money. But another is
to help fix legal processes that waste everyone's money in administrative costs or otherwise systematically produce unfair results. Again, I would guess that many lawyers
see this kind of framework repair and reform work as a kind of pro bono philanthropy: they are glad that some prominent lawyers are doing it, but see it as an optional task for the private bar. From this view, working on the framework is only
in the actual job description of public officials—legislators, administrators, judges.
And again, I would argue, that view can't be right—for reasons of both history and
principle.

As a matter of tradition, in America private lawyers have assumed a large share of the public role—sufficiently long-standing and ingrained into customary practice so that you could reasonably call it a *constitutional* role—of safeguarding the framework and adapting it to changing conditions. This role devolved on lawyers at the founding of the republic, when private lawyers assumed the major share of responsibility for making the legal case for the Revolution and in drafting the basic charters of government, the state and federal constitutions. In the early decades of the republic, private lawyers undertook the task of producing an Americanized common law to serve as the basic ground rules for commercial life. In the Progressive era, the creation of the modern state, government through administrative commissions and professional associations, was also largely the work of practicing lawyers—though academic lawyers also got into the act in a big way in drafting the legislation of the New Deal and staffing its agencies. Lawyers have of course dominated the legislative bodies of the country, especially at the federal level, for its entire history. Lawyers temporarily on leave from practice have run the foreign policy of this country for most of its existence.[4] Private lawyers don't play this role in every society; they have played it in America, primarily because with our Revolution we rejected the European model of government through a centralized bureaucracy staffed by an elite career civil service. Our senior levels of statecraft have had to come from part-time volunteers—more often than not lawyers—like Alexander Hamilton, Thomas Jefferson, John Adams, Daniel Webster, John Quincy Adams, Charles Evans Hughes, Elihu Root, Henry Stimson, Dean Acheson, John J. McCloy, John Foster Dulles, Cyrus Vance, and Warren Christopher, just for a short list.

But there is more to this story than the conspicuous lawyer-statesmen on the commanding heights of government. It's no accident that most of the names I've just mentioned were primarily active in foreign policy. In the domestic field, after the basic institutions of government had been established, Americans of the Jeffersonian persuasion turned away from Hamilton's aristocratic model of "energetic government" managed by elites drawn from professional classes.[5] Under the new ethos America was to be dominantly a commercial republic, one in which happiness was to be pursued by those free to pursue it (which at the time meant mostly white males) through labor, trade, manufactures, land cultivation, and speculation. From an early date the market economy, the sphere of "free enterprise," was naturalized, made to appear as if it were a machine that would run of itself. The background frameworks that it presupposed and helped make it run, the infrastructures of law and government and custom, because they were relegated to the background, became invisible to many of the enterprisers who depended on them without realizing it.

In fact, of course, those networks of law and government and custom were everywhere: the United States was even at the outset a thoroughly "well-regulated society"[6]—every aspect of social life was criss-crossed with legal and customary regulations of family and employment relations; of land use and common resources; of nuisances, contracts, and debt collection. Much of this regulation was decentralized and localized—government by local commissions and juries, by public enforcement actions brought by private informers and prosecutors, by county courts, and the case-by-case governance of the common law; or by special bodies like corporations created by government to serve public purposes.[7] In a country lacking strong centralized bureaucracies, the operation of these regulatory bodies and processes was to a large extent, by default, given over to lawyers. Tocqueville commented on this fact, that lawyers were the de facto governing class, and shrewdly guessed the reason for it: in a commercial society, as Adam Smith had warned, most people's energy and attention turns inward upon their private ambitions—getting ahead, making money; in such a society, people are likely to turn away from public life, to neglect or ignore (what I have been calling) the frameworks of law, government, and public custom on which a successfully functioning system of market exchange ultimately must depend. Enter lawyers—a professional class by training and usage devoted to the legal framework and to assuming a natural leadership role in civic life.[8]

Now obviously there's a lot of disagreement about how well lawyers have discharged the public stewardship that fell into their hands at the founding of the republic. There is nothing new in complaints about lawyers—that they exact a heavy monopolists' rent for running the public machinery, that they are excessively devoted to clumsy, cumbersome, expensive procedures, that they sow complexity, confusion, and ambiguity wherever they go, that they gratuitously stir up trouble, all for their own interest and profit. Some critics persistently charge that the regulatory frameworks they have built and interpret to clients tend to shackle and overburden enterprise; while others charge to the contrary, that lawyers have managed the framework far too often to the particular benefit of their principal business clients. These are complex debates that I clearly can't try to resolve here. The point I want to make is that, whatever you think of how lawyers have taken care of their civic responsibilities, those responsibilities, in our political-economic structure, are inescapable. If lawyers do not perform them, no one else can fully substitute.[9]

So it's absurd to pretend, as libertarian lawyers often like to do, that private lawyers just take care of their clients while relinquishing the public realm to officials. In fact, of course, lawyers are anything but inactive toward the public sphere. The public framework is dynamic, malleable, negotiable. Lawyers don't just passively follow framework rules: they take on active political roles—trying to change the ground rules in their clients' favor.

Here it seems to me is the area where the lawyers have to do the most complex balancing of their roles as agents for clients and agents of the general long-term welfare of the legal system and the public sphere. Adversary practice at the individual case or transactional level is relatively cabined and contained. At the policy level, where clients are pushing for major legislative change or alteration in basic doctrine, zealous representation of immediate client interests with no regard for anything or anyone else has the potential to turn political life into an uncontained war of all against all—litigation writ large, a Darwinian zero-sum struggle among social groups for their share of the pie—at the expense of the institutions of restraint, cooperation, and social bargaining that link the fates of the fortunate elites to those of the middling ranks and lower orders and thus promote the general welfare. The classical fears are of "rent-seeking" politics, of groups seeking public favors that milk the government for spending levels that threaten either fiscal crisis or confiscatory levels of taxation that destroy incentives to save and produce. The opposite, and in the United States more likely, danger is of public paralysis, brought about by groups that so successfully resist taxation or regulation that they exercise a practical veto on the government's being able to provide the public goods of defense, justice, order, ecosystem protection, health and safety, and the conditions of equal opportunity that most people in fact want provided; or simply of the capture of the legal system by the powerful, who use it to grab the largest shares of income, wealth, and public resources for themselves, and to neutralize and repress any other groups who might try to challenge their claims. An example of such wasteful struggle from our own history would be labor-capital relations in the United States between 1877 and 1937, relations of fairly constant zero-sum warfare, interrupted by intermittent truces and periods of exhaustion, polarizing public opinion, sharpening class conflict, leading to enormous losses through work stoppages and, just as important, to enduring legacies of bitterness and mutual distrust whose effects are still being felt in some industries today.[10]

How to reconcile these interests? What should a lawyer do whose client wants the public framework altered in its favor, when the lawyer has reason to believe that the change may do serious damage to the commons, the public sphere? Louis Brandeis, one of the earliest lawyers to address this problem, believed that in his own time most of the country's top legal talent had been recruited to the service of a single faction of civil society, that of large corporate interests. He believed that on issues of major framework change lawyers had sometimes to take a completely independent view from their clients—that they ought not to be partisan at all.[11]

Perhaps unfortunately, the Brandeis view has never taken hold and is probably no longer a practical option, if it ever was. My own view is that in the policy arena, as in ordinary transactional and litigation work, the lawyer is entitled to pursue the client's interests but without risking sabotage of the general public–regarding norms of the framework that link the client's interest with that of other social groups in a long-term relational bargain. Any number of examples would serve, but since it's a hot topic, let's take tort reform. Companies and their insurers want to minimize liability; plaintiffs want to ensure that they are compensated. To some extent these interests conflict, though the parties have common interests, even if it's sometimes hard for them to see this, in making products safer while reducing the costs of products and the transaction costs of the injury compensation system. What are the lawyers involved in tort litigation actually doing? Very little that's constructive. The plaintiffs' bar fights to hold on to the current system, remarkably unconcerned with its inherent problems: the vast majority of victims of personal injury, other than auto accident victims, are unable to reach the justice system to obtain any compensation at all, and the tort system is so expensive that half or more of its recoveries are eaten up in administrative costs, including payments to lawyers.[12] The defendants' bar has if anything been even less constructive in its public positions. Corporate and insurance counsel help to propagate the wildly exaggerated myths that the United States is in the midst of a personal-injury "litigation explosion" and "liability crisis" that add billions to the costs of products and seriously injure American competitiveness. (These are, by the way, clearly myths: filings for individual personal-injury tort claims have fallen, not risen, in the last decade; the big increases in federal civil suits are mostly increases in inter-corporate contract claims. The myths also tend to include in the count of the greatest "costs" of the system the *benefits* that victims receive in compensation for injuries.[13]) These interests promote political "reforms" of the process that would limit liability and reduce damages without substituting alternative proposals for ensuring that the system will in fact adequately compensate for injuries and keep in place incentives to make safer products; or for universalizing access to medical care so that treating accident victims could be financed outside the tort and workers-compensation systems. (In my view corporate counsel are more at fault in this debate than the plaintiffs' bar, because their own livelihoods would not be jeopardized by sensible and just reforms. One cannot expect complete objectivity from parties under threat of extinction.)

In my model, the lawyers ought to see the parties to policy conflicts like the conflict over the tort system much as one would see parties to a long-term relational contract. The aim is to make a good deal for one's clients *in the context of an ongoing relation with other interests*, not to extract everything possible for one's own side; and to build long-term collaborative relationships. The kind of negotiation I have in mind resembles that undertaken toward the beginning of this century by the National Civic Federation, a sort of private-corporatist institution that brought together (relatively) progressive employers and (relatively) conservative unions and had their lawyers try to work out institutional solutions for social disputes. The NCF was one of the main backers of the first Worker's Compensation system that moved industrial accidents out of the tort system, which was expensive and risky for both employers and employees.[14]

I think it will be apparent that what I have been mainly arguing for so far is a remarkably conservative view of the legal framework, and a very conservative role for the legal profession: oriented toward maintenance and improvement of existing frameworks. I should make clear that I think the current set of rules, procedures, institutions, and conventions of democratic capitalism is a very long distance away from a legal/social framework that would effectively realize the promise of American life. Nothing I've said should be taken as designed to restrain lawyers from working to revise the framework's ground rules, especially if they fight for revision openly rather than through surreptitious undermining of the system. And I certainly don't want to exclude the possibility that at any time, including our own time, aspects of the framework may be fundamentally unjust or unsound, and thus in need of radical revision; and that in such times lawyers may legitimately feel a calling to a morally activist, framework-transforming politics. There are times when the lawyers' most demanding conceptions of their calling may demand principled resistance to public norms they believe to be unwise or unjust. There are times when fire must be fought with fire, unscrupulous tactics met with fierce counter tactics—though lawyers use this justification far too often as an excuse for antisocial behavior, which might be avoided by collaborative efforts to reform systems. There are times when whole segments of society must be mobilized to overturn an unjust order. Lawyers have played important parts in such movements—like the movements to abolish slavery and racial segregation—and will, one hopes, do so again.

But in our time, even the most conservative view of the lawyer's public functions, that he is to respect the integrity and aid the functioning of the existing system and its purposes, has become controversial—in a way that would really have astonished the lawyers of the early republic, the lawyers of the Progressive period, and leading lawyers generally up until around 1970 or so, who took the idea of their public functions completely for granted.[15] The dominant view of most lawyers today—not all, but seemingly most—is one that denies the public role altogether if it seems to conflict with the job of aggressively representing clients' interests the way the client perceives them.

Yet, as I've said, a legal system that depends for its ordinary enforcement on information and advice transmitted by the private bar, that depends for its maintenance and reform on the voluntary activities of the private bar, and that relies on lawyers to design the architecture of private legislation, cannot survive the repeated, relentless battering and ad hoc under-the-counter nullification by lawyers who are wholly uncommitted to their own legal system's basic purposes. Lawyers in fact probably do serve the civic frameworks better than they occasionally like to pretend; they refrain from pushing every client's case, in every representation, up to just short of the point where no plausible construction of law or facts could support it. But it seems clear that like many other groups in American social life, the legal profession in the last twenty years or so has adopted an increasingly privatized view of its role and functions. The upper bar in particular has come to see itself simply as a branch of the legal-and-financial services industry, selling bundles of technical "deliverables" to clients. There are many reasons for this trend, chief among which is the increasing competition among lawyers (and in European markets, between lawyers and accountants) for the favor of business clients. That competition has brought many benefits with it in more efficient delivery of services, but one of those benefits cannot be said to be incentives to high-minded public counseling or the expenditure of time on legal and civic reform.

Our legal culture, in short, has mostly fallen out of the habit of thinking about its public obligations (with the significant exception of the obligation of pro bono practice, which has gained increasing attention from bar associations and large law firms). I expect therefore that if the idea of lawyers as trustees for the public good—

the framework norms and long-term social contracts that keep our enterprise afloat—is going to stage a comeback, the impulse will have to come from some set of external shocks, such as legislation or administrative rules or rules of court that explicitly impose gatekeeper obligations on lawyers as independent auditors of clients' conduct. We have seen some steps taken in that direction already, in rules regulating tax shelter lawyers, securities lawyers, and the banking bar.

It would be much better, however, if the impulse were to come from the legal profession itself—especially to build and to finance organizations in which lawyers can carry out their public function of recommending improvements in the legal framework that will reduce the danger of their clients' and their own subversion of that framework. Many of the existing bar organizations, unfortunately, are losing their capacity to fulfill that function. Even the august American Law Institute has become a place which lawyers, instead of checking their clients at its door, treat as just one more forum for advancement of narrow client interests.[16]

Think of lawyers as having the job of taking care of a tank of fish. The fish are their clients, in this metaphor. As lawyers, we have to feed the fish. But the fish, as they feed, also pollute the tank. It is not enough to feed the fish. We also have to help change the water.

Notes

An early version of this essay was given as a Daniel Meador Lecture at the University of Alabama School of Law. Thanks to Deborah Rhode for helpful comments.

1. See Jon Elster, *The Cement of Society: A Study of Social Order* (Cambridge: Cambridge University Press, 1989), 192–95.

2. Henry Hart and Albert Sacks Jr., *The Legal Process: Basic Problems in the Making and Application of Law* (Westbury, N.Y.: Foundation Press, 1994; William N. Eskridge Jr. and Philip P. Frickey, eds.; prepared for publication from 1958 Tentative Edition), 183–339.

3. The best account and critique I know of this "dominant view" is in William H. Simon, *The Practice of Justice: A Theory of Lawyers' Ethics* (Cambridge: Harvard University Press, 1998), 30–46.

4. James Willard Hurst, *The Growth of American Law: The Law Makers* (Boston: Little, Brown, 1950), 352–56; Mark C. Miller, *The High Priests of American Politics: The Role of Lawyers in American Political Institutions* (Knoxville: University of Tennessee Press, 1995), 57–75.

5. Joyce Appleby, *Liberalism and Republicanism in the Historical Imagination* (Cambridge: Harvard University Press, 1992), 271–76, 304–19, 326–39.

6. This phrase, and the content of much of the paragraph that follows, is taken from William J. Novak, *The People's Welfare: Law and Regulation in Nineteenth-Century America* (Chapel Hill: University of North Carolina Press, 1996).

7. See generally Novak, *People's Welfare*; and Oscar Handlin and Mary Flug Handlin, *Commonwealth: A Study of the Role of Government in the American Economy: Massachusetts, 1774–1861* (Cambridge: Harvard University Press, 1969).

8. Alexis de Tocqueville, *Democracy in America* (New York: Alfred A. Knopf, 1946; Phillips Bradley, ed., Henry Reeve, trans.), 1:208, 272–80; 2: 98–99.

9. In this century lawyers have been displaced from their once near-total dominance of

legislative and appointive positions, policy elites, and reform vanguards. They now share these roles with other public actors, such as economists, think-tank intellectuals, issue and area specialists, lobbyists, and grass-roots organizers. Nonetheless the role of lawyers, as public officials, public-interest advocates, and private lawyers advising clients, remains critical, especially as translators of public initiatives into legislative form, administrative rule and procedure, and practical enforcement.

10. For an epic history, see David Montgomery, *The Fall of the House of Labor* (Cambridge: Cambridge University Press, 1987).

11. See Louis Brandeis, "The Opportunity in the Law," in Brandeis, *Business: A Profession* (Boston: Small, Maynard, 1914), 329, 340–41.

12. See Deborah R. Hensler et al., *Compensation for Accidental Injuries in the United States* (Santa Monica: Rand, Institute for Civil Justice, 1991).

13. The literature on the tort "crisis" is enormous. For useful surveys of the data and assessment of the various positions, see Marc Galanter, "Real World Torts: An Antidote to Anecdote," 55 *Maryland Law Review* 1093 (1996); and Deborah Rhode, "Too Much Law, Too Little Justice," *Georgetown Journal of Legal Ethics* (forthcoming).

14. The NCF has been sharply criticized, with reason, as a basically conservative organization that promoted Workers' Compensation schemes in large part to co-opt and blunt the edge of movements for more generous industrial-accident compensation schemes. See, e.g., James Weinstein, *The Corporate Ideal in the Liberal State, 1900–1918* (Boston: Beacon Press, 1968). It takes something like the partisan posturing of belligerents in the current battle over the tort system to make the NCF look good.

15. One of the best statements to be found anywhere on the lawyer's public functions appeared in the report that launched the American Bar Association's 1969 Model Code of Ethics. "Professional Responsibility: Report of the Joint Conference [on Professional Responsibility of the American Bar Association and Association of American Law Schools, Lon L. Fuller and John D. Randall as co-chairs]," 44 *American Bar Association Journal* 1159 (1958): "Thus partisan advocacy is a form of public service so long as it aids the process of adjudication: it ceases to be when it hinders that process, when it misleads, distorts and obfuscates, when it renders the task of the deciding tribunal not easier, but more difficult. . . . [The lawyer as negotiator and draftsman] works against the public interests when he obstructs the channels of collaborative effort, when he seeks petty advantages to the detriment of the larger processes in which he participates. . . . *Private legal practice, properly pursued, is, then, itself a public service*" [emphasis added]. "Professional Responsibility," 1162.

16. On politics within the American Law Institute, see Alan Schwartz and Robert E. Scott, "The Political Economy of Private Legislation," 143 *University of Pennsylvania Law Review* 595 (1995).

PART II

Ethical Theory, Ethical Rules, and Ethical Conduct

4

Moral Thinking in Management

An Essential Capability

LYNN SHARP PAINE

In recent years, many corporate leaders have begun to pay serious attention to ethics.[1] Some have introduced special ethics or values programs in their organizations. Many have created corporate ethics offices, board-level ethics committees, or company task forces to deal with difficult ethical issues their companies are facing. Training programs to heighten awareness of ethical issues and integrate ethical considerations into decision making are becoming more common. Such company initiatives vary widely in their design and effectiveness. But most of them rest on the idea that attention to ethics will strengthen the organization and contribute to its performance in the marketplace. In short, many are coming to believe that ethics is good for business.

These initiatives defy conventional wisdom which says that ethics and business are inimical, that business ethics is a contradiction in terms, or that business is a moral "free-zone" where ethics has no place. They also fly in the face of arguments purporting to show that moral thinking by corporate decision makers is illegitimate, a violation of their fiduciary duty to shareholders. Recent interest in business ethics has even prompted some experts to become concerned that companies are embracing ethics for the wrong reason. According to these critics, ethics is something companies should care about because it is right, not because it will enhance their effectiveness. It is said to be naive and career-threatening or, alternatively, incompatible with a truly moral perspective to believe that moral thinking can contribute to business success.

I want to argue that the business leaders who are taking ethics seriously are on the right track. I am not suggesting that every company ethics initiative is effective, or that the right thing to do is always the most profitable thing to do. But I will argue that the basic idea behind these initiatives is correct: moral thinking is an essential capability for corporate decision makers. Moreover, though this is not a theme I will develop here, it is a capability that must be supported by the formal and informal systems of an organization if it is to be exercised effectively.[2] I suggest that if anyone is naive or at risk, it is those who consider ethics and moral thinking (terms I use interchangeably) unrelated to or inconsistent with good management.

This essay will explain what moral thinking is, show why it is an essential capability, and address the most common reasons for considering it inappropriate or irrelevant to managerial practice. If the argument is correct, it has far-reaching implications not only for corporate managers but also for their advisers. It has particular relevance for corporate attorneys—both in-house and outside counsel—who play an increasingly important role in corporate decision making and who are frequently called on to advise management on matters of ethics.

What Is Moral Thinking?

To understand why moral thinking is an essential capability for corporate decision makers, it is necessary to have a conception of what moral thinking is all about. In the broadest sense, of course, moral thinking is about how we ought to live—as a society, as individuals, and as individuals in relation to one another. These are rather large questions to which few people give systematic or sustained thought. Nevertheless, they are questions that cannot be easily avoided. In fact, we address them repeatedly in our day-to-day choices and decisions. The thought processes and criteria we use to make such choices reflect the nature of our commitments to one another and to certain personal and social ideals. They embody our understanding of our authority to act and our responsibilities to others.

When I use the term "moral thinking," I am referring to the various thought processes used in everyday life to give explicit voice to such considerations. Although the concept of morality may be understood very broadly to include purely personal and self-regarding concerns, a central problem of morality is how we should live in relation to others—others with whom we interact personally, as well as those more distant who may be affected by what we do. A central purpose of morality is to manage that problem in a way that enhances the well-being of individuals and their communities.

It is sometimes thought that morality or ethics is concerned only with what is good for others as distinct from what is good for oneself. This way of thinking, which sets morality in opposition to self-interest and personal well-being, should not be confused with the conception of morality offered here. The moral point of view requires not that individuals deny their personal needs and aspirations and consider only the interests of others, but rather that individuals see their personal interests and objectives in relation to those of others.

Moral thinking, then, is the vehicle through which the individual seeks an accommodation between self and others. To look at a problem or choice from the moral point of view is to invoke a perspective that relates the actor to those who may be affected by the actor's choices. This may be done directly by considering the affected parties; or indirectly through the various norms and ideals that govern our behavior in relation to others.

Two modes of moral thinking are particularly important. One mode involves seeing our choices through a filter of moral principles—general principles of social morality as well as the special principles associated with the roles we occupy and with our personal ideals. This mode, which may be called "principled thinking," is what we do when we rule out a course of action because it would be deceptive, unfair, unlawful, a breach of trust, a violation of rights, and so on. Or when we embrace a possibility because it is our duty, would help someone in need, or would realize an important ideal. For some people in some contexts, this type of thinking is intuitive. It may happen spontaneously, without conscious deliberation. For others, or in other cases, however, it may require focused attention and careful deliberation. It is not always a clear-cut matter to determine, for instance, whether a statement would be misleading or a course of action would violate an obligation of confidentiality.

A second mode of moral thinking involves a very different thought process. This mode, which may be called "consequentialist thinking," utilizes our capacity to think ahead and to anticipate the impact of our actions. It involves several distinct activities: projecting the likely consequences of alternative choices; achieving a sympathetic understanding of the rights and interests of those affected by the choice; and identifying the course of action likely to do the most good, considering impartially the legitimate claims of each affected party. While principled thinking calls on us to find consistency between our day-to-day conduct and the demands of our guiding principles, consequentialism calls on us to attend to the broader social impact of what we do.

Each of these modes serves a different, but equally valuable, function. In general, principled thinking is what we do every day as we size up our choices against important values, obligations, and ideals. This type of routine, day-to-day, moral thinking has been called "level one" thinking.[3] As mentioned earlier, it is frequently an instinctual rather than an explicit deliberative process: we shy away from breaking a promise or revealing a confidence more out of habit than analysis.

However, level one is not the whole of moral thought. Level-one thinking with principles is only possible if we have previously internalized or in some other way adopted a "code of conduct" comprising the principles we regard as moral imperatives. This is where consequentialism has its greatest value. It provides a critical or "second level" perspective from which to evaluate and select our level-one principles.[4] This higher-order perspective is also essential for adjudicating among level-one principles when they conflict—as they inevitably do. When we must choose between breaking a promise to one party and protecting the confidence of another, a consequentialist approach can help us decide on the better course in the particular circumstances of the case.

When I urge that moral thinking is an essential capability for corporate decision makers, I have in mind both modes. As I argue below, these individuals, like others, need routinely to evaluate their actions against a framework of moral principles. They also need an approach to selecting those principles and dealing with conflicts among them. Those who are leaders will very likely be called on to prescribe principles of conduct for their organizations and, in some cases, for the conduct of business in general, on a national or even global basis. As leaders, they will face many decisions that involve trade-offs among competing principles.

While these two modes of moral thinking are usefully distinguished, they are obviously related and overlapping. The correspondence between the two levels and the two modes is only a rough one. Insofar as one's general principles prohibit inflicting harm on innocent people, consequentialist thinking is a necessary component of principled thinking. Consequentialism, moreover, depends on a set of principles for evaluating alternative outcomes. Nevertheless, it is useful to distinguish these modes of moral thought. They involve very different cognitive capacities, decision rules, emotions, and sensitivities. Both are essential elements in a corporate decision maker's repertoire of perspectives.

Moral philosophers have devoted much attention to exploring the relationships between these types of thinking and the problems and conflicts within them. How should decision makers respond when duties conflict? Should they act in fulfillment of duty if it will bring about a great harm? Should rights be violated in order to bring about a great good? Are all types of moral thinking ultimately reducible to a single type? These are important questions, but for the purposes at hand, it is not necessary to address them in full. The immediate concern is less with problems internal to moral thinking and more with the role of moral thinking in relation to other types of thinking characteristically used by corporate decision makers.

However, I will note that these modes of thought are best understood not as rivals but as complementary ways of thinking, though they certainly can come into conflict. As a practical matter, the conflict can be quite wrenching. Consider the corporate decision maker who is compelled to choose between acting on an important principle and doing what is best considering the consequences for the affected parties. The decisions of organizational leaders are regularly scrutinized from multiple perspectives, both as particular cases and as instances of the espoused principles of the organization. For this reason, conflicts between principle-based and consequence-based reasoning can be even more acute for organizational leaders than for individuals acting solely in a personal capacity.

Despite the potential for conflict, however, principled and consequentialist thinking are best seen as complementary modes serving distinct purposes. The framework for everyday moral thinking that I recommend to corporate decision makers recognizes a role for both. It might be called "principled consequentialism," given its basic tenet that within a framework of general moral principles, corporate decision makers should seek to define and achieve business goals in ways that advance the well-being of those affected by the company's actions. So, for example, if two possible actions are consistent with the decision makers' rights and obligations, it is morally better to choose that which makes a greater contribution to the well-being of those affected. In substance, the general principles to be respected are those of what is sometimes called "common morality" at the core of which are the virtues of "conscientiousness": honesty, fidelity to commitments, fair dealing, obedience to law, respect for the rights of others. Successful implementation of this approach requires a readiness and a facility for principled as well as consequentialist thinking on a routine basis.

Consider, for instance, the senior executive of a firm specializing in health care, medical devices, and personal hygiene products who must decide between funding the development of a deodorant for children or funding a new medical test to evaluate the likely effectiveness of chemotherapy as a treatment for cancer. All other things being equal, it would be better to choose the product which serves the more important social need, presumably, in this case, the medical test. While few actual cases are clear cut in this way, the point is that an assessment of social consequences should be part of the decision process. However, welfare enhancement should not be sought at the expense of basic obligations of truthfulness. For example, submitting false test results to regulatory authorities in order to secure speedy approval of the device is not permissible within this approach, even if the motive is to enhance welfare by getting the product to market sooner.

While principled and consequentialist thinking are in many ways quite different, it should be emphasized that both provide essential connective tissue for coordinating individual choice with the social context in which it occurs. Moral thinking of both types affirms the individual's connections to the social community and its members. An important feature of this moral framework is its rich vocabulary of moral assessment. It recognizes conduct that is exemplary or in some degree better than it has to be as well as conduct that is unethical, falling short of minimal requirements. Such a vocabulary is necessary to create conditions favorable for moral leadership and improvement.

Moral thinking may be contrasted with another important type of thinking necessary for the conduct of life and routinely employed by corporate decision makers: strategic or instrumental thinking. This type of thinking has many other names: means-end, pragmatic, purposive, results-oriented. Within a strategic or instrumental frame of reference, the central question is whether a course of action will achieve a desired objective—often, but not necessarily, a self-regarding objective. Strategic thinking focuses the attention on an outcome and how it is to be accomplished: the building of a bridge, the provision of financial services, the protection of the environment, the production of apparel for sale worldwide. Results-oriented thinking is second-nature to managers who are regularly urged to clarify their company's objectives, translate them into individual performance objectives, and continually measure progress toward them.

To summarize, my central thesis is that moral thinking as sketched above is as essential for decision makers in profit-making businesses as the strategic or instrumental thinking which comprises the bulk of the curriculum in business and other professional schools today.

Is Moral Thinking Legitimate?

If moral thinking is roughly as I have described it, does it have a role in corporate decision making? Many people would say that moral thinking is something everyone should do—no matter what their profession or vocation. But some maintain—explicitly or implicitly–that moral thinking has little place in the corporation. This objection is grounded in the decision maker's role as a fiduciary for shareholders with an obligation inherent in that role to protect and promote shareholders' interests.

Within free enterprise capitalism as practiced in the United States, shareholders typically entrust their capital to management with the expectation of earning a competitive return and the hope of substantially increasing their wealth. This system grants shareholders the right to demand that managers use their best efforts to achieve this result and that managers not advantage themselves at shareholders' expense. This right correlates with manager's duties of care and loyalty to the corporation, two fundamentals of fiduciary law.[5]

Moral thinking requires decision makers to consider whether their actions respect the rights and interests of all those affected and sometimes to refrain from acting in ways that injure others or infringe their rights. This requirement of moral thinking is sometimes thought to be in conflict with the obligations to protect and promote the interests of shareholders. This objection to moral thinking is, itself, a moral objection based on the view that corporate decision makers have only a single responsibility: to enhance shareholder wealth.

The fiduciary objection is not merely a theoretical possibility. Several years ago, for example, it was raised when I argued on moral grounds that producers of hazardous agricultural chemicals should take steps to reduce the human health and environmental harm caused by the products they were shipping to developing countries.[6] These products were being marketed without adequate warnings to people lacking any knowledge of the risks and trade-offs involved in using them. The result: serious environmental problems and thousands of deaths and illnesses each year.

My argument was criticized on the grounds that it would violate management's fiduciary obligation to shareholders if the corporation voluntarily incurred costs to reduce health and environmental harms associated with these products since the products were quite profitable and entirely lawful under the laws of both exporting and importing countries. In many nations, laws governing the safety of agricultural chemicals do not apply to exports; many importing countries, especially those in the developing world, lack an effective system for regulating hazardous chemicals. The manager's only obligation, argued one commentator, is to maximize shareholder wealth within the law. It would be wrong to reduce or forego profits to benefit—or even to avoid harm to—a third party.

On close examination, however, the single responsibility view can be seen to be profoundly incomplete. One can readily grant that by assuming the role of manager, executive, or advisor, a person acquires a responsibility to shareholders to protect and enhance the capital they have contributed to the enterprise. We may even say, as some economists do, that the decision-maker is an agent for the shareholders, though lawyers would dispute this characterization at least under some circumstances.[7] Unlike other principals in principal-agent relationships, for example, shareholders have traditionally had no right to direct the operations of the business. Moreover, there is a longstanding debate in the legal literature concerning whether the manager is a fiduciary for shareholders or for the corporation as an institution.[8] If the corporation is conceptualized not as the private property of shareholders but as a cooperative venture among suppliers of capital, knowledge, labor, and other resources, the initial plausibility of calling managers the agents of shareholders is even more problematic.

But, even if it is accepted that corporate decision makers are agents of shareholders with a fiduciary obligation to them, it would not follow that these decision makers have no obligations to other parties or that ordinary principles of morality cease to apply to their behavior. In the absence of special circumstances, assuming an obligation to one party does not automatically extinguish a person's existing obligations to other parties. This principle of continuity applies with special force to obligations flowing from membership in the human community. If, as a human being, a person is obligated to respect the rights of others, to refrain from fraud, to avoid imposing unconsented-to harm on innocent people, she does not escape those duties by assuming an obligation to promote the interests of a third party. To take an obvious case, if it is wrong to steal to enrich oneself, it does not become right to steal to enrich someone else.

Just as an agency relationship with shareholders does not cancel out decision makers' responsibilities to other parties, it does not insulate shareholders from responsibilities they would otherwise have as individuals deploying their capital. In other words, if there is an ethical problem with undertaking an action on one's own behalf, there is an ethical problem with hiring an agent to do it in one's stead. This is not a radical or even a novel view. U.S. Supreme Court Justice Louis Brandeis long ago insisted that the shareholder has an "obligation to see that those who represent him carry out a policy which is consistent with the public welfare."[9]

The view that corporate decision makers have a single responsibility is often coupled with the view that shareholders have a single interest: to make as much money as possible while acting within the law.[10] While few would doubt that shareholders wish to acquire wealth, it cannot be assumed that wealth enhancement is their only or even their overriding interest. Shareholders are also citizens of society, parents of children, consumers of goods and services, and employees of companies.

As such, they have multiple interests and varying priorities, including an interest in a coherent and effective system of social morality.

It is sometimes supposed that the law of fiduciary obligation effectively rules out moral thinking by corporate decision makers. Yet, as the American Law Institute's authoritative summary, *Principles of Corporate Governance,* makes clear, management may take into account "ethical considerations that are reasonably regarded as appropriate to the responsible conduct of business" even if "corporate profit and shareholder gain are not thereby enhanced."[11]

Of course, reasonable people may disagree about the specific nature and scope of decision-makers' obligations. They may debate whether one course of action is morally preferable to another, just as they debate the market potential for a product or the suitability of a particular organizational structure.

The central point, however, is this: the claim that decision makers have only one responsibility—to maximize shareholder wealth—because they are shareholders' agents does not follow from any traditional or plausible understanding of the agency relationship.[12] Corporate decision makers function in a morally complex world of multiple, and sometimes conflicting, responsibilities flowing from their humanity, from their citizenship, from their social roles, from their agreements and promises, and from their power. Among these is a responsibility to protect shareholders' capital and to use their best efforts to increase shareholders' wealth. Not only do decision makers have discretion in choosing how to create shareholder value, but in doing so they, like others, are subject to the demands of social morality.

To be sure, charting a responsible path through this constellation of moral claims requires more than moral thinking alone. It also requires knowledge, imagination, perseverance, courage, and other important qualities and capabilities. And without an understanding of core business subjects such as marketing, finance, production, and organizational design, the chance of success would appear rather slim.

Is Moral Thinking Important?

Even if it is accepted that moral thinking in corporate decision making is legitimate, many people wonder whether it is really all that important. According to one commonly held view, moral thinking is important when individuals are acting as citizens, as friends, or as family members, but not when they are acting for corporations. In this context, moral thinking is often considered a frill—something nice, but not necessary—on the grounds that corporate decision makers only rarely experience moral problems and can conveniently side-step them when they do.

This position rests on dubious foundations. For one thing, the frequency of felt moral problems is a poor indicator of their importance, given that the failure to experience a moral problem may be due to the decision-maker's lack of receptivity rather than the absence of the problem itself. According to corporate ethics officers, failure to "see" the issue is a common source of ethical problems.[13] And contrary to the implicit assumption that frequency equates with importance, a single moral lapse can in certain circumstances have severe consequences. As a case in point, consider the failure of former Salomon Brothers' executives to report improprieties on the company's government trading desk. The handling of this incident, which has been called the "billion dollar error in judgment," led to a crisis in confidence which cut short several careers and put the firm's very survival in question. Finally, the assumption that moral problems in corporate decision making are extremely rare is unsupported by the facts. In one reputable large company, for example, the ethics office received more than 9,000 calls in the course of a year.[14]

More fundamental, however, this position misses the point that there are different types of ethical problems, some of which are likely to be less frequent or salient and others, more so, when managers routinely practice moral thinking. To assess the importance of moral thinking, it is critical to understand how it affects the presentation and resolution of different types of problems.

One type likely to be less frequent in organizations where moral thinking is routine is the problem of feeling pressured to engage in unethical or ethically questionable practices. This result can be seen at Wetherill Associates, Inc. (WAI), a small, highly successful supplier of electrical parts to the automotive aftermarket.[15] This 350-person company founded in 1980 has a well-developed approach to decision making, called the "right-action ethic," which directs employees to consider the interests of customers, suppliers, the community, as well as employees and the company, when making decisions. Employees are told they will never be asked to do anything that is wrong or dishonest. In turn they are expected to practice honesty and right action in all they do.

Wetherill employees report that one of the things they like best about the company is the relative scarcity of ethical problems, compared with other environments where they have worked. One long-time employee explains that a major predicament in many companies is weighing the seeming advantage of a dishonest act with the advantages of honesty, but at WAI, he says, "This is not a dilemma." One of WAI's cofounders notes that in a lot of companies, people "go to great pains to weigh, decide and justify [a wrong action]. . . . We just don't do it. Decisions become easy. . . . This simplifies life rather than complicating it."[16]

It would be a serious error to conclude from the scarcity of ethical problems that moral thinking is therefore unimportant for WAI. Quite the opposite. Company employees, customers, suppliers, and competitors all attribute WAI's successful entry into the industry and its remarkable growth to the company's ethical stance and the trust and cooperation it has generated. In a mature industry not known for high ethical standards, the company's revenues grew from $1 million to $60 million in the first decade and reached more than $150 million by 1997. WAI has also been credited with professionalizing the entire industry.

Of course, a commitment to ethical thinking does not eliminate all ethical problems. Moral uncertainty, moral conflict, and moral disagreement may in some contexts become more salient for ethically aware decision makers. In a fast-paced business environment characterized by rapid technological change, these individuals often face conflicts between competing responsibilities or novel moral claims which cannot be resolved by appeal to familiar general level-one principles. Such problems are often complicated by factual ambiguities. Hence, the need for moral thinking at the critical level.

For example, two companies became targets of moral criticism when they announced that they were jointly developing an innovative database product to help small businesses and nonprofit organizations identify potential customers. Critics charged that the product, which contained the names, addresses, estimated incomes, and buying habits for 80 million U.S. households, infringed upon consumer privacy. During the development process, the project managers had consulted a privacy expert and built several privacy protection mechanisms into the product. But once the product was publicly announced, critics argued that it involved the secondary use of consumer data without the data subject's consent. The project's managers had to assess the legitimacy of these privacy concerns and decide whether to ship the product as planned. In the end, they canceled the product. Some managers felt the privacy concerns were valid and could not be addressed adequately within the existing product design.

It is not hard to find obvious candidates for moral thinking: situations in which a moral question is a major, if not dominant, dimension. One needs only to read the newspaper to see the possibilities. Such issues come up regularly in a host of contexts, ranging from the hiring and promotion of employees, to the development and marketing of products, to the restructuring and sale of whole companies. Many of these situations are unavoidable and the stakes can be significant: a product line, a company, human lives. In the face of these facts, it is hard to maintain that ethics is a frill or a topic of minor importance for managers.

Is Moral Thinking Necessary?

But do corporate decision makers really need moral thinking to address problems like these? Can they not be adequately dealt with using familiar economic concepts and analyses: minimize costs, maximize revenues, expand market share, increase profits, maximize net present value, boost return on equity, etc.?

To see some dangers of omitting moral analysis, consider the case of the Beech Nut Nutrition company executive who discovered that a company supplier was providing adulterated ingredients. In fact, the vendor was supplying sugar water instead of apple concentrate for use in bottled apple juice labeled "100% pure" and marketed as "all natural." Struggling to regain profitability after several years of losses, the 900-person company had been anticipating a profit of only $700,000 on sales of about $80 million when the discovery was made. The executive terminated the supplier and returned the unused bogus concentrate, but the question remained: what to do about the bad juice already in the distribution system and in inventory.

Company documents and later trial testimony indicate that management approached the decision not in moral terms but simply as a problem of cost minimization. As stated in a summary prepared by the company's lawyers, the company's objectives were "To minimize . . . potential economic loss . . . conservatively estimated at $3.5 million (the cost of destroying unused inventory); and . . . to minimize any damage to the company's reputation."[17] In furtherance of these objectives, the company continued sales of the juice and other products made from the adulterated concentrate and sought to prevent regulatory authorities from gaining information they would need to remove the products from the marketplace before the inventory was depleted.

The company was successful in delaying regulatory action and successfully negotiated a recall of the then-small amount of remaining questionable inventory. However, several months after company management thought the matter closed, a member of the research department alerted regulatory authorities to the full facts of the situation. Ultimately legal action, both criminal and civil, was taken against the company and its executives, resulting in estimated financial costs of some $25 million and serious personal costs to everyone involved. Several years after the conclusion of legal proceedings, the company was still struggling to regain market share and restore consumer trust in the product.

Advocates of a purely economic perspective might argue that the problems experienced by this company flowed not from any flaw in the decision framework itself but from its improper application. Had the company's managers accurately estimated the potential costs associated with each alternative, they would have chosen a different course of action: probably one consistent with what moral thinking would have yielded.

But a critical question is how decision makers could have arrived at an accurate estimate of the potential costs of the alternatives without understanding the moral issues involved: that marketing a questionable product as 100 percent pure is dishonest; that it is incompatible with the company's obligations to consumers and the public; that it is harmful to purchasers of the product, to the nation's system of food production and distribution, and potentially to users (such as diabetic babies). All these features are surely relevant to the decision to continue marketing. Moreover, these features generate potential costs to the company such as those associated with legal action initiated by public and private parties and with loss of consumer and public trust. But such features are invisible to decision makers unskilled in moral thinking.

More general, and perhaps paradoxical, a thought process focused only on the cash value of alternative courses of action is not a reliable guide even to the financial implications of those actions. As U.S. Supreme Court Justice Oliver Wendell Holmes Jr. once pointed out, even a dog knows the difference between being kicked and being tripped over.[18] Though this difference may have a dramatic impact on the dog's behavior, it is not captured in the veterinarian's bill for treating the dog's injuries. As in this and other cases involving questionable conduct or wrongdoing, there is no ready monetary measure of the harm done. But there is no doubt that the damage occasioned by wrongs such as fraud, unfairness, or breach of commitment is real, often leading to costly consequences for the wrongdoer, not to mention harm to the victim and to the level of social trust. Moral thinking is clearly related to financial thinking, since it is essential for understanding the full meaning and impact of managerial choices. But moral thinking is not reducible to financial thinking in any way that is useful to a practicing corporate decision maker.

Moral thinking brings a distinctive point of view to the decision-making enterprise, a point of view not fully captured by the traditional business disciplines. It places management decisions squarely within a social and normative context, thus highlighting important factors that might otherwise be overlooked in the search for opportunities, the identification of problems, the analysis of decisions, and the implementation of action. Managers and corporate advisers who avoid moral thinking deny themselves access to this perspective. They run the risk of neglecting important considerations related to the welfare of their organizations, their communities, and their personal lives.

Moral Thinking and Profits

So far, the argument has shown how moral thinking can contribute to better decision making by corporate managers and their advisers. This line of reasoning should not be confused with the mistaken view that there is a one-to-one correspondence between ethical actions and profitable actions. As noted earlier, moral thinking and financial thinking involve differing frames of reference and decision criteria whose application is overlapping but not co-extensive. While many profitable activities are fully consistent with the demands of moral thinking, others are not.

History and experience tell us that unethical behavior can sometimes be financially rewarding, at least so long as its victims are ignorant or powerless. The adulterated apple juice situation illustrates this possibility. It also illustrates the vulnerability of such strategies when they are dependent on secrecy for their success. If it is difficult to maintain the secrecy of individual misconduct, it is even more difficult to conceal corporate misbehavior in today's increasingly transparent business environment. Though ethically weak strategies can sometimes be profitable, they are also subject to a higher level of reputational, legal, market, and political risk than strategies which are ethically sound.

But the relevant question for corporate leaders is not whether it is ever possible to make money by acting unethically. (It is.) The question is whether an ethical orientation enhances or diminishes the organization's ability to sustain itself and create economic value over time. A case-by-case analysis of the advantages and disadvantages of acting ethically cannot address this question adequately because it overlooks the systemic implications of choosing a basic orientation to other people and the world. As illustrated in the earlier discussion of WAI, the choice affects the habits of mind, the search strategies, the identification of opportunities, the information sources, and the profile of issues and decisions that arise for the organization. It also affects how the organization is perceived by others and, hence, the opportunities and challenges presented by those outside the organization.

In his book *Moral Thinking*, Professor R. M. Hare suggests an approach to deciding whether it is prudent to be moral: he asks us to consider how we would bring up a child if our only objective were to promote that child's interests and well-being.[19] Would we teach her always to seek her own interests? Would we try to instill a set of moral principles, but encourage her to ignore them whenever it was in her interests to do so and she thought she could get away with it? Or would we try to instill a firm commitment to a set of moral principles and encourage respect for the aims and needs of others? Professor Hare concludes that he would choose the latter course for a variety of reasons.

We may pose a somewhat analogous question for corporate leaders. If your only objective were to secure the long-term survival and profitability of your company, what would be your stance on ethics? Would you urge company managers, advisers, and employees to disregard ethics? Would you urge them to adhere to a set of ethical principles except when it was more profitable not to do so? Or would you urge them to behave ethically and seek profits in ways that were morally acceptable? I submit that anyone who has thought through what it takes to achieve sustained profitability would select the latter option.

This conclusion may be surprising or even unpalatable to those who conceive of ethics as, by definition, in conflict with self-interest. Such an arrangement of the conceptual furniture underlies many allegedly "hard-headed" arguments purporting to show that ethics is in conflict with business. For example, Professor Milton Friedman writes in a well-known *New York Times* article, "What does it mean to say the corporate executive has a 'social responsibility' in his capacity as a businessman? If this statement is not pure rhetoric, it must mean that he is to act in some way that is not in the interest of his employers."[20] In a single sentence, Professor Friedman draws a sharp line between acts that are socially responsible and those that are in the company's interests. His conceptual world is such that self-interested thinking and moral thinking generate mutually exclusive classes of acts.

But there is a problem with this conceptual foundation. It presupposes that the interests and needs of the self are independent of the interests and needs of others. If this starting point is problematic in the case of the individual person, it is even more so in the case of a corporation which is essentially a collection of relationships. As such, the interests of the corporation cannot be disengaged from the interests of its constituencies. Most effective decision makers realize that the corporation's success depends on securing the trust and ongoing cooperation of participants in all these relationships, whether they be shareholders, customers, employers, creditors, suppliers, or the public. That trust and cooperation, in turn, depend on observing certain ethical principles and serving important interests of each constituency on an ongoing basis.

As noted earlier, moral thinking is not the only thing needed for managerial effectiveness. The best moral thinking in the world cannot save a company whose production methods are too costly, whose marketing is ineffective, or whose information systems are inadequate. But given what moral thinking is about—our relationships and responsibilities to others—the surprising result would be that moral thinking had nothing to do with organizational effectiveness and business success.

Conclusion

My argument for moral thinking in corporate decision making is based on the needs and experiences of corporate managers and their advisers. I have tried to show that moral thinking offers a distinctive way of seeing the world and evaluating choices which is important for corporate decision makers. This bottom-up approach to understanding the importance of moral thinking sheds a somewhat different light from the more usual top-down approach.

The more usual arguments for business ethics start with society's need for the efficient utilization of resources and then reason to the inadequacy of a purely profit-oriented norm of business behavior.[21] As many economists and others have demonstrated, profit-maximizing behavior does not necessarily lead to the efficient use of society's resources nor does it always contribute to social welfare, more broadly conceived. Information asymmetries, externalities, and the absence of vigorous competition all create opportunities for firms to reap profits that are not justified from a resource-efficiency point of view. Hence, the need for moral norms. Many economists have pointed to the role of moral norms of honesty and reliability in sustaining the social trust necessary for economic activity.

By focusing on the everyday problems and challenges faced by corporate decision makers, I have tried to show that the need for moral thinking grows out of the nature of management itself. It need not be seen as some requirement emanating from without.

The importance of moral thinking in corporate decision making relates to what Dr. Martin Luther King Jr. called the "inescapable network of mutuality"[22] in which managers, more than other professionals, succeed or fail. Without the good will and cooperation of other people, they can accomplish very little. And it is hard to see how they could secure the good will and cooperation of others, at least in a modern democratic society, without a well-developed capacity for moral thinking. What is really puzzling is how anyone could take seriously the idea that business is an ethical "free-zone," where moral thinking has no application.

Notes

The original version of this paper was prepared for a conference held at the University of Florida in 1994 to honor Professor R. M. Hare, White's Professor of Moral Philosophy at Oxford University from 1966 to 1983 and a Graduate Research Professor of Philosophy at the University of Florida. The paper, whose title takes its inspiration from Hare's book *Moral Thinking*, was first published in *Business Ethics Quarterly* 6, no. 4 (1996), 477–92. It appears here in modified form.

1. See, e.g., Ronald E. Berenbeim, *Corporate Ethics Practices* (New York: The Conference Board, Rep. No. 986, 1992); *Ethics Policies and Programs in American Business* (Washington, D.C.: Ethics Resource Center, 1990).

2. See Lynn Sharp Paine, "Managing for Organizational Integrity," *Harvard Business Review* (March–April 1994), 106–17.

3. R. M. Hare, *Moral Thinking: Its Levels, Method, and Point* (Oxford: Clarendon Press, 1981). My account of the structure of moral thought draws heavily on Professor Hare's two-level theory.

4. Hare, *Moral Thinking*.

5. See ABA, "Corporate Director's Guidebook—1994 Edition," 49 *The Business Lawyer* 1243, 1252–56 (May 1994).

6. Lynn Sharp Paine, "The International Trade in Hazardous Pesticides: Prior Informed Consent and the Accountability Gap," in *Ethical Theory and Business*, 4th ed. (Norman E. Bowie and Tom L. Beauchamp, eds., Englewood Cliffs, N.J.: Prentice-Hall, Inc., 1993), 547–56.

7. E.g., Robert C. Clark, "Agency Cost versus Fiduciary Duties," in *Principals and Agents: the Structure of Business* (John W. Pratt and Richard I. Zeckhauser, eds., Boston: Harvard Business School Press, 1985), 56–62.

8. See E. Merrick Dodd Jr., "For Whom Are Corporate Managers Trustees," 45 *Harvard Law Review* 1145 (1932).

9. *Guide to a Microfilm Edition of the Public Papers of Justice Louis Dembitz Brandeis.* In the Jacob and Bertha Goldfarb Library of Brandeis University. Document 128. Testimony before the Senate Committee on Interstate Commerce, 62nd Congress, 2nd Session, Hearing on Persons and Firms Financed in Interstate Commerce 1 (Pt. XVI), pp. 1146–91 (Dec. 14–16, 1911). Quoted in Robert A. G. Monks and Nell Minow, *Watching the Watchers: Corporate Governance for the 21st Century* (Cambridge, Mass.: Blackwell, 1996), 103.

10. E.g., Milton Friedman, "The Social Responsibility of Business Is to Increase Its Profits," *New York Times Magazine*, September 13, 1970.

11. American Law Institute, "Principles of Corporate Governance: Analysis and Recommendations," vol. 1, §2.01 (1994) at 55.

12. Perhaps the claim is not that agency, as commonly understood, extinguishes all obligations other than furthering the financial interests of shareholders within the law, but that corporate and legal institutions should be structured to make this the case. (Notice, at this point, the argument is shifting to level two: rather than considering management's obligations within the existing moral structure, the structure itself is being questioned.) To evaluate this proposal would go far beyond the scope of this paper. However, there is little reason to believe that such an arrangement would have much social merit, especially given the state of the law around the world.

13. Source: Author's field research.

14. Ibid.

15. Lynn Sharp Paine, *Wetherill Associates, Inc.*, Harvard Business School case no. 9-394-113 (Boston: Harvard Business School Publishing, 1994).

16. Ibid., 1.

17. *United States v. Beech-Nut Nutrition Corporation*, 871 F.2d 1181, 1186–1187 (2nd Cir. 1989).

18. Oliver Wendall Holmes Jr., *The Common Law* (Boston: Little, Brown and Company, 1881), 3.

19. Hare, *Moral Thinking*, 191–98.

20. Friedman, "The Social Responsibility of Business," 32.

21. See, e.g., Alan Goldman, *The Moral Foundations of Professional Ethics* (Totowa, N.J.: Rowman and Littlefield, 1980), 230–82.

22. Martin Luther King Jr., *Letter from the Birmingham Jail* (San Francisco, Ca.: Harper, 1994).

5

Law Practice and the Limits
of Moral Philosophy

GEOFFREY C. HAZARD JR.

Inasmuch as ye have done it unto one of the least of these my brethren,
ye have done it unto me.

—Matthew 25:40

In this essay I explore the relationship between law practice and several virtues identified in some main branches of traditional moral philosophy.[1] "Law practice" refers
to the ordinary activities of ordinary lawyers, in the United States in particular but
also in modern political regimes generally. These activities include conducting litigation, giving confidential counsel to clients, and drafting legal documents such as
contracts, wills, and mortgages. The specific virtues I have in mind are autonomy,
impartiality, and truthfulness. These virtues find expression in classic Greek philosophy and are an integral part of our moral traditions and are postulates of most contemporary moral philosophy. Simply stated, my argument is that in the practice of
law, considered unromantically, one cannot fulfill these virtues. In my view the same
is true for most roles of people in modern life, so that the contradiction in law practice is simply a special case, although a salient one, of a general moral phenomenon.
The contradiction is between professed moral virtues and the virtues required in our
work and lives. Lawyers' experience is peculiar in that it continually requires kinds of
"unvirtuous" conduct that are required less often and less systematically by people in
other roles and walks of life.

If this thesis is sound, then much of contemporary moral philosophy is either irrelevant to law practice—and, by extension, to many moral problems of everyday
life—or, perhaps worse, an apparatus for disparaging people engaged in doing some
of society's dirty work: lawyers as highly compensated untouchables.

The implication of the argument is not that there are no limits to conduct that a
lawyer—or anyone else—may justifiably undertake. Nor is it that moral reflection is
inappropriate, particularly as it reminds us of the human condition that has made
law (and hence law practice) a socially necessary enterprise. It is simply that the gen-

eralities in conventional moral philosophy do not much "illuminate" the limits on justifiable conduct or the terms of justification.[2]

By "ethics" I refer to choosing among courses of action where values or moral issues are at stake. Courses of action, or "action," signifies real-world events occurring over real time rather than hypothetical possibilities. "Issues" refers to the dilemmas of assigning priority among interests where all relevant interests cannot be equally conserved or furthered in a specific course of action.

The dominant strand in moral philosophy has struggled to address these problems in terms of universals. That is, problems of assigning priority among competing interests are considered to be susceptible of being addressed and resolved by methods applicable in all contexts wherever value issues or moral issues arise, quite as epistemology and semantics and science proceed in terms of universals. Universality signifies all places and times. Along a different dimension, it also signifies all instances and circumstances. Moral universalism contrasts with "applied ethics," which refers to problems of choice posed in specific historical, cultural, and situational context. The significance of specific context is simple but fundamental: A specific context frames an ethical problem in terms of "local" standards—traditions, understandings, rules of law, ways of life in a specific community, and relationship specific people such as family, neighbors, clients, and fellow countrymen. I use the term "situational standards" to refer such frameworks. The situational standards applicable to lawyers include, notably, the legal profession's codes of ethics.[3]

My view is that the only genuine problems of ethics are those posed in a framework of situational standards. Accordingly, the term "applied ethics" entails a redundancy, in that genuine moral problems or problems of "appropriate conduct" arise only in, and in terms of, standards recognized in a specific institutional context. In support of this disrespectful approach, one can refer back to Aristotle's *Nicomachean Ethics*. In sober conclusion after much circumlocution, Aristotle recognized the determining significance of "particular circumstances":

> [I]t is a hard task to be good. . . . It is for this reason that good conduct is rare, praiseworthy, and noble. . . .
> There are times when we praise those who are deficient in anger and call them gentle, and other times when we praise violently angry persons and call them manly. . . . It is not easy to determine by a formula at what point and for how great a divergence a man deserves blame . . . determinations of this kind depend upon particular circumstances. . . .[4]

I also invoke Sir Isaiah Berlin's thesis that the history of philosophy—that is, the analysis of thought at particular historical stages and places—exhausts the possibilities of "philosophy" as regards ethics.[5] By the same token, I submit that moral philosophy divorced from specific historical context is mostly vacuous—a more pointed if less polite way of saying that there are "limits" to philosophy in matters of ethics. [6]

The practice of law is a useful instance through which to develop this thesis.

Practice of law epitomizes the techniques of political discourse in modern life, particularly the definition and resolution of disputed issues through formal procedure based on objectively manifested evidence, through participants who have definite roles in the process. A substantially similar technique is employed, more or less, in modern electoral and parliamentary decision making, in business management, and in management of public bureaucratic agencies. Although law practice is distinctive in being governed by highly specific and long-established standards, the basic concepts in legal ethics have counterparts in politics and business and bureaucratic management. As will be developed below, these concepts are agency, partisanship, and confidentiality. All office-holders public and private—hereafter referred to as "politicians"—are partisan agents in that they have special responsibility to limited constituencies, and in that they all are required and expected to withhold sensitive information.

Ethics and the Problem of Knowledge

A place of beginning in ethical analysis is the problem of the actor's knowledge. Ethics involves problems of choice among alternatives apparent at the point when choice must be made. Alternatives apparent to an actor can be considered hypothetically or by estimates of a real-world actor's knowledge at the point of choice. Knowledge attributed to lawyers and politicians is especially significant because they often know things that are unknown to others.

Specification of circumstances requires some source from which the specifics are to be derived. One source is hypothetical formulation, thus: "*If* A confronted situation X, then A should. . . ." By definition such a specification is unreal. To bring forth a real ethical problem, it is necessary to posit what Mr. A knew about the circumstances confronting him in situation X. Ethical *philosophy* is necessarily hypothetical when it comes to a factual appreciation attributed to an actor. Whether any set of facts was actually apparent to a real-world actor can be inferred only on the basis of specific circumstantial evidence. Circumstantial evidence is all we have as a basis for decisions and evaluations in everyday life, in family matters, and in business, as well as in legal proceedings. But circumstantial evidence by definition cannot establish the actual or "real" content of an actor's state of knowledge. Accordingly, many statements about actors' thoughts and choices, and hence about their ethics, are no more than guesses, and sometimes officious for that. It seems to me that the necessary reliance on hypotheticals itself is a source, if not the source, of the severe and insuperable limits to philosophy in ethics.

There is nothing malign about performing ethical analysis on the basis of hypotheticals or, what is much the same thing, doing it on the basis of assumptions about what a real-world actor knew or was in a position to ascertain. The point is that there is an impenetrable limitation on how "far down" we can go in such a discussion, concerning real choices available to real actors. There is a fundamental difference—an existential one—between hypothesizing a choice and acting out a choice. The difference is signified in colloquialisms such as "he talks a good game, but . . ." and in the distinction in any calling between a rookie and a veteran. This is the import of an observation by Hilary Putnam: "What some philosophers say about [a morally problematic] situation is that the [actor] should look for a policy such that if everyone in a similar situation were to act on that policy the consequences would be for the best, and then do that. Sometimes that is reasonable; but in [a specific actor's] situation it isn't. One of the things that is at stake in [the specific actor's] situation is his need to decide who [he] *is*."[7]

I take it that by these observations Professor Putnam means, first, that action guided by a Kantian or utilatian policy might be not "reasonable" because the actor discerns herself to be situated differently from the situation specified in the universial. Of course the universal could be redinfed to fit the course of action preferred by the actor, but this would only transform the supposed universal into a rule for the specific case. His observation that the actor needs to decide who he "*is*" refers, I think, to the existentialist proposition that a course of action chosen, as distinct from merely hypothesized, effects a transformation of the actor himself. Hence, in choosing a course of action the actor is redefining himself.

Each of us can imagine someone else's mental world—the world of that person's imagination—quite as fiction authors do so, but our estimation of someone else's mental world is itself an act of imagination.

A Lawyer's Imaginary World

Each lawyer has a mental or imaginary world. I use the term "imaginary" to emphasize the creative, dynamic, evanescent, and wholly subjective nature of a state of mind. That state of mind is the resultant of a lawyer's encounters with her surrounding community—clients, opposing counsel, opposite number clients, interacting third parties, government officials, and the transactions giving rise to those encounters. The lawyer's world of course also includes the encounters with the nonprofessional community in which a lawyer is immersed—family, relatives, friends, neighbors, former schoolmates, etc. Each of us makes a unique personal construct out of the buzzing and blurred images through which we experience life. For me at least, the best account of such personal knowledge is that by William James, of which the following is a sample: "No one ever had a simple sensation by itself. Consciousness, from our natal day, is of a teeming multiplicity of objects and relations, and what we call simple sensations are results of discriminative attention, pushed often to a very high degree."[8] The lawyer's mental world is in this respect like everyone else's, but has additional dimensions resulting from professional responsibilities as an advocate or as a legal counselor.

This "interior" focus does not deny that there is a real world out there. I have assumed that the external world really exists, having often stubbed my toe in imitation of Bishop Berkeley's demonstration. Indeed, no one knows better than lawyers that the external world can be decisively real. I mean only to say that each of us makes sense of what is "going on out there" as best we can, in a way that we cannot completely share with others.

The lawyer's mental world has special characteristics derived from the lawyer's function in society. These characteristics include:

- acting as agent for another, i.e., a client;
- serving as partisan advocate in systems that have power to inflict serious but lawful consequences on the client;
- giving confidential counsel to a client leading to courses of action that can have serious adverse effects on others.

As noted earlier, the lawyer's world is simply a special case of the situation in which many others find themselves.

Clients

Clients are people whose conduct may be subject to legal question and coercive intervention by government authority. People engaged in more or less transparent transactions, with more or less transparent purposes, do not ordinarily need lawyers and hence do not become clients. Most ordinary people in fact employ lawyers only a few times during their lives, for example, to draft a will or handle a vehicle problem. However, honest people enter transactions or encounter misfortunes that may later appear in adverse light, whether by misunderstanding or malevolence, and often can use a lawyer's help in these contexts. An honest client can have a claim that someone refuses to acknowledge, have money that someone else wants, or be at risk of criminal prosecution. Furthermore, many people are not completely honest in their purposes in the exacting sense that they are prepared to stand before the community as they would stand before God. Part of lawyers' assistance to clients involves maintaining a separation between what is known between lawyer and client and what is known to others.

Agency

An essential characteristic of legal practice is acting for a client, rather than acting on one's own account. The lawyer's typical function is endeavoring to induce some third party to take actions that could assist the client's interests. People other than lawyers act as agents for others in many everyday relationships. Parents act as agents of sorts in children's education; spouses act as agents in dealings on behalf of families; employees act as agents for their employers, etc. In this sense, nearly everyone acts as an agent some of the time. (Indeed, perhaps only academics speaking as such do not act as agents.) The distinctive feature of a "lawyer" is that agency is definitional in the role. To speak of a lawyer without a client may accurately describe a jurist or a legal scholar, but it does not describe a lawyer.

The lawyer's agency function involves taking positions on the basis of loyalty to the client regarding relationships with third persons. Third persons include private parties or governmental officials in a position to affect the client. The paradigmatic government official is of course a judge.[9] The term "judge" generically refers to first instance and appellate decision makers. Government officers can include building inspectors, regulators, and prosecutorial and other officials who may have authority comparable to that of a judge, although their exercise of such authority generally can be subjected to judicial review. Persons who exercise authority within private organizations, such as business corporations or universities or labor unions, have positions similar to government officials. All such personages are potentially subjects of a lawyer's efforts on behalf of his client.

The lawyer's world is best understood by considering it in terms of the judge's world—the mental dynamic of judges and other officials invested by government with power to make authoritative decisions. The judge is central in the legal scheme of things because the judge in the generic sense has authority to determine the relationships that may be coercively enforced between the lawyer's client and other private parties or government officials. The lawyer's function is derivative from the judicial function in that we can envision the functioning of judges without lawyers but not the functioning of lawyers without judges.

A Judge's Imaginary World

A judge's responsibility is to decide disputes over legal rights and duties according to an informed and disinterested interpretation of the law and facts.[10] That task can be compressed into a single function of authoritatively deciding the meaning to be attributed to words (what the law "is") and the meaning of evidence (what the facts "are"). This function takes on practical significance when it is performed in the face of some uncertainty about those issues.

There are essentially two epistemological foundations upon which the judicial function rests. One foundation is religious; the other is secular-procedural.[11] Adjudication based on religious authority is characteristic of relatively small traditional societies, for example the role of King Solomon as recounted in the Bible or that of elders or priests in tribal societies. Exercise of this kind of authority presupposes that all members of the community share most of its experience. As Aristotle observed: "[I]f the citizens of a state are to judge . . . according to merit, then they must know each other's characters; where they do not possess this knowledge the decision of lawsuits will go wrong."[12] This communally shared knowledge reinforces and is reinforced by a religious faith, in terms of which authority is taken to have divinely inspired capacity.[13]

Members of the community in a modern society cannot share most of their experience or obtain knowledge of others' character first hand, and in many countries they no longer have common religious faith. Since the modern unbelieving mentality no longer regards divine inspiration as sufficiently reliable for making final judgments, the judicial function is performed by functionaries whose connection to divine authority is nominal at most. Accordingly, the accepted epistemological foundation of judicial authority in developed legal systems is secular-procedural, a humanistic technique employing systematic procedures to discern objective manifestations of the law and facts.

Underlying this procedural foundation is a two-fold assumption. On the one hand, it is assumed that judges are subject to such human failings as incomprehension, inattention, impatience, and bias. On the other hand, it is assumed that legal procedures can mitigate these failings by requiring the judge to consider plausible alternative versions of the law and the facts. The judge must consider these plausible alternative versions on the way to, and as the means of, finding the truth of the matter.

Of course, it is possible to adopt different assumptions about judges. With regard to questions of law, it could be assumed that the judges already know the law well enough, having been systematically and uniformly trained in it. Something like this is the underling theory of civil law systems.[14] The "objective theory" of law indeed can be understood as referring to the fact that, where a judiciary has a homogeneous understanding of the law, their legal knowledge *is* the law, not necessarily requiring illumination by the parties. Even in systems where the judges are presumed to know the law, however, the advocates may make suggestions about its application. In any event, factual issues cannot be approached on the same assumption. In the Western tradition, the defendant in a criminal case, and interested parties in a civil case, can offer competing evidence.

This is an appropriate point to note, that "local" standards specify the roles of judges. There is no single, universal concept of the judicial function. The role of a king-judge in a closed religious society obviously differs from that of judge in a modern secular society. Modern societies also reflect significant variations in judicial role, particularly differences between the common-law judges and their civil-law counterparts. Thus, a lawyer's brief addressing the rule governing child custody would be contempt of court, or worse, if submitted to King Solomon, whereas failure to submit such a brief before a common-law judge could be professional malpractice.

Rhetoric and Truth

The recognized possibility that a judge can be wrong is the predicate for the requirement that judges consider plausible alternatives. This requirement is the mirror image of the right to be heard. Lawyers as advocates effectuate the right to be heard by providing the judge with plausible alternatives concerning the law and the facts. (An advocate who provides an *implausible* alternative has failed in her preliminary responsibility to refrain from "frivolous" contentions, a matter to which I return below.)

The advocate engages in what is classically categorized as rhetoric, as distinguished from philosophic or scientific discourse. In philosophic discourse, according to this categorization, the protagonist and all participants in the inquiry directly seek truth, without regard to consequences. The rhetorician, in contrast, addresses a doubtful matter with a precommitment to consequence. The distinction is classically drawn in Plato's *Gorgias*, where Socrates says: "I . . . begin by asking, whether [the rhetorician] is as ignorant of the just and unjust . . . as he is of medicine and the other arts; I mean to say, does he know anything actually of what is good and evil . . . just or unjust; or has he only a way with the ignorant of persuading them . . . .?"[15] Aristotle had a more analytic and somewhat less disparaging characterization: "[Rhetoric's] function is . . . concerned with . . . deliberation about matters that appear to admit of being one way or another. . . ."[16]

An advocate as agent for the client, when appearing before the judge in a contested matter, is precommitted to the proposition that the client's cause is just according to the law and the facts, and accordingly that the client should prevail. The advocate's engagement is to present to the judge, with fullest lawful force and skill, a plausible version of legal and factual issues that will have favorable consequence for the client. The judge, on the other hand, is engaged in directly questing the truth.

The relationship between judge and advocate thus involves a profound paradox: The advocate is to provide a nondisinterested and precommitted version of the doubtful matter in order to facilitate the judge's arrival at a disinterested conclusion proceeding from an uncommitted predisposition. The explanation for the paradox is of course the recognition that judges are not divinely inspired and the related supposition that they are less likely to commit error if presented with alternative versions. The same reasoning leads to recognition that the advocate should be *obliged* to present a partisan version, as distinct from some "neutral" or disinterested exposition similar to that at which the judge is to arrive.[17] The reason here, of course, is that a "neutral" advocate would be subject to the same failings as a judge in seeking to arrive at truth through unilateral inquiry.

Of course, the parties to a legal dispute can speak for themselves, and some do so, appearing *in propria persona*. However, experience demonstrates that parties are often inept compared to practiced advocates. Typically a party will also have difficulty getting beyond his own subjective perceptions in trying to present his situation in terms that are comprehensible to the judge.

The Advocate's Imaginary World

The advocate's role requires maintaining multiple images. The advocate seeks to produce a resultant "truth" through her presentations to the court. In another more encompassing view, the advocate must visualize her presentation to the judge, anticipate the competing alternative version presented by the opposing party, and imagine how the production as a whole will be received.

The term "production" implies that the advocate's endeavor is essentially theatrical, which indeed it is. The advocate produces a picture that, if artful, will appear to the judge as truth regarding the events in dispute. Like a theatrical producer, the advocate views her production as it will appear to the audience, not simply as it "is." A trial compresses some aspects of historical time, renders other events in slow motion, omits "irrelevant" detail, sharpens focus on crucial details, etc. Some evidence of course is "real," notably documents, but only as to items whose authenticity is not disputed. When a document is challenged as forged or postdated or the like, the document is no longer unequivocally "real." So also, the parties are "real" but appear in their forensic Sunday best and not as they were in the underlying transaction.

An advocate by no means has a free hand in presenting these portrayals. There is always some evidence that is irrefutable and some opposing evidence that is highly plausible. It is a truism in advocacy that it is foolish to dispute every disputable issue; many trials turn not on direct resolution of a crucial evidentiary issue but on an adverse inference drawn from a party's unwarranted disputation of some secondary issue. Another constraint is the counter-production by opposing counsel that aims to tear off costumes and wipe off grease paint, so to speak. Above all, there is the neutralizing effect of the judge's and jurers' skepticism. The advocate's production must appear to the decision makers as *cinéma vérité* or it is a failure.

Other constraints on the advocate consist of procedural and ethical rules that prohibit fabricated evidence and require disclosures such as identification of intended witnesses.[18] The subject of "legal ethics" addresses the content, meaning, and enforcement of these and other rules.[19] The advocate functions within the legal constraints imposed by these procedural and ethical rules and within the practical constraints of having to produce a scenario plausible to the judge. Within these constraints, the duty of loyalty to clients and the interest in craft as a professional impel the advocate to maximum rhetorical effectiveness.

All this is familiar but profoundly unattractive. It is shocking that matters of great moment, including life and death in some criminal cases, are resolved in a proceeding that technically speaking is a theatrical enterprise. This fact is not readily acknowledged by the professionals. The judges are unhappy knowing that the best they can get is verisimilitude. Advocates solemnly pronounce that trials are searches for truth and justice, which is quite true, but are less forthcoming about the ambiguity of their role in the process.

Many lay critics and some academicians condemn both the advocates' artifice and the artificers, without coming to terms with the fundamental difficulty that begets the role of advocate in the first place. An advocate who took on the judge's direct truth-finding obligations would no longer be an advocate, and the parties would have no advocates. We would be relegated to trusting divine intervention or constituting the advocate as "both prosecutor and judge," as the saying goes.

It may be observed that there is a similar dichotomy of roles in the vocations of politician in constitutional regimes and business manager in capitalist systems. In the domestic affairs of constitutional regimes, the governing party is supposed to make policy that is truly public, much as a judge is supposed to find the truth. However, constitutional systems involve an opposition party (sometimes more than one) committed to continually challenging whether the governing party's policies fulfill that standard. The "loyal opposition" is precommitted to oppose, quite like the precommitment of the advocate and on the same justification: the risk of error by those in authority. In the private sector of capitalist regimes, a similar function is performed through the force of competition. Advertising, for example, is advocacy by a business competing for the customers' decision.

The Legal Counselor's Imaginary World

A lawyer's responsibility goes beyond making an advocate's artful presentation if a dispute goes to trial. The lawyer must previously consider, as objectively as possible, the risk of losing in a trial. That is to say, an advocate is also a legal counselor.

A trial is a future contingent event and hence a gamble. Similarly contingent, and therefore something of a gamble, is any transaction with official authority that depends on interpretation of rules or determination of facts—for example, an encounter with tax authorities or the environmental regulators. The same kind of contingency is entailed in more or less contentious "private" transactions, for example between landlord and tenant, seller and buyer, borrower and lender. All such transactions potentially can be resolved by a trial before a judge, with corresponding contingencies. But short that, contentious transactions are resolved by bargaining—give and take between the parties, or a decision by one of them to lump it and retire. The bargaining postures are adopted in terms of the contours of legal rights—"bargaining in the shadow of the law."[20]

In the language of gambling, the lawyer as counselor must give advice to the client as to whether to raise, hold, or fold. The advice is in confidence and is supposed to be loyal but objective. Objectivity in an advocate's advice requires analysis informed by discerning appreciation of the client's interests, not improperly colored by the lawyer's own interests. The obligation to give candid advice is reinforced by the advocate's personal interest in avoiding an avoidable defeat, which translates into future financial returns, reputation, and, not the least, a personal sense of craftsmanship in navigating troubled social waters. A legal counselor is obliged to assess the client's interest as the client interprets that interest, not as the lawyer would interpret it.[21] However, a client can be startled to receive in private a dour and pessimistic estimate of a cause that his lawyer had boldly championed in court and to the opposing party.

There are of course cases in which a legal counselor need not weigh the contingency in adjudication. A conspicuous example is a death penalty case, where the accused has no practical choice except to take the risk of a trial. However, most cases going to trial do so because the opposing advocates have made substantially different estimates of their risks of loss.[22] Hence, the aphorism that a trial represents a failure of settlement. A more formal statement is that a trial often constitutes a failure by one or both advocates to make an adequately objective estimate of the risk of loss.

The Transaction Lawyer's Imaginary World

Most services provided by lawyers involve legal documentation, not trials or advice concerning litigation. "Transaction practice," as it is generally referred to, consists of drafting contracts, mortgages, wills and trusts, corporate prospectuses regulatory compliance statements, and myriad other documents.

Functionally, transactional practice is like the theatrical production of an advocate, except that it is at an earlier stage in a chain of events. Without documentation, parties to a transaction—a sale, a loan, and so on—rely, first of all, for compliance on each other's good faith and on private sanctions such as bad-mouthing and refusals to deal in the future. If the matter comes to litigation, the parties are governed by the law's general "default rules." However, modern regimes recognize that these default rules can be superseded by provisions in contracts and other documents. For example, the default rule governing family inheritance is that decedents' property goes to their spouse or children, but law permits a will that directs property to charities or other relatives. And so on for the myriad contracts that govern ordinary transactions in modern life. Transaction work thus establishes different legal frameworks for the parties' situation and for their bargining possibilities. In drafting a legal document, the transaction lawyer tries to envision all the contingencies that could disrupt the transaction—fire, flood, bankruptcy, death, etc. In addressing these contingencies, lawyers devise language favorable to clients but likely also to be acceptable to other parties and not so one-sided as to be unenforceable in court.[23] In effect, the hand and mind of the lawyer envelop the transaction in a different local reality.

Secrecy

Much of the lawyer's work in all these functions—advocacy, counseling, drafting—is secret from everyone but his client. The courtroom advocate creates impressions for consumption by the judge, reserving the rest of what the advocate knows. The legal counselor gives confidential advice to the client concerning the risks and alternatives in litigation and negotiation. The transaction lawyer discloses only the document itself and not the scenarios to which the language of the document might apply. These secrets are protected from the court's inquiry by the attorney-client privilege and from others by the lawyer's duty to maintain secrecy of the client's confidences.[24]

Marvin Frankel brilliantly expounded how the advocates' productions can appear misleading to a judge, but without further discussing the ethics of the situation "back stage."[25] Professor Monroe Freedman has vigorously defended the role of advocate[26] but has not much explored similar problems that arise in legal counseling. Dean Anthony Kronman has articulated the angst of many lawyers who evidently wish they were engaged in what they (or at least Dean Kronman) would consider a more noble enterprise, but without plumbing the enterprise in which lawyers actually are engaged.[27] Retired corporation lawyers, such as Sol Linowitz, know what is involved in being legal counselor for a corporate client but typically address legal process from a judicial viewpoint, or even an Olympian one.[28]

The hard facts are that a lawyer's functions include being a partisan rhetorician and keeping secrets to the advantage of favored parties (clients) and to the disadvantage of others who could benefit from the information. Each of these functions is morally disreputable according to central themes in modern ethical and religious traditions.

Agency Further Considered

Moral philosophy has generally aimed at universal application, that is, formulations of what a person—in principle, any person—ought to do in one or another circumstance. One notable exception is the Judaic tradition, which prescribed highly specific rules for a specific people.[29] Another exception to this universal orientation is recognition of situational moral dilemmas such as circumstances where a parent sees that one of her children is drowning but where attempted rescue would risk loss of the parent's life and as well thereby loss to the rest of the family.

One fact of special relevance in modern moral philosophy is that most agency relationships are between unequals. If the client-lawyer relationship, if the client could provide himself with advice and assistance equal to that available from a lawyer, the lawyer would be unnecessary. The lawyer's training and experience thus effectuate the purposes of the "community" formed by client and lawyer better than those purposes can be effectuated by the client acting for himself. At the same time, under principles of agency law and the rules of professional ethics, the client has final authority of objectives of the representation—for example, whether to settle in litigation or to walk away from a proposed transaction.[30] It is therefore inappropriate to talk of equality or "democracy" among the participants in the relationship, instead of recognizing that the participants make different contributions.

The agency relationship also involves expense by or on behalf of the client. There is much caviling about whether lawyers' fees are too high, and whether lawyer overbilling or outright fraud are rampant. However, there would still be costs even if lawyers—or other politicians—were paid the same as public school teachers and if all such agents were completely honest in their fee charges. Because expense is involved, access to lawyer services necessarily depends on resources available to pay. I do not see how this problem can be overcome. Even if legal services were rationed, administration of such a scheme would require differentiation between "meritorious" claims for assistance and other claims, and that task would encounter the discrepancy between reality and appearance described earlier. If public policy aimed at perfect equality in providing legal assistance, it seems safe to predict the evolution of bribery, black markets or auxiliary services, performing equivalent functions."[31] Under any of these regimes, access to lawyers' assistance would be unequal. "Equality before the law" can be achieved only imperfectly. This hard fact not only poses a dilemma for a society committed to democracy but it also enfeebles any discussion of lawyers' social responsibilities that assume true equality before the law, as distinct from the adequacy of representation.

Each of these aspects of agency entails difficulties that seem to me insoluble according to general principles. How far should the lawyer's duty to client be constrained by responsibilities to others—for example, the responsibility not to mislead?[32] What is the appropriate degree of paternalism by the lawyer, given that the client and lawyer are unequal?[33] How much is "enough" legal assistance, especially for a client who cannot pay the full cost? And at what point, and to what lawful purposes, should a skillful practitioner refuse assistance to a client with abundant resources but a cause that appears to the lawyer, having an insider's knowledge, as unjust or antisocial? (Tobacco companies and O. J. Simpson come to mind.) In my opinion, lawyers as citizens with special information on these issues should urge ameliorative measures in the political forum—for example, funding for legal aid. However, as far as I can see, lawyers as such have no special capability to discern appropriate solutions to these distributional problems. I do not see how these questions can be answered in general terms, any more than general terms can respond to similar questions on the public agenda involving health care, educational opportunity, and housing standards.

More fundamental, the concept of agency contravenes a basic theme in some ethical traditions. It violates a Christian ideal of equality and equal access to God's grace and mercy[34] and a Greek ideal of democratic equality of citizens. It violates the Kantian Categorical Imperative: The categorical imperative . . . is: act upon [subjective grounds] that can also hold as a universal law.[35] Agency by definition entails commitments to some indentifiable principal, with at least partial subordination of the interests of others. In my view, the Kantian universal presupposes a world devoid of relationships involving parties who stand in various relationships with each other-parent and child and "others," husband and wife and "others," partners, lawyer and client, fellow countrymen, etc.

Partisanship Further Considered: "Who Counts"

The correlate of agency is partisanship. One who undertakes to be another's agent cannot be impartial as regard third parties. This in turn poses the question of "Who counts?" and for what.

At the extremes, nearly all agree that everyone counts—everyone is entitled to compassionate treatment—in answering the question of whether genocide is evil. The difficult questions begin short of that extreme—for example, whether a particular war is "just"[36] or whether abortion is always wrong.[37] Similar questions arise in legal ethics because invoking legal sanctions has similarities to going to war or otherwise causing harm to innocents. Litigation can impose an unjust result through decision by an authority from whom there is no recourse, whereby an advocate for the winning party becomes the instrument of injustice. In legal ethics, the client is the one "who counts" more than others.

Prevailing moral philosophy has great difficulty with the idea that an actor can properly give preference to one individual as compared with others, or to one group compared with another. I have seen no satisfactory resolution of this problem in universal terms. Professor Michael Walzer, for example, proposes a peculiar concept of equal treatment: "The principle of equal consideration would . . . apply only within [legally separated] groups. Equality is always relative; it requires us to compare the treatment of this individual to some set of others, not to all others." I cannot distinguish between that formulation and segregation, which also distinguished between groups separated by law.

A recent attempt to address the problem of "who counts" is a thoughtful analysis by Onora O'Neill, *Towards Justice and Virtue*. In her pivotal section, "Constructing the Scope of Ethical Concern, Dr. O'Neill concludes: "[The]underlying idea is that for *practical* purposes it is not necessary to have a comprehensive theory of ['who counts']. Agents do not need a comprehensive account of ethical standing that covers all possible cases; but they do need *procedures* that can be deployed in circumstances they actually face." The qualifying term "practical" in this passage seems to translate into much-despised applied ethics. The interlinked reference to "procedures" might seem promising and would be welcome to lawyers, who are proceduralists. However, when Dr. O'Neill explains the procedures, they hinge on preexisting assumptions that in some unexplained way have been fashioned by the actors themselves: "[The actors] will need to construct rather than to presuppose an account of ["who counts."] . . . The presuppositions of activity commonly include rather specific assumptions about others who are taken to be agents and subject. . . ."[38] O'Neill does not tell us what an actor is "to construct," or out of what materials. This seems to me a concession that problems of ethics are necessarily situational and cannot be based on impartiality. It would follow that the only way someone can decide "who counts" is in terms of the actor's situation, such as being a lawyer and therefore governed by norms of legal ethics.

Secrecy Further Considered

The rules of truthfulness governing lawyers are designed to permit lawyers to keep secrets, but also to prevent lawyers from lying to a judge or to an opponent. Under current ethical rules, however, withholding relevant information is not "lying" unless being fully forthcoming is required in specified situations. These situations are quite limited. One is where disclosure of confidential information will further the client's interests. (Partisanship again.) A second is in response to a direct question that the court is authorized to ask. However, the rules and conventions sharply limit permissable questions. General rules of law governing all individuals, including lawyers, prohibit materially misleading statements. Where a question has arisen concerning the lawyer's own legal probity in a matter undertaken for a client, lawyers may disclose confidences to protect themselves. Attorneys are not required to risk going to jail for assisting clients who turn out to be crooks. But apart from these circumstances, lawyers must avoid disclosing confidential information. As a result they speak through clenched teeth.

At the same time, there are also practical constraints on a lawyer's freedom to conserve the truth. These arise primarily from the necessities of productive negotiation, an activity in which most lawyers engage. Productive negotiation requires a combination of openness about matters to be conceded and secrecy about one's reserve position, and a game of hide and seek within those limits. Positively misleading statements are destructive because they frustrate achieving a positive result— "getting to 'yes'" in the jargon of negotiation. Care in expression and wariness in attention are therefore required in playing the game.

Being less than fully forthcoming with the truth violates commonly pronounced standards of proper behavior, especially when employed to advantage a client's interest over the interest of another, perhaps with resulting injustice.[39] It is therefore impossible to reconcile an ethical demand for "the whole truth" with what lawyers do. Yet everyone beyond the age of four realizes the uses of imperfect truth and often resorts to them. Public opinion generally acknowledges the need to be less than fully forthcoming in various circumstances, despite the pronounced standards to the contrary.[40]

Concluding Reflections

The practice of law thus considered is incompatible with traditional virtues of autonomy, impartiality, and openness. It is, on the contrary, a Machiavellian calling, like politics, management, and other relationships in ordinary life. Machiavelli's key proposition was that in affairs of state it was necessary "to be a great feigner and dissembler."[41] In such matters "force alone will [not] ever be found to suffice, whilst it will often be the case that cunning alone serves the purpose."[42] So also in the practice of law, with the client standing in the place of the state.

Machiavelli still has a bad name, although his reputation has improved through the respectful attention he received from Sir Isaiah Berlin.[43] Yet Machiavelli had profound insights, particularly in the claims that institutional structures are extremely vulnerable and that dissimulation is a useful alternative to physical force. Clients are also vulnerable or consider themselves so; otherwise, they would not be seeking lawyers' assistance.

It might be useful, therefore, to begin analysis of legal ethics—and political and business ethics and ethics in ordinary life as well—with several Machiavellian premises. That is:

- lawyers, politicians, and business leaders cannot be impartial because they are agents, as are most ordinary people in many situations;
- an agent's responsibility to "relevant others" requires providing protection of those others in preference to those outside the pale;
- being not fully forthcoming with truth is a cheap and generally peaceful means of providing effective protection.

From this perspective, the serious ethical questions do not involve the justification for partisanship and secrecy, but rather the terms of situational norms that limit partisanship and confidentiality. Legal ethics, on this view, involves important moral, political and legal problems, but ones that are not much illuminated by traditional moral philosophy.

There is a more fundamental difficulty in trying to make use of traditional moral philosophy in matters of legal ethics. This is the problem of gradients, i.e., the specification of morally acceptable positions within extreme limits. For example, agents generally are not permitted to use lethal force on behalf of their constituents, but it is recognized that this limitation does not apply to soldiers in war or to policemen under some circumstances. A lawyer is not permitted to lie to a court, but in some situations can present evidence that he would conclude was false if it were his role to determine that issue. The partisanship involved in agency is prohibited on the part of such functionaries as judges, teachers, and auctioneers, but not on the part of legislative representatives or salesmen. All regimes impose limits on secrecy in domestic affairs but fewer ones in foreign affairs.

The concepts of agency, of partisanship, and of confidentiality thus all are conditional upon gradients. Moral philosophy has had difficulty with degrees since Aristotle sought to explicate a "mean" of virtue located intermediate on a continuum between vices on either end, for example a mean of "truthfulness" between "boastfulness" and "understatement."[44]

One interpretation for this difficulty is that specification of gradients *is*—is equivalent to—specification of situations or local conditions. That is, inelligibly addressing whether boastfulness or understatement or fulsome truth is appropriate requires such a specification. Yet to specify "the" situation or "a" situation is also to exclude all other situation and, thereby, to preclude universal statements.

The approach taken here follows that of Sir Isaiah Berlin, whose thought is aptly summarized by John Gray: "The implication of Berlin's thought for philosophical method is that the conception of the prescriptive authority of philosophy, and its pretensions to govern practice, which pervades the work of Aristotle, of Plato, of Hobbes, of Spinoza, of Kant, or J. S. Mill and (in a distinct but no less manifest way) of at least the earlier Rawls, say, cannot be accepted: philosophy's pretensions must be far humbler."[45]

Notes

I thank Professor Susan Koniak and Howard Lesnick for their helpful comments, and Mathew Applebaum for research assistance.

1. I use the term "moral" philosophy because that is the conventional description of philosophical discussion of normative issues. In my opinion, the term "ethical" philosophy might be most appropriate because that term denotes intersubjective deliberation as contrasted with wholly subjective reflection, for which the term "moral" might be more appropriate. See G. Hazard, "Law, Morals and Ethics," *So. Illinois U.L.J.* 447 (1995).

2. A rather difficult kind of criticism is in R. Posner, "The Problematics of Moral and Legal Theory," 111 *Harv. L. Rev.* 1638 (1998).

3. A detailed comparison of rules of professional ethics in various countries is Ed Godfrey, ed., *Law Without Frontiers: A Comparative Survey of the Rules of Professional Ethics Applicable to Cross-Border Practice of Law* (Amsterdam: Klumers, 1995).

4. Aristotle, *Nichomachean Ethics, Book Two* (Martin Ostwald, trans.; Indianapolis: Bobbs-Merrill, 1962), 9.

5. See Isaiah Berlin, *Vico and Herder: Two Studies in the History of Ideas* (New York: Viking Press, 1976); *Concepts and Categories: Philosophical Essays* (London: Hogarth Press, 1978); and *The Crooked Timber of Humanity: Chapters in the History of Ideas* (New York: Knopf, 1991). See also John Gray, *Isaiah Berlin* (Princeton, N.J.: Princeton University Press, 1996).

6. See Bernard Williams, *Ethics and the Limits of Philosophy* (Cambridge: Harvard University Press, 1985)

7. Hilary Putnam, *Renewing Philosophy* (Cambridge: Harvard University Press, 1992), 190–91.

8. William James, "The Principles of Psychology," in Bruce Wilshire, ed., *William James: The Essential Writings*, 44 (Albany: State University of New York Press, 1984).

9. The classic statement of judicial authority is in *Marbury v. Madison*, 1 Cranch 137, 177, 5 U.S. 137 (1803): "It is emphatically the province and duty of the judicial department to say what the law is." An observation by Justice Robert Jackson applies to judges generally: "We are not final because we are infallible, but we are infallible because we are final." *Brown v. Allen*, 344 U.S. 443, 540 (1953).

10. See, e.g., 28 U.S.C. Sec. 455; and American Bar Association, Model Code of Judicial Ethics. I bypass consideration of the salient function of the jury in deciding issues of fact, particularly in the American legal system. In the framework of this analysis, in a trial lawyer's imaginary world the jury has the same significance as a judge.

11. The distinction between religious-based authority and rational-bureaucratic authority is that drawn by Max Weber, who identified a third basis of authority—the charismatic. See Weber, *The Theory of Social and Economic Organization* (trans. A. M. Henderson and Talcott Parsons) (New York: Oxford University Press, 1947). The commonly employed distinction between the "legal" and "political," for example in the American conception of separation of powers, roughly corresponds to Weber's distinction between bureaucratically rational and charismatic processes.

12. Aristotle, *The Politics, Book 7*, 1326:15 (Jonathan Barnes revision of B. Jowett, trans., Cambridge: Cambridge University Press, 1988).

13. Compare Deuteronomy 14:2: "For thou *art* a holy people . . . and the Lord hath chosen thee to be a peculiar people unto himself, and above all the nations that *are* upon the earth."

14. See G. Hazard, "Discovery and the Role of the Judge in Civil Law Jurisdictions," 73 *Notre Dame L. Rev.* 1017 (1998).

15. *Dialogues of Plato* (B. Jowett, trans., New York: Appleton, 1898).

16. Aristotle, *The Art of Rhetoric* 76–77 (H.C. Lawson-Tancred trans. London: Penguin, 1991).

17. Some academicians seem unable to countenance such a role, or its epistemological and social foundations. See William H. Simon, "Ethical Discretion in Lawyering," 101 *Harv. L. Rev.* 1083 (1988).

18. See ABA, Model Rules of Professional Conduct, Rules 3.3 and 3.4.

19. E.g., American Law Institute, Restatement of the Law Governing Lawyers, Proposed Final Draft No. 1 (1996), Proposed Final Draft No. 2 (1998); G. Hazard and W. Hodes, *The Law of Lawyering: A Handbook on the Model Rules of Professional Conduct* (2d ed. Englewood Cliffs, N.J.: Prentice Hall Law & Business, 1990); C. Wolfram, *Modern Legal Ethics* (St. Paul, MN: West Publishing Co., 1986).

20. See R. Mnookin and L. Kornhauser, "Bargaining in the Shadow of the Law," 88 *Yale L. J.* 950 (1979).

21. Restatement of the Law Governing Lawyers, Proposed Final Draft No. 1 (1996) §28(1) See also §§31–33.

22. See F. James, G. Hazard, and J. Leubsdorf, *Civil Procedure* §6.3 (4th ed., Boston: Little, Brown, 1992).

23. See Restatement Second of Contracts Sec. 208 (unconscionable contract or term).

24. See, e.g., Restatement of the Law Governing Lawyers Proposed Final Draft, No.1, §118; see ABA, Model Rules of Professional Conduct, Rule 1.6.

25. See M. Frankel, "The Search for Truth: An Umperial View," 123 *U. Pa. L. Rev.* 1031 (1975).

26. See M. Freedman, *Understanding Lawyers' Ethics* 156 (New York: Matthew Bender, 1998).

27. Anthony Kronman, *The Lost Lawyer* (New Haven: Yale University Press, 1997).

28. Sol M. Linowitz with Martin Mayer, *The Betrayed Profession: Lawyering at the End of the Twentieth Century* (New York: C. Scribner's Sons, 1994).

29. See n. 12 above

30. See ABA, Model Rules of Professional Conduct, Rule 1.2(a).

31. See Paul Brand, *The Origins of the English Legal Professional* (Cambridge, Mass.: Blackwell Publishers, 1992).

32. For some "local" rules on this subject, see ABA, Model Rules of Professional Responsibility, Rules 1.6, 3.1, 3.3, 3.4, and 4.1.

33. Local rules addressing this problem include Rules 1.13(b) and 1.14.

34. Matthew 25:40: "Inasmuch as ye have done *it* unto one of the least of these my brethren, ye have done *it* unto me."

35. Immanuel Kant, *The Metaphysics of Morals* 17 (Mary Gregor, trans., Cambridge: Cambridge University Press, 1996).

36. See Michael Walzer, *Just and Unjust Wars: A Moral Argument with Historical Illustrations* (New York: Basic Books, 1977).

37. See, e.g., Cynthia Gorney, *Articles of Faith: A Frontline History of the Abortion Wars,* (New York: Simon and Schuster, 1998).

38. Onora O'Neill, *Towards Justice and Virtue: A Construction Account of Practical Rea-*

soning (Cambridge: Cambridge University Press, 1996), 99; Cf. G. Hazard, "Dimensions of Ethical Responsibility: Relevant Others," 54 *U. Pitt. L. Rev.* 965 (1993).

39. See Sissela Bok, *Lying: Moral Choice in Public and Private Life* (New York: Vintage Books, 1979); and Sissela Bok, *Secrets: On theEthics of Concealment and Revelation* (New York: Vintage Books, 1983).

40. Compare Janny Scott, "Bright, Shining or Dark: American Way of Lying," *NY. Times*, Aug. 16, 1998, p. 3: "It is okay to lie to hide something that will be used unfairly against you or others, or to conceal information that an inquisitor has no right to have (the classic Nazis-at-the-door-while-the-Jews-are-in-the-attic exception, stretched in contemporary life to justify paying the baby sitter off the books because the employer cannot afford child care otherwise)." The foregoing "cases" are among those in which people consult lawyers.

41. Niccolo Machiavelli, *The Prince,* Book 18 (Luigi Ricci, trans., New York: Modern Library, 1950).

42. Niccolo Machiavelli, *The Discourses,* Chap. 13 (Luigi Ricci, trans., New York: Modern Library, 1950).

43. Isaiah Berlin, "The Originality of Machiavelli," in *Against the Current: Essays in the History of Ideas* (New York: Oxford University Press, 1979).

44. See Aristotle, *Nichomachean Ethics,* Book, 2 viii (J. A. K. Thomson, trans., London: Penguin, 1955).

45. John Gray, *Isaiah Berlin* 7 (Princeton, N.J.: Princeton University Press, 1996).

6

The Ethics of Wrongful Obedience

DAVID J. LUBAN

A century ago the legal realists taught us that the real law is the law in action, not just the law in books. They taught us to think things, not words, and placed their faith in the power of the still-youthful social sciences to think legal things accurately and rigorously. In legal ethics, I think most scholars would agree on the single biggest discrepancy between the law in books—the profession's ethics codes—and the law in action. The ethics codes are almost entirely *individualist* in their focus. They treat lawyers (clients, too, for that matter) largely as self-contained decision makers flying solo. In fact, however, lawyers increasingly work in and for organizations. While most lawyers continue to practice in small firms, and sole practitioners still form the largest single demographic slice of the profession, the trend is toward organizational practice. The largest law firms and corporate legal departments have more than a thousand lawyers, and the biggest firms in the country three decades ago would not make this year's top hundred.

The importance of these trends for legal ethics can hardly be exaggerated. Psychologists, organization theorists, and economists all know that the dynamics of individual decision making change dramatically when the individual works in an organizational setting. Loyalties become tangled, and personal responsibility gets diffused. Bucks are passed, and guilty knowledge bypassed. Chains of command not only tie people's hands, they fetter their minds and consciences as well. Reinhold Niebuhr titled one of his books *Moral Man, Immoral Society,* and for students of ethics no topic is more important than understanding whatever truth this title contains.

My own students, I might add, think about it constantly without any prompting. No dilemma causes them more anxiety than the prospect of being pressured by their boss to do something unethical. Not only do they worry about losing their jobs if they defy the boss to do the right thing, they also fear that the pressures of the situation might undermine their ability to know what the right thing is.

An Example: The Berkey-Kodak Case

One of the best-known and most painful examples of this phenomenon was the Berkey-Kodak antitrust litigation in 1977, a bitterly contested private antitrust action brought by Berkey Photo against the giant of the industry. In the heat of adversarial combat, Mahlon Perkins, an admired senior litigator for the large New York law firm representing Kodak, snapped. For no apparent reason, he lied to his opponent to conceal documents from discovery, then perjured himself before a federal judge to cover up the lie. Eventually he owned up, resigned from his firm, and served a month in prison. Perhaps this sounds like an instance of chickens coming home to roost for a Rambo litigator. But by all accounts, Perkins was an upright and courtly man, the diametrical opposite of a Rambo litigator.[1]

Joseph Fortenberry, the associate working for him, knew that Perkins was perjuring himself and whispered a warning to him; but when Perkins ignored the warning, Fortenberry did nothing further to correct his mistatements. "What happened" recalls another associate, "was that he saw Perkins lie and really couldn't believe it. And he just had no idea what to do. I mean, he . . . kept thinking there must be a reason. Besides, what do you do? The guy was his boss and a great guy!"[2]

Notice the range of explanations here. *First*, the appeal to hierarchy: the guy was his boss. *Second*, to personal loyalty: the guy was a great guy. *Third*, to helplessness: Fortenberry had no idea what to do. *Fourth*, Fortenberry couldn't believe it. He kept thinking there must be a reason. The last is an explanation of a different sort, suggesting that Fortenberry's own ethical judgment was undermined by the situation he found himself in.

As a matter of fact, the same may be said of Perkins. He wasn't the lead partner in the litigation; he belonged to a team headed by a newcomer to the firm, an intense, driven, focused, and controlling lawyer.[3] In a situation of supreme stress, Perkins's judgment simply failed him.

In Berkey-Kodak, neither Perkins nor Fortenberry received an explicit order to break the rules, but sometimes lawyers do. (And in Berkey-Kodak, Perkins's behavior, ignoring Fortenberry's whispered warnings, amounts to a tacit order to Fortenberry to say nothing.) What guidance do the ethics rules give when this happens? ABA Model Rule 5.2(a) denies the defense of superior orders to a subordinate lawyer ordered to behave unethically, but Rule 5.2(b) states that a subordinate may defer to "a supervisory lawyer's reasonable resolution of an arguable question of professional duty." The problem is that the pressures on subordinate lawyers may lead them to misjudge when a question of professional duty is arguable and when the supervisor's resolution of it is reasonable. Remember Fortenberry, who "kept thinking there must be a reason" when he heard Perkins perjure himself before a federal judge. This was not even close to an arguable question, and there's nothing reasonable about perjury—but the very fact that it was Fortenberry's respected supervisor who committed it undermined his own confidence that he understood what was reasonable and what was not. When that happens, Rule 5.2(b) will seem more salient to an associate than the bright-line prohibition on wrongful obedience that the first half of the rule articulates.[4]

The Milgram Obedience Experiments

I want to see what we can learn about wrongful obedience from the most celebrated effort to study it empirically, Stanley Milgram's experiments conducted at Yale thirty-five years ago. Even though these experiments are very well known, it is useful to review what Milgram did and what he discovered.[5]

Imagine, then, that you answer Milgram's newspaper advertisement, offering twenty dollars if you volunteer for a one-hour psychology experiment.[6] When you enter the room, you meet the experimenter, dressed in a gray lab coat, and a second volunteer, a pleasant, bespectacled middle-aged man. What you don't know is that the second volunteer is in reality a confederate of the experimenter.

The experimenter explains that the two volunteers will be participating in a study of the effect of punishment on memory and learning. One of you, the learner, will memorize word-pairs; the other, the teacher, will punish the learner with steadily increasing electrical shocks each time he makes a mistake. A volunteer, rather than the experimenter, must administer the shocks because one aim of the experiment is to investigate punishments administered by very different kinds of people. The experimenter leads you to the shock-generator, a formidable-looking machine with thirty switches, marked from 15 volts to 450. Above the voltages, labels are printed. These range from "Slight Shock" (15–60 volts) through "Danger: Severe Shock" (375–420 volts); they culminate in an ominous-looking red label reading "XXX" above 435 and 450 volts. Both volunteers experience a 45-volt shock. Then they draw lots to determine their role. The drawing is rigged so that you become the teacher. The learner mentions that he has a mild heart problem, and the experimenter replies rather nonresponsively that the shocks will cause no permanent tissue damage. The learner is strapped into the hot seat, and the experiment gets under way.

The learner begins making mistakes, and as the shocks escalate he grunts in pain. Eventually he complains about the pain, and at 150 volts announces in some agitation that he wishes to stop the experiment. You look inquiringly at the man in the gray coat, but he says only, "The experiment requires that you continue." As you turn up the juice, the learner begins screaming. Finally, he shouts out that he will answer no more questions. Unflapped, the experimenter instructs you to treat silences as wrong answers. You ask him who will take responsibility if the learner is injured, and he states that he will. You continue.

As the experiment proceeds, the agitated learner announces that his heart is starting to bother him. Again, you protest, and again the man in the lab coat replies,

"The experiment requires that you continue." At 330 volts, the screams stop. The learner falls ominously silent, and remains silent until the bitter end.

But it never actually gets to the bitter end, does it? You may be excused for thinking so. In a follow-up study, groups of people heard the Milgram experiment described without being told the results. They were asked to guess how many people would comply all the way to 450 volts, and to predict whether they themselves would. People typically guessed that at most one teacher out of a thousand would comply—and no one believed that they themselves would.[7]

In reality, 63 percent of subjects complied all the way to 450 volts.[8] Moreover, this is a robust result: it holds in groups of women as well as men, and experimenters obtained comparable results in Holland, Spain, Italy, Australia, South Africa, Germany, and Jordan; indeed, the Jordanian experimenters replicated the 65 percent result not only among adults but among seven-year-olds. Originally, Milgram had intended to run his experiments in Germany, to try to understand how so many Germans could participate in the Holocaust; his American experiments were merely for the purpose of perfecting his procedures. After the American dry run, however, Milgram remarked: "I found so much obedience, I hardly saw the need of taking the experiment to Germany."[9]

In my view, we should regard the radical underestimates of subjects' willingness to inflict excruciating shocks on an innocent person as a finding just as important and interesting as the 65 percent compliance rate itself. The Milgram experiments demonstrate not only that in the right circumstances we are quite prone to destructive obedience, but also that we don't believe this about ourselves, or about our neighbors—nor do we condone it.[10] Milgram demonstrates that each of us ought to believe three things about ourselves: that we disapprove of destructive obedience, that we think we would never engage in it, *and, more likely than not, that we are wrong to think we would never engage in it.*

Milgram was flabbergasted by his findings. He and other researchers ran dozens of variations on the experiment, which I won't describe, although I'll mention some of them shortly. His battery of experiments, which lasted for years and ultimately involved more than 1,000 subjects, stands even today as the most imaginative, ambitious, and controversial research effort ever undertaken by social psychologists.

The Milgram experiments place moral norms in conflict. One is what I will call the *performance principle*: the norm of doing your job properly, which in hierarchical work-settings includes the norm of following instructions. The other is the *no-harm principle:* the prohibition on torturing, harming, and killing innocent people. In the abstract, we might think, only a sadist or a fascist would subordinate the no-harm principle to the performance principle. But the Milgram experiments seem to show that what we think in the abstract is dead wrong. Two out of three people you pass in the street would electrocute you if a laboratory technician ordered them to.

The question is why. At this point, I'm going to run through several explanations of the Milgram results. None of them fully satisfies me. After exploring their weaknesses, I turn to the explanation that seems to me most fruitful.

The Agentic Personality; The Classical Liberal Personality

Each of the explanations I will discuss focuses on a different aspect of human personality, and I will label them accordingly. There is, first, Milgram's own explanation. He describes the mentality of compliant subjects as an *agentic state*—a state in which we view ourselves as mere agents or instruments of the man giving the orders. The terminology is entirely familiar to lawyers, of course, because it is agency principles that govern the relationship between lawyer and client.

The problem with this explanation is that it merely relabels the question rather than answering it. *Why* do we turn off our consciences and "go agentic" when an authority figure starts giving us orders? Saying "because we enter an agentic state" is no answer; it's reminiscent of Molière's physician, who explains that morphine makes us sleepy because it possesses a "dormative virtue."

Admittedly, Milgram's subjects usually offered the agentic explanation in their debriefing. But as we all know, "I was just following orders" is often an insincere rationalization. Remember that in the follow-up studies, no one who heard the Milgram experiment described stated that they would comply, and that is another way of saying that none of them accept "just following orders" as a valid reason for complying. Even if the subjects offered the agentic explanation sincerely, we should never accept it at face value, because we human beings are not very gifted at explaining our own behavior.

Indeed, one of Milgram's experiments dramatizes this fact. Many of Milgram's subjects insisted that they went along with the experiment only because the learner had consented. Their response is, of course, quite different from the agentic explanation. Here, subjects claim to be impressed by the learner's consent, not the experimenter's orders. Their consent-centered explanation of why they complied is a hallmark of classical liberalism, so we might as well call them "Classical Liberal Personalities"—if, that is, their understanding of why they complied is correct. To test this classical liberal explanation, Milgram ran a variation in which the learner expressly reserved the right to back out of the experiment whenever he wanted. He did this out loud, in the presence of the teacher and the experimenter. But even so, 40 percent of the subjects followed the experimenter's instructions to the bitter end despite the learner's protests; and three-fourths of the subjects proceeded long past the point where the learner withdrew his consent. Apparently, whether the learner consented or not is actually not especially relevant to whether subjects are willing to administer high-level shocks to him regardless of his subsequent protests. We simply can't take subjects' own explanations for their obedience at face value.

The Authoritarian Personality

If the *Agentic Personality* doesn't explain Milgram's results, how about the *Authoritarian Personality*? A group of researchers in the early 1950s devised a famous questionnaire to measure the cluster of personality traits that they believed characterized supporters of fascist regimes—traits that include an emotional need to submit to authority, but also an exaggerated and punitive interest in other people's sexuality, and a propensity to superstition and irrationalism. They called this measure the *F-scale*—'F' for fascist.

Interestingly, Milgram's compliant subjects had higher F-scores than his defiant subjects.[11] Indeed, isn't it mere common sense that authoritarians are more obedient to authority?

Unfortunately, the answer is no. For one thing, subsequent research has largely discredited the authoritarian personality studies. The F-scale turns out to be a good predictor of racism, but a bad predictor of everything else politically interesting about authoritarianism (such as left-right political orientation).[12] For another, people who volunteer for social psychology experiments are generally low-F, which makes Milgram's subjects at best atypical authoritarians.[13] For a third, high-F individuals typically mistrust science, so it rather begs the question to assume that they regard the experimenter as an authority to be deferred to. Finally, remember that the F-scale measures other things besides emotional attachment to hierarchy. We might as well call high-F something other than the Authoritarian Personality: we might call it the Superstitious Personality, or even the Perverted Prude Personality. In that case, the explanation only raises new questions. Why should Perverted Prudes or believers in alien abduction be specially prone to obedience?

The Sadistic Personality

Some researchers, perhaps with the Perverted Prude in mind, argued that the true explanation for Milgram's results is the *Sadistic Personality*: the experimenter's orders remove our inhibitions, and permit us to act on our repressed urge to hurt other people for pleasure.

The problem is that there is no evidence that we *have* such an urge. None of Milgram's compliant subjects seemed to take even the slightest pleasure in administering punishment, and many of them seemed downright agonized. They protested, they bit their lips until they bled, they broke into sweat or hysterical giggles. One went into convulsions. Milgram writes, "I observed a mature and initially poised businessman enter the laboratory smiling and confident. Within twenty minutes he was reduced to a twitching, stuttering wreck, who was rapidly approaching a point of nervous collapse. . . . At one point he pushed his fist into his forehead and muttered: 'Oh God, let's stop it.' And yet he continued to respond to every word of the experimenter, and obeyed to the end."[14] This hardly describes a sadist at work.

And, as it happens, the researchers who proposed the Sadistic Personality had an ax to grind.[15] They claimed, based on Rorschach tests done on the Nuremberg defendants and Adolf Eichmann, that every last one of the top Nazis was a psychopath. Like Professor Goldhagen today, they wanted to show that there was nothing ordinary about Hitler's executioners, nothing banal about Nazi evil. Their interest in Milgram seemed largely a competitive interest in shoring up their own theory of Nazism.

But their studies were flawed and their argument fallacious. Without interviews and other evidence of clinical pathology, Rorschach diagnoses are quack psychiatry; in any case, the researchers used a discredited method to analyze their Nazi Rorschachs. More basically, Rorschach diagnoses are based on deviations from statistical norms—and Milgram compliance *is* the statistical norm! To say on the basis of Rorschachs that two-thirds of adults are sadists is arithmetically impossible, like saying that all the children are above average.[16]

The Deferential Personality

A very different kind of explanation grows out of the cognitive psychology of the past three decades. Much of this research has revolved around the claim that we all rely on heuristics—rules of thumb—to make everyday judgments. Life is too short for us to be Cartesian rationalists, thinking everything through to the bottom, and natural selection is not kind to Cartesian rationalists. Instead, evolution statistically favors creatures who make snap judgments by applying largely reliable heuristics— even though, in atypical situations, the heuristic gets things badly wrong.

One of these is what might be called the *Trust Authority* heuristic. And this suggests that what drives Milgram's compliant subjects is not the Agentic Personality, nor the Authoritarian Personality, nor the Sadistic Personality, but the *Deferential Personality*. Indeed, some of Milgram's subjects said in their debriefings that they went along with the experimenter because they were sure he knew what he was doing. Remember the Berkey-Kodak associate, who "kept thinking there must be a reason" for Perkins to lie. Ordinarily, we do well to follow the Trust Authority heuristic, because authorities usually know better than lay people. At times, though, even the best heuristic fails—and Milgram devised one such situation.[17]

This is a sophisticated explanation, but I think that Milgram's own findings cast serious doubt on it. In one experiment, Milgram places the naive subject who draws the role of teacher with two experimenters instead of one. Before the session begins, one experimenter announces that a second volunteer has canceled his appointment. After some discussion of how they are going to meet their experimental quota, one of the experimenters decides that he himself will take the learner's place. Like the learner in the basic set-up, he soon begins complaining about the pain, and at 150 volts he demands to be released. Indeed, he follows the entire schedule of complaints, screams, and ominous silence.

Surely, if subjects were relying on the Trust Authority heuristic, the fact that one of the authorities was demanding that the experiment stop should have brought about diminished compliance. Indeed, in another version of the experiment, in which two experimenters disagree in the subject's presence about whether the subject should go on shocking the learner after the learner begins protesting, all of the subjects broke off the experiment immediately. Here, however, the usual two-thirds of the subjects complied to 450 volts. Apparently, it isn't deference to the experimenters' superior knowledge that promotes obedience.

Another variant of Milgram's experiment reinforces this conclusion. In this version, the experimenter gives his orders from another room, in a situation where it is clear that he cannot see what level of shock the teacher is actually administering. Unsurprisingly, compliance drops drastically; and yet the experimenter's superior knowledge is no different than if he was standing directly behind the teacher. Again, it appears that whatever causes the teacher to obey, it is not the experimenter's perceived expertise.

The Situationist Alternative

Perhaps the most radical suggestion is that *nothing* in the subjects' personalities accounts for their compliance. The so-called situationist view holds that situational pressures, not personalities, account for human behavior. Indeed, situationists argue that attributing behavior to personality is one of the fundamental delusions to which human beings are prey—it is, in their terminology, the "fundamental attribution error." Situationists point out that small manipulations of Milgram's experimental set-up are able to evoke huge swings in compliance behavior. For example, in some experiments Milgram placed the teacher on a team with other "teachers," who were actually actors working for Milgram. When the fellow teachers defied the experimenter, compliance plunged to 10 percent; but when they uncomplainingly delivered the shocks, compliance shot up to 90 percent. Obviously, variation like this arises from the situation, not from the subjects' personalities.[18] As a consequence, situationists argue that the only reliable predictor of how any given person will behave in a situation is the baseline rate for the entire population. The person's observable character traits are by and large irrelevant.

Situationism offers an important reminder that human character and will do not operate in a vacuum. The Achilles' heel of situationism is explaining why anyone deviates from the majority behavior. If individual personality and idiosyncrasy are largely irrelevant to subjects' responses, we should find more-or-less uniform compliance behavior. In the Milgram experiments, situationists must explain why one-third of the subjects defy the experimenter. Remember that in the follow-up questionnaire studies, where subjects were asked whether they would comply in the Milgram experiment, 100 percent said no. What, if not individual personality and idiosyncrasy, causes a one-third/two-thirds split when the situation changes from filling out a questionnaire to performing in the actual experiment?

The situationists' explanation is that even though people respond similarly to similar situations, different individuals perceive situations differently from each other. Idiosyncrasy operates at the level of perception and not the level of behavior.

On this theory, the defiant minority simply don't perceive the experiment in the same way as the compliant majority.[19] Yet I find this explanation a little too convenient, particularly because there is no evidence to back it up—no independent study of how Milgram's subjects perceive the experiment, and no attempt to correlate perception with response. Just what do the defiant subjects perceive in the experiment that their compliant brethren perceive differently? Without an answer to this question, and evidence to support it, it seems to me that the situationist explanation of individual differences fails, and with it the situationist explanation of Milgram compliance.

A Proposal: The Corruption of Judgment

And yet I agree that the key to understanding Milgram compliance lies in features of the experimental situation. The feature I wish to focus on is the slippery-slope character of the electrical shocks. The teacher moves up the scale of shocks by 15-volt increments, and reaches the 450-volt level only at the thirtieth shock. Among other things, this means that the subjects never confront the question "Should I administer a 330-volt shock to the learner?" The question is "Should I administer a 330-volt shock to the learner *given that I've just administered a 315-volt shock?*" It seems clear that the latter question is much harder to answer. As Milgram himself points out, to conclude that administering the 330-volt shock would be wrong is to admit that the 315-volt shock was probably wrong, and perhaps *all* the shocks were wrong.[20]

Cognitive dissonance theory teaches that when our actions conflict with our self-concept, our beliefs and attitudes change until the conflict is removed.[21] We are all pro se defense lawyers in the court of conscience.[22] Cognitive dissonance theory suggests that when I have given the learner a series of electrical shocks, I simply won't view giving the next shock as a wrongful act, because I won't admit to myself that the previous shocks were wrong.

Let me examine this line of thought in more detail. Moral decision making requires more than adhering to sound principles, such as the no-harm principle. It also requires good judgment, by which I mean knowing which actions violate a moral principle and which do not. Every lawyer understands the difference between good principles and good judgment—it is the difference between knowing a rule of law and being able to apply it to particular cases. As Kant first pointed out, you can't teach good judgment through general rules, because we already need judgment to know how rules apply. Judgment is always and irredeemably particular.

Let's assume that most of Milgram's subjects do accept the no-harm principle, and agree in the abstract that it outweighs the performance principle—again, the questionnaire studies strongly suggest that this is so. *The subjects still need good judgment to know at what point the electrical shocks violate the no-harm principle.* Virtually no one thinks that the slight tingle of a 15-volt shock violates the no-harm principle: if it did, medical researchers would violate the no-harm principle every time they take blood samples from volunteers. Unsurprisingly, only two of Milgram's thousand subjects refused to give any shocks at all.

But how can 30 volts violate the no-harm principle if 15 volts didn't? And if a 30-volt shock doesn't violate the no-harm principle, neither does a shock of 45 volts.

Of course we know that slippery-slope arguments like this are unsound. At some point, the single grains of sand really do add up to a heap, and at some point shocking the learner really should shock the conscience as well. But it takes good judgment to know where that point lies. Unfortunately, cognitive dissonance generates enormous psychic pressure to deny that our previous obedience may have violated a fundamental moral principle. That denial requires us to gerrymander the boundaries of the no-harm principle so that the shocks we've already delivered don't violate it. However, once we've kneaded and pummelled the no-harm principle, it becomes virtually impossible to judge that the next shock, only imperceptibly more intense, crosses the border from the permissible to the forbidden. By luring us into higher and higher level shocks, one micro-step at a time, the Milgram experiments gradually and subtly disarm our ability to distinguish right from wrong. Milgram's subjects never need to lose, even for a second, their faith in the no-harm principle. Instead, they lose their capacity to recognize that administering an agonizing electrical shock violates it.

What I am offering here is a *corruption of judgment* explanation of the Milgram experiments. The road to hell turns out to be a slippery slope, and the travelers on it really do have good intentions—they "merely" suffer from bad judgment.

The corruption-of-judgment theory fits in well with one of the other classic experiments of social psychology, Freedman and Fraser's 1966 demonstration of the so-called foot-in-the-door effect. In this experiment, a researcher posing as a volunteer asks homeowners for permission to erect a large, ugly "Drive Carefully!" sign in their front yards. The researcher shows the homeowners a photo of a pleasant-looking home completely obscured by the sign. Unsurprisingly, most homeowners refuse the request—indeed, the only real surprise is that 17% agree to take the sign. (Who *are* these people?)

Within one subset of homeowners, however, 75 percent agree to take the sign. What makes these homeowners different? Just one thing: two weeks previously, they had agreed to place a small, inconspicuous "Be a Safe Driver" sticker in their windows. Apparently, once the public service foot insinuated itself in the door, the entire leg follows.[23] Perhaps what is surprising is only that such a small foot could provide an opening for such a large and unattractive leg. The slippery slope from sound judgment to skewed judgment is a lot steeper than we may have suspected.

According to this explanation of the Milgram experiments, it is our own previous actions of shocking the learner that corrupt our moral judgment and lead us to continue shocking him long past the limits of human decency. In a sense, then, we "do it to ourselves"—Milgram compliance turns out to be the result of cognitive dissonance and our need for self-vindication, rather than obedience to authority. In that case, what role does the man giving the orders play in this explanation?

The answer, I believe, is twofold. First, his repeated instruction—"the experiment requires that you continue!"—prompts us to view the shocks as morally indistinguishable, to downplay the fact that the shocks are gradually escalating. After all, his demeanor never changes, and his instructions never vary. The authority of the superior lies in his power to shape our perceptions, by making us regard everything he asks us to do as business as usual. The experimenter's unflappable demeanor communicates a message: "This experiment is as worthwhile now as it was at the outset. Nothing has changed." Good judgment lies in drawing distinctions among near-indiscernables, whereas authoritative instructions reinforce the theme that indiscernables are identical. The experimenter undermines our judgment, rather than over-mastering our will. Second, his orders pressure us to make our decisions quickly, without taking adequate time to reflect. Together, these two effects of orders subtly erode the conditions for good judgment, and contribute to judgment's self-corruption.

The idea that obedience to evil may result from corrupted judgment rather than evil values or sadism is central to the most famous philosophical study of wrongful obedience in our time, Hannah Arendt's *Eichmann in Jerusalem*.[24] Adolf Eichmann, on Arendt's account, was neither a monster nor an ideologue, neither an antisemite nor a sadist. He was a careerist—an organization man through and through, who could never understand why doing a responsible job well might be regarded as a crime against humanity.

Arendt was struck by the many statements Eichmann made that showed that he never perceived anything at all extraordinary about mass murder. Eichmann would relate the "hard luck story" of his failure to win promotion in the S.S. to an Israeli policeman whose parents he knew had been murdered by the Nazis; or describe the "normal, human" conversation he had had with an inmate of Auschwitz, who was actually begging for his life.[25] He was utterly oblivious to the way that his listeners would regard these war stories. For Arendt, who understood that thinking is the inner dialogue by which we examine our situation from various perspectives, Eichmann's inability to think from another person's point of view meant that he could not think at all. Instead, he fell back on the slogans and party euphemisms that had structured his experience throughout his career. Eichmann insulated himself from reality with an impenetrable wall of routines, habits, and cliches.

The result was a man who was incapable of judging reality for what it was; he could experience the world only through the arid, Newspeak categories of a functionary. Eichmann's inability to think from another's point of view deprived him of the ability to think from his own point of view, perhaps even the capacity to *have* a point of view of his own. As in the Milgram experiments, Eichmann allowed his superiors to define the situation he was in; and that is why Eichmann, "an average, 'normal' person, neither feeble-minded nor indoctrinated nor cynical, could be perfectly incapable of telling right from wrong."[26]

The parallels between Arendt's account and the corruption-of-judgment theory offered here are straightforward. To begin with, consider the slippery slope that led Eichmann to the dock in Jerusalem. Eichmann "knew" that his conscience was clear about his casual decision to follow a friend's advice and join the Nazi Party, about which he knew very little at the time. As for his subsequent decision to transfer into the S.S., that was a simple mistake: he thought he was joining a different service with a similar name. He regarded his early work in Jewish affairs as something close to benevolent, as he expedited the deportation of Jews from Austria by making it easier for them to obtain their exit papers (in return for all their property). When the mission changed from expelling Jews to concentrating them in camps in the East, Eichmann persuaded himself that this was the best way to fulfill the Zionist ambition of "putting firm ground under the feet of the Jews."[27] As for the Final Solution, all the glitterati in the Nazi hierarchy embraced it enthusiastically; so after six weeks of bad conscience, Eichmann came to see things their way. In his own eyes, each step on Eichmann's road to damnation seemed innocent, sanctioned, almost inevitable. There was no sticking point, no clear moment of demarcation that his judgment, accustomed to functioning solely in terms of conformism and career advancement, could grab ahold of. The ordinary incentives of career-making colluded with his sense of dutifulness (the performance principle) to launch Eichmann on his slippery slope. His own thoughtlessness and *amour-propre* prevented him from seeing it for what it was; as a result, his judgment became entirely corrupt without Eichmann ever ceasing to believe in his own rectitude.

For Arendt, the case of Adolf Eichmann posed profound questions in moral psychology, questions she wrestled with for the rest of her life. What is thinking? What is judgment? How can thought, which is not the same as judgment, insulate us, at least in part, from bad judgment?[28] These are ultimate questions that I shall not even try to answer here. But the corruption-of-judgment account presented here can at least provide us with a point of connection between Arendt's philosophizing and the empirical phenomena revealed in social psychology experiments such as Milgram's.

To many readers, the idea of analogizing issues of legal and organizational ethics to the Eichmann case will be preposterous and even offensive. On the one side, the analogy demonizes the Joseph Fortenberrys of the American workplace; on the other, it trivializes the Holocaust. But this objection misses the point. Obviously, I am not suggesting that wrongfully obedient law firm associates are the moral equivalent of Eichmann, nor that genocide is just one more form of wrongful obedience in the workplace. Rather, the point for both Arendt and Milgram is that if an ordinary person's moral judgment can be corrupted to the point of failure even about something as momentous as mass murder—or shocking an innocent experimental volunteer to death!—it is entirely plausible to think that the same organizational and psychological forces can corrupt our judgment in lesser situations. The extreme situations illuminate their ordinary counterparts even if, in the most obvious ways, they are utterly unlike them.

Explaining Berkey-Kodak through Corruption-of-Judgment Theory

With these thoughts in mind, let me return to the Berkey-Kodak case and see what light the corruption-of-judgment theory may shed on it. The theory suggests that we should find the partner's and associate's misdeeds at the end of a slippery slope, beginning with lawful adversarial deception and culminating with lies, perjury, and wrongful obedience. Following this lead, one fact leaps out at us: *the misdeeds occurred during a high-stakes discovery process.*

Every litigator knows that discovery is one of the most contentious parts of civil litigation. Civil discovery is like a game of Battleship. One side calls out its shots—it files discovery requests—and the other side must announce when a shot scores a hit. It makes that announcement by turning over a document. There are two big differences. First, unlike Battleship, it isn't always clear when a shot has scored a hit. Lawyers get to argue about whether their document really falls within the scope of the request. They can argue that the request was too broad, or too narrow, or that the document is privileged, or is attorney work-product. Second, unlike Battleship, lawyers don't always get to peek at the opponent's card after the game. When the opponent concludes that a shot missed her battleship, she makes the decision ex parte—she doesn't have to announce it to her adversary, who may never learn that a smoking-gun document (the battleship) was withheld based on an eminently debatable legal judgment.[29]

Every litigation associate goes through a rite of passage: she finds a document that seemingly lies squarely within the scope of a legitimate discovery request, but her supervisor tells her to devise an argument for excluding it. As long as the argument isn't frivolous there is nothing improper about this, but it marks the first step onto the slippery slope. For better or for worse, a certain kind of innocence is lost. It is the moment when withholding information despite an adversary's legitimate request starts to feel like zealous advocacy rather than deception. It is the moment when the no-deception principle encoded in Model Rule 8.4(c)—"It is professional misconduct for a lawyer to engage in conduct involving dishonesty, fraud, deceit or misrepresentation."—gets gerrymandered away from its plain meaning. But, like any other piece of elastic, the no-deception principle loses its grip if it is stretched too often. Soon, if the lawyer isn't very careful, every damaging request seems too broad or too narrow; every smoking-gun document is either work-product or privileged; no adversary ever has a right to "our" documents. At that point the fatal question is not far away: *Is lying really so bad when it is the only way to protect "our" documents from an adversary who has no right to them?* If legitimate advocacy marks the beginning of this particular slippery slope, Berkey-Kodak lies at its end.

Are Compliant Subjects Morally Blameworthy?

The Milgram experiments lead quite naturally to the depressing reflection that human nature is much more readily disposed to wrongful obedience than we might have expected or hoped. Milgram seems to have established that in situations where obedience struggles with decency, decency typically loses. What does this conclusion imply about moral responsibility for wrongful obedience? Let us consider two possible lines of thought, which, for reasons that will become clear, I shall call the *Inculpating View* and the *Exculpating View*.

The Inculpating View holds that no matter how widespread wrongful obedience is, and no matter how deep its roots within human nature, wickedness remains wickedness; the fact that wickedness is the rule rather than the exception excuses no one. Suppose that experimenters were to demonstrate that two out of three people will walk off with someone else's hundred-dollar bill if they are sure they can get away with it. The experiment suggests that greed has roots deep within human nature, but that creates no excuse for theft. The temptation to obey is like greed or any other temptation. It is perfectly natural to give in to it—that's why they call it temptation!—but being perfectly natural excuses nothing.[30]

It might be objected that the analogy between Milgram obedience and greed is a bad one. No matter what his rationalizations, the thief knows that theft is wrong, or so we may suppose. He simply allowed his baser drives to override his moral judgment, and that is why we don't allow his greed to excuse him. If our earlier corruption-of-judgment explanation of Milgram obedience is correct, however, the drive to obey operates at a deeper level, undermining our very capacity to distinguish right from wrong.

But this objection overlooks the fact that we generally do *not* excuse wrongful behavior because it resulted from bad judgment—if anything, the fact that the wrongful choice was the product of judgment rather than passion or pathology condemns it even more. So the corruption-of-judgment explanation supports rather than undermines the Inculpating View.

Or does it? Try a thought experiment. Suppose a group of high school seniors is given a test of judgment, such as the familiar multiple-choice analogies test. And suppose that the test's difficulty is calibrated so that every student in a control group passes it. This time, however, the test is administered under extraordinary conditions: throughout the test, a large-screen television in the testing room broadcasts a video of a good-looking couple making enthusiastic, noisy, and improbably athletic love. Under these conditions, we will suppose, two-thirds of the students fail the test.

Clearly, we should conclude that passing the test under such distracting conditions is really hard. The numbers prove it.[31] We would be foolish to blame the students for failing; and we would be cruel to punish those who failed, for example by refusing to admit them to college because of their bad scores. Surely we would blame the situation, which obviously undermined their capacity to judge.

The analogy to Milgram is straightforward. When people had the Milgram experiments described to them, they all passed the "test" of moral judgment: without exception, they predicted that they would break off the experiment well before the 450-volt maximum (and it should be clear that their prediction is in reality a moral judgment that complying to 450 volts would be wrong). But in the actual experiment, two out of three failed their test. Pursuing the parallel, we would be foolish to blame them for failing, and cruel for punishing them. The situation excuses their compliance. This is the *Exculpating View.*

In short, the Inculpating View holds people responsible for their wrongful obedience, regardless of how common wrongful obedience is, or how deeply rooted it may be in human nature. The Exculpating View excuses wrongful obedience whenever it is the statistical norm, because that fact shows how unreasonably difficult it must be to disobey under such circumstances. One view accuses, the other excuses.

How are we to decide between the Inculpating and the Exculpating Views? I propose approaching the problem indirectly, by looking at parallel puzzles in the treatment of psychologically based defenses in the criminal law. Admittedly, criminal responsibility raises different issues from moral responsibility, and the psychological defenses the law recognizes do not include the deep-seated propensity to obey. Despite these obstacles, there are enough suggestive parallels that examining the criminal law issues will allow us to triangulate toward our own question.

Consider the "heat of passion" or "extreme emotional disturbance" defense in homicide cases, which reduces murder to manslaughter.[32] In its formulation in the Model Penal Code, the defense is available whenever a "homicide which would otherwise be murder is committed under the influence of extreme mental or emotional disturbance for which there is reasonable explanation or excuse."[33] The canonical situation is a husband murdering his wife and her lover when he finds them in bed.

Surprisingly, however, this cliched bit of melodrama is *not* the typical situation in which the defense actually arises. Victoria Nourse recently examined every reported heat-of-passion decision in U.S. courts between 1980 and 1995, and discovered a disturbing pattern. The paradigm case for heat of passion turns out to be men angry at women for exiting a relationship: boyfriends upset that their girlfriends have left them; long-separated husbands whose wives finally file for divorce; long-divorced husbands who learn that their ex-wives are remarrying; and men served with protective orders forbidding them from approaching wives or girlfriends they have battered. In other words, the typical heat-of-passion "provocation" turns out not to be infidelity, but a woman's attempt to lead her own life free from her killer's dominion; and the killer's "passion" seems not to be sexual jealousy so much as the overwhelming desire to control and own a woman.[34]

The Model Penal Code aimed to reform the criminal law by taking a scientific approach to human psychology. It treats passion and irrationality as demonstrable facts of human existence that must be acknowledged rather than denounced. In this respect, it holds what Dan Kahan and Martha Nussbaum label the "mechanistic conception" of emotion—he idea "that emotions . . . are energies that impel the person to action, without embodying ways of thinking about or perceiving objects or situations in the world."[35] From a clinical point of view, it hardly matters what circumstances provoke an emotional disturbance. All that matters is whether the emotional disturbance undermines the defendant's self-control. The MPC embodies the idea that psychological drives are causes, not reasons, for human behavior, and that it is senseless to moralize about nonrational causes. For that reason, juries in MPC jurisdictions are asked to determine whether, *from the killer's "subjective" point of view*, a woman's declaration of independence is a reasonable explanation of murderous anger.[36] Sadly enough, from the killer's point of view, it often is.

Nourse is critical of the Model Penal Code's approach, and I am as well. Her findings about the circumstances under which the heat-of-passion defense gets invoked provide a virtual reductio ad absurdum of the mechanistic treatment of provocation. Mitigations reflect judicial and legislative compassion for wrongdoers who have committed crimes under unusually trying circumstances. Does a man who flies into a murderous rage because his wife dates someone else three years after they separated really deserve our compassion?[37] Surely not; and surely it *is* appropriate to moralize about whether his murderous rage was justified.

In line with this thought, Nourse proposes a different approach to extreme emotional disturbance, based on the concept of a *warranted excuse*.[38] Begin with the philosophically attractive idea that emotions can be appropriate or inappropriate—that they embody (or at least correspond with) evaluative judgments of objects and situations that can be true or false, warranted or not warranted.[39] If a man flies into a murderous rage because his wife has been raped, his emotion reflects a warranted evaluative judgment about the rape—that rape is wicked and horrible. If the enraged man kills his wife's rapist, his extreme emotional disturbance provides a warranted excuse that rightly mitigates the murder to a manslaughter.[40]

If, on the other hand, the killer has become enraged because his wife is leaving him, his emotion corresponds with the evaluative judgment that she is not entitled to leave him—perhaps even that wives are never entitled to leave their husbands. This evaluative judgment is absurd and repulsive. Even assuming that he was in the grip of extreme emotional disturbance when he killed her, the heat-of-passion excuse should be unavailable to him, because the emotion is unjustified. In line with this reasoning, Nourse proposes a legal test to distinguish warranted from unwarranted extreme-emotional-disturbance excuses for homicide. If the killer's emotional disturbance is provoked by an act, like rape, which the law condemns, the excuse is warranted; if it is provoked by an act that the law protects, like leaving a relationship, the excuse is unwarranted.

There is one way in which the "warranted excuse" terminology can be misleading. It is important to realize that what makes the excuse unwarranted is not just that the actor's emotion corresponds with a *false* evaluative judgment. The excuse is unwarranted because the actor's emotion corresponds with an *evil* evaluative judgment—one that reflects badly on the actor's character. The excuse fails not because its underlying evaluative judgment is epistemologically unwarranted; the excuse fails because its underlying evaluation is morally detestable.

Admittedly, it runs deeply against the modern temper to moralize about psychological forces over which we arguably have no control. That is what the warranted-excuse approach does, inasmuch as it relies on moral judgments to distinguish causal explanations for behavior that mitigate liability from causal explanations that do not.

Yet assigning responsibility in a world of causal explanations is what compatibilism (the approach to the free-will problem that insists that moral responsibility is *compatible* with determinism) is all about—and the criminal law is compatibilist through and through. Criminal lawyers are rightly agnostic about the possibility that all behavior can be causally explained, but they will insist that even so the law must ascribe responsibility to some people but not others for their actions. Given that we inevitably make such judgments, it seems plausible to make them on moral grounds—in effect, blaming agents for their susceptibility to morally obnoxious causes.

Viewed abstractly, then, the strategy for separating warranted from unwarranted heat-of-passion excuses amounts to this. First, we make explicit the underlying judgment that the emotion reflects. Second, we ask whether the judgment is warranted. Third, if the judgment underlying the emotion is unwarranted, we ask whether in addition it is morally condemnable. If so, the excuse is unwarranted.

How can we apply these ideas to Milgram obedience? Notice first that the propensity to obey is not an emotion. It is more like a hankering, like wanting to smoke a cigarette or scratch an itch. But even though the urge to obey is not an emotion, we can treat it along the same lines as the heat-of-passion defense: first, by making explicit whatever underlying judgments it corresponds with, second, by asking if they are justified, and third, if they are unjustified, by asking whether they are in addition morally condemnable.

What underlying judgments correspond with Milgram obedience? That depends on what the explanation of Milgram obedience is. Here, I will assume that the corruption-of-judgment explanation I defended earlier is the right explanation. Subjects obey, according to the corruption-of-judgment account, because the experiment manipulates them into misjudging the point at which an electric shock violates the no-harm principle. The experiment begins innocuously, and each incremental step implicates the teacher a bit further in the project of shocking the learner. The experimenter's repeated instruction—"The experiment requires that you continue"—reinforces the idea that every shock level is morally indistinguishable from those that went before. As a result, breaking off the experiment for moral reasons generates cognitive dissonance, because it suggests that the teacher has willingly participated in wrongdoing. The teacher cannot eliminate the dissonance by undoing what he's already done. Instead, he eliminates the dissonance by gerrymandering the scope of the no-harm principle so that participating in the experiment doesn't appear to violate it. As one psychologist puts it, "Dissonance-reducing behavior is ego-defensive behavior; by reducing dissonance, we maintain a positive image of ourselves—an image that depicts us as good. . . ."[41] In other words, our judgment gets corrupted because only by corrupting our judgment can we continue to think well of ourselves. Conscience must be seduced into flattering our self-image.

On this analysis, the propensity to obey corresponds with the following line of (unconscious) reasoning: "If the next shock is wrong, the one I just administered was wrong as well. If so, I would have to believe that I had done something morally wrong; I would have to think badly of myself. That's unacceptable. So the next shock can't be wrong."

That this line of reasoning is unsound goes without saying. It takes one's own inevitable moral uprightness as a given, and our inevitable moral uprightness is never a given. But the reasoning is more than merely unsound. It reflects badly on our character. It reveals us as so childishly resistant to moral self-criticism that we will distort our sense of right and wrong to avoid admitting that we have done wrong. We are willing to electrocute the learner if the alternative is feeling a little bad about ourselves. *Amour-propre über alles!*

The Milgram experiments demonstrate that two-thirds of us are fatally susceptible to this kind of unconscious reasoning, from which it follows that avoiding it must be rather difficult. On the Exculpating View, the difficulty of avoiding it mitigates our moral culpability. But the argument I have been elaborating leads to the opposite conclusion. Compliance originates in corruption of judgment, and corruption of judgment in this case corresponds with the line of reasoning that I have summarized as *amour-propre über alles!*—a line of reasoning that is not only unsound but morally repugnant. Our susceptibility to self-corrupted judgment reflects badly on us, and no mitigation is warranted. In this case, at any rate, the Inculpating View seems closer to the truth.

It is important to understand what I am *not* arguing. I am not arguing that whenever a bad choice arises from fallacious unconscious reasoning that corrupts our judgment we bear full responsibility for making the bad choice. We bear full responsibility only when the unconscious reasoning is not only fallacious but morally reprehensible. Sometimes, fallacious unconscious reasoning casts no discredit on us, and in those cases the difficulty of avoiding it *does* mitigate our blame.

For example, cognitive psychologists have discovered that when we face risk-decisions we unconsciously employ quick-and-dirty heuristics that in trick cases can lead us to faulty probability-judgments. Presumably, natural selection bred these heuristics into us because they make up in ease and speed what they sacrifice in reliability. They are useful rules of thumb, and Mother Nature is a rule-utilitarian. The principle is the same as in optical illusions: our brain learns quick-and-dirty optical heuristics like "small-is-far-and-big-is-near," which can be exploited by illusionists to fool the eye. The rule "small-is-far-and-big-is-near" is fallacious; but it does not reflect badly on us that we unconsciously follow it. Even if following it leads us to a fatal mistake, we aren't to blame. In the same way, we aren't to blame for mistakes arising from our quick-and-dirty cognitive heuristics, because it doesn't reflect badly on us that we employ them. Finite creatures like us must and should employ them.[42]

Milgram compliance is different, because the unconscious reasoning compliant teachers follow *does* reflect badly on them. What follows from these observations is that neither the Inculpating View nor the Exculpating View is entirely right, because each holds sway in some cases but not others. Suppose psychologists discover that under some experimental condition *C* most people suffer a failure of judgment. The Inculpating View says that the large number of people suffering the failure doesn't excuse the failure, while the Exculpating View says that it does. What we have discovered instead is that when susceptibility to *C* reflects badly on our character, the Inculpating View is true; when susceptibility to *C* does not reflect badly on our character, the Exculpating View is true. In Milgram, the Inculpating View is true; compliant subjects are to blame for their wrongful obedience, even though it resulted from bad judgment, and their judgment was corrupted by dynamics they were unaware of. That is because their susceptibility to corruption of judgment reflects badly on them.

Warranted Excuses and Free Will

Those who hold the Exculpating View are likely to find this analysis question-begging. If it is extraordinarily difficult to avoid fallacious unconscious reasoning based on excessive self-regard, as the two-thirds Milgram compliance rate suggests, giving in to it should not reflect badly on us. That, recall, was the argument behind the Exculpating View, and the analysis offered here seems to assume at the outset that it fails. Hence the concern that the analysis begs the question.

The point of the objection is that we should be held responsible only for choices that are ours to make, and if we cannot help reasoning as we do—it is, remember, *unconscious* reasoning—it follows that the choice is not really ours. Let us use the term "moral self" to describe those aspects of a person that engage in moral choice. Unconscious reasoning that we can't easily avoid seems to come from outside the moral self, and for that reason it does not reflect badly on the moral self.

Take an extreme illustration. Suppose that a Milgram subject believes he is morally infallible, but he believes it only because a brain tumor has given him delusions of grandeur. And suppose that because of this belief he becomes a Milgram complier in just the way that the corruption-of-judgment theory suggests. He is, in other words, a typical Milgram complier, with the one difference that excessive self-regard has become part of his make-up only because of the misfortune of the brain tumor. Surely, we should hold him blameless, because his judgment has been corrupted by something foreign to his moral self.

If that is right, however, we must consider the possibility that even in less extreme cases—everyday cases where we can't point to an obvious cause like a brain tumor—susceptibility to excessive self-regard also derives from causal factors foreign to the moral self (brain chemistry, psychological laws, upbringing). According to psychologist Melvin Lerner, "as any reasonable psychologist will tell you, all behavior is 'caused' by a combination of antecedent events and the genetic endowment of the individual."[43]

Clearly, we are here treading in the vicinity of the general question whether moral responsibility and determinism are compatible—an aspect of the Problem of Free Will, which one writer has aptly described as the most difficult problem in philosophy.[44] I have no reason to believe myself equipped to solve that problem. A distinguished philosopher once warned that "it is impossible to say anything significant about this ancient problem that has not been said before."[45] He wrote these words in 1964; obviously they remain true now. Instead, I will simply lay out, with a minimum of argument, the views about free will and compatibilism that underlie the argument of this chapter. More importantly, though, I will show how these views respond to the objection I have just rehearsed.

Melvin Lerner's deterministic line of argument suggests a blanket disclaimer of responsibility for all bad acts, and—as legal theorist Michael Moore rightly argues—this implication amounts to a reductio ad absurdum of the theory that caused action is blameless action.[46] Not that everyone would regard the implication as a reductio. Lerner believes "that (a) the way people act is determined by their past experience and their biological inheritance, and (b) this perspective neutralizes the condemning or blaming reaction to what people do."[47]

Yet Lerner finds that he himself blames members of his family for actions of which he disapproves. His explanation: "I want to, must, believe that people have 'effective' control over important things that happen, and I will hang on to this belief, even when it requires that I resort to rather primitive, magical thinking. . . ."[48] A few moments' reflection will reveal that to abandon this "primitive, magical thinking" is to abandon all the reactive attitudes such as gratitude, resentment, forgiveness, and indignation—that is, to abandon the cement of the social universe.[49] That is one reason Moore calls the argument a reductio ad absurdum.[50] Before accepting its drastic conclusion, we should explore the possibility that praising and blaming do not require primitive, magical thinking, even in a deterministic universe.

Moore's preferred alternative is to insist that we are morally responsible for our choices, whether or not determinism is true. To avoid the counter-intuitive argument that his position blames people for acting even though they could not do otherwise, he adopts G. E. Moore's analysis of the phrase ". . . could have done otherwise": it means "could have if the actor had chosen to do otherwise."[51] According to this analysis, even an actor whose behavior is determined could have done otherwise, as long as the causal laws that link choosing with doing remain valid. For then, the actor could have done otherwise if he had chosen to.

I cannot accept this alternative, however, because it falls prey to the well-known objection that "he could have done otherwise if he had chosen to do otherwise" can be true even of someone who could not have chosen to do otherwise. As Susan Wolf illustrates the objection, "the fact that a person attacked on the street would have screamed if she had chosen cannot possibly support a positive evaluation of her responsibility in the case if she was too paralyzed by fear to consider, much less choose, whether to scream."[52] Indeed, "she could have screamed if she had chosen to" may be true (in a hypothetical sort of way) even if the victim had fainted—hardly a condition under which it is reasonable to insist that she could have screamed!

Wolf suggests a better characterization of the ability to do something, namely that one possesses the necessary skills, talents, and knowledge to do it, and nothing interferes with their exercise.[53] And indeed, this may come close to another of Michael Moore's ideas, namely that one can do something if one has the capability and opportunity to do it.[54] If this characterization of freedom is right, atom-by-atom physical determinism seems pretty much beside the point.[55]

A worry nevertheless arises about whether Wolf's alternative will help us understand the Milgram experiment or similar cases where psychological forces distort our judgment. Moore rightly maintains that "[t]he freedom essential to responsibility is the freedom to reason practically without the kind of disturbances true [psychological] compulsions represent"[56]; and Wolf likewise insists that "agents *not be psychologically determined* to make the particular choices or perform the particular actions they do.[57] But what if we aren't free in that way? In that case, even Wolf's definition of ability will lead to the conclusion that Milgram's compliers were unable to act differently. After all, in social psychology the determinist argument is not that agents are unfree because the motions of every particle in the Universe are determined by the laws of physics. The argument is that psychological forces distort the judgment even of sane, healthy people.

However, the numbers in the Milgram experiments suggest that such distortion does not rise to the level of determination. If every last one of Milgram's thousand subjects had complied with the experimenter, we would undoubtedly conclude that some powerful psychological force, as irresistible as the brain tumor in our earlier example, compels our obedient behavior and excuses otherwise-wrongful compliance. Our only remaining puzzles would be isolating and identifying the force, and explaining why naive observers don't predict the result. Furthermore, if only one or two of the thousand subjects complied, we would likewise suspect that pathology had something to do with it, precisely because the experimenter's orders prove so easy for normal people to resist.

In the actual experiment, the numbers fall in between. The two-thirds compliance rate provides strong evidence that some previously-unsuspected psychological force distorts the judgment of otherwise-normal people. But, because a third of the subjects did not comply, the evidence hardly supports the hypothesis of an irresistible compulsion.

The corruption-of-judgment theory I have defended here grounds the urge to comply in cognitive dissonance, a dynamic that all people share. But it links the subjects' susceptibility to the urge to excessive self-regard, which two-thirds of us (apparently) have despite our conscious beliefs to the contrary, and the rest do not. This difference, no doubt, results from differences in how we are put together and brought up.

What makes the warranted-excuse theory distinctive is its insistence that such differences are not morally neutral brute facts about us that excuse bad judgment. When distorted moral judgment arises from bad values like excessive self-regard, it seems wrongheaded to release the actor from blame for his actions. That, at any rate, is the idea underlying the warranted-excuse strategy defended here: because susceptibility to corruption of judgment reflects badly on the agent, corruption of judgment provides no excuse for wrongdoing. A person's character flaw, or so I am assuming, provides a basis for criticism, not a basis for excuse.

Notice that on this approach, we blame people only for their chosen actions, not for their characters; the warranted-excuses approach should not be confused with the theory that actions are wrong only because they manifest bad character. Michael Moore criticizes this "character theory" because it implies that people of bad character deserve to be punished even if they do nothing blameworthy.[58] It is important to understand why his objection does not apply to the warranted-excuses approach. On our approach, the ground for criticizing Milgram compliers is not that they have bad characters. It is that they knowingly administered lethal electrical shocks to an innocent person pleading with them to stop. The character-trait that renders them susceptible to authoritarian pressure is a moral fault, but that fact functions only to rob them of an excuse, not to explain why shocking the learner is wrong.

The warranted-excuses approach does share features with the character theory. First, as Moore observes, it recognizes two very different sorts of moral judgments we make about persons—judgments that they are blameworthy because of their wrongful actions, and judgments that their characters are bad.[59] Second, it accepts Moore's point that the latter judgments are "a kind of aesthetic morality"[60] which in effect judges people by how well-formed their souls are. But, unlike Moore, it rejects any implication that "aesthetic morality" is illegitimate. What should we judge people (as distinguished from their actions) by except the content of their characters?

Moore confuses matters when he marks the distinction between the two sorts of moral judgments by describing them as judgments holding people responsible for their chosen actions and judgments holding them responsible "for being the sort of people that they are."[61] To be sure, this makes character-based moral judgment sound irrational, because holding people responsible for being who they are sounds irrational. But that is only because Moore has inadvertently collapsed two very different meanings of the word "responsibility"—responsibility as authorship, and responsibility as blameworthiness (or, for that matter, praiseworthiness). He is right that a person is not the author of her character, but that does not mean she can't be morally judged according to her character. She is praised or blamed for her character not because she created it, but because in an important sense she *is* her character— there is no moral self beneath or beyond it. The distinction between judgments of deeds and judgments of character does not rest on extravagant Romantic ideas about self-creating selves.

Both kinds of moral judgments are legitimate, and the warranted-excuse approach utilizes both. It assigns blame by judging actions, and accepts or rejects excuses by judging character. This procedure is fair, because it grounds blameworthiness solely in what we do, and withholds deterministic excuses only when the bad acts result from judgment corrupted by bad character. Deterministic excuses remain available whenever our judgment is corrupted by forces beyond our moral selves— forces outside of us in the way that bad character in not outside of us. But doubts surely remain, unless there is something we can do to guard against corrupted judgment and wrongful obedience.

There is no reason to believe that corruption of judgment is inevitable in organizations or in the adversary system. But neither do I have a fail-safe remedy to protect lawyers or anyone else from the optical illusions of the spirit that authority and cognitive dissonance engender. Perhaps the best protection is understanding the illusions themselves, their pervasiveness, the insidious way they work on us.[62] Understanding these illusions warns us against them, and forewarned truly is forearmed, at least to some extent. One of Milgram's compliant subjects wrote him a year after the experiment, "What appalled me was that I could possess this capacity for obedience and compliance to a central idea, . . . even at the expense of another value, i.e. don't hurt someone else who is helpless and not hurting you. As my wife said, 'You can call yourself Eichmann.'"[63] It's hard to believe that this man will obey orders unreflectively in the future.

The point is that to understand all is *not* to forgive all. But if I am right, to understand all may well put us on guard against doing the unforgivable.

Notes

I presented an early version of these ideas as the Keck Award Lecture to the Fellows of the American Bar Foundation, and a later version became my Condon-Faulkner Lecture at the University of Washington School of Law. Later versions were presented at the University of Maryland, the Georgetown Philosophy Department, the Industrial College of the Armed Forces, the Program in Ethics and the Professions at Harvard University, and the Wharton School. I wish to thank the many listeners for their probing questions and perceptive comments. Thanks go also to Laura Dickinson, Deborah Rhode, and Wibren van der Burg for helpful comments on the penultimate draft. I owe a special debt of gratitude to Alan Strudler and David Wasserman, who have sparred with me for years about these issues.

1. For an extended account, see James B. Stewart, *The Partners: Inside America's Most Powerful Law Firms* (New York: Simon & Schuster, 1983), 327–65.

2. Steven Brill, "When a Lawyer Lies," *Esquire* 23–24 (Dec. 19, 1979).

3. Stewart, *The Partners*, 338.

4. See Carol M. Rice, "The Superior Orders Defense in Legal Ethics: Sending the Wrong Message to Young Lawyers," 32 *Wake Forest L. Rev.* 887 (1997).

5. I draw all my descriptions of the Milgram experiments and their variations from Stanley Milgram, *Obedience to Authority: An Experimental View* (New York: Harper Torchbooks, 1974).

6. Milgram actually offered $4, but this was in 1960 dollars.

7. Arthur G. Miller, *The Obedience Experiments: A Case Study of Controversy in Social Science* (New York: Praeger, 1986), 13, 21.

8. The fact that those who hear the experiments described vastly underestimate compliance may result in part from the "false consensus effect," the well-confirmed tendency to exaggerate the extent to which others share our beliefs. Lee Ross and Richard E. Nisbett, *The Person and the Situation: Perspectives of Social Psychology* (Philadelphia: Temple University Press, 1991), 83–85. That is, once a subject in the follow-up surveys had concluded that *she* would defy the experimenter in Milgram's set-up, she is also likely to conclude that most people would. A sophisticated subject aware of the false consensus effect should compensate for it by upping her initial estimate of how many people would comply, say from one percent to five percent. Yet even this 500 percent compensation would drastically underestimate what Milgram actually found. Something more than false consensus is evidently at work here. Moreover, the follow-up subjects' belief that they would defy the Milgram experimenter is itself an unwarranted prediction, since we know that in the basic experiment two-thirds of them would comply to the 450-volt maximum. That is, the very premise for their false consensus—their prediction of their own behavior—is itself most likely false.

9. Quoted in Robert B. Cialdini, *Influence: Science and Practice* (3d ed. 1993), 176 n. 2. In 1970, David Mantell repeated some of the Milgram experiments in Munich, obtaining an 85 percent compliance rate in the basic experiment. David Mantell, "The Potential for Violence in Germany," 27 *J. Social Issues* 101 (1971). So perhaps destructive obedience is a German pathology after all!—except that a similar 85 percent compliance rate appeared in an American replication as well (17 compliant subjects out of 20—David Rosenhan, "Some Origins of Concern for Others," in *Trends and Issues in Developmental Psychology* (P. Mussen, J. Langer and M. Covington eds. 1969), 143). Interestingly, Mantell introduced still another variation, in which the subject would see a prior "teacher"—a confederate of the experimenter—refuse to proceed with the experiment and indignantly confront the experimenter. At that point, the experimenter revealed that he was actually an unsupervised undergraduate, and not a member of the institute where the experiment was conducted. In this version, more than half the subjects nevertheless complied, even after having observed the melodramatic scenario just described; and in subsequent interviews many of them criticized the previous teacher who had broken off the series of shocks. In his American replication, Rosenhan also obtained a compliance rate over 50 percent when it was revealed the experimenter was an unsupervised undergraduate.

10. In another experiment, subjects had the Milgram set-up described to them, and were shown the photograph of a college student who had supposedly participated in the experiment as a "teacher." They were asked to rate the student in the photograph (weak-strong, warm-cold, likable-not likable), based on appearance. Unsurprisingly, the ratings varied drastically depending on what level of shock the student had supposedly proceeded to—the higher the shock, the weaker, colder, and less likable the subject. Miller, *The Obedience Experiments*, 28–29. The natural explanation of the "likability" finding is that subjects found the teacher unattractive to the degree that they found her behavior unattractive—from which it follows that they disapproved of her compliance.

11. Alan C. Elms and Stanley Milgram, "Personality Characteristics Associated With Obedience and Defiance Toward Authoritative Command," 1 *J. Experimental Res. in Personality* 282 (1966).

12. John J. Ray, "Why the F Scale Predicts Racism: A Critical Review," 9 *Political Psychology* 671 (1988).

13. Indeed, it is unclear whether the compliant Milgram subjects were high-F compared with the population at large, or only compared with the defiant subjects. The latter alternative is fully compatible with the compliant subjects being normal, or even low-F, compared with the population at large.

14. Stanley Milgram, "Behavioral Study of Obedience," 67 *J. Abnormal & Social Psych.* 371, 375-77 (1963).

15. Florence Miale and Michael Selzer, *The Nuremberg Mind: The Psychology of the Nazi Leaders* (New York: Quadrangle, 1975); Michael Selzer, "The Murderous Mind," *N. Y. Times Magazine,* Nov. 27, 1977, 35–40.

16. See, e.g., Stephen W. Hurt et al., "The Rorschach", in *Integrative Assessment of Adult Personality* (Larry E. Beutler and Michael R. Berren, eds., New York: Guilford Press, 1995), 202; Zillmer et al., in *Integrative Assessment of Adult Personality,* 73–76, 94; 1 John E. Exner, Jr., *The Rorschach: A Comprehensive System—Basic Foundations* (New York: Wiley, 1993), 330.

17. Alan Strudler and Danielle Warren, "Authority, Wrongdoing, and Heuristics," forthcoming in David Messick, John Darley, and Tom Tyler (eds.), *Social Influence in Organizations.*

18. A clear and forceful statement of situationism may be found in Ross and Nisbett, *The Person and the Situation.*

19. Ibid., 11–13.

20. Milgram, *Obedience to Authority,* 149.

21. This formulation of dissonance theory—a refinement of Lionel Festinger's original hypothesis of cognitive dissonance—comes from Elliot Aronson, *The Social Animal* (7th ed., New York: W. H. Freeman, 1995), 230–33.

22. I take the lawyer metaphor from Roderick M. Kramer & David M. Messick, "Ethical Cognition and the Framing of Organizational Dilemmas: Decision Makers as Intuitive Lawyers," in *Codes of Conduct: Behavioral Research Into Business Ethics* (David M. Messick and Ann E. Tenbrunsel, eds., New York: Russell Sage, 1996), 59.

23. Jonathan L. Freedman and Scott C. Fraser, "Compliance Without Pressure: The Foot-in-the-Door Technique," 4 *J. Personality & Social Psych.* 195 (1966).

24. Hannah Arendt, *Eichmann in Jerusalem: A Report on the Banality of Evil,* rev. ed. (New York: Viking, 1963).

25. Ibid., 49–51.

26. Ibid., 26.

27. Ibid., 76.

28. See Arendt's paper "Thinking and Moral Considerations: A Lecture," 38 *Social Research* 417 (1971).

29. On the game-playing aspects of discovery, see William J. Talbott and Alvin I. Goldman, "Legal Discovery and Social Epistemology," 4 *Legal Theory* 93, 109-22 (1998).

30. On this point, see Ferdinand Schoeman, "Statistical Norms and Moral Responsibility," in *Responsibility, Character, and the Emotions* (Ferdinand Schoeman, ed., New York: Cambridge University Press, 1987), 296, 305.

31. "[T]he mere fact that most people fail in a given environment suggests that succeeding in that environment is difficult." Schoeman, 304. Schoeman takes this idea from Fritz Heider, *The Psychology of Interpersonal Relations* (New York: Wiley, 1958), 89. Heider was one of the founders of attribution theory, the psychological study of how we make judgments attributing causal responsibility for the actions of others as well as ourselves. Doing the right thing in the Milgram set-up is emotionally as well as cognitively difficult. In an Austrian replication of the Milgram experiment, the pulse rates of defiant subjects went *up* at the moment they broke off the experiment, signaling that defiance generates physiological stress. Thomas Blass, "Understanding Behavior in the Milgram Obedience Experiment: The Role of Personality, Situations, and Their Interactions," 60 *Journal of Personality and Social Psychology* 404 (1991).

32. In the ensuing discussion, I closely follow the brilliant treatment of the emotional disturbance defense in Victoria Nourse, "Passion's Progress: Modern Law Reform and the Provocation Defense," 106 *Yale Law Journal* 1331 (1997).

33. Model Penal Code, §210.3(1)(b).

34. Nourse, "Passion's Progress," 1342–68.

35. Dan M. Kahan and Martha C. Nussbaum, "Two Conceptions of Emotion in Criminal Law," 96 *Columbia Law Review* 269, 278 (1996).

36. Even though the MPC requires a reasonable explanation or excuse for the emotional disturbance, it insists that "[t]he reasonableness of such explanation or excuse shall be determined from the viewpoint of a person in the actor's situation under the circumstances as he believes them to be"—a subjective, rather than an objective, test of reasonableness. Model Penal Code, §210.3(1)(b).

37. Nourse, "Passion's Progress," 1360, discussing *State v. Rivera,* 612 A.2d 749 (Conn. 1992) (common-law husband kills his wife's lover three years after he and the wife separated).

38. In the present essay I follow Nourse's examples and terminology. But the same approach was proposed several years earlier in Andrew von Hirsch & Nils Jareborg, "Provocation and Culpability," in Schoeman, *Responsibility, Character, and the Emotions,* 241–55.

39. Kahan and Nussbaum refer to this as the "evaluative conception" of emotion.

40. To avoid confusion, notice that this does not say that killing the rapist is justified. Justified emotions can lead to unjustifiable actions. That is why the appeal to heat of passion is only a partial excuse, reducing murder to manslaughter, and not a full excuse or a justification.

41. Aronson, *The Social Animal,* 185.

42. On this point, see Christopher Cherniak, *Minimal Rationality* (Cambridge, Mass.: MIT Press, 1992).

43. Melvin J. Lerner, *The Belief in a Just World: A Fundamental Delusion* (New York: Plenum Press, 1980), 120.

44. Susan Wolf, *Freedom Within Reason* (New York: Oxford University Press, 1990), vii.

45. Roderick M. Chisholm, "Human Freedom and the Self," reprinted in Gary Watson, ed., *Free Will* (Oxford: Oxford University Press, 1982), 24.

46. Michael Moore, *Placing Blame: A General Theory of the Criminal Law* (Oxford: Oxford University Press, 1997), 504–05

47. Lerner, *The Belief in a Just World,* 121.

48. Ibid., 122.

49. See Peter Strawson, "Freedom and Resentment," 48 *Proceedings of the British Academy* 125 (1962), reprinted in Watson, *Free Will,* 59–80.

50. Moore, *Placing Blame,* 542–43.

51. Moore, *Placing Blame,* 540–41; again at 553. The analysis comes from G. E. Moore, *Ethics* (Cambridge: Cambridge University Press, 1912), 84–95.

52. Wolf, *Freedom Within Reason,* 99. This objection originally comes from Chisholm, "Human Freedom and the Self," in Watson, *Free Will,* 26–27.

53. Wolf, *Freedom Within Reason,* 101.

54. Moore, *Placing Blame,* 541.

55. Wolf skillfully argues this point in *Freedom Within Reason,* 103–16.

56. Moore, *Placing Blame,* 525.

57. Wolf, *Freedom Within Reason,* 103.

58. Moore, *Placing Blame,* 584–87.

59. Ibid., 571.

60. Ibid.

61. Ibid.

62. This is Robert Cialdini's general strategy for immunizing us, to the extent possible, against those who use built-in psychological mechanisms, such as consistency-seeking or reciprocation of favors, to manipulate us. See Generally Cialdini, *Influence: Science and Practice.*

63. Milgram, *Obedience to Authority,* 54.

PART III

Adversarial Premises
and Pathologies

7

The Limits of
Adversarial Ethics

CARRIE MENKEL-MEADOW

Imagine a world in which you have a problem. You know you need help so you look for an advocate and a counselor. If the problem involves law, you may pay generously for this "special purpose" friend. And this friend will typically respond by viewing others involved as potential adversaries.

Welcome, you have entered the world of adversarial lawyering. Here, a special friend will be able to do a great deal on your behalf, including some things that you probably wouldn't want or wouldn't be able to do for yourself if you were acting alone. This assistance may very well be appropriate when you have a clear conflict of values with other parties, when state intervention is essential to resolve a dispute, when you are defending yourself against criminal charges, and when you can readily afford an adversarial battle. But for many other modern transactions, disputes, and social problems, such an approach may not be the best way to accomplish your goals. It may be particularly inappropriate if your problem involves multiple parties, multiple issues, and multiple remedial possibilities.

This essay explores limitations in our adversary legal system and the ethics of advocacy it implies. After examining the attributes of the current system, my analysis suggests that our "culture of adversarialism" has distorted how we think about solving human problems at both societal and individual levels; and that the legal ethics derived from this model are often outmoded, inconsistent, inefficient, and unjust. Most of what passes for legal ethics (a phrase considered oxymoronic by some) rests on the assumption that an adversary system is self-evidently preferable to other possible ways of organizing a legal system. Adversarial processes are often presented as the best way to learn the truth and to protect the legal rights and liberties of disputants. The preference for an adversary system over more inquisitorial, bureaucratic, or mediational forms of dispute resolution implies a central role for lawyers. The defining feature of that role is "partisanship"; the lawyer must work resolutely for her client's interests.[1] Although prevailing rules place some limits on this partisan function, it dominates our understanding of legal ethics and marginalizes other conceptions of what lawyers actually do as planners, problem solvers, government officials, advisers, and policy makers. Despite the varied contexts in which lawyering occurs, we still tend to think of litigation as the lawyer's "habitat" and partisanship as the lawyers' central responsibility.[2]

The adversary model and the ethical norms it has inspired underpin virtually all aspects of our social life, including politics, education, the media, and the family.[3] Robert Kutak, chair of the drafting committee of the ABA's Model Rules of Professional Conduct, underscored the importance of this influence:

> Our legal system is not cooperative but competitive, or adversarial. The basic premise of virtually all our institutions is that open and relatively unrestrained competition among individuals produces the maximum collective good. That idea permeates all aspects of American life, and accordingly, is given effect by laws governing the conduct of individuals and the state. . . . A fundamental characteristic of the competitive theory is that competing individuals have no legal responsibility for the competence of their counterparts on the other side of the transaction and, consequently have no obligation to share the benefits of their own competence with the other side. . . . The principles of individual monopolization of personal competence and indifference to the incompetence of others imply a "survival of the fittest" theme. In the adversary system, there is no obligation, as a general rule, to aid others.[4]

Although there is much to value in a system of party-controlled presentations before a neutral decision maker, the adversary system, as currently practiced, also has structural, remedial, and behavioral flaws. These, in turn, affect ethical practices within the system and the fairness of its outcomes.

The relationship between the adversarial system and the behaviors it demands or encourages is, of course, complex. It is difficult to know how much an adversarial structure is responsible for limited outcomes and strident behaviors, and how much disputes themselves are responsible for contentious relationships. Underlying those issues are other, equally difficult questions. How much can rules of practice or ethical codes affect such structures? To what extent are the rules and codes themselves the product of a less controllable "culture of adversarialism"?

This essay places such questions in sharper focus. Despite the centrality of the adversarial ethic in American legal and cultural institutions, we lack evidence that it is the best way for a dispute resolution system to be organized. This essay illustrates what the adversary system may provide us and what it may prevent us from achieving as professionals dedicated to assisting clients, resolving conflict, and promoting justice.

The Elements of the Adversarial Paradigm

The adversarial paradigms that inform our Anglo-American legal system emphasize a variety of core concepts. It remains unclear how many are "essential" to an adversarial system, and whether the system is itself philosophically, constitutionally, or empirically justified.[5]

In the United States, the adversary system has long been associated with important social, political, and economic values. It is consistent with a system in which: the power of the state remains limited; competition rather than strong governmental officials controls market structures; and individualistic, rights-based values assume priority over broader communitarian values. Yet whether there is, in fact, any necessary relationship between these adversarial structures and our political economy remains to be seen. As we view other nations' transition from centralized, socialist states to more market-based democratic governments, we may gain a better sense of whether particular legal systems and advocacy practices are critical for particular economic arrangements.[6]

The adversarial system of dispute resolution is often distinguished from the European inquisitorial model with several key differences. Adversarial frameworks emphasize party-initiated actions, including production of evidence and presentation of law and fact before relatively passive, neutral decision makers. By contrast, inquisitional systems rely on judges to direct the investigation of factual and legal issues and may control the presentation of evidence (more often in written affidavits than oral testimony). Cases are often heard piecemeal until enough information has been gathered, rather than in the continuous trial proceeding that Americans know best.

However, these two "oppositional" systems are becoming more alike than different.[7] In most European inquisitorial systems, lawyers play an "adversarial," argumentative role. And with the advent of American "managerial judges," our once passive decision makers have become far more active in controlling the timing and factual development of cases. American judges have further expanded their roles by performing settlement and mediation functions.[8]

There are also other models of dispute resolution less familiar to American audiences. Indeed, the juxtaposition of adversarial to inquisitorial frameworks itself illustrates a primary deficiency of adversarial thinking—an assumption of two presumed opposites. In fact, mixed models prevail in a variety of other cultures. Disputants, either directly or through representatives, often present grievances or issues to third parties who are not neutrals but wise elders, or the equivalent of the modern-day expert.[9] These "interested" third parties may decide issues, facilitate an agreement between the parties themselves, or call on the larger community present at such events to help resolve the dispute.[10] In many such community settings, the focus is less on who is "right" or "wrong" about past events than on what resolution will best serve community values and reestablish relations between parties who live or work near each other. Values other than finding the truth or protecting individual rights play a crucial role.

Cultural choices about the goals and priorities of a dispute resolution system vary widely. While the Anglo-American adversarial model is often assumed to be the "best" for securing justice, or, more recently, "the rule of law," it is not the only system, and it is not self-evidently preferable for all communities. To this extent, justice systems and the legal ethics that support them are chosen, not given.

Moreover, there is no inherent relationship between the organization of a dispute resolution system and the goals it seeks, even within an adversarial framework. More mediation-oriented problem-solving approaches would be possible if third-party neutrals used the information presented by advocates to craft future-oriented solutions that served community needs and multiple interests. Indeed, many American judges in law-reform cases have moved in that direction.[11]

Whether formal doctrine, "justice," "fairness," or "the parties' needs" should assume priority remains debatable at both jurisprudential and practical levels. But there are advantages to confronting those questions directly. And adversarial frameworks have too often ducked those issues by relying on some idealized vision of legal processes to justify adversarial practices.

First, as critics note, the adversarial model presumes that fact finders must choose "one" solution or result even if the real truth lies someplace in between or at a different point altogether.[12] Pure adversarialism presupposes a passive, third party neutral decision maker. But in modern litigation, judges, like lawyers, in fact serve a full spectrum of roles, including case manager, mediator, settlement officer, rule enforcer, and monitor of court decrees. Many of these roles include much more active participation in the case than a pure adversarial model would suggest, and raise complex questions about appropriate relations between judges and advocates. To the extent that legal solutions occur in out-of-court negotiations, the solutions preferred by binary adversarial models may be inadequate expressions either of justice or of satisfactory solutions to the parties.[13]

Similar inadequacies arise from the assumption that the adversarial model is the appropriate paradigm for all of legal ethics. As critics have noted, bar ethical rules often prescribe norms appropriate for the most extreme form of adversarialism–the criminal trial. Yet practices that may be appropriate when a powerful state places an individual defendant's rights at risk may be less satisfying in other, far more common legal settings. In response to such concerns, the bar's most recent code, the Model Rules of Professional Conduct has taken account of other lawyer roles—civil advocate, adviser, prosecutor, or lawyer for governmental organizations. Yet even these roles are too often defined to serve adversarial functions.[14]

Third, the classic idealized descriptions of the adversarial model do not capture the reality of how that model actually operates. Current frameworks do not simply pursue truth and protect rights. They also spawn procedural pathologies. Our adversarial preferences obscure questions about the extent to which "zealous representation" and client confidentiality thwart other values of the justice system. For example, withholding evidence or aggressively cross-examining truthful witnesses may serve client interests at the expense of fairness to third parties and the proper administration of justice.

Finally, while ethical rules are intended to police the excesses of "zealous advocacy," many of these rules suffer from indeterminate or internally inconsistent mandates. "Zealous advocacy within the bounds of the law" is an example.[15]

Because the simplified descriptions of the "ideal type" of adversary system usually emphasize only a few core principles, other key elements of that system remain implicit and unexamined. But these elements also structure ethical rules on which we rely. For example, one of the basic premises of the adversarial model is that there are two sides to every case—a plaintiff and defendant, a prosecution and defense, a petitioner and respondent, an appellant and appellee. If the matter proceeds to trial (which occurs in less than 10 percent of all cases), one of these sides will win and the other will lose. Thus, the adversary system is structured along a procedural and substantive binary model. It assumes that there are two sides—but only two sides—to every question, and that there is one right and one wrong answer to each issue. In reality, of course, the legal system is more complicated and allows multiple parties through class actions, joinder, and cross-claims. However, most cases result in binary alignments on either side of the "versus."

This dualistic structure distorts problem solving in several respects. Such an approach to winning and losing assumes that presentation of two self-interested versions of the facts will produce, if not the ultimate truth, then a "single" solution to a problem or decision. But if we have learned anything from twentieth-century philosophical and postmodern theories of knowledge, it is clear that many questions are not reducible to single, simple truths.[16] This does not mean that answers are entirely indeterminate, but rather that there may be a spectrum of "truths" and a continuum of solutions, some of which may be better than others.

The dangers of binary processes and outcomes are that they may lead to exaggerated claims on each side, and may fail to reveal information that partisan advocates do not consider helpful to their case. By contrast, one advantage of an inquisitorial approach is that it authorizes judges to explore evidence that neither side has chosen to develop. Such an alternative approach is of particular value in cases involving "battles of the experts," when each side has retained specialists favorable to its position, and the court needs access to less partisan information.

In most realms of human inquiry—science, academic research, investigative journalism—we look for all possible sources of information and do not confine ourselves to adversarial presentations or either/or answers.[17] Many critics of the current system have noted that leaving factual development and legal argument solely to opposing advocates often yields partisan and partial information, which, in turn, yields distorted outcomes. As one seasoned litigator acknowledged, "A jury trial is not about an altruistic search for the truth. Rather, in our adversarial system of justice, a jury trial is simply a forum that provides an opportunity for the party bearing the burden of proof to convince the jury that his or her side should prevail. . . . As we prepare for trial, do we think 'Oh, I hope the truth comes out!' No, We play to win."[18]

But who defines a "win"? The client? The lawyer? The side that loses? Does a judgment in favor of one party count as winning when it proves too costly to enforce? If an adversarial battle alienates parties who must continue to deal with each other, has either side truly won?

Defenders of the adversary system sometimes concede that truth is not the only goal and that in some circumstances winning is not a preeminent objective. For example, prosecutors are ethically obligated to seek "justice," not simply convictions.[19] Moreover, in supporters' view, the weaknesses of an adversarial process are counterbalanced by the protections it offers individuals against arbitrary action of the state and by its ability to provide final, clear, and definitive outcomes. If the system sometimes fails to achieve truth, it can at least achieve some forms of justice, efficiency, and clarity.

But those virtues are often insufficient compensations for both the parties inside the dispute and the rest of us outside of it. What may be a good system for many criminal prosecutions may be an inappropriate framework for cases involving multiple issues, multiple parties, and broad policy implications. Adversary models have their place, but they should not dominate the entire legal system.[20]

Partisan adversarial models are also inappropriate when the lawyer serves in nonadvocacy roles, such as planning and counseling. An increasing variety of attorneys' work falls somewhere in between the paradigmatic litigator and the out-of-court adviser. For example, lawyers representing governmental or corporate organizations and lawyers serving as policy makers or as mediators between two clients, provide a variety of planning and dispute-resolution services.[21] These different roles may require different skills, tasks, and capabilities than adversarial models presume. In these contexts, many legal issues arise with individuals who are not clients' adversaries. To assume an oppositional position may prevent important alliances from developing. As conflict theory demonstrates, it is often much harder to defuse a controversy than to escalate one.[22] To the extent that the lawyer's role reflects adversarial assumptions, lawyers may fail to provide appropriate advice or achieve desirable outcomes.

Whole categories of cases are inappropriately assigned to adversary treatment where on/off, yes/no decisions simply will not solve the problem. Common examples include child custody cases, environmental siting and clean-up disputes, mass tort litigation, and remedial situations that require continuous monitoring and adaptation to new parties or new factual developments. Adversarial frameworks focused on "adjudicating" the past often fail to supply future-looking solutions that require different priorities. As long as these frameworks operate as a default model for many lawyers, other useful options will be too often overlooked. For these reasons, many jurisdictions are adopting aspirational, if not mandatory, rules calling for lawyers to counsel their clients about the availability of other forms of dispute resolution.[23]

In short, the adversary system is structurally and ethically sound for some purposes, but not for all of what lawyers do. Yet courtroom trials have remained the preeminent cultural symbol of the lawyer's work, and courtroom conduct has "bled" into other (and in fact, more empirically common) forms of lawyering where such conduct may be less appropriate.[24]

The Ethics of Adversarialism

America's current adversary system has produced a variety of troubling behaviors, which may or may not be necessary to the proper functioning of an adversarial structure but which are now reinforced by both the formal rules and shared culture of the profession. In a profession that borrows heavily from sports and war metaphors, winning has become such a preeminent goal that it has obscured other values.[25] "Solving the problem," or "achieving justice" are often lost in translation. Although bar ethical codes proclaim that lawyers' advocacy should remain within the "bounds of the law" and their obligations as "officers of the court," the profession's disciplinary rules and practice norms make client loyalty and confidentiality the paramount values.

More specifically, the Model Rules of Professional Conduct require lawyers to preserve client confidences except in highly limited circumstances.[26] Attorneys have no affirmative duty to disclose relevant factual information or witnesses (unless required by procedural, not ethical, rules). Nor are they required to be "truthful" or forthcoming with adversaries, especially in non-courtroom settings.[27] Unless they are prosecutors, lawyers have no obligation to "seek justice" or fairness. Not only are advocates absolved from any responsibility to promote truth, they have a right (and some argue a responsibility) to cross-examine and impugn the credibility of "truthful" opposing witnesses.[28]

To be sure, ethical codes impose some limits on adversarial conduct. For example, lawyers must inform courts of certain adverse legal authority (Rule 3.3). Lawyers may not knowingly use false or perjured testimony and must take remedial action if they have knowledge of a fraud perpetrated on a court (Rule 3.3). They may not assist a client in committing fraudulent or criminal acts (Rule 1.2) (although they may counsel the client about the likely legal consequences of any course of conduct). Bar ethical rules also prohibit lawyers from filing claims or pursuing tactics designed solely to harass the other side, but inventive lawyers can usually escape compliance by identifying some other purpose.

Over the years, any number of proposals to impose greater obligations of candor, justice, and fair dealing have largely failed. For example, in the last effort to rewrite the rules, the Model Rules Commission initially proposed mandatory pro bono service, obligations to disclose material adverse facts, requirements to be truthful in negotiations, and prohibitions on drafting unconscionable agreements.[29] None of these proposals were acceptable to the ABA House of Delegates.

The result has been that adversarial polarizing tactics have too often substituted for thoughtful problem solving.[30] And, as others have suggested, such adversarial models of legal work have affected the legislative process as well, especially where a two-party political system reflects some of the same limitations of a binary litigation framework. It may be no coincidence that European countries manage (if sometimes stressfully) to work with political structures that share power among multiple parties and legal structures that share control among litigants and judges.

What Can Be Done about Adversarialism?

Proposals to reform the adversary process are in ample supply. Most have focused on modifications in ethical rules, although for some of the concerns raised above, more structural or cultural change may be necessary.

Reforms in both ethical and procedural rules could remedy some of the problems of obfuscation of truth by requiring more disclosure by attorneys and more active participation by courts. Some of these changes are already under way. Amendments to federal civil procedural rules have demanded more exchange of discovery information, and have encouraged more active managerial judging.[31] Further reforms could borrow some aspects of the inquisitorial system. For example, we could follow England's proposed example and curtail battles between adversarial experts by more often authorizing one court-appointed expert.[32] We could also rely more heavily on magistrates to provide active supervision of discovery. Other reforms could include mandatory disclosure of material adverse facts. Such a requirement could help challenge the mindset that no attorney should ever have to "do the work" of another, however unjust the result.[33]

Other aspects of the litigation system also require reform. Not only is withholding information a problem, so, too, is deluging opponents with factual material and legal motions that drive up litigation costs. Such "Rambo" tactics have been the source of much rhetorical condemnation and many aspirational civility standards.[34] But significant reform will require more demanding disciplinary rules and stiffer sanctions. Reform proposals also need to address distortions of the truth-seeking process that include overzealous cross-examination, overpreparation of witnesses, inequalities in expert evidence, and failure to investigate dubious client claims.[35]

When preparing for trial, judges or other case managers often seek to "narrow" the issues in order to clarify and expedite the decision-making process. However, reducing issues may also reduce the range of possible solutions. The adversary mindset encourages a view of litigation as a zero-sum game and deflects attention from other possible solutions, such as in-kind exchanges, or apologies.[36] Dispute-resolution experts find that it is usually helpful to broaden, rather than narrow, the issues in order to permit more trades and more ways to maximize complementary interests.[37] Effective reform proposals need to include adequate attention to problem-solving techniques.[38]

Other problems in adversarial practice involve costs, delay, and inequalities. However, whether adversarial procedures are in fact more expensive or time consuming than other systems is open to question. Countries with different systems experience similar or greater problems of delay. And experimentation with court-approved alternative dispute resolution programs (ADR) have failed to produce demonstrable evidence of savings in cost and time.[39] Although ADR supporters have noted that these surveyed programs may not be representative examples, we clearly need more experimentation and research to craft adequate reform proposals.

We also need better responses to the inequalities in representation that distort outcomes under the current adversarial structure. Partial solutions would include increased access to legal assistance through provision of more services for the poor (e.g., through government funding and more pro bono assistance), and less expensive services for the middle class through prepaid legal plans and other nonlawyer providers. While all of these efforts to expand access to justice make sense, they fail to respond to disparities in the quality of service. It seems unlikely that we will ever be able to fully equalize the brainpower of lawyers on both sides, even if we strengthen the ethical rules of competence and diligence. Thus, some inequalities will likely remain and the structure of the adversary system makes them critical in affecting outcomes.

This is not to say that other systems escape such problems. One major criticism of mediation and mandatory arbitration is that there are vast power and resource disparities between parties and that these disparities are especially difficult to monitor and correct when they occur in nonpublic dispute-resolution settings.[40] Some ADR approaches, such as those used in mediating environmental disputes, have attempted to address the problem of unequal resources by relying on funds from foundations or other neutral third parties to equalize resources for fact finding, experts, and related costs. Other innovative strategies are clearly needed. One of the advantages claimed for more inquisitorial systems is the equalization of information that occurs when the judge, and not the parties, controls the investigation and production of evidence.

A further problem with adversarial frameworks involves their lack of opportunity for direct participation by parties. Dispute-resolution research generally finds that individuals prefer processes that permit such personal involvement. In some forms of arbitration or mediation, parties can "tell their stories" and play a direct role in crafting solutions.[41] Such opportunities could become more common in adversarial processes.

Other forms of dispute resolution also offer an alternative to the unduly oppositional win/lose structure of the adversarial system. Even the most well respected defenders of that system often buy into this limited worldview. For example, Lon Fuller's classic defense of adversarialism rested on its ability to prevent judges from making premature diagnoses and allowing them instead to "hold the case . . . in suspension between two opposing interpretations."[42] But why assume there are only two interpretations? Such oppositional frames may restrict judicial decision making in ways that can be as problematic as premature evaluation. Our willingness to permit partial concurrences and dissents, and our reliance on doctrines like comparative negligence implicitly recognize that legal disputes may have more than two sides and need more than either/or solutions. Oppositional frameworks limit the vision of parties as well as judges. Assigning individuals narrowly defined adversarial roles may restrict what parties can hear about and from each other as well as how they conceive of remedies (blameworthy/innocent; winner/loser).

The limited remedial imagination of adversarial processes, which focus on compensatory and backward-looking solutions, may prolong, without resolving, painful past disputes.[43] Even where adversarial processes are most justified, where crucial individual "rights" are at issue, the win/lose solutions may not deliver justice. Some rights, while conflicting, may be equally valuable (e.g., two parents' custodial rights of a child, protection of "free" speech and protection from hurtful "hate" speech). Alternatively, the "right" resolution as a matter of legal doctrine may not be "right" as a matter of social justice.[44] Lower court decisions that adhered to the "separate but equal" holding of *Plessy v. Ferguson* are obvious cases in point.[45] So, too, enforcement of a generally defensible legal rule may work an injustice in a particular case. That is why parties sometimes prefer mediation or other ADR systems that can consider nonlegal factors in dealing with their disputes.

For many modern legal problems, adversarial, dualistic legal structures cannot take account of the complexity of multiparty, multiissue controversies with broad social consequences. Consider matters such as labor-management disputes, environmental siting, billion-dollar mass torts, international trade agreements, corporate reorganization, or municipal budgeting processes. Such matters involve a matrix of possible parties, interests, issues, and responses. A crucial question for legal policy and legal ethics is how to adapt current institutions to meet these complex challenges of contemporary dispute resolution.

Toward an Ethic of Problem-Solving Lawyering

Our profession is in a state of transition. As we consider how to structure effective problem-solving processes, we could draw insights from other professional approaches with different values and different intellectual paradigms. These approaches have influenced processes lumped together as "alternative dispute resolution": for example, mediation, arbitration, minitrials, summary judge or jury trials, early neutral evaluation, med-arb, or other hybrid forms.[46] Experts refer to choices about these systems as "Appropriate Dispute Resolution." A crucial function for lawyers is to determine what kind of process is most likely to be effective for a particular legal matter.[47]

Beyond ADR, however, are innovative approaches and orientations toward problem solving that represent a profound change in culture, and that require a new "ethics" to match. These approaches focus on outcomes such as party satisfaction, problem solving, collaboration, and sharing, rather than simply as restitution, compensation, or punishment.[48] The goal is to promote self-reliance and empowerment, instead of dependence on professionals. Lawyers in these situations need ethical principles that reflect more than adversarial expectations and values.

The relationship between adversarial and ADR processes remains in dynamic and ongoing tension. Thus far, adversarial practices seem to have influenced ADR processes more than the other way around. Participants talk about "winning at mediation" or "mediation advocacy," and warn that "I am filing an ADR against you."[49] Such references reflect the application of win/lose, zero-sum strategies to processes that aim at joint gain and mutual problem solving. Similar tensions arise from the role of relatively rigid legal standards in processes seeking flexible, participatory solutions. For example, consensus-building approaches in environmental and land-use disputes must still yield results that satisfy zoning requirements or administrative agency regulations. Accommodating these competing needs remains a dialectic challenge of accountability and legitimacy.[50]

These new problem-solving approaches take a variety of forms but share some common elements. Examples include facilitative mediation, consensus building, dialogues, public forums, partnering, study circles, strategic planning, ombudsing, and negotiated rule-making (reg-neg).[51] Such approaches assume that parties have different, often opposing, positions, but also that they are likely to share some common ground, or at least complementary views from which solutions may emerge. Rather than focusing on differences and contentions, they begin with commonalities. Rather than cultivating "toughness," participants value creativity, patience, persistence, flexibility, and resilience.[52] They recognize that some solutions must be provisional and dynamic, based on changes in information, interests, resources, and party alignments. The outcomes are not simply winning and losing but points in a continuum of best case, slightly better case, middle case, or slightly worse case.[53] A multidimensional matrix, rather than a two-sided courtroom contest, structures the alignment of parties and information. As a consequence, participants may develop different configurations or formats than opening/closing, direct/cross-examination, plaintiff/defendant.

Third-party neutrals in such settings seldom "decide" the case or "find" the facts. Rather, these neutrals give form and coherence to the process, monitor participant behaviors, and enforce procedures that participants have jointly chosen. These facilitators are usually trained to help probe for parties' underlying needs and interests, and not simply accept their stated positions.

This is not the place to describe these processes in depth, but a few examples might help to illustrate the variety of different goals that such processes might serve and the different ethical structures that they require. On contested legal and public policy issues such as abortion and affirmative action, various groups have sponsored "dialogues" and "public conversations" that bring together those who hold opposing views. Goals vary from reducing the violence at abortion clinics or developing public policy to understanding the effects of affirmative action in different social environments. Participants agree to rules of conversation that permit them to speak from personal experience and expose their own assumptions while asking each other to address "the grey areas in your own thinking."[54] Imagine an advocate acknowledging some uncertainty in his position! In some communities, participants have gone on to form action groups to prevent violence and lobby for new regulations, while in other communities, such groups continue as verbal sounding boards to diffuse antagonisms before they fester.

In other settings, conflict is recognized as natural and productive and is harnessed to alternative forms of civic problem solving. Public mediation or study circles have been used to rebuild democracy in contexts involving cases of failed municipal governments, community financial crises, and block-grant funding allocations. Such processes are highly participatory and often contentious; they allow expressions from a wide variety of interest groups (not just two) who, in dealing with each other face to face, can explore the factual issues and remedial possibilities involved.[55] Such groups may ultimately rely on conventional techniques such as voting or consensus building but they may get to the end point in different ways. These processes seek to avoid the acrimony of lawsuits challenging governmental action.

"Partnering" is a preventative approach first used by federal and military construction contractors (not those commonly associated with "touchy-feely" methods). It brings together participants in a project before it begins, in order to troubleshoot potentially difficult issues and personalities. The goal is to develop guidelines and procedures for resolving problems that may arise during the project and avoid later time-consuming litigation or formal grievances.[56]

Environmental disputes have utilized a wide variety of consensus-building processes to deal with the clean-up of toxic or polluted sites, or the new location of developments and waste dumps often labeled NIMBYs (Not in My Backyard). Such disputes often involve multiple parties with different levels of knowledge and resources, and multiple issues involving competing long-term and short-term considerations. In this area, ongoing participation, monitoring, and adaptation are necessary. A single yes/no court decision will seldom resolve the problem, especially in geographic areas where the parties have ongoing relationships.[57]

Some judges have begun to adapt these techniques to modify adversarial processes. "Integrated" court systems now deal with all family issues such as custody, abuse, neglect, support, delinquency, violence, drugs, and "vice." These systems employ a variety of remedial options, including prevention and treatment as well as sanctions and resolution of contested issues. At least one state supreme court justice proudly, and not defensively, calls these "creative social problem solving courts." She is less interested in distinguishing the formal legal aspects of the courts from the "social-work" and "treatment" aspects of their work.[58]

State courts that have established "future commissions," often have envisioned not only conventional, adversarial dispute-resolution services, but also procedures that allow the judicial system "to solve problems, rather than merely processing the cases that come before it."[59] Many of these commissions have drawn from disciplines other than law, and from public members who are consumers of law. One lesson emerging from this analysis is that legal solutions are sometimes necessary to define and legitimate rules, but are inadequate to provide innovative answers and broad participation to many social and legal problems. Legal processes that can evaluate and judge post-hoc may not be effective for more creative experimentation at the programmatic level.

Some commentators now speak of "broad" (preventative, policy-oriented, many issued, multiplex, multipartied) ADR or "narrow" ADR, focused on resolving one issue or one case.[60] To the extent that lawyers participate in both kinds of processes (and if they don't, they will lose this work to others), new behaviors and ethics will have to develop.[61] Many professionals, including myself, are currently engaged in drafting best practices and rule formulations for the different activities that ADR requires in areas such as conflicts of interest, confidentiality, neutrality, fees, counseling, legal advice, self-determination, and impartiality, both for lawyers who serve as third-party neutrals, and those who serve as representatives or "advocates" within an ADR process.[62] However, the real issue is whether lawyers with adversarial mindsets and adversarial ethics can really learn to "shift paradigms" and change cultural assumptions and behaviors.

Proposals have emerged for different kinds of lawyers—"collaborative" lawyers who will work under assumptions of good faith, fair dealing, and full disclosure of relevant facts—to solve the problem. Under some approaches, if settlement fails, a new lawyer takes over and changes the character of the dispute.[63] Other proposals involve reforming ethical rules, revisiting the question of whether lawyers should be more candid in negotiations or other out-of-court contexts. Some commentators suggest that with increased use of mediation and problem-solving techniques, both in court-mandated programs and in private, voluntary settings, the practice of law will become less adversarial. [64] Others fear, as do I, that increased use of lawyers within mediational processes will do just the opposite—make problem-solving processes more adversarial.[65]

Yet a less adversarial mindset or "problem-solving" orientation to legal issues might inspire a new ethical orientation for all lawyers. Just as William Simon suggests a "contextual approach to legal ethics" with justice as his reference point, I suggest that a "problem-solving" approach to legal ethics might also usefully direct us to some different mileposts.[66] If lawyers were to see their social and legal role less as "zealously representing" clients' interests and more as solving clients'—as well as society's—problems, what legal ethics would follow? Lawyers might have to learn different skills beyond research, argumentation, analysis, and persuasion.[67] They would have to learn to think about "the other side" in a different way—as a "joint venturer" as well as an opposing challenger. They would have to learn to "facilitate" and "synthesize," as well as analyze and criticize. Lawyers would learn to listen better and pronounce less. Perhaps with difficulty, lawyers would have to learn creativity, to "think out of the box," a somewhat countercultural approach to looking for the "best precedent."[68]

When recently asked what I would suggest as the "ten most important things to add to the existing ethical codes" to encourage more mediational, less adversarial, approaches to lawyering, I suggested the following examples:

1. Lawyers should have an obligation to consider and inform the client about all the possible methods of resolving a dispute, planning a transaction, or participating in legislative, administrative, or other processes that might best address the client's needs. Lawyers should educate themselves and their clients about all available options for handling the client's matter.
2. Lawyers should promptly communicate all proposals to resolve disputes by any process suggested by other parties, clients, or decision makers.
3. Lawyers should consider and promptly communicate all substantive proposals for dispute resolution or transactional agreements to their clients, including both legally based remedies and resolution and those which address other needs or interests. Lawyers should assist a client to consider nonlegal concerns including social, ethical, economic, psychological, and moral implications.
4. Lawyers should not misrepresent or conceal a relevant fact or legal principle to another person (including opposing counsel, parties, judicial officers, third-party neutrals, or other individuals who might rely on such statements).
5. Lawyers should not intentionally or recklessly deceive another or refuse to answer material and relevant questions in representing clients.
6. Lawyers should not agree to a resolution of a problem or participate in a transaction that they have reason to know will cause substantial injustice to the opposing party. In essence, a lawyer should do no harm.
7. Lawyers serving as third-party neutrals should decline to approve or otherwise sanction an agreement achieved by parties that the lawyer has reason to believe would cause substantial injustice to the opposing party and/or another person.
8. Lawyers serving as third-party neutrals (such as arbitrators or mediators) should disclose all reasons that the parties might consider relevant in determining if the neutrals have any bias, prejudice, or basis for not acting fairly and without proper interest in a matter.
9. Lawyers serving as representatives of clients or as third-party neutrals should fully explain to their clients any and all processes and procedures used to facilitate solutions, make claims, or plan transactions.
10. Lawyers should treat all parties to a legal matter as they would wish to be treated themselves and should consider the effects of what they accomplish for their clients or others. In essence, lawyers should respect a lawyer's golden rule.[69]

I have no expectation that such "golden rules" of lawyer behavior would ever be adopted by any regulatory or bar disciplinary body.[70] Nor do I assume that we can mandate by ethical rules a change in lawyers' mindset to be a creative problem solver or facilitator, rather than a "warrior," neutral partisan, or "gladiator." I know that a myriad of other, substantial issues and objections can be raised about the role of lawyer as "problem solver." Under such a role definition, what happens to rights and legality? Is law to be completely lost in a utilitarian calculus of party satisfaction and external effects? And, as has so often been argued in the debates about ADR, what constitutes justice and by whom should it be measured?[71] Does a problem-solving, joint-gain approach to legal matters assume a model of communitarian justice and social responsibility that conflicts with basic American legal, economic, and cultural commitments to individual rights?

Yet for many of us, it is time to question some of the well-worn aspects of our profession. We became lawyers in order to leave the world in a better state than we found it, to right individual, as well as systematic, wrongs, and to "assist in improving the legal system."[72] To that end, we need not junk the adversary system. Let that system do its work when we need a contest to find facts, declare legal rights and responsibilities, and clarify values. But to the extent that the adversary system and the ethics it inspires has caused us to lose the confidence of our own clients and the better parts of ourselves, we must open up our profession to a greater diversity of approaches. We need better ways of doing justice in the many different forms in which justice is experienced by participants in legal processes. We need an ethics of practice that would seek to solve problems, rather than to "beat the other side" by tenaciously advocating one single "truth." That ethical system would, in turn, require a different orientation to both the parties and the substance of legal problems. Winning would not be everything. Nor would "how you play the game."[73] What would matter is whether more people would be better off with the intervention of a "solution-seeking" lawyer than with a partisan gladiator, or with no intervention at all.

Notes

1. For one of the most extreme, as well as eloquent, defenses of the ethics of the lawyer as advocate who must treat the practice of law as a game ("identifying with the client as with the hero of a novel"), see Charles Curtis, "The Ethics of Advocacy," 4 *Stanford Law Review* 3, 20 (1951).

2. See Kimberlee Kovach, "Lawyers' Ethics in Mediation: Time for a Requirement of Good Faith," *Dispute Resolution Magazine* 5, 6 (Winter 1997).

3. See Deborah Tannen, *The Argument Culture: Moving from Debate to Dialogue* (New York: Random House, 1998); Lon L. Fuller, "The Adversary System," in *Talks on American Law* (ed. Harold J. Berman, New York: Vintage Books, 1961); David Luban, "The Adversary System Excuse," in *The Good Lawyer* (ed. David Luban, Totowa, N.J.: Rowman & Allanheld, 1983); Monroe Freedman, *Understanding Lawyers' Ethics* (New York: Matthew Bender, 1990); and Deborah Rhode, *Professional Responsibility: Ethics by the Pervasive Method,* 2d ed. (New York: Aspen Law and Business, 1998), chap. 5. Perhaps the most classic statement of the advocate's role in the adversary system is Lord Brougham's defense of his role in defending Queen Caroline in her 1820 divorce and adultery trial before the House of Lords: "An advocate, by the sacred duty which he owes his client, knows in the discharge of that office but one person in the

world, that client and none other. To save that client by all expedient means, to protect that client at all hazards and costs, to all others and among others to himself, is the highest and most unquestioned of his duties." David Mellinkoff, *The Conscience of a Lawyer* (St. Paul: West Publishing Co., 1973), 189. For a richer description of the political context and complexities against which this statement was made, see Deborah Rhode, "An Adversarial Exchange on Adversarial Ethics: Text, Subtext and Context," 41 *Journal of Legal Education* 29 (1991).

4. Robert J. Kutak, "The Adversary System and the Practice of Law," in *The Good Lawyer* (ed. David Luban, Totowa, New Jersey: Rowman & Allanheld, 1983), 173–78.

5. Monroe Freedman, for example, has argued that certain elements of the adversary system are constitutionally required (Freedman, *Understanding Lawyers' Ethics*, 13–25). Textual references such as requirements of due process, or rights to confront witnesses, can justify appeals to a constitutional foundation for dispute resolution frameworks.

6. In the transition to market-based economies, many nations have looked for certainties and predictability through "rule of law" systems. A host of Americans have helped to design legal systems, including constitutions, court systems, and mediation. GATT and NAFTA are now exploring various forms of arbitral and mediational dispute resolution, so that it seems relatively clear that American adversarial frameworks are not necessary for market economies. Other legal forms may turn out to be not only more efficient, but more legitimate in transcultural settings. See Herbert Jacob et al., *Courts, Law and Politics in Comparative Perspective* (New Haven, Conn.: Yale University Press, 1996). For an interesting argument that there is currently a competition for legal systems and cultural-legal approaches to international dispute resolution, see Yves Dezalay and Bryant Garth, *Dealing in Virtue: International Commercial Arbitration and the Construction of a Transnational Legal Order* (Chicago: University of Chicago Press, 1996).

7. In a recent report calling for reforms of the British civil justice system, Lord Woolf suggested reforms that were derived both from American judicial court management practices and German administrative practices. See Lord Harry Woolf, Master of the Rolls, *Access to Justice* (London: HMSO, 1996).

8. However, the advocacy which goes on in a settlement conference looks much more like traditional adversary practice than alternative mediation modes of problem solving. See Carrie Menkel-Meadow, "For and Against Settlement: The Uses and Abuses of the Mandatory Settlement Conference," 33 *UCLA L. Rev.* 485 (1985); Marc Galanter, ". . . A Settlement Judge, Not a Trial Judge: Judicial Mediation in the United States," 12 *J. L. & Soc'y* 1 (1985).

9. Martin Shapiro, *Courts: A Comparative and Political Analysis* (Chicago: University of Chicago Press, 1981), 6.

10. Laura Nader and Harry F. Todd Jr., *The Disputing Process: Law in Ten Societies* (New York: Columbia University Press, 1978).

11. Many modern lawsuits are complex multiparty disputes, such as school desegregation suits, environmental siting and clean-up cases, and mass torts (involving injured parties, manufacturers, insurers, and employees, etc.). For an argument that courts, as institutions, should be "creative problem solvers," rather than simple "adjudicators," see Judith Kaye, "Changing Courts in Changing Times: The Need for a Fresh Look at How Our Courts Are Run," 48 *Hastings L.J.* 851 (1997).

12. See Owen Fiss, "Against Settlement," 93 *Yale L. J.* 1073 (1984); David Luban, "Settlements and the Erosion of the Public Realm," 83 *Geo. L. J.* 2619 (1995); and Carrie Menkel-Meadow, "Whose Dispute Is It Anyway? A Philosophical and Democratic Defense of Settlement (In Some Cases)," 83 *Geo. L. J.* 2663 (1995).

13. Carrie Menkel-Meadow, "Toward Another View of Legal Negotiation: The Structure of Problem-Solving," 31 *UCLA L. Rev.* 754 (1984). See John Coons, "Approaches to Court Im-

posed Compromise: The Uses of Doubt and Reason," *58 NW U. L. Rev.* 750 (1964), and his "Compromise as Precise Justice" in *Nomos XII, Compromise in Ethics, Law and Politics* (ed. Pennock and Chapman, New York: New York University Press, 1979), for a description of how binary court solutions often do not reflect either factual or legal truth, accuracy, liability, or justice.

14. Much of the controversy surrounding the proper role of the lawyers for the Lincoln Savings and Loan Bank turned on whether the lawyers were "counselors" with a duty to reveal information in a regulatory context or whether, as litigators, those lawyers were barred from revealing client confidences in an on-going adversarial litigation posture. See, e.g., David Wilkins, "Making Context Count: Regulating Lawyers after Kaye Scholer," *66 S. Cal. L. Rev.* 1145 (1993); William Simon, "Further Thoughts on Kaye Scholer," 23 *Law & Soc. Inquiry* 365 (1998). Even the most extreme defenses of advocacy ethics, like Curtis, "The Ethics of Advocacy," often admit the necessity for different rules in the courtroom when the lawyer serves as an advocate rather than a counselor.

15. See William H. Simon, *The Practice of Justice* (Cambridge: Harvard University Press, 1998), for a discussion of the indeterminacy of the law, and the practices of zealous advocacy, 39–52. Landsman, "Readings on Adversial Justice, argues, for example, that the adversary system employs ethics rules to control the behavior of counsel, while at the same time "the rules of ethics are designed to promote vigorous adversarial contests by requiring that each attorney zealously represent his client's interests at all times" (5). See also discussion of contradictory definitions of "fraud" in Model Rules of Professional Conduct in Arthur Isak Applbaum, *Ethics for Adversaries: The Morality of Rules in Public and Professional Life* (Princeton: Princeton University Press, 1999), 105–107.

16. I have more fully elaborated these issues in Carrie Menkel-Meadow, "The Trouble with the Adversary System in a Postmodern, Multicultural World," 38 *William and Mary L. Rev.* 5 (1996).

17. See Michael Michalko, "The Art of Genius: Eight Ways to Think Like Einstein," *Utne Reader,* 73 (July-Aug. 1998), for a useful discussion about the differences in reproductive (using old and rigid solutions) and productive (creative, multifaceted definitions) problem solving.

18. Cheryl Bush, "Should Jurors Be Allowed to Ask Questions of Witnesses?," 45 *Federal Lawyer* 49 (May 1998).

19. ABA, Model Rules of Professional Conduct (Chicago: ABA, 1998), Rule 3.8.

20. The standard defense of the adversary system often points to criminal proceedings as the quintessential expression of adversarialism. On the prosecution side, we need clear rules of wrongdoing and definite, equitably delivered punishments. On the defense side, we need to put the state to its proof, and insure that it respects constitutional safeguards concerning searches and seizures. In fact, even the criminal justice system is looking at less adversarial approaches to decision making and justice. Examples include plea bargains that seek to treat defendants' underlying problems and efforts to involve victims. See Pamela Utz, *Settling the Facts: Discretion and Negotiation in Criminal Court* (Lexington, Mass.: Lexington Books, 1978). See also Kaye, "Changing Courts"; and Mark Umbeit et al., *Victim Meets Offender: The Impact of Restorative Justice and Mediation* (Morsey, N.Y.: Criminal Justice Press, 1994).

21. Rule 2.2 of the Model Rules of Professional Conduct permits this controversial role of the lawyer acting as an intermediary for two clients at the same time, modeled on the ill-fated phrase of Justice Brandeis, "lawyer for the situation." This role should be distinguished from the lawyer as mediator, since in the latter case the lawyer represents no client.

22. Dean Pruitt and Jeffrey Z. Rubin, *Social Conflict: Escalation, Settlement and Stalemate* (New York: Random House, 1986).

23. See, e.g., Colorado Rules of Professional Conduct (1996), Rule 2.1; Stuart Widman, *Attorneys' Ethical Duties to Know and Advise Clients about ADR, "The Professional Lawyer"* (Chicago: ABA Center for Professional Responsibility, 1993), 18; and Arthur Garwin, "Show Me the Offer," 83 *ABA Journal,* 84 (June 1997), (reporting on ethics opinions from Kansas, Pennsylvania, and Michigan, requiring advice and transmittal of offers to use particular forms of dispute resolution, besides conventional litigation). Some jurisdictions treat the issue of advice about alternative dispute resolution as a mandatory counseling issue like transmittal of substantive settlement offers (Rule 1.2), and others treat the issue as a lawyer-client discussion of either objectives or means of representation.

24. It remains an interesting question why journalism and popular culture continue to focus on the trial lawyer, when the vast majority of attorneys never appear in court and the pinnacle of the profession in terms of income and prestige is the corporate deal maker. Dramatic appeal may be part of the explanation, but most modern litigation bears little resemblance to what the media popularizes.

25. See Elizabeth Thornburg, "Metaphors Matter: How Images of Battle, Sports and Sex Shape the Adversary System," 10 *Wisc. Women's L. J.* 225 (1995).

26. ABA, Model Rules of Professional Conduct, Rule 1.6.

27. Compare ibid, Rule 3.3, with Rule 4.1.

28. Ibid., Rules 1.3, 3.1.

29. ABA Commission on Model Rules of Professional Responsibility Discussion Draft (1980), Rules 4.2, 4.3, 8.4.

30. One example involves "puffing," a form of misrepresentation allowed by the Comments to Rule 4.1. Under the current rules, negotiators have no obligation to truthfully represent the price they will actually pay, the clients they represent, or the "bottom line" settlement they will accept.

31. Judith Resnik, "Managerial Judges," 96 *Harvard L. Rev.* 376 (1982).

32. Woolf, *Access to Justice,* at 140.

33. See *Hickman v. Taylor,* 329 U.S. 495 (1947).

34. Robert Saylor, "Rambo Litigator: Why Hardball Tactics Don't Work," 74 *ABA Journal* 79 (March 1988). See also Louis Pollack, "Professional Attitude," 84 *ABA Journal* 66 (August 1998); Marvin Aspen, "The Search for Renewed Civility in Litigation," 28 *Val. Univ. L. Rev.* 513–530 (1994). Indeed, the D.C. Bar Civil Code goes further and seeks, through "voluntary civility" standards, to enact some substantive rules of "good faith and fair dealing" in representations in business transactions and other negotiations. See "D.C. Bar Voluntary Standards" (Washington, D.C.: D.C. Bar Board of Governors, March 11, 1997), 11–12. See also Marvin Frankel, "The Search for Truth: An Umpireal View," 123 *Univ. Penn. L Rev.* 1031 (1975); and Discussion Draft, Kutak "Commission on Professional Responsibility, Proposed Sections" (1980), 4.2, 4.3, 8.4.

35. See Morley Gorksy, "The Adversary System," in *Philosophical Law: Equality, Adjudication, Privacy* (ed., Richard Bronaugh, Westport, Conn.: Greenwood Press, 1978).

36. For an eloquent argument that our legal system reduces compensable harms to a limited number of injuries (mostly "male-defined") and then also limits remediation to (often) inadequate monetary compensation, see Robin West, *Caring for Justice* (New York: New York University Press, 1997), chap. 2.

37. Howard Raiffa, *The Art and Science of Negotiation* (Cambridge: Harvard-Belknap Press, 1982).

38. A classic text in the legal interviewing field suggests that a good lawyer use the principle of "exhaustion" to identify all the clients' needs, interests, and concerns in the course of representation. See David Binder et al., *Lawyers as Counselors: A Client Centered Approach* (St.

Paul: West Publishing Co., 1991). Both the Code of Professional Responsibility (EC 7–7, 7–8) and the Model Rules of Professional Conduct, Rule 1.2, suggest that lawyers give not only legal, but nonlegal, advice.

39. See James Kakalik et al., RAND Institute for Civil Justice, *Just, Speedy and Inexpensive? An Evaluation of Judicial Case Management under the Civil Justice Reform Act* (Los Angeles: RAND Institute, 1996); James Kakalik et al., RAND Institute for Civil Justice, *An Evaluation of Mediation and Early Neutral Evaluation under the Civil Justice Reform Act* (Los Angeles: RAND Institute, 1996). Cf. Donna Stienstra et al., Federal Judicial Center, *A Study of the Five Demonstration Programs Established under the Civil Justice Reform Act of 1990* (Washington, D.C.: Federal Judicial Center, 1997), demonstrating reduced case-processing time and costs in at least two federal district courts.

40. See Carrie Menkel-Meadow, "Do the Have's Come Out Ahead in Alternative Judicial Systems?: Repeat Players in ADR," 15 *Ohio St. J. on Disp. Resolu.* 19 (1999).

41. Alan Lind et al., *The Perception of Justice: Tort Litigants' Views of Trial, Court Annexed Arbitration and Judicial Settlement Conferences* (Los Angeles: RAND Institute for Civil Justice, 1989).

42. Fuller, "The Adversary System," 40.

43. To anticipate one of the often-stated criticisms of future-oriented mediational approaches, looking to the future for solutions does not mean that one should not or cannot deal with hurt, blame, and the past as well. See Carrie Menkel-Meadow, "What Trina Taught Me: Reflections on Mediation, Inequality, Teaching and Life," 81 *Minn. L. Rev.* 1413, 1419 (1997); and Harlon Dalton, *Racial Healing: Confronting the Fear Between Blacks and Whites* (1995).

44. See, e.g., Simon, *The Practice of Justice;* Luban, "Settlements and the Erosion of the Public Realm"; Judith Maute, "Public Values, Private Justice: A Case for Mediator Accountability," 4 *Georgetown Journal of Legal Ethics* 503 (1991); and Jacqueline Nolan-Haley, "Court Mediation and the Search for Justice Through Law," 74 *Washington University Law Quarterly* 47 (1996).

45. Some of the richest texts in the law and literature canon explore conflicts between laws of nature and laws of the state (Sophocles, *Antigone*), as well as conflicts between the rule of law and justice in particular cases and strict legal interpretation or enforcement (Herman Melville, *Billy Budd;* Nathaniel Hawthorne, *The Scarlet Letter*).

46. For a basic review of these terms and descriptions of the processes, see Center for Public Resources—Institute for Dispute Resolution Glossary of ADR, *Alternatives* 147 (November 1996).

47. See Stephen Goldberg and Frank Sander, "Fitting the Forum to the Fuss," 10 *Negotiation Journal* 49 (1994).

48. As one expert has noted, lawyers now need to become "conceptual thinkers and problem-solvers," not just litigation or transactional strategists. Conversation with Noel Brennan, deputy assistant attorney general, U.S. Department of Justice. At the Justice Department's Office of Justice Programs, lawyers are being organized into new working groups, e.g., "lawyers for public safety," uniting prosecutors, defenders, land-use lawyers; "lawyers for community governance," uniting government, private sector land-use, municipal finance, and election lawyers.

49. See, e.g., John W. Cooley, *Mediation Advocacy* (South Bend, Ind.: National Institute for Trial Advocacy, 1996), in contrast to Eric Galton, "Representing Clients in Mediation" (Dallas: American Lawyer Media, 1994), and Bennett Picker, *Mediation Practice Guide: A Handbook for Resolving Disputes* (Bethesda, Md.: Pike & Fisher–BNA, 1998).

50. See Jody Freeman, "Collaborative Governance in the Administrative State," 45 *UCLA*

L. Rev. 1 (1997), for a detailed exploration of these questions in connection with analysis of empirical case studies. See also Dwight Golann and Eric E. Van Loon, "Legal Issues in Consensus Building," in *Consensus Building Handbook* (ed., Lawrence Susskind, Thousand Oaks, Calif.: Sage Publications, 1999).

51. While it was once easy to distinguish the collaborative problem-solving process of mediation from decisional and adversarial processes like arbitration, recently, mediation itself has decomposed into facilitated or "pure" mediation (with party responsibility for solution crafting) and evaluative mediation in which the third-party neutral takes a more active role in evaluating the merits of cases and even suggesting particular solutions. For definitions and illustrations of these processes, see Susskind, *Consensus Building Handbook;* and "Innovations in Process: New Applications for ADR," 4 *Dispute Resolution Magazine* 3–27 (Summer 1998).

52. Imagine how differently we would consider our leaders if instead of criticizing them for being "wimps" who didn't rigidly adhere to their positions, we valued them for flexibility and the ability to acknowledge mistakes.

53. I recall a dispute with my insurance company in a comparative negligence state that would not acknowledge a 50/50 split of responsibility. The insurance company's position was that at least one of the parties had to be at least 51 percent "at fault" so that the entire loss could be allocated "to the really guilty party."

54. See Menkel-Meadow, "The Trouble with the Adversary System," 34–35; Margaret Herzig, "Public Conversations: Shifting to Dialogue When Debate Is Fruitless," 4 *Dispute Resolution Magazine* 10 (Summer 1998); and Michelle LeBaron and Nike Carstarphen, "The Common Ground Dialogue Process on Abortion," in Susskind, *Consensus Building Handbook.*

55. See Catherine Flavin-McDonald and Martha McCoy, "What's So Bad about Conflict? Study Circles Move Public Discourse from Acrimony to Democracy Building," 4 *Dispute Resolution Magazine* 14–17 (Summer 1998); Paul Martin DuBois and Jonathan Hutson, "Bridging the Racial Divide: A Report on Interracial Dialogue in America"; and Susan Podziba and John Forester, "Social Capital Formation, Public Building and Public Mediation: The Chelsea Charter Consensus Process," in Susskind, *Consensus Building Handbook.*

56. Lindsay Peter White, "Partnering: Agreeing to Work Together on Problems," 4 *Dispute Resolution Magazine* 18–20 (Summer 1998). I used my own minipartnering clause in a home-renovation project with an agreed-to, on-the-driveway, in-the-moment ADR process involving architect, contractors, subcontractor, and owner. Such processes are now utilized in hospitals, government agencies, universities and some corporations, especially where people work on transient projects or who need to develop a dispute resolution system for their specific time-based or specialized subject matter issues.

57. Pat Field and Edward Scher, "Finding the Way Forward: Consensus Building and Superfund Clean-Up," in Susskind, *Consensus Building Handbook* (describing the rescue of an ill-fated multiyear effort to clean up the soils and groundwater of a vast polluted site on Cape Cod with multiparty consensus building and a facilitated solution that resulted in a monitored and staged clean-up effort).

58. See Kaye, "Changing Courts in Changing Times." I know there are shades of nineteenth-century legal paternalism in juvenile courts if rights are not fully recognized, but I wonder how many neglected and abused children or drug addicts would prefer to have full recognition of "rights" or an "effective" alternative to their problems.

59. "To Serve All People," A report from the Commission on the Future of the Tennessee Judicial System (1996).

60. See International Association for Public Participation, Conference Announcement for Synergy, Participation, Involvement, Community, Enrichment (Alexandria, Va., 1998).

61. I have been training the major accounting firms in ADR skills for many years, and, being of an entrepreneurial bent, they have been less resistant to change than lawyers. These accounting firms are offering ADR as part of their litigation analysis, valuation, strategic planning, or business consulting services.

62. See Carrie Menkel-Meadow, "Ethics in Alternative Dispute Resolution: New Issues, No Answers from the Adversary Conception of Lawyer's Responsibilities," 38 *South Texas L. Rev.* 407 (1997); and CPR-Georgetown Commission on Ethics and Standards in ADR, Proposed Model Rule for the Lawyer as Third Party Neutral; Joint Standards for the Conduct of Mediators (AAA-ABA-SPIDR, 1994). See "The Ethics of Representation in Mediation: On the Horns of a Dilemma," Vol. 4, No. 2 *Dispute Resolution Magazine* (Winter 1997); and Carrie Menkel-Meadow, "Ethics in ADR Representation: A Road Map of Critical Issues," 4 (2) *Dispute Resolution Magazine* 3 (Winter 1997).

63. Robert W. Rack, "Settle or Withdraw: Collaborative Lawyering Provides Incentive to Avoid Costly Litigation," Vol. 4, No. 4 *Dispute Resolution Magazine* 8 (Summer 1998). There have been earlier efforts to separate the problem-solving functions from the adversarial litigation functions. See Roger Fisher, "Why Not a Negotiation Speciality?" 68 *ABA Journal* 1220 (1983).

64. One group of researchers, for example, has identified a group of "reasonable lawyers" in a divorce-practice setting where mandatory mediation has introduced more lawyers to this approach. See Craig McEwen et al., "Bring in the Lawyers: Challenging the Dominant Approaches to Ensuring Fairness in Divorce Mediation," 79 *Minn. L. Rev.* 1317 (1995); and "Lawyers, Mediation and the Management of Divorce Practice," 28 *Law & Society Rev.* 149 (1994).

65. John Lande, "How Will Lawyering and Mediation Practices Transform One Another?" 24 *Fla. S. L. Rev.* 125 (1997).

66. Simon, *The Practice of Justice.*

67. See Carrie Menkel-Meadow, "Narrowing the Gap by Narrowing the Field: What's Missing from the MacCrate Report—Of Skills, Legal Science and Being a Human Being," 69 *Wash. L. Rev.* 593 (1994); and "To Solve Problems, Not Make Them: Integrating ADR in the Law School Curriculum," 46 *SMU L. Rev.* 801 (1993) and "Taking Problem Solving Pedagogy Seriously," 49 *J. Legal Educ.* 14 (1999).

68. See, e.g., Martin Gardner, *Aha! Insight* (New York: W. H. Freeman & Co., 1978); James L. Adams, *Conceptual Blockbusting* (Reading, Mass.: Addison-Wesley Publishing Co., 1990); and *The Care and Feeding of Ideas: A Guide to Encouraging Creativity* (Reading, Mass.: Addison-Wesley Publishing Co., 1995). In a clinical setting, I recently heard a brilliant, creative, and I think legally "correct," new argument. The judge rejected it with the observation, "If you can give me no authority approving that reasoning I cannot use it." How can the law develop, if not from lawyers and judges willing to turn innovation into precedent?

69. In another context I have suggested that lawyers should abide by a golden rule of truth telling: the lawyer should inform a client of information the lawyer would want to know if the lawyer was a client. See Carrie Menkel-Meadow, "Lying to Clients for Economic Gain or Paternalistic Judgment: A Proposal for a Golden Rule of Candor," 138 *U. Penn. L. Rev.* 761 (1990). See also Carrie Menkel-Meadow, "Is Altruism Possible in Lawyering?" 8 *Georgia State L. Rev.* 385 (1992).

70. Some of these aspirational rules are extensions of current rules (such as Rule 8.4 prohibiting dishonesty, fraud, deceit, or misrepresentation) such as requiring more candor and explicitness about facts and law than Rule 4.1 currently requires in negotiation and other contexts (as contrasted to the more forceful requirements for truth before tribunals in Rule 3.3). Similarly, Rules 1.2, 1.3 and 1.4 require lawyers to transmit settlement offers (substantive of-

fers as noted in my aspirational standard 3) and to generally inform clients about information pertinent to their cases (including presumably process), but current Rule 1.2 permits a lawyer simply to "consult" a client about means of representation (while abiding by the client's decisions "concerning the objectives of representation") while my standards 1, 2, and 9 require lawyers to educate themselves and clients about all possible means and to transmit offers of "process" of dispute resolution or transactional matters, as well as substantive solutions. Some state ethics codes now either recommend such client counseling about process (Colorado) or require it (Georgia). My aspirational standards go beyond current rules by requiring "substantive" justice in the lawyer's participation in dispute resolution or transaction formation (standards 6, 7, and 10 which include both "objective" and "subjective" standards of justice), which, as a proposed rule, was rejected the last time an ABA ethics rule committee considered substantive justice in dispute resolution activity. See Proposed Rules 4.2 and 4.3, Kutak Commission on Model Rules of Professional Responsibility, Discussion Draft (1980). Finally, my aspirational standards explicitly focus on the roles of lawyers as third party neutrals (standards 7, 8, 10) and as representatives in ADR-like settings (standards 9 and 10) which are not currently addressed in the rules at all. See Carrie Menkel-Meadow, "The Silences of the Restatement of the Law Governing Lawyers: Lawyering as Only Adversary Practice," 10 *Geo. J. Legal Ethics* 631 (1997) and "Ethics and Professionalism in Non-Adversarial Lawyering," 27 *Fla. St. L. Rev.,* 153. (1999).

71. Another way to put this in recent language is, who should decide what dispute resolution is "appropriate"?

72. See Canon 8 of the Code of Professional Responsibility.

73. For an elegant argument that even games with rules may not be morally justified see Applbaum, *Ethics for Adversaries,* 113–35.

8

Ethics in Litigation

Rhetoric of Crisis, Realities of Practice

AUSTIN SARAT

Periodically the legal profession, or more precisely some part of the profession, discovers or declares that the profession is in "crisis." Crises in the profession do not just happen; they are marketed by particular segments of the bar hoping to mobilize their colleagues to deal with particular issues.[1] Because the profession is experiencing important shifts in the demographics and conditions of law practice,[2] large segments of the bar feel that values to which they are deeply attached are today endangered. As a result, during the late 1980s and the 1990s, some claims about crisis have been well received by both the bar and the media.

One of the most important of the recently marketed crises concerns ethics and civility in litigation. In this narrative, market forces propel escalating incivility and ethical breaches and threaten to overwhelm the values associated with "professionalism."[3] There is, some believe, a new culture in large firms. Previously taken-for-granted ways of doing business among the most prestigious sectors of the bar can no longer be assumed. Lawyers at all levels of the profession today ask themselves, with unusual urgency, whether their work is really more of a business than a profession, and whether the allegedly genteel ways of a romanticized by-gone era can, or should, be recaptured.[4]

At the heart of the idea of lawyer professionalism is a vision of autonomy and ethical practice,[5] of civility and decorum in the daily life of lawyers, of lawyers committed to—and regulated by—a set of principles encoded in, but not limited to, the profession's Model Rules as well as to canons of civility and respect.[6] Professionalism so conceived envisions a horizontal, peer-oriented system of social control in which each lawyer is responsible for his or her own conduct and accountable solely to peers within the profession as a whole.[7] Part of what the recently marketed crisis in the profession reveals is that this idea of professional self-regulation is being put to the test by the fact that many lawyers today practice in large organizations—law firms—which are arranged hierarchically and in which lawyers are exposed to behavioral norms and pressures distinctive to work life in megascale organizations.[8] In these organizations, demands for loyalty and responsiveness to the explicit directions or the implicit desires of superiors are real and pressing.[9] Yet in these organizations profitability is today as much a watchword as professionalism. New forces acting on, and in, firms put new pressures on ethics in litigation as in other forms of practice. Among large firm litigators there is, as Nelson and Trubek point out, a "general sense that lawyers have lost control of their markets, their workplaces, and careers."[10]

In addition, some of the most visible and damaging breaches of professional norms now occur within large, respected law firms at the metropolitan center of the bar.[11] The working lives of lawyers in these firms are filled with daily pressures to cut corners, evade rules, and respond to incompatible demands for high-quality work at cut-rate prices. In this context, neither professionalism nor legal ethics should be regarded as a set of essential attributes or a singular tool produced and used by powerful lawyers in a struggle to suppress marginal practitioners.

Professional ethics no longer is, if it ever was, the unquestioned, hegemonic value to which all lawyers proclaim adherence. In the face of that fact, the identification of an allegedly "common" crisis in professional values seems unlikely to mobilize anything like universal recognition and assent. One lawyer, working as house counsel for a major corporation, recently suggested, "The language of professionalism is a smokescreen." This lawyer's critique of professionalism is but one of an increasing number of such criticisms from within the profession itself.[12] Important voices now openly proclaim that law is, and should be, a business, that business values are themselves more than adequate in policing lawyers' conduct, and in ensuring the efficient, cost-effective delivery of high-quality legal services and that existing ethical rules are biased or out of date.

In such a climate what some regard as uncivil, if not unethical, others will regard as just a new way of doing business. Advocates for business values suggest that sound professional practice requires that lawyers understand the limits of their own knowledge and competence. The good lawyer knows enough not to try to substitute either his moral values or his business judgment for that of someone who "knows his own business."[13] Lawyers are supposed, above all else, to know what they are talking about and to talk only about what they know. And civility is important only to the extent it facilitates productivity.

The research reported below is part of an effort to understand how participants in litigation experience and understand these conditions.[14] It brings legal realism to the study of lawyers' ethics.[15] Just as legal realists discovered a gap between law on the books and law in action and urged prudent lawmakers to attend to the social factors that explained why rules were followed, so today, if we are to understand the ethical climate in litigation, we must attend to the social factors, incentives, and cultural norms that shape the decision making of lawyers in their daily practice.

In the legal profession, as elsewhere, ethical behavior and high levels of professionalism are variable achievements. Professionalism is a social product enacted, and defined, in the decision making and behavior of lawyers. The practice of law is socially organized, and the social organization of law practice shapes the extent to which litigation will be conducted in an ethical and civil fashion. This conception recognizes that among the most important of the contextual factors shaping enactments of professionalism is the large law firm. As Nelson and Trubek rightly suggest, "it is in the workplace that we find real conflicts over how practice should be organized. It is there that the presence and power of professional ideology often is least visible and least understood."[16] Particular environments, structures, and incentives may encourage lawyers to behave in an ethically appropriate fashion; others send different signals.[17]

What follows is a description of accounts of ethics and professionalism in litigation, of the growing commercialism of large firm practice and its consequences, of problems of incivility and hyper-adversarial behavior and of responses to the "crisis" in ethics and civility provided by a small group of participants in litigation practice in two large cities.[18] This paper provides a description of how corporate defense counsel, plaintiff lawyers, in-house counsel, and judges talk about their work, in particular their work as participants in, and managers of, civil litigation, and about their own behavior and the behavior of others.

This talk is significant in its own right; it tells us about the way judges and lawyers see their worlds and about the extent to which perceptions and beliefs are or are not shared. It helps map patterns of agreement and conflict in recognition of, and responses to, ethical and professional problems as well as the extent to which there is a common understanding of the crisis in big-firm, litigation practice. This paper focuses on accounts of the nature of the adversary system and its impact on litigation ethics, of the importance of large law firms in controlling lawyer behavior in litigation, and of the dynamics of law practice and the impact of those dynamics in leading otherwise responsible professionals into what some perceive to be professionally questionable or undesirable conduct.[19]

Adversarial Ethics

Talk among judges and lawyers about problems of ethics and civility in litigation is, perhaps not surprisingly, inextricably linked to talk about the adversary system As reflected in comments by the lawyers and judges who participated in this study, the adversary system and the ideal of zealous advocacy is alive and well. All of the participants—though to varying degrees—subscribe to a version of what Luban calls the "dominant conception" of the lawyer's role. In this conception, lawyers "have a heightened duty of partisanship toward their own clients and a diminished duty to respect the interests of their adversaries or of third parties. The adversary system thus excuses lawyers from common moral obligations to non-clients."[20]

This commitment to adversarialism was manifest as large firm lawyers discussed, among other things, counseling their clients about disclosure obligations in discovery, their own obligations of candor, and preparing witnesses in depositions. In each of these situations, being "tough" and being ready to fight for the interests of their client was, as Luban's argument suggests, defined as the first prerequisite to being a good lawyer. Large firm lawyers, both partners and associates, plaintiffs' lawyers, and in-house counsel agreed, even as they deeply disagreed about many other things, that the ethical climate in litigation is established by an adversary system which is "set up to be a fight" and in which the norm is, "When in doubt—be tough."

This norm is played out throughout the litigation process, including in discovery. As one judge explained, "gamesmanship is the norm in discovery. This is firm taught. Associates often feel that what they do in discovery is make or break. . . . Young lawyers are afraid; they fear releasing documents that may turn out to be relevant." "Discovery," one plaintiffs' lawyer quipped, "is antics with semantics." The structure of the adversary system itself, along with the default norm of toughness, was seen by some lawyers and judges to be in tension with the norms of disclosure which are, at least in theory, supposed to govern discovery. Contentiousness and hyper-adversarialism arise, these accounts suggest, in part because lawyers are unable (or unwilling) to disconnect the adversarial norms that govern litigation from their behavior in the discovery process. In some instances, as one judge put it, "The adversary system seems to have become an end in itself. It is almost as if lawyers play the game for its own sake."

Luban's "dominant conception" of the lawyer's role was reflected in the fact that several of the participants in this research confidently asserted the distinction between the rules by which their conduct is governed and ordinary morality. In making this distinction they provide an excuse for engaging in conduct that "ordinary" people would neither understand nor condone. As they see it, they are not "priests" whose responsibility it is to engage in moral counseling with their clients, nor do they have a duty to temper their representation in light of some set of moral criteria external to the legal system itself. As one lawyer put it, "I don't want to have a moral dialogue. The client didn't hire me to be a philosopher." Or, as another said, "The fundamental problem . . . is that the justice system is not established for moral judgment. . . . The system is not set up to answer moral questions." Litigation ethics are inscribed within a system that values aggressiveness more than sensitivity and defines success as winning within a set of rules whose basic soundness most of the participants did not question. If there are problems in litigation, this argument would suggest, they are problems endemic to the adversary system.

Embrace of the adversary system as the default position also was in the background of the explanations by both partners and associates provided in response to questions having to do with "coaching" witnesses in preparation for depositions. While several lawyers denied that they "coach" witnesses ("educate" or "prepare" were the preferred terms), all talked about the need to get witnesses ready by reminding them to tell the truth and not to try to win the case during discovery. But the injunction to tell the truth means to tell only that part of the truth which is necessary to be minimally responsive to the questions as they are asked. Such a position is not considered either unethical or uncivil; it is part of an adversary process in which each side carries the burden of making their own case.

Typically witnesses are told to "give answers that will not seem unresponsive, but that also won't open up areas of inquiry." Some lawyers also report that they prepare witnesses by informing them of what others have said on the subject and by reminding them that it is "okay to say you don't remember." Each of these practices reinforces adversarialism—the truth, but not the whole truth until and unless asked. This is, of course, the lawyer's skill, namely to know what has to be said to be responsive, and, at the same time, to say that and nothing more.

When asked to put this adversarial view of truth in the context of complaints about unethical or uncivil behavior in litigation, most large firm litigators seem to have a well-honed sense of the kinds of tactics that are involved in simply being good, aggressive advocates as well as the kinds that go beyond aggressiveness to incivility. While it is okay to make repeated objections as to form or to use breaks to throw off questioners in depositions, or to take advantage of a less experienced lawyer, it is not okay routinely to threaten to seek sanctions or to call the opposing counsel or party names.

Yet finding the line between aggressiveness and incivility may not be so easy for lawyers in other positions in large firms; thus associates often are "chastised for not being aggressive enough." As one said, "People are passed over for depositions when they lack a reputation for aggressiveness." Or, as another explained, "It is valuable to have a reputation as a hardball litigator." At the same time, partners believe that associates sometimes may go too far in the direction of aggressiveness early in their careers; associates, some partners suggest, tend to think of the other side as "the enemy." With experience, so several partners said, the good lawyer finds ways to be aggressive without being uncivil. In this climate associates have to figure out for themselves the limits of tolerable behavior within a complex framework of rules.

Despite the effort to market a "crisis" concerning behavior in litigation, there was no consensus among those who participated in this project (nor, I suspect, in the profession as a whole) as to what constitutes aggressiveness without incivility. There was, however, agreement among the judges and lawyers that *clearly* ethically problematic behavior rarely occurs in discovery. As one lawyer said, "Lawyers don't want to lose their licenses by engaging in clear misconduct." The ethically problematic behavior that would bring such a sanction is forbidden by applicable rules of the legal system and the legal profession. Beyond that is the "adversary system excuse," which treats behavior that would be ethically problematic in other contexts as not problematic[21]—even if it is not desirable—and which assigns ultimate responsibility for the moral content of a client's position to the client himself.[22]

Here, as elsewhere, when they talk about the standards that they set for themselves, lawyers produce accounts which focus on the specifics of particular situations. How they behave is, as one lawyer put it, a function of "the case, the client, and the opposition." Lawyers, as another explained, are "hired for their judgment" and must be left to make judgments about the limits of adversariness. Yet the conditions for exercising (good) judgment are often not present. One judge remembered that as an associate in a large firm, "I did document production myself. It was often at three o'clock in the morning that I had to decide whether some document was relevant. I received little mentoring, and I operated under great pressure. Both make it difficult to exercise judgment."

As they accounted for the judgments that they did make, many of the lawyers in this research seemed somewhat inconsistent. They sometimes said that they strictly "played by the rules." At other times they spoke about the rules as providing only the minimum content of professionalism or the floor above which they have individual aspirations or standards. They claimed that those aspirations or standards as much as the rules help them distinguish between appropriate and inappropriate tactics and behavior. Thus, most found it permissible to use tactics that lead opponents down dead-ends, to delay in order to raise costs, and to use discovery to "harass" opponents.

The widely shared norm of discovery is, as I have already suggested, "make the other side work." Under this norm, the obligation is on the lawyer seeking information to know what he wants and to frame a request which is both accurate and comprehensive. Even if one knows what the other side is after, one should not produce it unless or until one is specifically asked. So strong is this norm that when lawyers were presented with a rendition of a case (*Washington State Physicians Insurance Exchange v. Fisons*, 858 P2d 1054 [1993]) in which defense lawyers initially responded to a discovery request in an unusually narrow and evasive fashion and in which eventually a highly relevant document was illegitimately withheld,[23] they focused almost as much on what they saw as the incompetence of the lawyer seeking that information, who did not adequately follow up on the initially evasive response, as on the ethically problematic behavior of the respondent. As one participant noted, "Refusal to answer [a discovery request] is not an ethical problem because plaintiff's counsel can remedy it [through motions to compel]." Or, as another said, "The limited response should have been a red flag. The plaintiff's lawyer must have been inexperienced. What we need to explain is what caused him to stop asking."

Moreover, many of the participants in this research said that the kind of behavior portrayed in the case—narrowing responses, delaying production, etc.—was typical. One of the judges talked about that case and observed, "There was nothing unusual about it. It happens in every case." Another judge expressed a similar view: "*Fisons* isn't unusual at all. The fact that documents are often hidden never comes out. There is usually no consequence at all to an attorney for hiding documents. What matters is keeping the client and winning the case." And, as an in-house counsel said when asked to speculate about why discovery problems like those in the *Fisons* case occur, "The norm is that one generally responds as narrowly as possible. You keep stonewalling and reply as narrowly as possible. You don't volunteer anything in the hope they'll wear down."

Responses to the *Fisons* case were not, however, all so accepting. Some participants insisted that instead of evading or consciously narrowing a response, lawyers have an obligation to state an objection and allow a judge to decide the question. Others suggest that it is always better to deal with a bad document—either by making an early and appropriate settlement offer or to disclose it in order to avoid later allegations of cover-up and misconduct.

Whatever their view of the propriety of what was done in *Fisons*, several judges and in-house counsel accounted for the persistence of the "discovery game" in terms of the economics of the large law firm in which discovery disputes run up billable hours. This game is reflected in what is widely perceived to be growing adversariness in discovery and in litigation. As one partner in a large firm put it, "Today people believe that you succeed by always being unreasonable and always bullying." Discovery and litigation, in this view, are fraught with what some lawyers saw as unnecessary rancor and unpleasantness. They attributed this change to the growth in the bar. In a large legal community, attorneys are less likely to know, and therefore to trust, the lawyer on the other side.

Accounting for growing adversariness in discovery, some associates note a "generational" difference within some of their firms in the litigation styles of older and so-called "middle generation" partners. The middle generation tend to be more aggressive, more prone to "asshole" behavior. Associates speculate that this difference is a function of the fact that the middle generation came of age during the 1980s when there was a substantial growth in the economic pressures on, as well as the economic opportunities for, large law firms. The generational shift explanation opens up the question of how, if at all, the large law firm functions to maintain and reproduce high standards of conduct in litigation, of whether there are distinctive firm cultures, and of whether those cultures matter in structuring lawyers' behavior.

The Firm and the Control of Behavior in Litigation

What role does the large law firm play in controlling behavior in litigation? How effective are firms at socializing their members into the highest standards of professionalism and at responding to problems of incivility or to breaches of ethics? Do firms have distinctive cultures which encourage ethical behavior and discourage abuses and uncivil behavior? The answers to these questions seemed to vary by the position of lawyers within firms.

While they acknowledged that the present is unlike the past, most partners nonetheless continue to believe that firms have distinctive cultures and that those cultures function effectively in socializing their members. As one said about her firm,"We do adhere to a culture. We have learned in this culture." Associates, however (even some in the same firms as partners who expressed confidence in the existence and significance of firm culture), were less ready to concede that firm culture existed and expressed greater uncertainty about the socialization processes of the firms in which they worked. In addition, while some judges, plaintiffs' lawyers, and in-house counsel spoke confidently of their ability to "identify a law firm by its style of litigation," others were uncertain and more comfortable with the view that litigation style varied more lawyer by lawyer than firm by firm.

Firm culture is reportedly reproduced through what one partner described as "conscious efforts to bring in 'people like us.'" Another suggested, "Core values exist and are transmitted to our associates. . . . 'Be honest with the court, your clients, and your opponents. You will follow the rules and more.'" Still another contended, that "Firms matter in exercising control over deviants. We have a firm culture that encourages our lawyers to be honest and ethical. This is our bread and butter." Throughout, where references to firm culture were made, they were phrased in rather abstract terms; the content of firm culture was equated with the *least controversial* content of professionalism. Questions of style and judgment in the daily conduct of litigation seem to exist below the threshold at which firm culture asserts itself.

Moreover, even among partners there was a recognition that firm culture today may not be all that it is cracked up to be. Many acknowledged that in the current environment there is less mentoring in their firms than once was the case. Rather than the informal learning by watching and close observation of an experienced lawyer over time, that they contend used to help socialize associates, there is now less time available for such activities. Responsibility for the decline in such informal mentoring is attributed to corporate clients who are no longer willing to absorb the costs of allowing associates to learn by observation. As one lawyer put it, "Clients used to invest in mentoring for young associates. Today because they aren't committed to the firm they don't want to invest in that anymore."

In response, many firms have instituted formal training programs for their associates. What was once an easy, accepted part of big firm practice has taken on a more studied and formal character. Firms create professional responsibility committees, institute lunches among partners to discuss targeted questions about professional conduct, and/or designate ombudsmen to whom questions about ethics and professionalism can be referred. Thus if one just looked at the organization chart one would think that firms were deeply invested in their socialization and social control functions.

However, even partners acknowledged that firm culture becomes harder to maintain and identify as firms get larger and more specialized. As one partner said, "We have a strong firm culture about misconduct within the litigation department, but the overall culture of the firm is weakening. . . . It is fraying around the edges." The fragmentation of firm culture into the cultures of its subdivisions may be especially consequential in litigation since it means that the aggressiveness which is the hallmark of the litigator is not tempered by regular, informal interactions with lawyers in other departments with different professional norms and styles.

This disaggregation also means that there may be less control of, and accountability for, individual behavior than might appear from the organization of committees, lunches, etc. As one partner bluntly said, "One doesn't monitor one's partners." Or, as another put it, "Given the large size of firms you end up having less confidence about the behavior of others." While several partners conceded that there may be uncivil, hyper-aggressive litigators in their firms, they suggested that there is little that could/should be done about them. Controlling their behavior is impossible so long as it stays within the range of the rules. Within that range everything is a matter of personal style and judgment.

The fraying of firm culture is not only a function of size and specialization. It is, in addition, attributed to the increased recruitment of laterals, people socialized into the culture of one firm who are brought into a different firm at a senior level and who are valued primarily for their skills at getting and keeping clients. "In the classic big firm," Galanter and Paley write, "almost all hiring was at the entry level. Partners were promoted from the ranks of associates. Those who left went to corporations or smaller firms, not to similar large firms. . . . But starting in the 1970s, lateral movement became more frequent."[24] Many partners noted the significance of laterals in explaining changes in, and the weakening of, the culture of the large law firm. "Having laterals," one said, "changes the level of assurance that one can feel that there would be a uniform response to any problematic situation in litigation." Or, as another noted in describing his firm, "It is now the internal culture versus the outside invaders."

Laterals thus play an important symbolic role in signaling the transformation of the values of the firm and in providing an ideological lightning rod. They provide convenient symbolic markers of the transition from the hegemony of professional values, of collegiality and community within the firm, to the hegemony of business concerns, from professionalism to profit.

Finally, the presence of laterals marks a significant transformation in the expectation of permanency and stability in firms. Where once firms provided and relied on an expectation of long-term membership, where once lawyers spent their entire careers with the same firm, today there is much greater mobility as lawyers sell themselves and their client gathering skills to the highest bidder. There is, in addition, much greater uncertainty among lawyers who can no longer assume that making partner means a lifetime of security. This uncertainty is, in these explanations, related to the way big firm lawyers behave in litigation. Indeed, one plaintiffs' lawyer quite emphatically insisted that incivility and hyper-adversarialism, where it occurs among large firm lawyers, is simply an external manifestation of what has increasingly marked the internal life of the firm. As he put it, "They live internally in a cannibalistic world. They have no regard for each other. . . . They don't act differently toward their adversaries than they do toward each other. If you are a great lawyer, but don't bring in fees, you are fired. The only common value among a firm of 300 lawyers is money. There will be no other common values."

Not surprisingly, the world of the firm seems quite different from the perspective of the associate than it does to partners. As I have already suggested, firm culture played a much less significant role in the accounts they provided. As a group associates were much less clear and certain about the existence of the firm culture. One noted, "Ethics is talked about the first day and never talked about again. There may be a culture at the top, but it doesn't filter down." Associates report that they learn most by observing senior associates as well as partners and that the firm most effectively transmits its values not through formal mechanisms but through the stories that are told about what happened in this or that case. "The problem deposition," one associate explained, "becomes part of the lore of the firm." Several associates argued that large firms want and expect "quality work" even if the definition of quality work is amorphous or idiosyncratic to particular partners. Most of the associates seemed to share the view of one who said, "I feel imprinted by the partners I work for—not by the firm." Or, as another explained, "My firm is very large. . . . You don't know what the standards are of most of the lawyers in the firm. You only know from the lawyers with whom you work directly."

Associates also say that the partners within their firms are less sensitive than they should be to the climate concerning ethics and professionalism. "Partners think everything is fine." Another suggested that partners "do not see that ethics is of inherent value. Ethics is treated as a matter of sanctioning people for bad behavior rather than rewarding good behavior." No consensus existed, however, about the extent to which they were "on their own" in making judgments and identifying norms of professionalism that their firm would value. Some associates confidently asserted that "unethical behavior is an aberration" and that "there is a clear sense that the firm matters in setting ethical expectations." Others reported considerable "give and take among associates about how to handle cases." But several associates shared the sentiment of one who, like the judge quoted earlier, said, "Most of the time you are working by yourself—collaboration is absent. As a result, I have no clue what our firm culture is."

Associates believe that there are a large range of things that their firms could/should do to encourage greater cohesion and promote higher standards of professional conduct. For example: Firms should refrain from rewarding associates and partners who engage in uncivil behavior. Firms also should stop catering to clients who want hyper-aggressive lawyering. Ethical practices should be talked about and used in evaluating associates. Associates who see the way partners conduct themselves in litigation should participate in their evaluation. Reliance on billable hours should be reduced.

Listening to the accounts of both partners and associates one cannot have great confidence that large firms today have distinctive cultures into which their lawyers can predictably be socialized. Such firms are too segmented and structured to maximize lawyer independence to sponsor a single set of values except at the most general level. And, even if firm cultures do exist, they do not seem to be geared to policing the everyday, often subtle, choices that lawyers make about their practice styles. Socialization seems too incomplete and social control in large firms seems too deferential, except when confronted with gross violations of *clear* ethical norms, to ensure uniformly admirable professional and ethical behavior in litigation.

Problems in Litigation? Someone Else Is to Blame

One might think that the willingness to concede that firm culture does not play a consistently reliable role in controlling lawyer conduct might be associated with a willingness on the part of those making such a concession to accept responsibility for problems in litigation. However, what is striking as one listens to judges and lawyers talk about ethics and civility in litigation is the extent to which each group presents itself as a "victim" of forces over which they believe they have little control, as responding and reacting to the taken-for-granted dynamics of litigation and a changed environment for law practice, as blaming others for "forcing" them to be more aggressive, and sometimes uncivil, than they would otherwise be. Some of the forces onto which blame is shifted have already been named or alluded to—economic pressures, increased competitiveness within the profession with a resulting emphasis on business and commercial values, the increased number of laterals, etc. Yet strategies for responding to, or for anticipating, changing environmental forces and taking control, strategies for preserving or promoting professional values, seem notably absent.

For partners in large firms, the chief source of problems is said to be the changing nature of their relationship with clients. While, at one time firms established long-term, continuing relations with clients, today, partners suggest, those relationships are more difficult to find. One partner explained, "There is no longer law firm–client loyalty. Clients are increasingly looking for and getting an attack dog. People are very eager to satisfy the client who often is sending a mixed message. They want someone who is tough, but they don't want to pay the cost." One judge agreed. He said, "Firms are not rewarded for being ethical." "Who is the client looking for?" this judge asked rhetorically, "The client is going to look for someone who will do almost anything to win their case." Another judge suggested that "clients are worse than the lawyers they are hiring. . . . Increasingly we are dealing with a business; the obligations of a profession run in the opposite direction." Still another noted, "Defense lawyers are under a lot of pressure. In-house counsel is the master. . . . No one is looking for a reasonable defense lawyer. The message sent is 'Take no prisoners.'"

In this environment, the emphasis is on pleasing the client rather than on developing a counseling relationship. Clients want to conduct their own document searches in response to discovery requests. In addition, there may be great pressure from clients to limit discovery. "In-house counsel," one lawyer told us, "generally want you to take a narrow interpretation of a document request. When they take this position it makes it harder to convince the business people to be reasonable." Big firm lawyers say that they are driven to heightened levels of aggressiveness to please clients who can easily take their business elsewhere.

They note that business clients take the same bottom-line attitude toward their legal work that they take toward everything else and seem less interested in supporting high levels of professionalism. If there are problems in litigation, corporate clients are responsible. Yet perhaps not surprisingly, the comments of in-house lawyers have a very different flavor to them. Typical were the comments of one who said, "I insist on a thorough cost-benefit analysis in every case. Outside counsel don't do this. . . . The outside lawyer starts with a 'leave no stone unturned' attitude. But every case does not require a Cadillac defense. We insist that they ask whether the cost justifies the benefit." Partners, in turn, respond by arguing that such cost-benefit thinking leads to great cost-cutting pressures, such that they often feel that the client is unwilling to pay for sufficient preparation. Incivility is one substitute for being well prepared.

Because business clients have established their own well-staffed in-house legal offices, they are today more sophisticated as consumers of legal services. They demand the highest-quality service at discount prices. At the same time, they often seem disdainful of, or hostile to, the large law firms with whom they deal. As one said, "Why should I pay $500 per hour. There is a lot of high quality lawyering around. I can get as good lawyering in Texas as I can in New York". Or, as another inside lawyer explained, "Outside firms whine and want to maintain their high incomes. Large firm lawyers need to face facts. There are a large number of top quality lawyers around who will do it for less. 'We want to lower your annual income.'"

In-house counsel blame outside lawyers for hanging onto an outmoded ethos of professionalism instead of embracing a business ethos. "They [large law firms] are behind on the learning curve," one in-house lawyer observed. "They look at bodies and billable hours to support partnership income." Moreover, in this view hyperadversarialism and incivility occur because "outside counsel only care about proving that they are the best lawyers in town. They end up creating more problems than they solve." As one participant said, "Law firms use everything to make things hard on the other side. They play on trivia, they play on tactics."

Several in-house counsel noted what they saw as the economic interest of the hourly fee lawyer to "churn" cases, to use discovery disputes to run up fees. In-house lawyers were thus deeply suspicious of large firm litigators who they said "are slow to respond to change. For the large firm lawyer the mere fact that we are asking them to do things differently means that it is by definition not as good." "Consumers of legal services," one in-house counsel explained, "are forcing change. For us efficiency is the key value. Law firms, he said, haven't yet caught up with the business environment."

Or, as another colorfully asserted, "It is like the family farm. Law firms will go the way of the family farm." Still another said that the complaints that one hears from large firm lawyers are a function of the fact that "the reigns on them are tighter. Many senior partners are disappointed with diminishing access to senior executives. . . . It is a threat to their ego to have to deal with the general counsel's office." From the point of view of in-house counsel, there is indeed nothing special about legal services; they can be purchased like any other fee-for-service commodity, and lawyers should be evaluated like any other supplier.

In relations between big firm lawyers and their corporate clients, we see the clash of two different, and deeply held, views of what law practice should be like, one of which emphasizes autonomy, the other responsiveness, one which imagines itself as the carrier of the practical wisdom of a learned profession, the other which seeks to subject lawyers to business values. In the words of one in-house lawyer, "Professional ethics are the same as business ethics." This difference of views cannot be overcome by the mere assertion that law is a profession, no matter how often that assertion is repeated. Unless or until the bar deals explicitly with this difference in perspective, mutual suspicion between big firm litigators and litigation managers of large corporations will continue.

But the externalization of responsibility, the "blame the other guy" approach to problems in litigation, is, in the accounts of in-house counsel, not limited to blaming big firms; they also blame plaintiffs' lawyers who, in their view, bring frivolous cases, who use the discovery process to try to figure out whether they have a case, and who seek to extort payments just for ceasing to be a nuisance. "I have had the experience," one lawyer explained, "of saying to a plaintiff's lawyer that we had been mistakenly named in a case. They said, 'How much is it worth to you to let you off the case.'" "We are abused," another contended, "by the extent of discovery. Litigation is often just a fishing expedition." Or, as another put it referring to what he said were unfair advantages available to plaintiff lawyers, "We are on an unfair playing field."

Plaintiffs' lawyers, in turn, argue that the litigation playing field is not even. The rules, they suggest, favor defendants who are able to gain advantage just by "playing the game" in which "delay" is for them itself a kind of victory. They say that defendants, with or without the cooperation of their lawyers, routinely withhold relevant information and seek to hide incriminating documents. "Defendants know that they can come out on top by withholding." In their accounts, several plaintiffs' lawyers explained that outside lawyers typically adopt "a win at all costs mentality in order to show how tough they are," and that that attitude is essential if they are going to keep their corporate clients. As one observed, "Defense lawyers cannot practice without withholding stuff. Having a reputation for honesty and being forthright means losing clients. . . . The result is that no one produces what they are supposed to produce."

Moreover, several plaintiffs' lawyers suggested, echoing the views of some of the in-house counsel, that there is a kind of mutuality of interest between themselves and outside counsel. "Defense lawyers love us. When I get in a case, it means that their fees will be run up." In this view, plaintiffs' lawyers and their big firm counterparts understand the nature of the "game," and inside counsel typically do not. Thus when the latter get involved, "they really screw up the works. They are the client, and they personalize the litigation. . . . They make it harder to do business." Indeed, from conversations with different groups of lawyers, this observation seemed true; in-house counsel display a deep sense of grievance about the behavior of plaintiffs' lawyers and the conduct of litigation.

To the extent that plaintiffs' lawyers push the limits of civility or adopt a hyper-adversarial posture, they, like other lawyers, argue that they are "forced" to do so. In this case, however, they have to do so in order to establish credibility with corporate defendants and their lawyers. "You have to get to the point where the defendant's lawyers respect you. To get to that point you have to keep on attacking. You have to make them fear you." Aggressiveness, as described by plaintiffs' lawyers, is then a defensive response to routine nondisclosure. "You have to beat up the defendant," one lawyer explained, "until they give up."

In this climate, in-house counsel, while conceding that everything depends on the case and the stakes, were divided about how tough and aggressive they want their outside lawyers to be in response. One said, "The lawyer who isn't aggressive enough doesn't get another case," Another said, "The general rule is that we do not want to be easy in depositions. . . . The tone set is to be aggressive within the rules, to zealously defend the company. . . . This often means reveal as little as possible as late as possible." However others noted that "outside counsel often go beyond where I think they should. They try to show how good they are by being tough." Another lawyer suggested that the "pitbull" loses credibility. A third described what he called "the life-cycle of litigation in large firms" which involves "over enthusiasm, followed by boredom, followed by cold-feet." Outside lawyers were said to "be afraid to lose a case. They try to avoid any risky strategies. They fear they will fall into disfavor." The response of in-house lawyers is to insist on close communication and "partnering" which large firm lawyers, in turn, tend to see as limiting their professional autonomy and turning them from lawyers into mere technicians.

If there is one source of ethical responsibility commonly identified in the accounts of all types of lawyers, it is the judiciary. If there is one thing that lawyers, whatever their type of practice and practice setting, agree upon it is that judges hate to get involved in discovery disputes, that most find managing discovery to be uninteresting, and that, as a result, they take a hands-off approach, leaving it to the lawyers to play the discovery game with relatively little supervision. One plaintiffs' lawyer suggested, "Discovery issues pose hard questions. Judges have to get into the nitty-gritty. It is a pain in the neck for judges."

Some judges agreed that they have great power to control behavior in litigation, power which, they conceded, many of them do not now use. As one said, "What the judge will tolerate sets the standard." Another said that "discovery abuses can be stopped by a judge. A lot of efforts to bend the rules come from a feeling of security that a judge will never look and see what they have done." Still a third noted that "discovery disputes are a nuisance. . . . If we get into the question of sanctions we have litigation within litigation. . . . Putting time into sanctions does not move the case toward resolution."

Yet judges, like others, do not typically accept responsibility. They, too, present themselves as "victims." They highlight caseload pressures and/or the view that judges should not get into the business of "doing the lawyer's job for them" to explain why many do not get involved in managing discovery. "To find sanctionable conduct takes a lot of time," one judge explained, "so judges tend not to find such conduct." And as another judge said, "If we do impose sanctions for discovery abuse, we almost always get reversed on appeal. The result is that lawyers know that there are no teeth in the authority of the court." If there are problems in litigation, the "don't blame us" attitude found among lawyers is alive in the judiciary as well.

Conclusion: Is There a Crisis in Litigation Ethics?

In the observations of the lawyers and judges who took part in this research, two things stand out: first, ethical problems are not high on their list of concerns and, second, when breaches occur, responsibility for incivility and for professional deviance is placed elsewhere—by large firm lawyers on plaintiffs' lawyers, in-house counsel and judges; by plaintiffs' lawyers on defendants and their lawyers who allegedly hide documents and abuse discovery and on a "defense oriented" judiciary; by in-house counsel on plaintiffs' lawyers who file frivolous cases and use discovery as fishing expeditions, on large firms which are reluctant to take risks and which are too interested in protecting their own privileges; and by judges on lawyers who do not take their professional obligations seriously enough and on appellate courts which routinely undo whatever trial judges try to do to manage the discovery process.

While lawyers and judges acknowledge problems in civil litigation, they believe that those problems are either inextricably bound up with the adversary system itself or the products of a few bad apples or "assholes." As to the latter, there is no possible response. As to the former, lawyers on all sides and judges continue to believe deeply in the adversary system. In their view it works; it serves our society well, even in the face of its excesses. Incivility and the occasional ethical lapse merely are part of the "price of doing business" in such a system.

While many of the lawyers and judges recognized the pervasiveness of hyper-adversariness in litigation and acknowledged that hiding documents was a daily occurrence, this perception existed side by side with the view that there is no "crisis" in the litigation system. "There is just a more thorough examination of big firm practices," one judge noted, "rather than a change of conduct." From these responses it seems that the effort to market a crisis in litigation has not succeeded, at least not at the level of persuading lawyers and judges that there are deep systemic problems requiring systemic solutions.

Yet hyper-adversarial orientations combined with a weakened, fraying, and segmented firm culture, pressures from clients driven by bottom-line, cost-benefit orientations, and inadequate and inconsistent judicial supervision all encourage lawyers to get close to the line at which aggression turns into incivility, adversariness into breaches of ethics. In such an environment, the tasks of socialization to appropriate conduct and social control of deviance are unusually difficult,[25] and it should not be surprising that lawyers sometimes miss the mark.

Were one to take seriously the need to respond to problems of ethics and civility in litigation, or to believe in the rhetoric of crisis marketed by some segments of the bar, then several things can be learned from the accounts provided by judges and lawyers. First, some of those problems are indeed endemic to the adversary system itself. They cannot, and will not be rooted out by this or that incremental reform. A serious commitment to address those problems will require a serious reexamination of the so-called adversary system excuse and the "dominant conception" of lawyering which it encourages.

Second, firms have a large role to play in monitoring and regulating the conduct of their lawyers—whether partners or associates. Surely a changed legal environment has placed great strains on the capacity of firms to play such a role. But unless and until firms muster the will to adapt to this changed environment in ways that are supportive of professional as well as commercial values, little progress can be made.

Third, the culture of denial and the externalization of responsibility is itself a problem. Each segment of the bench and bar has earned its share of the blame for a litigation process that almost everyone concedes constantly grows less and less civil and more and more unmanageable. Until that blame is acknowledged, the attitude of "It's the other fellows fault" will continue to be matched with an attitude of "Let others clean up their act." Both attitudes ensure that little impetus for significant change is likely to come from within the profession itself.

Finally, one of the most important products of this research is a greater awareness of the real diversity in the profession, a diversity born not just of the different social backgrounds from which lawyers come, but also of the distinctive perspectives which are cultivated by those in different kinds of practices. In the face of this diversity we might ask: "For whom do problems of hyper-adversariness and incivility, and the occasional, though highly publicized, breach of ethics, constitute a crisis and what power or influence can they mobilize to persuade others to change?" In the answer to that question we may get one angle from which to understand where energy for reform is likely to emerge and what its likelihood of success might be.

Notes

I am grateful to my colleagues in the American Bar Association's Section of Litigation's Project *Ethics: Beyond the Rules* for their stimulating intellectual companionship and to Douglas Frenkel and Deborah Rhode for their helpful comments on an earlier draft of this essay.

1. Understanding crisis within the legal profession as constructed or marketed is not meant to suggest that problems are themselves *simply* matters of perception. It does not deny the importance of the underlying events (e.g., hyper-adversarial tactics in litigation, uncivil behavior, etc.) which may occasion the use of the label "crisis". Yet it may be useful in reminding us that one person's crisis is another person's healthy change.

2. See Richard Abel, "The Transformation of the American Legal Profession," 20 *Law & Society Review* 7 (1986).

3. Robert Nelson and David Trubek, "Introduction: New Problems and New Paradigms in Studies of the Legal Profession," in *Lawyers Ideals/Lawyers Practices*, ed. Robert Nelson, David Trubek, and Rayman Solomon (Ithaca, N.Y.: Cornell University Press, 1992).

4. For a discussion of comparable concerns in an earlier era, see Champ Andrews, "The Law: A Business or a Profession?" 22 *American Bar Association Journal* 188 (1907).

5. Robert Gordon and William Simon, "The Redemption of Professionalism?" in Nelson, Trubek, and Solomon, *Lawyers Ideals/Lawyers Practices*.

6. The image of lawyer as statesman looms large as the unspoken model to which lawyers should aspire. In this image, lawyers' ethics go beyond strict adherence to professional rules and reflect the dictates of practical wisdom, a capacious sense of the public interest, and a judicious ability to see and reconcile the client's long-term interest with the best interests of both law and the society it serves. See Anthony Kronman, *The Lost Lawyer: Falling Ideals of the Legal Profession* (Cambridge: Harvard University Press, 1993). As Gordon describes it, that conception entrusts lawyers "with a distinctive political mission in a commercial republic, that of being the bearers of an autonomous, public-regarding civic culture, to make them real and effective not just in the occupation of public office but in every corner of social life, including most definitely the practice of advising and representing clients." Robert Gordon, "Lawyers as the American Aristocracy," unpublished essay, n.d. 2–3.

7. David Wilkins, "Who Should Regulate Lawyers?" 105 *Harvard Law Review* 799 (1992).

8. Marc Galanter, "Larger than Life: Mega-Law and Mega-Lawyering in the Contemporary United States," unpublished manuscript, 1980. See also Robert Nelson, *Partners with Power: The Social Transformation of the Large Law Firm* (Berkeley: University of California Press, 1988).

9. David Wilkins, "Everyday Practice Is the Hard Case: Confronting Context in Legal Ethics," in *Everyday Practices and Trouble Cases*, ed. Austin Sarat et al. (Evanston: Northwestern University Press, 1998), 30.

10. Nelson and Trubek, "Introduction," 14.

11. David Wilkins, "Making Context Count: Regulating Lawyers after Kaye, Scholer," 66 *University of Southern California Law Review* 1145 (1993).

12. William Simon, *"Babbit v. Brandeis:* The Decline of the Professional Ideal," 37 *Stanford Law Review* 565 (1985).

13. For an analysis of the decline in the so-called counseling function of corporate lawyers, see Robert Kagan and Robert Rosen, "On the Social Significance of Large Firm Law Practice," 37 *Stanford Law Review* 399 (1985).

14. For a more extended discussion, see Austin Sarat, "Enactments of Professionalism: A Study of Judges' and Lawyers' Accounts of Ethics and Civility in Litigation," LXVII *Fordham Law Review* 809 (1999).

15. See David Wilkins, "Legal Realism for Lawyers," 104 *Harvard Law Review* 468 (1990).

16. Robert Nelson and David Trubek, "Arenas of Professionalism: The Professional Ideologies of Lawyers in Context," in Nelson, Trubek, and Solomon, *Lawyers Ideals/Lawyers Practices*.

17. Wilkins, "Everyday Practice Is the Hard Case," 30.

18. For a complete discussion of the background and methodology of this research, see Douglas Frenkel, Robert Nelson, and Austin Sarat, "Editorial Introduction: Bringing Legal Realism to the Study of Ethics and Professionalism," LXVII *Fordham Law Review* 697 (1999).

19. In evaluating those accounts, it is important to keep in mind the elasticity of professionalism and the ways it is mobilized in struggles within the bar. In this paper I am interested in professionalism as ideology, or, more particularly, the way ideologies of work, framed as accounts of conduct in litigation, are presented by judges and lawyers.

20. David Luban, *Lawyers and Justice: An Ethical Study* (Princeton: Princeton University Press, 1988), xx.

21. See David Luban, *The Good Lawyer* (Totowa, N.J.: Rowman & Allanheld, 1983).

22. William Simon, "The Ideology of Advocacy: Procedural Justice and Professional Ethics," *Wisconsin Law Review* 29 (1978).

23. The case used was based on the events reported in *Washington State Physicians Exchange and Association v. Fisons Corp.*, 122 Wash2d 299, 858 P2d 1054 (Wash. 1993).

24. Marc Galanter and Thomas Paley, *Tournament of Lawyers: The Transformation of the Big Law Firm* (Chicago: University of Chicago Press, 1991), 50.

25. See Diane Vaughan, *The Challenger Launch Decision: Risky Technologies, Culture, and Deviance at NASA* (Chicago: University of Chicago Press, 1996), 408. As Vaughan puts it, talking about the behavior of NASA officials before the Challenger disaster, "[R]ather than contemplating or devising a 'deviant' strategy for achieving the organization's goals and then invoking techniques of neutralization in order to proceed with it or rationalize it afterward, they never see it as deviant in the first place. How influential can the deterrent effects of punishment and costs be when environmental contingencies, cultural beliefs, and organizational structures and processes shape understandings so that actors do not view their behavior as unethical, deviant, or having a harmful outcome?"

PART IV

Client Interests and Professional Obligations

9

Lawyer Advice and Client Autonomy

Mrs. Jones's Case

WILLIAM H. SIMON

In one influential view, the lawyer's most basic function is to enhance the autonomy of the client. She does this by providing information that maximizes the client's understanding of his own situation and minimizes the influence of the lawyer's own views.

This autonomy or "informed consent" view is often contrasted with a paternalist or "best interest" view most strongly associated with official decisions about children and the mentally disabled. Here the professional's role is to make decisions for the client based on the professional's view of the client's best interests.[1]

I am going to argue against the autonomy view that any plausible conception of good practice will often require lawyers to make judgments about clients' best interests and to influence clients to adopt those judgments. The argument, however, does not amount to an embrace of paternalism. The issue of paternalism does not arise until we can clearly distinguish a judgment that a client choice is autonomous from a judgment that a choice is in the client's best interests. My argument is that in practice we often cannot make such distinctions. The argument builds on an illustration from my own experience.

I

The only criminal case I ever handled involved defending the housekeeper of the senior partner at the firm where I worked. The client, Mrs. Jones, was charged with leaving the scene of a minor traffic accident without stopping to identify herself. According to her, she had stopped to identify herself. It was the other driver—the complainant—who had caused the accident by hitting her car in the rear and who had left the scene without stopping. The other driver then called the police and reported Mrs. Jones as leaving the scene.

Mrs. Jones was black; the other driver was white. The police, without investigation, had taken the other driver's word for what had happened, and when Mrs. Jones came down to the station at their insistence, they reprimanded her like a child, addressing her—a sixty-five-year old woman—by her first name, while referring to the much-younger complainant as "Mrs. Strelski."

Mrs. Jones lived near Boston in a lower-middle-class black neighborhood with a history going back to the Civil War. She was a homeowner, a churchgoer, and a well-known and respected member of the community. This was her first brush with the police in her sixty-five years. Nervous and upset as her experience had made her, she was a charming person. As far as I was concerned, her credibility was off the charts.

Moreover, I had a photograph of her car showing a dent and a paint chip of the color of the other driver's car in the rear—just where she said the other driver had struck her. When we got to the courthouse, we located the other car in the parking lot. We found the dent and a paint chip of the color of my client's car in the front, and I took a Polaroid picture of that.

The case seemed strong, and the misdemeanor procedure gave us two bites at the apple. First, there would be a bench trial. If we lost that, we were entitled to claim a trial de novo before a jury.

Mrs. Jones's main problem was that her lawyer—me—was incompetent. I had never tried a case and had never done any criminal work. But I sought to remedy that by enlisting a friend with a lot of experience in traffic cases to co-counsel with me. The first thing my friend did was to dismiss, with a roll of his eyes, my plan to expose the police's racism through devastating cross-examination. The judge and the police were repeat players in this process who shared many common interests, he told me. We could never get a dismissal on a challenge to prosecutorial discretion, and if an acquittal would imply a finding of racism against the police, it would be all the harder for the judge to give one.

The second thing my friend did was to start negotiation with the prosecutor, which he told me was the way nearly all such cases were resolved. He told the prosecutor some of the strengths of our case and showed him my photographs, but he didn't say a word about racism. The prosecutor made the following offer. We would enter a plea of, in effect, nolo contendere. Under the applicable procedure, the plea, if accepted by the judge, would guarantee a disposition of six months' probation. Mrs. Jones would have a criminal record, but because it would be a first offense, she could apply to have it sealed after a year.

We considered the advantages: It would spare her the anxiety of a trial and of having to testify. In the unlikely but possible event that we lost this trial, the plea bargain would have spared her six further months of anxious waiting and the anxiety of a second trial. In the even more unlikely but conceivable event that we lost both trials, it would have spared her certain loss of her driver's license, a probably modest fine, and a highly unlikely but theoretically possible jail term of up to six months.

What was the downside? I couldn't say for sure that the criminal record Mrs.

Jones would have for at least a year wouldn't adversely affect her in some concrete way, but I doubted it. (She was living primarily on Social Security and worked only part time as a housekeeper.) What bothered me was that the plea bargain would deprive her of any sense of vindication. Mrs. Jones struck me as a person who prized her dignity, deeply resented her recent abuse, and would attach importance to vindication.

Mrs. Jones had brought her minister to the courthouse to support her and serve as a character witness. Leaving my friend with the prosecutor, I went over to her and the minister to discuss the plea bargain. I spoke to them for about ten minutes. For about half this time, we argued about whether I would tell her what I thought she should do. She and her minister wanted me to. "You're the expert. That's what we come to lawyers for," they said.

I insisted that, because the decision was hers, I couldn't tell her what to do. I then spelled out the pros and cons, much as I've mentioned them here. However, I mentioned the cons last, and the final thing I said was, "If you took their offer, there probably wouldn't be any bad practical consequences, but it wouldn't be total justice." Up to that point, Mrs. Jones and her minister seemed ambivalent, but that last phrase seemed to have a dramatic effect on them. In unison, they said, "We want justice."

I went back to my friend and said, "No deal. She wants justice." My friend stared for a moment in disbelief, and then said, "Let me talk to her."

He then proceeded to give her his advice. He didn't tell her what he thought she should do, and he went over the same considerations I did. The main differences in his presentation were that he discussed the disadvantages of trial last, while I had gone over them first; he described the remote possibility of jail at slightly greater length than I had; and he didn't conclude by saying, "It wouldn't be total justice." At the end of his presentation, Mrs. Jones and her minister decided to accept the plea bargain. As I said nothing further, that's what they did.

II

My guess is that most people will have some doubts about whether Mrs. Jones's ultimate decision was autonomous. Before we explore these doubts, however, we should consider a prior set of circumstances that seems to represent a paradox for the autonomy view.

Mrs. Jones did not want to be autonomous in the way that the autonomy view contemplates. She asked me to make the decision for her. She would have been immensely relieved if I had told her without explanation what to do, and she would have done it.

Now most people recognize that a commitment to individual autonomy requires the condemnation of some individual choices that, however seemingly autonomous in themselves, would preclude capacity for further autonomous choice.

Choosing to sell yourself into slavery is the classic example. So long as these choices seem crazy or highly unusual, the contradiction they pose for the commitment to autonomy is not that serious.

However, I don't think that Mrs. Jones's desire for an "escape from freedom" was crazy or highly unusual. Decision making of this kind involves anxiety. Moreover, some people may reasonably believe that they are not very good at it. In such circumstances, the opportunity to put your fate in the hands of an apparently benevolent expert may seem attractive.

I've had experiences of this kind. For example, I recall our pediatrician advising my wife and me as to whether we should have our then two-month-old son vaccinated against whooping cough, several cases of which had occurred in our area. There was a specified small probability of an adverse reaction to the vaccine, and given an adverse reaction, a specified small probability of death, and specified small probabilities of less extreme bad outcomes. Without the shot, there was a specified small probability of contracting the disease, a specified small probability given contraction of death, and specified small probabilities of various bad results short of death. I found this explanation, which went on for several minutes, overwhelmingly oppressive, and I felt a sense of relief when she concluded by saying, "In the case of my own child, I decided to give him the shot." I felt, and still do, that that sentence was all that I needed or wanted to know.

Such attitudes pose a dilemma for the autonomy view. In the legal context, the lawyer must either acquiesce in the client's choice to put her fate in the lawyer's hands or "force her to be free" by denying her the advice that she considers most valuable. Neither seems consistent with the mainstream idea of autonomy.

In Mrs. Jones's case, I think I was right not to permit her to delegate the decision to me at the outset. I correctly doubted my legal competence in the relevant area, and I didn't know Mrs. Jones very well. (In both respects, my relation to our pediatrician at the time of the vaccination decision was different.) Thus, it was a good idea both to try to involve her in the decision and to learn more about her. But I don't think of this conclusion as distinctively supported by respect for Mrs. Jones's autonomy. It was contrary to her expressed wishes, and it did not and probably could not have made her more capable of a genuinely autonomous subsequent decision. My decision to withhold my own views could be supported as well by saying that it was not in Mrs. Jones's best interests for her to delegate the decision to someone as ignorant about both the law and her as I was then.

III

Mrs. Jones's ultimate decision illustrates a point that is now widely acknowledged. Even where they think of themselves as merely providing information for clients to integrate into their own decisions, lawyers influence clients by making judgments, conscious or not, about what information to present, how to order it, what to emphasize, and what style and phrasing to adopt.[2]

As you probably surmised from the way I told the story, I think Mrs. Jones's initial decision not accept the plea bargain was influenced by the facts that I went over the disadvantages of the plea bargain last, that I concluded by saying, "It wouldn't be total justice," and that my tone and facial expressions implied that justice should have been a decisive consideration for her. I think her ultimate decision was influenced by the facts that my friend discussed the advantages of the plea bargain last, went over the jail possibility at more length, omitted any reference to justice, and implied by his manner that he thought she should accept the bargain.

Proponents of the autonomy view are likely to respond that the problem illustrated by Mrs. Jones's case is not the implausibility of the autonomy ideal, but the failure to implement it competently on the part of her lawyers. They would suggest that the discussion was too hurried and pressured and the advice was less informative and neutral than it should have been. Although such criticisms have substance, they tend to underestimate some intractable problems. Time is scarce in nearly all practice situations, and the difficulties of framing unbiased advice are often overwhelming.

As an illustration of these problems, consider two specific issues in counseling Mrs. Jones. My friend and I made clear to her that there was a theoretical possibility of a jail term if she were convicted, even though we both thought this probability tiny, and this knowledge visibly evoked anxiety and fear in Mrs. Jones. At the same time, we never discussed with her the possibility that we might defend on the ground that the prosecution was racially discriminatory.

Most practicing lawyers would probably approve our conduct. Such judgments are based on assumptions that lawyers necessarily rely on about what a client's goals are likely to be. Most lawyers would assume that even a small probability of jail would be important to most clients, and that in a case with strong conventional defenses, a defense with little probability of success and a strong potential for alienating the judge would be of little importance to most clients. The compatibility of such assumptions with the autonomy view depends on the extent to which the assumption accurately reflects client ends. My own impression is that they are often too crude to serve as reliable guides. For example, in Mrs. Jones's case, I think the conventional assumptions about the jail penalty and the discrimination defense were wrong.

Going to jail would have been a disastrous outcome for Mrs. Jones. However, it was also a very unlikely outcome. As a purely cognitive matter, most people have difficulty rationally (that is, consistently) making decisions about risk. When the decision involves an outcome that evokes strong emotions and vivid images, the difficulty is compounded.[3] And of course, where the circumstances in which the decision must be made involve strain and discomfort, the difficulty is further compounded. Such factors account in part for my feeling that it was not helpful to me in deciding whether to vaccinate my son against whooping cough to hear about the probability that he might die from the vaccination or from not having it.

I once met a client who had received a notice from the welfare department accusing her, more or less accurately, of some small-time fraud. She sobbed and fidgeted uncontrollably and couldn't focus on my questions or tell a coherent story. After a few minutes, she said, "Please tell me there's no chance I could go to jail." I replied, "There's no chance you could go to jail," and she relaxed and achieved some composure.

My statement was inaccurate in two respects. It implied that I had a professionally adequate basis for such an opinion, when in fact I did not know either what the law said or what the relevant official practices were. Moreover, there was in fact a chance, albeit a small one, that she could have gone to jail. I did not correct my statement when I learned more. Had I done so, I don't think she would have been able to focus on anything else or to achieve enough composure or confidence to engage in anything that could plausibly be called decision making.

In Mrs. Jones's case, I think my friend and I should have either omitted mention of jail entirely or characterized it in the way I did to the welfare client. Mrs. Jones was a considerably more self-possessed woman; she was intelligent, and her anxiety was not greater than what I'd guess the average person's would be in her situation. Still, I think she was bound to be disabled by any description of jail as a real, even if small, possibility.

What about the option of the race discrimination defense? The defense is almost impossible to establish, and we had no evidence for it other than Mrs. Jones's testimony of some vaguely racist police statements and the fact that the police had insisted on prosecution after the other driver had withdrawn her complaint. The probability that the client, when fully informed, would want to assert the defense, seems low. It would have consumed a lot of scarce time to fully discuss this option. Moreover, there's some danger that the client wouldn't have fully understood the situation and would have chosen to assert the defense without appreciating its disadvantages.

Some such reasoning probably underlies the practice of criminal defense lawyers of encouraging (instructing) novice defendants to plead not guilty at arraignment without discussing the possibility that there might be moral, expiatory reasons why a defendant might wish to confess guilt even at the cost of making herself vulnerable. A small number of clients might, when fully informed, decide to plead guilty for such reasons, but lawyers do not explore the possibility for fear of wasting the time of or confusing the others.

However, I don't find this line of reasoning as convincing in Mrs. Jones's case. Mrs. Jones's chances of success on the discrimination claim were no less than her chances of going to jail. She clearly thought she was the victim of official racism. An acquittal would not have specifically vindicated this dimension of her grievance. The opportunity to bear witness in public to the grievance, even if it were not officially vindicated, might have been of some value to her.

In any event, the reasons that lawyers tend to find adequate for not mentioning the racism defense are hard to distinguish from the reasons they tend to find inadequate for not mentioning the jail penalty. The tendency to attach more importance to the prescribed penalty than the defense seems to arise in part from influences other than understanding of clients. One such influence is the Positivist strain in the legal culture that tends to conflate law with express command and tangible sanction. In this light, the racism defense, which rests on vaguely formulated principle and, in Mrs. Jones's case, would serve largely nonmaterial, dignitary interests, seems further from the core of legality and, hence, from the lawyer's core representational function.

Another influence may be a selfish risk aversion that leads the lawyer to give priority to minimizing the chance of disappointing the client (and of provoking malpractice claims) over achieving some benefit that the client does not anticipate. By not alerting the client to the possibility of asserting the discrimination claim, the lawyer eliminates the risk that the client will blame him if the claim is asserted and fails.

IV

I should now acknowledge a point that often bothers people about Mrs. Jones's case. Mrs. Jones was elderly, black, and of modest means; my friend and I were none of these. She probably had a vast lifelong experience of subordination and marginalization of kinds that we knew only through imagination. In these circumstances, the dangers were great that we would fail to understand her, that we would compound her oppression by interpreting her in terms of inappropriate assumptions conditioned by the dominant culture.

Indeed, ever since I entered Mrs. Jones's plea, I have believed that my friend succumbed to just such dangers: class and race prejudice inclined him to see avoiding sanctions as the only thing Mrs. Jones really cared about. On the other hand, even as I have reproached myself for deferring to my friend, I have flattered myself that I have appreciated Mrs. Jones's sense of dignity and the likely importance to her of vindication by acquittal.

However, recently, friends have convinced me that I failed to adequately consider the possibility that my own views were biased. Perhaps I was just smugly attributing my own liberal upper-class moralism to her. I never considered how the fact that I had no reason to fear the kind of risks facing Mrs. Jones might lead me to overly discount them and how my generally more satisfying experience with official institutions might lead me to overvalue official vindication.

Now that I have considered these possibilities, I still think my original interpretation was right. (I just can't see Mrs. Jones's moralism as a projection of my own. I had lots of observations to support my interpretation. After all, the only initiative she took in the whole relation was to bring her minister with her to testify to her character.) But I have considerably less confidence in my judgment about Mrs. Jones than I used to have, and I recognize that in more ambiguous situations the dangers of misinterpretation would be high.

Such observations might lead some to conclude that lawyers like me are so ill-equipped to understand clients as socially distant as Mrs. Jones that it would be better if we didn't try. Or that we are likely to do more harm than good if we challenge the client's initially articulated choice or if we tell the client what we think the better choice would be. Perhaps, for example, the effort to empathize and establish rapport with a client like Mrs. Jones threatens to unleash in the lawyer unconscious feelings of prejudice that are more likely to be held in check if the relation remains more formal and emotionally sterile.[4] Binding the lawyer to the client's initially stated choice would have the virtue of a relatively determinate rule. More complex judgments based on a wider range of factors would leave greater room for bias to operate. Moreover, there's the danger that the effort to connect more than superficially with the client will induce an inappropriate trust and dependence in the client.

I don't agree with these views, at least when put categorically. I think they underestimate the capacity of people to empathize across social distance (though I agree this requires training and effort). Moreover, social distance from the client is not entirely a disadvantage; we associate distance with detachment as well as alienation. A lawyer socially closer to Mrs. Jones might have been less conscious of the distance that remained and more ready to attribute his own values to her than I was.

Even if I'm wrong about this point, however, I don't think it affects my principal argument. The point that establishing empathy and rapport can be dangerous is not an argument against paternalism or for autonomy. Empathy and rapport are no less important for autonomy than for paternalism. If at all plausible, the judgment that the lawyer should not strive for empathy and rapport will be based in part on an assessment of whether the outcomes associated with such an effort are, on balance, in clients' best interests.

V

Consider some formulations of the contrasting approaches to counseling in the autonomy and paternalism views. Begin with a crude but nevertheless influential version of the autonomy view: The lawyer's job is to present to the client, within time and resource constraints, the information relevant to the decision at hand. The lawyer discharges her function when this information has been presented, and whatever decision the client then articulates is deemed autonomous.

This crude formulation is unworkable and implausible. It is unworkable because it does not provide any criteria of relevance, and because it ignores the fact that the most obvious criteria—the client's goals and values—are not immediately accessible to the lawyer. It is implausible because it measures autonomy simply in terms of the information the lawyer presents without regard to whether the way she presents it influences the decision or whether the client is emotionally or cognitively able to make effective use of the information. On the crude autonomy view, my pediatrician could have fully discharged her duty by telling me the probabilities associated with the vaccination decision even though I felt unable to make any use of this information.

Thoughtful autonomy proponents do not argue for this crude view. In their refined version, the lawyer's duty is to present the information a typical person in the client's situation would consider relevant except to the extent the lawyer has reason to believe that the particular client would consider different information relevant, in which case she is to present that information. The lawyer has to start by imputing the goals of a typical client to the actual client because, before she knows the client, she has no other basis for understanding.

But in this refined autonomy view, the lawyer has a duty both to educate herself about the particular client's concerns and to assist the client in making use of the information the lawyer provides.[5] Here the client's autonomy is as much a goal as a premise of the counseling relation.[6] The refined view contemplates a dialogue in which the lawyer adjusts her presentation as she learns more about the client's concerns and abilities and in which she is as much concerned with relieving the client's disabling anxieties and enhancing her cognitive capacities as she is with simply delivering information.

Now consider the paternalist view—first in a crude version. In this version, the lawyer simply consults her own values; she asks what she would do in the client's circumstances or what she thinks a person with some general characteristic of the client should do and tries to influence the client to adopt that course.

More refined versions of paternalism appear in two of the best-known defenses of paternalism in the lawyering literature. David Luban has argued that paternalist coercion is justified when, among other conditions, the client's explanation of his decision fails to meet a minimal test of objective reasonableness. Luban's test is basically procedural. He asks whether the client can explain his decision in a way that suggests that "any process is going on in [his] mind that can be called 'inference from real facts.'"[7] The test is objective in the sense that it turns on abstract principles of reason rather than appreciation of the particular personality of the client.

On the other hand, Duncan Kennedy has argued for paternalistic coercion on the basis of "lived intersubjectivity".[8] Kennedy's approach is more substantive than Luban's. It is triggered by a sense of the particular client's personality. Here the paternalistic judgment does not look to an external standard such as reasonableness, but rather to an interpretation of the subject's own projects and commitments. The paternalist works for the choice that seems most consistent with her understanding of who the client is. When she disregards the client's articulated choice, she has concluded that the client has misunderstood either herself or how the options relate to her deepest goals. The Luban and Kennedy approaches are not incompatible, and the refined view should make room for them both.

The two aspects of the refined paternalist view can be readily applied to Mrs. Jones's case. The concerns about Mrs. Jones's request for me to make the decision for her seem to resonate with Luban's perspective. It wasn't reasonable for her to want to put her fate in the hands of someone as inexperienced and ignorant as me. This would be a bad decision for anyone to make under the circumstances.

On the other hand, the concerns about her ultimate decision seem to resonate with the Kennedy perspective. There's nothing unreasonable in any general sense about the decision to accept the plea bargain. It would be the right choice for many people—for example, for someone with no strong sense of dignity, with no respect for authoritative public pronouncements, and with no tolerance for the conflict or stress of self-presentation in public. But Mrs. Jones seemed to be a different person. There's at least a suspicion that I let her make the wrong choice, *given who she was*.

My claim is that, once we get beyond the crude versions, it is hard to distinguish the autonomy and paternalist views. Each refined view contemplates a dialogue with the client that it recognizes is both essential to understanding her and fraught with dangers of oppressing her. Each refined view involves a dialectic of objective constructs (the "typical client" presumption or the minimal reasonableness test) and efforts to know the client as a concrete subject.

The paternalist view is intensely individualistic to the extent that it aspires to keep knowledge of the client as a concrete individual and grounds the lawyer's decision in the client's self-realization. Even where it disregards client choices because they fail the minimum reasonableness test, it is not denying the value of autonomy, just that the particular client has the capacity for autonomous choice. Conversely, the refined autonomy view is quite collectivist to the extent that it licenses the application of objective "typical" client presumptions to the particular client. And to the extent that it differs from the paternalist view in failing to apply a minimum reasonableness test, that difference, though perhaps defensible on other grounds, is not plausibly grounded in the value of autonomy, since that value presupposes a capacity for rational choice.

David Luban suggests that the defining and problematical feature of paternalism is its commitment to particular "conception[s] of the good life."[9] But the most notable theory of "the good" to come of the law schools in recent years—Roberto Unger's—defines the good in terms of the "choices" people make when not under "domination."[10] This sounds very much like a theory of autonomous choice.

A genuine conflict between autonomy and paternalism would require a view that contained both a thick theory of the good that did not depend on individual choice and a notion of individual choice capable of envisioning choices that violate the good as autonomous. We find such views in many religious doctrines, but within the culture of the legal profession it is hard to find one.

If the debate between the autonomy and paternalist views is so often moot, why does it inspire so much energy and emotion? My guess is that the debate expresses the anxiety that lawyers, especially those who represent clients socially distant from themselves, feel about getting to know their clients and about assuming responsibility for them. The process of learning to understand and communicate with a stranger is usually difficult and often scary. Moreover, as I've emphasized, in this process the lawyer inescapably exercises power over the client. The issues that have to be decided can be tremendously difficult, and the stakes can be high. In such circumstances, lawyers may find the demands of connecting with the client and the responsibilities of power emotionally overwhelming.

The crude autonomy view is attractive to lawyers because it absolves them of the burdens of connection and the responsibilities of power by suggesting that they can perform their duties simply by presenting a professionally defined package of information. Both the crude and the paternalist views are frightening because both emphasize the inescapableness of lawyer power, and the latter emphasizes as well the duty to connect with the client. So, of course, does the refined autonomy view, but perhaps the rhetorical association of the refined autonomy view with the crude one evokes some of the comforting associations of the latter and makes it more palatable than refined paternalism, even when they are functionally indistinguishable.

VI

I don't claim that we can never plausibly conceive of a meaningfully autonomous choice that is not in the chooser's best interests. But I would argue, at least, that there is a large category of cases involving legal decisions, where, given the circumstances in which decisions must be made, we have no criteria of autonomy independent of our criteria of best interests. Many of the best reasons we have for thinking that Mrs. Jones's choice was not autonomous are the reasons we have for thinking that it was not in her best interests.

Notes

William H. Simon is William and Gertrude Saunders Professor of Law at Stanford University. An earlier version of this essay was given as the Stuart Rome Lecture at the University of Maryland Law School on May 3, 1990, and published in 50 *Maryland Law Review* 1 (1991). I received valuable assistance the first time around from David Luban, Lucie White, Jerry Lopez, Michael Wald, Bill Hing, Mari Matsuda, Deborah Rhode, and David Rosenhan. This revised version benefitted from further comments by Deborah Rhode and from a critical response by Mark Spiegel published as "The Case of Mrs. Jones Revisited: Paternalism and Autonomy in Lawyer-Client Counseling," 1997 *Brigham Young University Law Review* 307 (1997).

   1. The autonomy view dominates the academic literature on lawyering. See, for example, David Binder and Susan Price, *Legal Interviewing and Counseling: A Client-Centered Approach* (St. Paul: West, 1977); Stephen Ellmann, "Lawyers and Clients," 34 *UCLA Law Review* 717 (1987); and Mark Spiegel, "Lawyering and Client Decisionmaking: Informed Consent and the Legal Profession," 128 *University of Pennsylvania Law Review* 41 (1979). However, the paternalist view has recently been defended in contexts involving conventional clients, as well as minors and disabled adults. Duncan Kennedy, "Distributive and Paternalistic Motives in Contract and Tort Law, With Special Reference to Compulsory Terms and Unequal Bargaining Power," 41 *Maryland Law Review* 563 (1982); David Luban, "Paternalism and the Legal Profes-

sion," 1981 *Wisconsin Law Review* 454. Both views seem well represented among practitioners. For example, a small survey of divorce lawyers found that their role conceptions divided more or less evenly between the two views. Hubert O'Gorman, *Lawyers and Matrimonial Cases* 163–64 (New York: Arno Press, 1963).

Respectful treatments of paternalism are most often encountered in discussion of juvenile clients and clients with mental disabilities. See, for example, Deborah Rhode and David Luban, *Legal Ethics* 609–19 (2d ed., New York: Foundation Press, 1995).

2. See, for example, Ellmann, "Lawyers and Clients," 733–53.

3. The cognitive and emotional obstacles to decision making about risk are explained and documented in Paul Slovic, Stanley Fischhoff, and Sarah Lichtenstein, "Facts versus Fears: Understanding Perceived Risk," in *Judgment under Uncertainty: Heuristics and Biases* 493–518 (ed. Daniel Kahnemann et al., Cambridge: Cambridge University Press, 1982). For example, psychologists find that it is difficult to educate people about risks such as nuclear disasters because "any discussion of nuclear accidents may increase their imaginability and hence their perceived risk" (487).

4. See Richard Delgado, Chris Dunn, Pamela Brown, Helena Lee, and David Hubbert, "Fairness and Formality: Minimizing the Risk of Prejudice in Alternative Dispute Resolution," *Wisconsin Law Review* 1370 (1986), arguing that form procedures that create role distance between professionals and subordinated people desirably inhibit the influence of prejudice on the professionals.

5. See, for example, the works cited in note 1 by Binder and Price and by Ellmann.

6. For an elaboration of this idea in the context of welfare rights, see William H. Simon, "The Invention and Reinvention of Welfare Rights," 44 *Maryland Law Review* 1, 16–23 (1985).

7. Luban, "Paternalism," 477 (quoting *In re Will of White*, 24 N.E. 935 [N.Y., 1890]).

8. Kennedy, "Motives," 638.

9. Luban, "Paternalism," 464.

10. Roberto Manabeira Unger, *Knowledge and Politics*, 242–46 (New York: Free Press, 1975).

In Hell There Will Be Lawyers
Without Clients or Law

SUSAN P. KONIAK AND GEORGE M. COHEN

More than twenty years ago, moral philosopher Richard Wasserstrom framed the debate in legal ethics by asking two questions:[1] Does the lawyer's duty to represent the client zealously, constrained only by the bounds of the law, render the lawyer "at best systematically amoral and at worst more than occasionally immoral in . . . her dealings with the rest of the world [?]"[2] And is the lawyer's relationship with the client likewise morally tainted in that it generally entails domination by the lawyer over the client rather than mutual respect?[3] Wasserstrom answered both questions affirmatively. Though these questions have preoccupied legal ethics scholars ever since,[4] they are the wrong questions. They were off-base when posed and, if anything, are even more off-base today. The problem with Wasserstrom's questions is that they presuppose individual clients and settled law. The truly troubling questions in legal ethics arise, however, when clients are entities and the law governing these clients and the lawyer's relationship to them is contested. Class actions, the subject of this essay, raise perhaps the most troubling questions of all.

Wasserstrom wrote in the wake of Watergate. The involvement of so many lawyers in that scandal embarrassed the profession and prompted the American Bar Association to require that all law students receive instruction in legal ethics.[5] The ABA's legal ethics requirement helped spark scholarship in the field, and Wasserstrom's article was one of the first serious entries in what would soon become a burgeoning area of research. Strangely, however, Wasserstrom, who specifically referred to Watergate as an example of lawyer misconduct, and many other legal ethics scholars who followed in his path, focused on questions that had little connection to what the lawyers of Watergate infamy did wrong.

The Watergate lawyers did not go wrong because professional ethics condoned all activity on the client's behalf short of actually breaking the law, Wasserstrom's first indictment of legal ethics. They went wrong because their personal morality condoned even lawbreaking.[6] As for Wasserstrom's second indictment of legal ethics, the domination critique, even if the Watergate lawyers had represented Richard Nixon in his personal capacity, the moral taint in that relationship would surely not have been that the lawyers imposed their will on their client. But even if they could have, none of the Watergate lawyers was representing President Nixon in his personal capacity. Those whose lawbreaking was even arguably undertaken as part of representing a client[7] had clients that the law had created, such as the United States or the Office of the President[8] and thus had lawyer-client relationships not subject to Wasserstrom's paternalism critique nor amenable to his remedy: a relationship in which the lawyer listened more and dominated less.

The questions articulated by Wasserstrom and accepted by so many legal scholars as central to legal ethics do not fit the patterns of later lawyer scandals any better than they fit Watergate. Just as in Watergate, lawyer involvement in the savings and loan debacle[9] and in the tobacco industry's longstanding pattern of deception[10] involved zealousness not within the bounds of law but outside those bounds. Similarly, all three situations involved not lawyers dominating individual clients but lawyers representing entities and deferring altogether too much, not too little, to dominant individuals acting in the name of those entity-clients. To understand any of this conduct, we need different questions. We need to explore how difficult it is for those trained in law to maintain a belief in its boundaries. Have modern theories of jurisprudence made the notion that the law has boundaries harder for lawyers to accept? Or was it ever thus? As for the lawyer-client relationship, we need to concentrate more on how that relationship should be structured when the client is an entity. Are the entities lawyers represent sufficiently similar to support one model of the lawyer-entity relationship, the approach reflected in the ABA's Model Rules of Professional Conduct,[11] or are multiple models needed?

Class action abuse is a particularly interesting area in which to explore both themes: when and why law might fail to affect lawyer conduct; and the complexity of the lawyer-entity relationship. By class action abuse, we have in mind three related problems: collusive settlements, inadequate representation of class interests, and payoffs to objectors and their counsel. The law condemns collusive settlements and the lawyers who make them. It demands that class counsel adequately represent the class. Paying objectors and their counsel to drop their challenges to class settlements is, at best, legally questionable behavior and, at worst, evidence of collusion and inadequate representation. If, as we contend, these practices have become commonplace, the law has proved a poor regulator of lawyer conduct. Why?

As to the complexity of the lawyer-entity relationship, class-clients differ significantly from partnership-clients and corporation-clients, to name just a few of the possible varieties of entity-clients. For example, class counsel plays an important, and typically exclusive, role in selecting and controlling the class representatives and shaping the size and purpose of the enterprise. By contrast, lawyers representing other entities typically do not select or control the managing agents, nor do they define the nature of the firm. Other entities typically have chains of command, and they have agents authorized to hire and monitor the entity's lawyers; classes typically have neither. With respect to the scope of the lawyer's representation, the law generally presumes that corporate counsel represents the corporation and *not* its officers, but class counsel necessarily represents both the class and its named representatives.

The Complex Relationship between Lawyers and Law

The traditional approach to legal ethics assumes that the "bounds of the law" are known and focuses on the fact that these boundaries permit much undesirable behavior. From this perspective, the moral dilemma for the lawyer is the conflict between promoting the client's interests within these known bounds and protecting the interests of society against client behavior that is lawful, yet harmful. But the premise underlying this dilemma is often false. By assuming that lawyers obey the law and concentrating on what more an ethic should demand of them, the traditional approach has contributed, however unwittingly, to the myth that law, unlike moral philosophy, is simple stuff. Even those who are not philosophers, such as legal economists, often write as if legal rules are fixed in some meaningful sense, which leads them to focus on problems of over- and underdeterrence and to seek "optimal" rules to solve those problems. Like the philosophers, the economists thus view the problem of legal advice as stemming from the fact that lawyers will obey the law, but nonetheless may be able to give advice that is socially undesirable.[12]

Yet to accept, without discussion or qualification, that lawyers generally obey the law, one must first believe that for lawyers, if not for everybody, determining what the law demands is relatively easy. One must further believe that, having identified what the law demands, lawyers will determine that obedience is the appropriate course of action. Neither proposition is sustainable. Not only is law more complex than this account suggests, but the relationship between law and lawyers is more complex.

Understanding what the law demands may sometimes be a simple matter: when the light is red, the law demands that you stop. But that is certainly not always so. Lawyers presumably advised Microsoft that the way it was responding to its competitors did not violate the antitrust laws, but the Justice Department's lawyers believed otherwise. Whether or not Microsoft's business practices were legal or illegal is, as we write this, the subject of an intense courtroom battle. If the case does not settle, there may someday be a final judgment on the matter, but that judgment will not end the difficult questions about the limits of lawful responses to competitors. It is not that there is no law on the matter—antitrust law exists—but its contours are not easy to discern; thus, obedience is no simple task.

Antitrust law is not uniquely uncertain. Uncertainty is inherent in law, if only because lawmakers cannot identify and address all possible problems in advance.

Thus, the meaning of a legal rule in a particular situation almost always demands a conscious act of interpretation, the creation of a story about the rule. Stories connect legal rules to facts, and in the process give meaning to both the law and the facts. A court decision, for example, embodies a story that explains what happened; what the law says should have happened; and whether what happened diverges enough from what the law demands to constitute an illegal act.

In counseling clients, lawyers must do more than read legal rules; they must use the stories embodied in court opinions, legislative debates and executive agency pronouncements to assess their client's proposed or past conduct. In assessing whether that conduct is legal or illegal, the lawyer must extrapolate, interpret. After all, the client's conduct will rarely, if ever, be precisely the same as the conduct that has already been ruled on by the courts or specifically contemplated by the legislature in enacting a rule. Thus, the lawyer is required to construct her own story—a story about stories told by others. In doing so, the lawyer in a sense makes law for the client.

To understand the inherent uncertainty of law is to begin to understand the complexity of the lawyer's relationship to law. Lawyers are not only trained to understand that law's boundaries are uncertain, but they "practice" by constructing stories, thereby helping to shape the law's boundaries. Lawyers are thus a part of, not apart from, law's boundaries, a fact of which they are all too well aware from their legal training and practice.

This knowledge, however, may lull lawyers into a false belief that law's boundaries either do not exist at all or do not apply to them.[13] In particular, lawyers may think that there are no constraints on their helping clients to do things that the lawyers imagine are lawful, only to find a court reaching the conclusion that the client's actions were unlawful and, worse yet, that the lawyers should have realized this based on existing law. At some level, of course, lawyers know that the law's limits are real; they affect events. Up close and on a regular basis, lawyers see damages awarded and fines and prison terms imposed in the name of those limits. Good lawyers understand that the ethical practice of law involves lawyers simultaneously shaping legal boundaries and recognizing the real limits to this manipulation. The most significant ethical dilemma for lawyers is therefore not the one traditionally posed by legal ethics scholarship, in which lawyers use their knowledge of certain legal boundaries to assist in legal, though morally questionable acts. Rather, it is that lawyers sometimes let their awareness of legal uncertainty delude them into thinking that they have more control over constructing legal boundaries than they in fact do. In this sense, the bounds of the law are inextricably intertwined with what lawyers are allowed to do in shaping those bounds.

The recent savings and loan scandal, in which lawyers were forced to pay millions in settlements arising out of their representation of savings and loans that became insolvent, provides a concrete example of this phenomenon. The harsh response of many courts to lawyer conduct in the scandal represents a collective refusal to allow the fuzziness of the law governing corporate fraud to become a rationalization for lawyers' complicity in such fraud. But in many other lawyering contexts—the class action situation we discuss below being the most notable—courts have frequently failed to apply the brakes.

The problem of legal uncertainty, however, is only one aspect of the complex relationship lawyers have with law, including the law governing lawyers, which so many legal ethicists take for granted that lawyers simply obey. Not only do lawyers in their role as counselors interpret law for their clients and themselves, but in their roles as advocates and public citizens, they occupy a privileged position in the construction of the legal meaning articulated by courts and in the construction of the legal rules to which meaning must be attached. In these latter roles, lawyers act in a very public way to help determine just what the "bounds of the law" are.

With respect to court-made law, lawyers are uniquely empowered by the state to present judges with alternative interpretations of what the law demands. Most judges most of the time consider the competing legal meanings offered by the lawyers in a case and simply adopt one, albeit generally with some modification, as that court's official interpretation of the law. Although judges are free to invest law with a meaning no lawyer advocated or imagined, they rarely do so. And even when a judge adopts her own interpretation, because lawyers frame the questions courts decide, the lawyers will still have significantly influenced the law-building process, a role that extends far beyond a particular client's case.

The special role lawyers play in constructing law is not limited to courtroom practice. Lawyers still dominate legislatures and other rulemaking bodies. In voluntary organizations, most notably the American Law Institute, lawyers draft model statutes, which legislatures often subsequently enact, and purport to codify the common law developed by judges in *Restatements of the Law* (themselves acts of interpretation that often go beyond pure restating), which judges often rely on in later cases. As to the law governing themselves, lawyers in other voluntary organizations, most notably the American Bar Association, draft model ethics rules, which almost every jurisdiction in the country has adopted as law. Although official lawmakers are free to, and often do, modify or (more rarely) reject these proposed statutes, *Restatements of the Law,* and ethics rules, lawyers' influence in promulgating these rules, like their influence in courtroom advocacy, is enormous.

The fact that lawyers play a privileged position in the construction of legislative and judicial law complicates lawyers' obedience to the law in at least two ways. First, lawyers, at least when a significant number of them act as a group, occupy a privileged position in constructing new statutes and new interpretations to counter or nullify existing official law. Other groups may propose new law; however, lawyers have a leg up on transforming their proposals into the real thing. This advantage is particularly troubling when lawyers use their privileged status to counter extant law directed at their own conduct. For example, many lawyers were unhappy with court rulings that forced them to testify before grand juries about matters such as their clients' fees. In response, various bar groups constructed and sought the adoption of an ethics rule making it unethical for prosecutors to demand such appearances without first obtaining court approval and meeting other hurdles.[14] Second, lawyers may refuse to play their part in the construction of official law, encouraging the maintenance of "free zones" in which the law plays little, if any, role in regulating conduct. This path is the one lawyers have taken in the class action area, as we will discuss shortly. The bar's rhetoric on the right of "self-regulation" can also be understood in this way, as a call for the state to leave most lawyer conduct unregulated by law.

Finally, the lawyer's relationship to law is complicated by the bar's understanding of its obligation to resist the state on behalf of clients and in the name of preserving the independence of the bar itself, an independence that sustains our democracy, at least according to the bar's ethos.[15] If resisting the state is noble, obeying the law may sometimes be wrong. Ethics opinions and commentary to the ethics rules, both promulgated by the bar, reflect a strong sense of noble resistance to official law. For example, a Statement of Policy adopted by the ABA House of Delegates on the duties to comply with the securities law in 1975 proclaimed:

> [A]ny principle of law which, except as permitted or required by the [Model Code of Professional Responsibility, a code written by the ABA and not itself official law], permits or obliges a lawyer to disclose to the [Securities and Exchange Commission] otherwise confidential information should be established only by statute after full and careful consideration of the public interests involved and should be resisted unless clearly mandated by law.[16]

This statement calls on lawyers to resist law embodied in something other than a clear statutory provision, for example, administrative regulations and court opinions interpreting the statute, when that law conflicts with the bar's self-generated rules of conduct. In a similar vein, the comment to Model Rule 1.6 of the ABA's Model Rules of Professional Conduct states that lawyers "must comply with the final orders of a court or other tribunal of competent jurisdiction requiring the lawyer to give information about the client."[17] Significantly, the rule does not say that a lawyer must comply with statutes, like the federal tax code, that require lawyers to disclose material that would otherwise be protected by the bar's ethics rule. The bar's rhetoric of resistance to official law is more than just talk. Many lawyers have refused to comply with statutes that require disclosure of material the bar believes lawyers should not be forced to disclose, on the theory that their acts of resistance fulfill their ethical obligations.[18]

Lawyers' skepticism about law's limits, their special role in the construction of law, and their ethic of noble resistance to law all help to undermine simplistic assumptions about lawyers living within the bounds of the law. How lawyers understand law, what it means to obey law, and when disobedience to law is justified are subjects that have been pushed off center stage by such simplistic assumptions. Only by concentrating on the many complexities in the lawyer's relationship to law can we adequately understand the lawbreaking that pervades the major lawyer scandals from Watergate to the present, and indeed the nature of law itself.

The Complexities of the Lawyer-Entity Relationship

Undoubtedly, much of the work that lawyers do involves the representation of entities, as opposed to individuals, though quantifying how much is difficult. The representation of corporations alone represents a significant percentage of the work of all lawyers, and if one adds to that all the work lawyers do representing partnerships (and, more recently, limited liability companies), labor unions, formal and informal associations, and governments and classes, there can be little question that the representation of entities is at the heart of what many, if not most, lawyers do. Although the Model Rules of Professional Conduct represents an improvement over its predecessor Model Code of Professional Responsibility in addressing the relationship between lawyers and their entity clients, the Model Rules are woefully inadequate to the complex task at hand. Policymakers and legal ethics scholars have similarly neglected the problems of entity representation. How does the representation of entity clients in general differ from the representation of individual clients? How do entity clients differ from one another? Do the ethics rules adequately deal with the representation of partnerships, or associations, or classes? These questions have received too little attention.[19] Our attention has been diverted to where the ball is not.

The less one's entity client resembles a large, publicly held corporation, the less sense the ethics rules make. The only rule specifically applicable to entity representation, Model Rule 1.13, addresses a particular crisis in the lawyer's relationship to an entity client: what a lawyer should do when she discovers that a constituent of the organization is violating duties to the organization or violating the law in a manner that might be imputed to the organization.[20] In the representation of large, publicly held corporations, this is *the* crisis: the crisis of the rogue manager or, worse yet, the rogue officers or directors. With its singular focus on this crisis, Rule 1.13 implies that in other situations, representing an entity is not much different from representing a person or at least is so simple a matter that no particular guidance is required. When the client is a corporation, this position is at least tenable, because in the absence of lawless management, it is reasonable for a lawyer to defer to directions from management or the board just as the lawyer would defer to directions from an individual client. Such a stance is consistent with, and indeed vindicates, the corporate form—a form that presumes that shareholders invest management and the board with the power to direct corporate activities, and insists that managers and directors act as faithful fiduciaries in exercising that power. The ethics rule on entity representation presupposes, and depends upon, the checks and balances that have evolved as a matter of corporate and agency law. To take an important example, corporate law is fuzziest when the corporation is on the verge of bankruptcy. With no clear answer in law on who speaks for the corporation in this situation, Rule 1.13 is of little use, as lawyers representing failing savings and loans discovered to their detriment. In general, however, the comprehensive legal backdrop makes it tenable to posit that only when management breaches its fiduciary duties must the lawyer cease to treat the decisions of managers as if they were comparable to the decisions of an individual client.

Not all entity-clients are corporations, however. They do not all share the same central crisis and, when an analogous crisis does present itself, lawyers for other entity-clients may find that the remedial measures dictated by Rule 1.13 make little sense, despite the bold insistence of the rule's comment that the lawyer's duties "apply equally to unincorporated associations."[21] Let's start with partnerships. Two of the central crises in the representation of partnerships involve seemingly analogous situations to the crisis most likely to occur in corporate representation. When a majority of the general partners breach fiduciary duties owed the minority of general partners and when general partners breach fiduciary duties to limited partners, the lawyer for the partnership is in an analogous position to that of the corporate lawyer who discovers a manager engaged in illegal conduct. Rule 1.13, however, provides much more guidance to the corporate lawyer and is relatively unhelpful to her partnership-lawyer counterpart. The Rule presumes a formal hierarchy of control within the entity-client, which the lawyer may use to help protect the entity from the lawlessness of its agents. In plain language, the Rule tells a lawyer to make her way up the entity's chain of command, bringing the misconduct to ever-higher levels of authority in an effort to bring the lawless agent into line. When general partners act in breach of fiduciary duties to limited partners or to a minority of their peers, to whom should the lawyer appeal? The partnership lawyer is likely to begin at the place Rule 1.13 marks as an end: advising the highest authority designated to act on behalf of the entity—typically all general partners—to abide by the law, and in all likelihood meeting resistance.

Many scholars criticized Rule 1.13, as adopted by the ABA, for prohibiting corporate lawyers from speaking out to the government or shareholders in the event that the corporation's highest authority, the board, refused to act in accordance with law.[22] Rule 1.13's resolution of the "lawless board" problem is that the corporate lawyer should resign and remain quiet about the violation of law. Whether this resolution strikes the right balance is subject to debate, if for no other reason than the fact that following it may leave lawyers vulnerable to liability.[23] The Rule requires a lawyer to leave her vulnerable client, the corporation, and that client's most vulnerable constituents, the shareholders, at the mercy of unfaithful agents. The power of this objection is, however, significantly muted as long as one assumes that in almost all cases the corporation's highest authority will comply with the lawyer's advice. Thus, as long as the corporation's central crisis takes place below board level, it is reasonable to require lawyers to work their way up the chain of command. The partnership's analogous crises, however, are much more likely to involve misconduct at the top, and, as a consequence, Rule 1.13 adds little to the general rule requiring all lawyers to resign if necessary to avoid assisting a client in unlawful conduct.[24]

More troublesome, the crises central to the representation of other entity-clients, like classes, are simply not analogous to those that plague corporations. In class actions, the big problem is not that those designated to represent the class as typical plaintiffs or defendants (the named representatives) are likely to act lawlessly and thereby harm the class; the problem is that class lawyers will subordinate the class's interest to their own. In fact, the class is entirely a creation of the lawyer: class counsel controls its beginning, its end, its shape, its conduct. Rule 1.13 assumes that a well-defined entity exists with a hierarchical structure protected by legal checks and balances, and that an agent other than the lawyer is available to monitor the lawyer and direct the lawyer's effort. The Rule therefore simply does not speak to the problem of lawyer domination of the entity-client, which is at the core of all the difficult situations that confront class counsel.

Class actions are merely an extreme example of a more general point about the lawyer-entity relationship. That relationship depends on the law that structures or fails to structure the entity-client. The more that internal and external rules structure an entity, for example, by designating the agents authorized to speak, listen, and act on behalf of that entity, the easier it is for lawyers, authors of ethics rules, commentators, and courts to conceptualize how lawyers should act in representing those entities, and to envision and address the crises likely to plague particular entities. On the other hand, the more formless the entity—the less defined it is by internal or external law—the more difficult it is to speak coherently about what lawyers should and should not do. In this regard, it is at least interesting, if not disturbing, that following the savings and loan crisis—and at least in part because of it—we have seen the blossoming of a dizzying array of new, limited liability business entities,[25] which create whole new areas of legal uncertainty in entity representation. This uncertainty exists not only because the statutes governing these entities are so new and unexplored, but also because the entities themselves are hybrids of partnerships and corporations, raising questions of how courts will interpret the rules applicable to them.

Thus, to some extent the two neglected questions in professional responsibility are related. The question of how lawyers should deal with their entity-clients is a question that requires not simply philosophical musings, but legal analysis and theoretical and empirical inquiry into the lawyer's relationship to the law, in particular the law—both old and new—governing entity-clients, as well as the law governing lawyers. That is the lesson we should have learned from previous lawyer scandals. It is the lesson we might learn now from the disgrace that class action practice has become. We turn to that subject now.

Class Action Abuse

The world of class action practice we see is one in which abuse flourishes.[26] It is a world in which lawyers make fabulous fees for achieving very little, if anything, on behalf of their clients; defendant-corporations make sweetheart deals to dispose of serious liability at bargain-basement rates; and absent class members end up with useless coupons or pennies on the dollar as compensation for their alleged injuries. While we believe abuse is rampant, others believe it is relatively rare: the exception, not the rule. There is no way to establish to a certainty which belief more accurately reflects the current state of class actions. There is no common definition of abuse. Many, although no one knows how many, court opinions in class action cases are not published. In those cases in which detailed court opinions are available, information critical to the determination of whether the settlement is abusive may not appear on the surface of the opinion, and the underlying record is likely to be either unavailable, skimpy or, at the other extreme, too voluminous to make an assessment of many cases a practical undertaking. Despite these difficulties, we need to begin by setting out the reasons for our conviction that abuse in class actions is pervasive. We have two: the incentives built into the present system, and available empirical and anecdotal evidence.

The incentives built into the current class action system suggest that abuse is pervasive. All lawyer-client relationships create conflicts because the interests of lawyers and clients are not perfectly aligned. Lawyers have a keen interest in the size of their fees. Clients are interested primarily in the size of their recovery. To the degree lawyers dominate the lawyer-client relationship, there is a danger that they will engage in conduct that increases their fees at the expense of the client's recovery. Economists refer to the misalignment of interests between agents, such as lawyers, and principals, their clients, as an agency problem. Class actions exacerbate agency problems considerably.

In ordinary lawyer-client relationships, clients can deal with the agency problem in two ways: by a contract between the lawyer and client that limits the lawyer's fee or ties it to the client's recovery, or by monitoring the lawyer's performance carefully as the representation proceeds. These solutions, imperfect enough in the ordinary client setting (especially when clients are unsophisticated individuals), are even more ineffective in the class action setting. The reason is that absent class members, by definition the majority of the class, can neither contract with the lawyer nor monitor the lawyer's actions. Class representatives, chosen and controlled by class counsel, are in no position to make restrictive fee contracts with class counsel. Nor have courts in general insisted that the class representatives be consulted about the progress of the suit. Indeed, they regularly approve class settlements even though the class representative has only the vaguest idea of what the settlement provides.[27] Thus, client monitoring of lawyer performance is effectively unavailable in almost all class actions.

Defendants and their lawyers in class action suits understand the agency problem just discussed and have every incentive to exploit it. Defendants have a strong interest in minimizing their liability exposure through a settlement. Defendants care only about the total amount they must pay out in settlement, not how the payoff is distributed between class members and the class lawyer. Thus, defendants have a strong incentive to offer class counsel a deal in which the defendants accede to increased class counsel fees in return for the class counsel's agreeing to a lower recovery for class members. There is every reason to believe that many class action settlements involve this trade of a smaller recovery pie for a larger fee slice. We call this a collusive deal.

Of course, honorable class counsel could try to resist the collusive settlement offers of defendants and their lawyers. But if class counsel balk at the prospect of selling out their clients, the defendant can try auctioning off the right to bargain on behalf of the class to lawyers more willing to cooperate. The fact that defendants have effective control over which lawyers represent the class may seem surprising. Defendants get that control because they have a very important bargaining chip: the ability to challenge class certification. In most mass tort cases, the defendant's agreement not to fight class certification is crucial, because the heterogeneity of the class would prevent certification if the defendant decided to challenge it.[28] Even in class suits not involving mass torts, the threat to challenge certification and impose high costs on uncooperative class counsel gives defendants great leverage. A lawyer who wages an expensive fight to get a class certified for trial and loses gets no fees.

The collusion between class counsel and defendants can and does take a variety of forms. One strategy is to make the class as big and undivided as possible, which means bigger fees for class counsel, greater finality for defendants, and fewer competing plaintiffs' lawyers to muck things up. This strategy can disadvantage some members of the class, for example, those few with relatively strong claims compared to others. But dividing the class into subgroups of people, known as subclasses, is not in the interest of class counsel or defendants.

Another strategy is to find methods to lock class members into settlements—methods to defeat the ordinary right of absent class members to "opt out." Transforming opt-out classes into non-opt-out classes is another way of ensuring as much finality as possible for defendants. The collusion here can take one of two forms. First, the defendant can get class counsel to tack a request for an injunction onto a class complaint for money damages. Injunctions are court orders directing a party to do or stop doing something. When a class action is brought to ask for an injunction to help the whole class group, the rule is that no one can opt out of the class.[29] That rule is based on the notion that the injunction will necessarily affect all members of the class, so all should be included in the suit as a means of ensuring that the interests of all will be taken into account in issuing and framing the injunction or in denying it. In the collusive version, however, the defendant tells the class lawyer that the defendant would settle the class's claims for money damages on the condition that class counsel tack on a request for a makeweight injunction, for example one ordering the defendant to put up a plaque to commemorate those who died as a result of the defendant's product.[30] That ensures that no one in the class can refuse to accept what the class settlement offered her in money damages (or coupons) and elect to sue as an individual.

The second method that has been developed to lock in the class is for the defendant and class counsel to agree to tell the court that the defendant's assets should be treated as if they were too small to pay all class members. Class action law allows the locking in of class members when there is a designated pot of money from which all claims must be paid and that pot is too small to pay everyone in the class all that they might be owed.[31] Of course, if the defendant and compliant class lawyers are free to designate the available pot of money, they will always designate an amount that is too small, which means they can always lock in all class members. Recognizing this problem, the Supreme Court, in its recent *Ortiz v. Fibreboard Corp.* decision, reversed a district court's approval of a class action settlement that had been upheld by the Fifth Circuit, in which this collusive technique was used.[32] The Court rejected the settlement in part because the only evidence that the pot of money—mostly insurance money—was insufficient was the settlement agreement between the defendant and class counsel, and an accompanying settlement between the defendant and its liability insurance companies.[33] It is too soon to tell, however, whether *Oritz* will succeed in killing off this collusive technique or whether class action participants will succeed in finding effective substitutes.[34]

Courts in class actions are supposed to thwart such collusive efforts, as the Supreme Court did in *Ortiz,* by fulfilling the monitoring role that the client cannot. Rule 23(e) of the Federal Rules of Civil Procedure requires district court approval of class action settlements. Ostensibly, the court stands in for the client as a fiduciary to ensure that the settlement is fair to the client and does not merely serve the lawyer's interest. But this rule simply replaces one imperfect agent (class counsel) with another (the court). Although the court has no monetary interest in the settlement, its interests are not perfectly aligned with the interests of class members. Courts generally favor settlements because they clear crowded dockets. Courts favor class action settlements because the alternatives—trying the class action or, worse yet, trying the multitude of suits that make up the class action individually—are particularly burdensome alternatives, taking up significant court time and resources.[35] Even if courts did not face these incentives, they may lack the information necessary to make an informed evaluation of the settlement.[36] Moreover, the court's institutional role as neutral arbiter limits its ability to serve as an effective fiduciary. Courts are not and cannot be advocates for the class. Although courts provide some constraint on collusive behavior, for the reasons just given it is predictable that courts would be generally unreliable monitors of class counsel's performance and ineffective protectors of class members' interests, and that they will resist the broader implications of cases like *Oritz.*

It is true that courts have an interest in promoting their reputation for fairness. That interest should encourage them to safeguard the interests of absent class members. At least so far, however, individual judges have little reason to expect negative reputational effects among the general public from approving bad class deals. The press and academia have imperfect access to class settlements. Even when settlement documents are readily accessible, they are likely to be so lengthy and complex that sorting out what happened is very difficult. Class settlements are, if nothing else, heavily lawyered affairs, and discerning fraud through pages and pages of legalese drafted to conceal any such activity requires effort few reporters and fewer academics have thus far invested. To the extent the public blames anyone for the abuse it believes is present, though finds difficult to document, that blame tends to land on the doorstep of lawyers, not the judiciary. And judges understand all this.

More important, courts worry not only about their reputation among the general public, but also about their reputation among other judges and lawyers. Rejecting a settlement that clears not only one's own docket, but the dockets of colleagues, is not apt to win a judge the praise of fellow judges. Nor should a judge expect to win praise from the bar for rejecting the efforts of lawyers and firms. The judge who has to work with these lawyers on a continual basis would be understandably reluctant to reject a settlement on the grounds that those lawyers colluded. Moreover, state judges who must stand for election may depend on lawyers for campaign contributions, and all judges, whether elected or appointed, may depend on the bar for endorsements. Judges may be wary of academic criticism, but this has far less practical impact. Indeed academic criticism can be—and often is in the class action area—dismissed as idealistic musing by people not sufficiently grounded in the "real world." More important, many legal academics are hesitant to criticize at least federal judges, perhaps in the hope that they may some day join their ranks. Legal academics have also developed something of a stake in the class action system by, for example, serving as special masters in evaluating settlements, who get paid only if a settlement is approved.

It is possible that trial courts' enthusiasm for settlement could be tempered by the possibility of reversal on appeal in cases like *Ortiz*. Appellate judges, one step removed from the mess, presumably have less interest in approving every class settlement that comes up on appeal. But being one step removed also means that appellate judges are to a large extent necessarily dependent on the findings of the trial judge as to the fairness of the terms, the adequacy of the representation, and the appropriateness of the request for attorney's fees. As a consequence of this distance, appellate courts review such matters under the abuse of discretion standard,[37] which seems appropriate, but which also will never lead to a high rejection rate. Cases like *Ortiz* may simply demonstrate that appellate courts are able to act only when the facts are egregious and apparent. If, in response to *Ortiz*, district courts acquiesce in the papering over of difficulties, appellate courts may not be in a good position to do anything about it.

The available empirical evidence supports the claim that courts are extremely reluctant to reject proposed class action settlements. A recent empirical study conducted by the Federal Judicial Center of class action practice in four federal district courts finds that of the 117 proposed class action settlements, around 90 percent were approved without changes and 98 percent were approved with changes. As for attorney's fees, although the study found that objections were made in 21 (18 percent) of the cases, in 19 of those cases the court awarded the full fee requested.[38] Thus, not only are proposed settlements routinely approved without change, but so are the proposed attorney's fees. Of the settlements approved in the study, only three were appealed, and only one of those three—the only appeal filed by objectors—was reversed.[39]

Moreover, if judges had no bias in favor of accepting class settlements and the standard on appeal were much more stringent, it is reasonable to believe that the vast majority of class settlements would still be approved no matter how dirty the conduct was that surrounded the settlement. The reason: most hearings on the fairness of class settlements are not adversarial proceedings. The Federal Judicial Center study found that in the four districts studied 42 percent to 64 percent of the fairness hearings were concluded without any presentation of objections to the proposed settlement by "class members and other objectors."[40] The study provides no information on whether in the cases where objectors made written objections or appeared at the hearing, they were represented by counsel or appeared pro se, but it is probably safe to assume that many of those objections were raised pro se. In the absence of a trained advocate to present problems with a proposed settlement, the likelihood that a judge could ferret out corruption or illegality surrounding a settlement that is presented jointly by class counsel and defendant's counsel as fair, legal, and just is quite small.

The current system provides little incentive for lawyers to seek out corruption or illegality in proposed settlements. Objecting lawyers stand little chance of receiving fees or even reimbursement of expenses incurred in mounting a challenge.[41] Lawyers are sometimes motivated to challenge proposed settlements in the hope of reaping some later economic benefit, such as success in one's own bid to be class counsel in a later suit or continued income from individual suits, which would be more lucrative than processing people through a claims procedure set up for class members under a proposed settlement. However, because the chances of convincing a trial judge to reject a settlement are so slim, and the chances on appeal are not much greater and entail added expenses, the expected benefit of derailing the settlement would have to be enormous to make it rational to launch a serious challenge.[42] Even when objectors and their lawyers have sufficient incentives and funding to challenge the class settlement, however, they are often motivated not by the chance to protect the class from a sellout settlement, but by the prospect of being paid off by class counsel and/or the defendant to drop their objections and walk away.[43]

The situation is thus ripe for abuse. It is in the interest of all the participants in the class action—save the absent members of the class—to settle class actions by collusively transferring money from the class to class counsel. As long as some plaintiffs' lawyers are willing to act in a self-interested way, they will be rewarded by defendants with extraordinary fees funded at the expense of the class. Courts will not effectively monitor the abuse due to their interest in seeing cases settled. Because abuse, by which we mean fraud and negligence as to the class's interest, is in the interest of the participants, it is reasonable to expect abuse to be pervasive. Combined with our experience and the available evidence of class action practice, our understanding of the incentives built into the present system sustains our conviction that collusion and inadequate representation are everyday features of the class action world—a scandalous state of affairs.

No There, There

If we are correct that collusion and inadequate representation are rampant in class actions, what does that say about Wasserstrom's two questions and our reframing of them? Let's start with the "bounds of the law" of class actions. That law condemns both collusion and inadequate representation, at least that's what the court opinions say. "[T]he proponents [of a proposed class action settlement] have the burden of proving . . . that the settlement is not collusive but was reached after arm's length negotiations."[44] The court is supposed to reject the settlement if that burden is not met. And the absence of collusion is not enough. Again, according to the law that courts purport to be applying, no class settlement may be approved unless the court finds that the class has been afforded adequate representation by counsel. The courts have interpreted the Constitution's Due Process Clause to guarantee the class adequate representation by the named plaintiffs and by counsel.[45] Moreover, the guarantee is so important that the initial court's determination of this issue may be reexamined not just on appeal but even after all appeals have been exhausted. In other words, an absent class member may sue the defendant at some later point in time and claim that the class settlement should be treated as a legal nullity because, despite what the trial and appellate courts ruling on the settlement said, the lawyers who proposed the settlement did not adequately represent the class. While recently some academic commentators have argued strenuously against this two-bites-at-the-apple treatment of the guarantee of adequacy, courts, at least thus far, maintain that a second (or what lawyers call a collateral) attack on adequacy is allowed.[46]

But a court (or, for that matter any institution or individual) may say something is law and treat it as if it were not. To be law, as opposed to a string of words, the phrases courts repeat must "mean" something. For words to mean something, two things must be true about them: they must divide actions that occur in the world into valid and void, lawful and unlawful; and they must entail real consequences. If any and all conduct meets a particular "standard," or if the violation of the standard never results in tangible consequences to the violator, we put it to you that the "standard" is no "standard" and certainly not a rule of law. It is at most a mantra, something that is repeated no matter what the circumstances. It is mumbo-jumbo, not law.

"Class counsel has adequately represented the class," is a mantra. Some form of that phrase can be found in virtually every class action settlement opinion, seemingly without regard to what class counsel has actually done. In most cases, the court does not even bother to construct a story describing class counsel's activities. Instead, courts content themselves by summarizing class counsel's resume in the most laudatory terms and by making conclusory statements about how well-respected, talented, and above reproach class counsel is.[47] In most cases, in other words, courts are too busy heaping praise on class counsel to describe what they have done to represent the class, to elaborate on what the rule of adequacy demands of class counsel, or to explain why it makes sense to hold that what class counsel did satisfies the law. It is true that some courts discuss class counsel's actions at length. But this is almost always to respond to an objector who has a lawyer to present a case challenging what class counsel has done, and that is a rare occurrence for reasons we explained earlier. More important, even in those cases, the courts manage not to create any law of adequacy, leaping as they do from the actions of counsel to the conclusion that those actions are adequate without pausing to explain the content of the standard they purport to be applying.[48]

Conduct described by class action lawyers and stamped as adequate has included the following: negotiating a class settlement that leaves some members of the class paying more in attorney's fees than they receive in recovery;[49] negotiating a deal for the class that is worse than the deal simultaneously negotiated by the same lawyers for identically situated people outside the class;[50] negotiating a deal that gives members of the class with no viable claims as good a recovery as those with viable, even strong, claims;[51] negotiating a deal without conducting any discovery;[52] and devising settlement notices that the average citizen could not hope to understand.[53]

In one recent case, the Ninth Circuit Court of Appeals broke from the pack and put some teeth in the standard of adequate representation.[54] In a very detailed opinion, the court explained what class counsel had done and why that conduct fell short of the standard. This glaring exception to the otherwise cavalier approach to adequacy demonstrated by our courts was soon relegated to the scrap heap by the very court that issued the opinion, however. Months after the decision was issued, the Ninth Circuit panel ordered reargument in the case and issued a new opinion on the matter of adequacy, vacating the prior opinion, with one judge from the prior panel switching his vote.[55] The new opinion effectively immunizes from collateral attack the cursory treatment courts typically give to adequate representation.

On the other hand, the Supreme Court in *Ortiz* undertook to pour some meaning into adequate representation. Recognizing that conflicts of interest among class members translate into a conflict of interest problem for class counsel, and that class counsel conflicts are relevant to whether or not the class has received adequate representation,[56] the Court held that if these conflicts are severe enough the class must be divided into subclasses with separate representation to insure adequate representation. Specifically, the Court held that two such conflicts existed in *Ortiz*: the conflict between holders of present and future claims, and the conflict between claimants exposed to asbestos before and after the expiration of the defendant's most significant insurance policy.[57] Although we find the Court's attempt to put some meaning into adequate representation encouraging, the Court did not give much guidance about what other kinds of conflicts might create problems of adequate representation. At this point it is uncertain what impact the Court's opinion will have on class action practice and the lower courts.

The extant "law" prohibiting collusion is as illusory as that guaranteeing adequacy.[58] One must search high and low for a court decision rejecting a class settlement on the ground that it was collusive. Unlike adequacy, collusion is sometimes defined by the courts. Nevertheless, the definition sets such a high bar for "collusive" conduct, equating it with acts that would constitute criminal fraud, that the definition itself seems to guarantee the "no collusion" result. After all, most judges would be highly unlikely to accuse class counsel and the defendant of the equivalent of criminal conduct on the basis of the scanty information likely to be available to the court on what these lawyers actually did in negotiating a class settlement and what their intent was in doing what they did. Whether the high bar for collusion is primarily responsible or not, the fact is that the collusion standard does not work any better than the adequacy standard to mark conduct as lawful or unlawful. Put another way, when nothing is collusive, the collusion prohibition is not functioning as law.

This state of class action law is, of course, not lost on class counsel and other lawyers in the class action world. Once again, their dilemma is not that they are tempted to act within the bounds of the law, yet immorally. Nor is their dilemma simply that class action law is uncertain, and so they are tempted to go beyond the bounds they convince themselves do not exist, or at least do not exist for them. Rather, their ethical problem is that in a very real sense they are operating in a world without law as we generally understand it. Their representation knows no bounds.

The absence of law to control lawyer conduct in class action cases extends much further than we have thus far suggested. Class action "law" imposes little structure on the entity of the class, and to the extent it fails to do so, it leaves class counsel with what amounts in practice to virtually unlimited discretion to create, control, and manipulate her client: the class. A class is a unique entity in our legal system. Its true "owners," the class members, do not voluntarily form the entity. In fact, unlike any other legal entity, there is no law of class formation, save for the skimpy requirements of Rule 23.[59] Nor, unlike any other legal entity, is there any law of "authority," that is decision-making power, within the class. Without this structural law as a foundation, ethics has nothing on which to build.

Let us be concrete. While class action law demands that each class have named representatives, the law nowhere defines what the responsibilities of those representatives are either in relation to the rest of the class or in relation to class counsel. The little courts do say about the responsibilities of the named representatives suggests that these "responsibilities" are nonexistent. For example, as we have already discussed, courts have said that named representatives may be adequate despite the fact that they know little, if anything, about the claims asserted on the class's behalf, the settlement negotiated by counsel or the actions or conflicts of interests of counsel for the class. Moreover, courts have held that class counsel may advocate and a court may approve a settlement of a class action despite the objections of some or even all of the named representatives.[60]

In *Amchem Products, Inc. v. Windsor*,[61] the Supreme Court referred to the "representational responsibilities" of the named representatives and insisted that separate named representatives be appointed for subgroups within the class with differing interests, ostensibly so that the named representatives could fulfill their "responsibilities" to those subgroups without being burdened by the need to advocate (or do whatever named representatives are supposed to do) on behalf of groups with widely divergent interests. But the Supreme Court never said what those representational responsibilities were. What point is there in insisting that separate named representatives be appointed for subgroups within a class, if class counsel need not follow the direction of the named representatives or even keep the named representatives informed of the case's progress? The Supreme Court's decision is coherent if one assumes, as the Court has since held in *Ortiz*, that the Court meant that separate *lawyers* would be necessary to represent subgroups with divergent interests within a larger class—as long, that is, as the courts take seriously the notion that adequate counsel must advocate for the interests of the class or subclass that she represents. But the Court's decision is incoherent if read against the backdrop of "law" that demands nothing of the named representatives and gives those people no power to affect what happens to the class.

Not only does class action law fail to structure the responsibilities or powers of the named representatives, it says virtually nothing about the relation of objectors to the class or to class counsel.[62] Although courts do say that the number of objectors is a factor to be considered by the court, again class counsel is permitted to advocate and a court is free to approve a settlement objected to by many or even most of the class.[63] Objectors are technically still members of the class, but the case law is silent on whether that means that objectors continue to be clients of class counsel, despite their representation by others (in the rare case when objectors appear through counsel), and is equally silent on what class counsel's duties, if any, are to objectors, whether one imagines them to be clients or not. Must class counsel give some *Miranda*-like warning to unrepresented objectors, who all will have been told in the class notice that their interests will be represented by class counsel?[64] No answer in law. May class counsel help objectors to get a different and better deal from the defendant to encourage the objectors to remain mute in court on the problems the objectors have with the settlement offered to the class? May class counsel help objectors to opt out of the class action after the opt-out period has passed? Although both of these practices occur, we believe, with some regularity, no law speaks to their propriety, as far as we have been able to ascertain.

The emptiness of the legal concepts of adequacy and collusion, together with the law's failure to define the rights and responsibilities of class counsel and the various constituent members of the class (named representatives, objectors, opt-outs, and absent members) combine to create a free zone of activity in which class lawyers can essentially do what they please. If one understands that in class action practice, defense counsel and plaintiffs' counsel have much to gain by cooperating to ensure that class counsel has wide discretion to dispose of the claims of the absent class, it is fairly easy to understand how this lawless state of affairs might result. Put simply, no subgroup within the bar has a strong interest in seeing any other subgroup involved in this area of practice constrained by the rule of law. With no subgroups within the bar to argue for or construct law constraining lawyer conduct in this field, we find no such law.

A better understanding of the relationship of lawyers to the law and the complexity of the lawyer-client relationship is helpful not only in illuminating what is happening in the world, but in identifying solutions that might have a chance at working as well as sifting out those that seem less promising. Expecting courts to develop the law of class actions in a manner sufficiently protective of the class would, for example, seem quite optimistic. Courts, even more than legislatures, are dependent on the assistance of lawyers in the construction of sensible law. Courts construct law, as we discussed earlier, largely by relying on the arguments of lawyers. With lawyers dedicated to preserving a lawless environment in which to operate, it is not surprising that class action law has developed in so anemic a fashion. Similarly, the Advisory Committee on the Rules of Civil Procedure, a committee of the Federal Judicial Center, would seem to be ill-suited to constructing class action law because it, like the courts, is too dependent on input from class action lawyers in framing its class action rules and in addition too sensitive to the concerns of those lawyers.[65] Indeed, the Advisory Committee's class action "reform" proposals have been aimed at increasing, not decreasing, the free zone of activity now enjoyed by lawyers in this field.[66] Legislatures, although also dependent on lawyers, are in a relatively more independent position with relation to class action lawyers than courts or the Advisory Committee. Not all legislators are lawyers and the legislature is more accessible than the courts or the Advisory Committee to nonlawyers and their concerns. If anything is to be done about class action abuse, the legislature is, in short, most likely to do it.

As to what needs to be done by the legislature and in the meantime by responsible judges willing to rely less on lawyers to help them construct law, the first step is to continue down the path the Supreme Court started in *Amchem* and continued in *Ortiz*: to exorcize the notion that the fact of a settlement is sufficient to determine either the settlement's reasonableness, the lawyers' adequacy, or the absence of collusion. To develop a standard that can serve as law, courts and the legislature cannot only look to existing class action practice, which as we have argued is effectively lawless, but instead must extrapolate from, and draw analogies to, practices in areas in which law binds and lends confidence, such as the law governing other types of entities.

Moreover, understanding that a lawyer's responsibilities to her entity client will inevitably be a function of that entity's structure helps provide some direction. To decide what a class lawyer is supposed to do—what constitutes adequate representation—the relationship of the various components of a class to one another and then to the lawyer must be fleshed out. The more ephemeral the client, the more abstract and ultimately empty the lawyer's duty to that client will be. In short, class action abuse will thrive as long as the components of a class are as ill-defined as they are now. When one's client is unknowable or incoherent, one's duty will always be unclear. The law needs to make the class client coherent by explicating how its parts fit together and how they are designed to interact with the lawyer. With meaningless law and shapeless clients, the lawyer's self-interest is her only guide. The unchecked self-interest of lawyers drives class action practice today. That needs to change and asking the right questions is the first step.

In hell there will be lawyers without clients or law.[67] It is time legal ethics scholars talked about that.

Notes

1. Richard Wasserstrom, "Lawyers as Professionals: Some Moral Issues," 5 *Human Rights* 1 (1975).

2. Ibid., 1.

3. Ibid.

4. See, e.g., David Luban, "Paternalism and the Legal Profession," 1981 *Wisconsin Law Review* 454–93 (1981) (arguing that a moral dilemma exists when a client's wishes do not meet with the attorney's approval or the attorney's assessment of the client's interests).

5. ABA Standards for the Approval of Law Schools, Standard 302(a)(iv) (1995), discussed in Roger C. Cramton and Susan P. Koniak, "Rule, Story, and Commitment in the Teaching of Legal Ethics," 38 *William and Mary Law Review* 145–98 (1996)

6. See, e.g., *U.S. v. Halderman et al.*, 559 F.2d 31 (D.C. Cir. 1976) (en banc) (former Attorney General John Mitchell and other top advisers to President Nixon convicted of conspiracy to obstruct justice and perjury). See also *U.S. v. McCord*, 509 F.2d 334 (D.C. Cir. 1975); *U.S. v. Liddy*, 509 F.2d 428 (D.C. Cir. 1974); *U.S. v. Mardian*, 546 F.2d 973 (D.C. Cir. 1976); *U.S. v. Barker*, 514 F.2d 208 (D.C. Cir. 1975); and *U.S. v. Mitchell*, 372 F.Supp. 1239 (S.D.N.Y. 1973).

7. Some of the Watergate lawyers were convicted for acts they committed while acting not as lawyers but in some other capacity. For example, Donald Segretti, although a lawyer, was convicted for activity he engaged in as a campaign worker. These activities included promoting and distributing posters saying, "Help Muskie Support Bussing [*sic*] More Children Now," and purporting to come from the Mothers Backing Muskie Committee; writing a letter on "Citizens for Muskie" stationery accusing Senator Jackson of being a homosexual and Senator Humphrey of cavorting with prostitutes at the expense of lobbyists; and putting out a "Humphrey" press release stating that Representative Shirley Chisholm had been committed to a mental institution in the early 1950s after being detained in Richmond, Virginia, as a transvestite, and that she was still under psychiatric care.

8. John Dean, who pleaded guilty to burglary, was Counsel to the President. In that role, his client could be conceived as the Office of the President and/or the United States government, but not as Richard Nixon, the individual. Cf. *In re Grand Jury Subpoena Duces Tecum*, 112 F.2d 910 (8th Cir. 1997) (holding that for White House Counsel, the client is "the White

House" and the attorney-client privilege created by these lawyers does not apply to the president or the first lady in their personal or professional capacities).

9. Some of the country's most prestigious law firms were implicated in the savings and loan scandal and were sued by both the government and individuals defrauded by thrift clients for having assisted their clients in committing fraud or for negligently failing to protect those clients from the misdeeds of the individuals managing the affairs of those entity clients. See, e.g., *In re American Continental/Lincoln Sav. and Loan Securities Litigation,* 794 F.Supp. 1424 (D. Ariz. 1992) (denying a summary judgment motion by the Jones Day firm in a case alleging misconduct arising out of the representation of Lincoln Savings and Loan, controlled by Charles Keating); Susan Beck and Michael Orey, "They Got What They Deserved," *American Lawyer* 69 (May 1992) (describing the Kaye, Scholer firm's $41 million settlement with the government arising out of its representation of Lincoln Savings and Loan).

10. See Milo Geyelin and Ann Davis, "Tobacco's Foes Target Role of Lawyers," *Wall Street Journal,* April 23, 1998, B1 (reporting that law firms have been named as codefendants with tobacco companies in several suits alleging a conspiracy to deceive the public about the dangers of tobacco).

11. ABA Model Rules of Professional Conduct, Rule 1.13.

12. See, e.g., Louis Kaplow and Steven Shavell, "Legal Advice about Information to Present in Litigation: Its Effect and Social Desirability," 102 *Harvard Law Review* 565 (1989); Stephen McG. Bundy and Einer Elhauge, "Knowledge about Legal Sanctions," 92 *Michigan Law Review* 261 (1993).

13. See David B. Wilkins, "Legal Realism for Lawyers," 104 *Harvard Law Review* 468, 478–84 (1990) (discussing how the indeterminacy of law, as espoused by legal realism, renders "the bounds of the law" an ineffective ethical constraint on the lawyer's zealous advocacy).

14. See Susan P. Koniak, "The Law Between the Bar and the State," *North Carolina Law Review* 70 (1992): 1389, 1398–1401 (describing this move by the bar). Other such examples are described, ibid., 1423–24.

15. Ibid., 1449.

16. Statement of Policy Adopted by the American Bar Association Regarding Responsibilities and Liabilities of Lawyers in Advising with Respect to the Compliance by Clients with Laws Administered by the Securities and Exchange Commission, reprinted in 61 *ABA Journal* 1085, 1086 (1975).

17. ABA Model Rules of Professional Conduct, Rule 1.6 and cmt.

18. See, e.g., David B. Wilkins, "In Defense of Law and Morality: Why Lawyers Should Have a Prima Facie Duty to Obey the Law," 38 *William and Mary Law Review* 269–95 (1996); William H. Simon, "Should Lawyers Obey the Law?," 38 *William and Mary Law Review* 217–53 (1996); and Susan P. Koniak, "When Courts Refuse to Frame the Law and Others Frame It to Their Will," 66 *Southern California Law Review* 1075–113 (1992).

19. For some recent exceptions, see, e.g., Fred C. Zacharias, "Reconceptualizing Ethical Roles," 65 *George Washington Law Review* 169, 192–94 (1997); James M. Fisher, "Representing Partnerships: Who Is/Are the Client(s)?" 26 *Pacific Law Journal* 961–88 (1995); and Frederic L. Smith Jr., "Partnership Representation: Finding the Client," 20 *Journal of the Legal Profession* 355–65 (1995–96).

20. The applicable provisions, Rule 1.13(b) and (c), read:

> (b) If a lawyer acting for an organization knows that an officer, employee or other person associated with the organization is engaged in action, intends to act or refuses to act in a matter related to the representation that is a violation of a legal obligation to the organization, or a violation of law which reasonably might be imputed to the organization, and is likely to result in substantial injury to the organization,

the lawyer shall proceed as is reasonably necessary in the best interest of the organization. In determining how to proceed, the lawyer shall give due consideration to the seriousness of the violation and its consequences, the scope and nature of the lawyer's representation, the responsibility in the organization and the apparent motivation of the person involved, the policies of the organization concerning such matters and any other relevant considerations. Any measures taken shall be designed to minimize disruption of the organization and the risk of revealing information relating to the representation to persons outside the organization. Such measures may include among others:

> (1) asking reconsideration of the matter;
> (2) advising that a separate legal opinion on the matter be sought for presentation to the appropriate authority in the organization; and
> (3) referring the matter to higher authority in the organization, including, if warranted by the seriousness of the matter, referral to the highest authority that can act in behalf of the organization as determined by applicable law.

(c) If, despite the lawyer's efforts in accordance with paragraph (b), the highest authority that can act on behalf of the organization insists upon action, or a refusal to act, that is clearly a violation of law and is likely to result in substantial injury to the organization, the lawyer may resign in accordance with rule 1.16.

ABA Model Rules of Professional Conduct, Rule 1.13[b], [c]

21. Ibid., cmt.

22. See, e.g., James R. McCall, "The Corporation as Client: Problems, Perspectives, and Partial Solutions," 39 *Hastings Law Journal* 623–40 (1988); and Stephen Gillers, "Model Rule 1.13(c) Gives the Wrong Answer to the Question of Corporate Counsel Disclosure," 1 *Georgetown Journal of Legal Ethics* 289–310 (1987).

23. See, e.g., H. Lowell Brown, "The Dilemma of Corporate Counsel Faced with Client Misconduct: Disclosure of Client Confidences or Constructive Discharge," 44 *Buffalo Law Review* 777–886 (1996); Stanley Pietrusiak, "Changing the Nature of Corporate Representation: Attorney Liability for Aiding and Abetting the Breach of Fiduciary Duty," 28 *St. Mary's Law Journal* 213–67 (1996); and Jonathan J. Lerner, "Traversing the Legal Ethics Minefield of the 1990's: When Does the Corporate Counsel Become a Cop?" 779 *PLI/Corp.* 9-51 (1992). But see, e.g., George H. Brown, "Financial Institution Lawyers as Quasi-Public Enforcers," 7 *Georgetown Journal of Legal Ethics* 637, 661 (1994) (arguing that if avoiding malpractice liability is the lawyer's goal, the lawyer's best bet is to remain silent in the face of management's violations of law and withdraw from the representation if necessary).

24. ABA Model Rules of Professional Conduct, Rule 1.16(a).

25. The new business forms are limited liability companies (LLCs), limited liability partnerships (LLPs), and limited liability limited partnerships (LLLPs). All states have adopted statutes permitting the creation of LLCs, and 47 states have statutes allowing LLPs. J. Dennis Hynes, *Agency, Partnership, and the LLC* (5th ed. Charlottesville, Va.: Lexis Law Publishing, 1998), 538. Law firms themselves have used limited liability entities to protect their members, raising some of the questions of lawyers' advantage in constructing law that we raised above. See Robert W. Hamilton, "Registered Limited Liability Partnerships: Present at the Birth (Nearly)," 66 *University of Colorado Law Review* 1065 (1995) (arguing that the LLP came about as a response to huge damages awards against accounting and law partnerships stemming from the savings and loan crisis, among other events). See also Martin C. McWilliams Jr., "Limited Liability Practice," 49 *South Carolina Law Review* 359–406 (1998); and Michael J.

Lawrence, "The Fortified Law Firm: Limited Liability Business and the Propriety of Lawyer Incorporation," 9 *Georgetown Journal of Legal Ethics* 207–28 (1995).

26. Much of the following discussion draws heavily on Susan P. Koniak and George M. Cohen, "Under Cloak of Settlement," 82 *Virginia Law Review* 1053–57, 1080–88, 1102–15 (1996).

27. See, e.g., *Lewis v. Curtis*, 671 F.2d 779, 789 (3d Cir.), cert. denied, 459 U.S. 880 (1982) (finding representation to be adequate despite the fact that the class representative "displayed a complete ignorance of facts concerning the transaction that he was challenging"); *Eggleston v. Chicago Journeymen Plumbers' Local Union No. 130*, 657 F.2d 890, 896 (7th Cir. 1981), cert. denied, 455 U.S. 1017 (1982) (stating that the class representative's role is limited, and citing a Supreme Court case for the proposition that it is not enough to defeat class certification that the named plaintiff did not understand the complaint or the nature of the lawsuit); *J/H Real Estate v. Abramson*, No. 95-4176, 1996 U.S. Dist. LEXIS 1546, at 8 n.3 (E.D. Pa., Feb. 9, 1996) ("class counsel, not the class representative, guides and orchestrates the litigation"); and *Hastie v. Community Bank of Greater Peoria*, 125 F.R.D. 669, 676-77 (N.D. Ill. 1989) (accepting as adequate a named plaintiff who was unfamiliar with the details of the claim).

28. See John C. Coffee Jr., "Class Wars: The Dilemma of the Mass Tort Class Action," 95 *Columbia Law Review* (1995): 1343, 1349.

29. Federal Rules of Civil Procedure, Rule, 23(b)(2), (c)(2).

30. See, e.g., Robert B. Gerard and Scott A. Johnson, "The Role of the Objector in Class Action Settlements: A Case Study of the General Motors Truck 'Side Saddle' Fule Tank Litigation," 31 *Loyola of Los Angeles Law Review* 409–31(1998).

31. Federal Rules of Civil Procedure, Rule 23(b)(1)(B), 23(c)(2).

32. 119 S. Ct. 2295 (1999).

33. The Court held that "in an action such as this settling parties must present not only their agreement, but evidence on which the district court may ascertain the limit and the insufficiency of the fund, with support in findings of fact following a proceeding in which the evidence is subject to challenge." Ibid. at 2316. See also ibid. at 2323 (stating that, assuming the Court would allow such a settlement at all, "it would be essential that the fund be shown to be limited independently of the agreement of the parties to the action").

34. Despite its broad statements that the class settlement agreement could not establish a limited fund, the Court's opinion contains language that appears not to rule out the possibility completely. In *Ortiz*, the alleged "limited fund" consisted mostly of insurance policies with no aggregate limits on their face, but whose applicability to the class's claims was being sharply contested by the insurance companies in pending state court litigation. Because of the uncertain outcome of the insurance coverage litigation, the class counsel and defendant had argued that the value of the insurance policies was not unlimited, but a discounted "settlement value." The Court stated that the settlement value of insurance policies might be sufficient to establish that only a limited pot of money existed, but found such a position acceptable only "if one can assume that parties of equal knowledge and negotiating skill agreed upon the figure through arms-length bargaining, unhindered by any considerations tugging against the interests of the parties ostensibly represented in the negotiation. But no such assumption may be indulged in this case, or *probably* in any class action settlement with the potential for gigantic fees." Ibid. at 2317 (emphasis added). The Court found that class counsels' agreement to the insurance settlement value was inherently suspect because they had a conflict of interest: they had separately settled claims of their individual clients at the same time as, and contingent on, the class action settlement, and so had a great incentive to agree to any settlement that could win court approval. This language seems to suggest that what the Court would do if class counsel did not suffer from such a severe conflict is an open question.

35. See Jonathan R. Macey and Geoffrey P. Miller, "The Plaintiffs' Attorney's Role in Class Action and Derivative Litigation: Economic Analysis and Recommendations for Reform," 58 *University of Chicago Law Review* 1, 45–46 (1991); John C. Coffee Jr., "Understanding the Plaintiff's Attorney: The Implications of Economic Theory for Private Enforcement of Law Through Class and Derivative Actions," 86 *Columbia Law Review* 669, 714 n.121 (1986); and Sylvia R. Lazlos, "Abuse in Plaintiff Class Action Settlements: The Need for a Guardian During Pretrial Settlement Negotiations," 84 *Michigan Law Review* 308, nn. 1, 2 (1985): (discussing the judicial policy of encouraging settlements in both ordinary civil and class action suits).

Judge Henry Friendly observed that "[a]ll the dynamics conduce to judicial approval of [the] settlement" once the adversaries have agreed. See *Alleghany Corp. v. Kirby*, 333 F.2d 327, 347 (2d Cir. 1964) (Friendly, J., dissenting), aff'd en banc by equally divided court, 340 F.2d 311 (2d Cir. 1965), cert. dismissed, 384 U.S. 28 (1966). Although the case law may require full and elaborate judicial review before a settlement is approved, it is doubtful that courts have much incentive to be very demanding. Their deferential attitude is probably best expressed by one recent decision which acknowledged that: "In deciding whether to approve this settlement proposal, the court starts from the familiar axiom that a bad settlement is almost always better than a good trial." *In re Warner Communications Sec. Litig.*, 618 F. Supp. 735, 740 (S.D.N.Y. 1985).

36. See Macey and Miller, "Plaintiffs' Attorney's Role," 46–47; Coffee, "Understanding the Plaintiff's Attorney," 714 n.121.

37. The abuse of discretion review is "the most deferential standard of review available with the exception of no review at all." Martha S. Davis, "A Basic Guide to Standards of Judicial Review," 33 *San Diego Law Review* 469, 480 (1988).

38. Thomas E. Willging, Laural L. Hooper, and Robert J. Niemic, "Federal Judicial Center, Empirical Study of Class Actions in Four Federal District Courts: Final Report to the Advisory Committee on Civil Rules" (1996): 58, 178 (Table 38).

39. Ibid., at 191 (Table 51), 193 (Table 53). The settlement reversed on appeal was *In re General Motors Pick-Up Truck Litigation*, 55 F.3d 768 (3d. Cir.), cert. denied, 116 S.Ct. 88 (1995). With respect to attorney's fees appeals, ten were filed, including the *General Motors* case. Of the other nine appeals, two courts affirmed the fee award, two courts dismissed the appeal, one court reversed a denial of fees, one court reversed a trial court's reduction of fees, one court remanded for reconsideration, and two other appeals were pending at the time of the study. Ibid., 77, 191–94 (Tables 51–54).

40. Willging et al., Federal Judicial Center study, 57, 178 (Table 38).

41. In the Federal Judicial Center study, the researchers found "no fee awards to, and few fee requests by counsel other than plaintiffs' counsel" (Ibid., 155). We have found no case in which a court has awarded attorney's fees to objecting counsel for raising arguments that caused the court to disapprove a class-action settlement. In *approving* a settlement, courts sometimes award fees to objectors upon a finding that the objectors conferred a monetary benefit upon the class by raising objections that resulted in the court modifying some part of the settlement (usually class counsel's request for attorney's fees). See *Uselton v. Commercial Lovelace Motor Freight*, 9 F.3d 849, 855 (10th Cir. 1993) (fee awarded to objecting counsel, citing to Herbert Newberg, *Attorney Fee Awards* § 2.24, at 84 [1986]); *Ace Heating & Plumbing Co. v. Crane Co.*, 453 F.2d 30 (3d Cir. 1971) (an objecting attorney should not be denied reasonable compensation for a benefit conferred on the class); *Bowling v. Pfizer, Inc.*, 922 F. Supp. 1261, 1285 (S.D. Ohio 1996) (awarding attorney's fees to objectors for their role in improving the settlement for the class); 1 Alba Conte & Herbert Newberg, *Attorney Fee Awards* § 2.25, at 91-92 (2d ed. 1993). But see *Grunin v. International House of Pancakes*, 513 F.2d 114, 126-27

(8th Cir.), cert. denied, 423 U.S. 864 (1975) (objector denied fees). See also *Alpine Pharmacy, Inc. v. Chas. Pfizer & Co.*, 481 F.2d 1045, 1053-54 (2d Cir.), cert. denied, 414 U.S. 1092 (1973); *Milstein v. Werner*, 58 F.R.D. 544, 552 (S.D.N.Y. 1973); *Newman v. Stein*, 58 F.R.D. 540, 543-44 (S.D.N.Y. 1973) (securities cases denying fees to settlement objectors who conferred no class benefit).

When a court *rejects* a settlement, there is by definition no common fund from which to award attorney's fees to objecting counsel. To award counsel fees to objecting counsel who exposed a settlement as the product of collusion, and thus unworthy of approval, would require the courts to find some other source of funds from which to pay those fees. Thus far, no court has taken that step.

42. It happens. See, e.g., *Georgine v. Amchem Products, Inc.*, 157 F.R.D. 246 (E.D. Pa. 1994), vacated, 83 F.3d 610 (3d Cir. 1996), aff'd sub nom. *Amchem Products, Inc. v. Windsor*, 521 U.S. 591 (1997). However, the economics suggest that it will happen rarely.

43. For examples of cases in which objecting counsel switched sides to become cooperating class counsel or mysteriously disappeared, see *Bowling v. Pfizer, Inc.*, 922 F. Supp.1261, 1265, 1271–73 (S.D. Ohio 1996) (most of the objecting lawyers became co-counsel for class and requested attorney's fees); *Price v. Ciba-Geigy Corp.*, No. 94-0647-B-S, (S.D. Ala. 1995) (all objecting counsel dropped their objections, although changes to settlement were minor).

44. See *International Union of Elec., Salaried Mach. & Furniture Workers v. Unisys Corp.*, 858 F.Supp. 1243, 1264 (E.D. N.Y. 1994).

45. See *Phillips Petroleum Co. v. Shutts*, 472 U.S. 797, 811–12 (1985).

46. "Federal courts, however, recognize that absent class members hold a due process right to attack collaterally the res judicata effects of a class action judgment if the absent class members establish that the class representatives inadequately represented the interests of the class." *Tompkins v. Alabama State Univ.*, 15 F.Supp. 2d 1160, 1163 (N.D. Ala. 1998) (citing *Hansberry v. Lee*, 311 U.S. 32, 42–43 (1940); *Guthrie v. Evans*, 815 F.2d 626, 628 (11th Cir. 1987); *Gonzales v. Cassidy*, 474 F.2d 67, 74 (5th Cir. 1973)). But see *Epstein v. MCA Inc.*, 179 F.3d 641 (9th Cir. 1999) (declining to allow collateral attack where court certifying the class action made findings on adequacy).

47. See, e.g., *Georgine v. Amchem Products, Inc.*, 157 F.R.D. 246 (E.D. Pa. 1994), vacated, 83 F.3d 610 (3d Cir. 1996), aff'd sub nom. *Amchem Products, Inc. v. Windsor*, 521 U.S. 591 (1997). The court not once but repeatedly praised class counsel: ibid., 293–94 (reciting the "impressive" credentials of class counsel and emphasizing their long experience as leaders of the asbestos plaintiffs' bar); ibid., 294 (finding class counsel to be "highly respected for their skills and experience in asbestos litigation" and to "have the knowledge and credibility necessary to negotiate on behalf of future asbestos victims"); ibid., 329 ("All three Class Counsel were unquestionably experienced, highly respected leaders of the plaintiffs' asbestos bar."); ibid., 335 (describing class counsel as "extraordinarily competent and experienced" and "highly respected" and asserting that it is "clear to this Court that they intended to negotiate this settlement in compliance with the ethical rules"). See also *South Carolina Nat'l Bank v. Stone*, 139 F.R.D. 325, 331 (D.S.C. 1991) ("Plaintiffs' counsel have now practiced before this court in a number of securities fraud class actions, and the court is aware from first-hand experience of their competency in this complex area of law. The Court is satisfied that the plaintiffs and their class counsel will fairly and adequately protect the interests of the class."); and *In re Washington Pub. Power Supply Sys. Secs. Litig.*, 720 F. Supp. 1379, 1392 (D. Ariz. 1989) ("Both Class Counsel and counsel for Chemical Bank deem the settlements to be fair, reasonable, adequate and deserving of the Court's approval. Counsels' opinions warrant great weight both because of their considerable familiarity with this litigation and because of their extensive experience in similar actions").

48. See generally Susan P. Koniak, "Feasting While the Widow Weeps: *Georgine v. Amchem Products, Inc.,*" 80 *Cornell Law Review* 1045, 1057, 1090–92 (1995).

49. *Hoffman v. BancBoston Mortgage Corp.,* No. 91-1880 (Ala. Cir. Ct. Jan. 24, 1994). A subsequent malpractice suit by a class member against class counsel and the defendant bank's lawyers was dismissed on procedural grounds without considering the merits of the claims against the lawyers. *Kamilewicz v. Bank of Boston Corp.,* 92 F.3d 506 (7th Cir. 1996). For a comprehensive discussion and critique of these cases, see Koniak and Cohen, "Under Cloak of Settlement."

50. *Georgine v. Amchem Products, Inc.,* 157 F.R.D. 246 (E.D. Pa. 1994), vacated, 83 F.3d 610 (3d Cir. 1996), aff'd sub nom. *Amchem Products, Inc. v. Windsor,* 521 U.S. 591 (1997); *Ahearn v. Fibreboard,* 162 F.R.D. 505 (E.D. Tex. 1995), aff'd, *In re Asbestos Litigation,* 90 F.3d 1363 (5th Cir. 1996), vacated and remanded for reconsideration in light of *Amchem Products, Inc. v. Windsor,* 521 U.S. 591 (1997), aff'd on remand, 134 F.3d 668 (5th Cir. 1998), rev'd sub. nom. *Ortiz v. Fibreboard,* 119 S. Ct. 2295 (1999); *Spencer v. Shell Oil Co.,* No. 94-074 (Ala. Cir. Ct. 1995).

51. See, e.g., *Broin v. Phillip Morris Companies, Inc.,* 641 So.2d 888, 891 (1994) (settlement provided that those flight attendants with claims barred by the statute of limitations would have the statute waived to allow them the same relief as those without time-barred claims); *In re Paine Webber Short Term United States Government Income Fund Securities Litigation,* 1995 WL 512703 (S.D.N.Y. 1995) (approving settlement in which those with claims barred by the statute of limitations were provided the same relief as those without time-barred claims). Susan Koniak, one of the authors of this essay, testified as an expert witness in the *Paine Webber* fairness hearing on behalf of the objectors. She was paid for the time she spent preparing to testify and testifying. In her testimony, she criticized the settlement, inter alia, on the ground that those with time-barred claims were treated as if they were similarly situated to those with timely claims. The court rejected her testimony on this and other points.

52. A practice known as "confirmatory discovery" has developed in the settlement of class actions. See, e.g., "SFX Broadcasting Announces Settlement of Lawsuits," *Business Wire,* March 18, 1998 ("The settlement is conditioned on the consummation of the merger, the completion of confirmatory discovery, and approval of the court."); Michael A. Riccardi, "Philadelphia Lawyers Negotiate $30 Million Settlement in Securities Class Action," *The Legal Intelligencer,* September 5, 1997 ("The company said that 'confirmatory discovery' must take place as well as the negotiation of a detailed settlement stipulation."); "Micro Warehouse, Inc. Settles Class Action Lawsuit," *PR Newswire,* September 3, 1997 ("The agreement [to pay $30 million is contingent on completion of confirmatory discovery. . . ."); "Cigna Designs, Inc. Announces Tentative Settlement of Shareholder Claims," *Business Wire,* January 14, 1997 (describing settlement subject to confirmatory discovery). Confirmatory discovery refers to discovery class counsel conducts *after* agreeing to a settlement on behalf of the class.

53. See, e.g., *In re Prudential Insurance Company of America Sales Practices Litigation,* 177 F.R.D. 216, 232 (D.N.J. 1997); and *Zimmer Paper Products, Inc. v. Berger & Montague, P.C.,* 758 F.2d 86, 93–94 (3d Cir. 1985) (recognizing cause of action by class member against class counsel for negligence in providing notice).

54. See *Epstein v. MCA, Inc.,* 126 F.3d 1235 (9th Cir. 1996). Shareholders for a corporation acquired in a tender offer brought two related actions, the first one making claims under state corporate law and filed in Delaware state court, and the second making claims under the federal securities laws and filed in a California federal court. The trial court in the federal case granted the acquiring corporation's motion of summary judgment. While the shareholders' appeal in that suit was pending, the Delaware Chancery Court approved a settlement extinguishing the shareholders' state and federal claims, even though the state court did not have

jurisdiction over the federal claims. Although the court of appeals reversed that approval, 50 F.3d 644, the Supreme Court reversed the court of appeals, holding that the state court's judgment approving the settlement had preclusive effect in the federal courts under the Full Faith and Credit Act (516 U.S. 367). On remand, the court of appeals held that the Supreme Court had left open the issue of whether the settlement could be collaterally attacked on grounds of inadequate representation. The court of appeals further held that the adequate representation issue was not fully and fairly litigated in the state court suit, and so the consideration of the issue was not precluded in the federal suit; that the objectors' participation in the state settlement hearing did not bind absent class members on the adequate representation issue; that the shareholders could collaterally attack the adequacy of their representation at the state settlement hearing; that a conflict of interest between class counsel in the state court action and the plaintiff class rendered representation inadequate; and that the state class counsel's failure to vigorously pursue the class members' federal claims was inadequate representation.

55. The two judges in the majority did not agree on the rationale for reversing the prior decision. One judge concluded that the Supreme Court, in its opinion holding that the state court judgment approving the settlement was entitled to full faith and credit in the federal courts, had already implicitly held that the state court judgment did not violate due process; thus, there could be no collateral attack on the judgment. 179 F.3d at 644 (Opinion of O'Scannlain, J.). The judge who switched his vote did not agree that the Supreme Court had conclusively resolved the due process issue, but nevertheless found that the state courts had fully and fairly litigated the adequacy of representation, despite his personal reservations about the settlement. Ibid. at 650–51 (Opinion of Wiggins, J., concurring in the result). The full and fair litigation consisted of the state court's conclusory statement that the settlement was in the best interest of the class despite the charges of inadequate representation that several objectors had raised.

56. 119 S. Ct. at 2319 n.31 (stating that "the adequacy of representation inquiry is . . . concerned [not only with the adequacy of the named plaintiffs, but also] with the 'competency and conflicts of class counsel') (quoting *Amchem Prods. v. Windsor,* 531 U.S. 591, 626 n.20 (1997)).

57. Ibid. at 2319–20. According to the Court: "While at some point there must be an end to reclassification with separate counsel, these two instances of conflict are well within the requirement of structural protection recognized in *Amchem.*" Ibid. at 2320.

58. The discussion in this paragraph is based on Koniak, "Feasting," 1161–62.

59. Rule 23(a), discussing the prerequisites to a class action, states:

One or more members of a class may sue or be sued as representative parties on behalf of all only if (1) the class is so numerous that joinder of all members is impracticable, (2) there are questions of law or fact common to the class, (3) the claims or defenses of the representative parties are typical of the claims or defenses of the class, and (4) the representative parties will fairly and adequately protect the interests of the class. Federal Rules of Civil Procedure Rule 23[a].

Only recently did the Supreme Court suggest that these requirements could not be bargained away as part of a compromise settlement. *Amchem Products, Inc. v. Windsor,* 521 U.S. 591 (1997).

60. See, e.g., *TBK Partners v. Western Union Corp.,* 675 F.2d 456, 462 (2d Cir. 1982) (opposition of majority of the class "cannot serve as an automatic bar to a settlement").

61. 521 U.S. 591, 594–95 (1997).

62. The Supreme Court last term had before it *California Public Employees' Retirement*

System v. Felzen, 119 S. Ct. 720 (1999) in which the question was whether objectors must intervene in the proceeding to have standing to appeal. The Court wound up equally divided and so affirmed the court of appeals without an opinion. It is amazing that the question of an objector's relation to the proceeding and standing to appeal has remained uncertain for so long. For an argument that absent class members should have to object to the adequacy of class counsel at the fairness hearing or lose their chance to raise this issue later on collateral attack, see Marcel Kahan and Linda Silberman, "The Inadequate Search for 'Adequacy' in Class Actions: A Critique of Epstein v. MCA, Inc.," *New York University Law Review* 73 (1998): 765–92. But see *Phillips Petroleum Co. v. Shutts*, 472 U.S. 797, 802–03 (1985) (stating that absent class members, unlike parties, need not do anything to preserve their rights).

63. For example, courts have approved class action settlements in which the sole value exchanged was warrants, even over the objections of class members. See, e.g., *Hertz v. Canrad Precision Indus., Inc.* [1973 Transfer Binder] Fed. Sec. L. Rev. (CCH) ¶ 97,594 (S.D.N.Y. July 18, 1980); *Blank v. Talley Indus., Inc.*, 64 F.R.D. 125 (S.D.N.Y. 1974); *In re Brown Co. Sec. Litig.*, 355 F. Supp. 574 (S.D.N.Y. 1973).

64. Compare ABA Model Rules of Professional Conduct, Rule 1.13(d): "In dealing with an organization's directors, officers, employees, members, shareholders or other constituents, a lawyer shall explain the identity of the client when it is apparent that the organization's interests are adverse to those of the constituents with whom the lawyer is dealing."

65. See, e.g., David L. Shapiro, "Class Actions: The Class as Party and Client," *Notre Dame Law Review* 73 (1998): 913–61, at 917, 947.

66. See Susan P. Koniak and George M. Cohen, "Under Cloak of Settlement," 1133–39.

67. This warning (repeated in the title of this essay) is inspired by Grant Gilmore's famous closing to his book, *The Ages of American Law*: "In Heaven there will be no law, and the lion will lie down with the lamb. . . . In Hell there will be nothing but law, and due process will be meticulously observed." Grant Gilmore, *The Ages of American Law* 111 (New Haven, Conn.: Yale University Press, 1977).

PART V

Personal Identities and Professional Values

11

Beyond "Bleached out" Professionalism

*Defining Professional Responsibility
for Real Professionals*

DAVID B. WILKINS

Consider the following cases:

1. Anthony Griffin, a black lawyer affiliated with the ACLU, agrees to defend the Grand Dragon of the Ku Klux Klan. The case involves the state of Texas's attempt to subpoena the Klan's membership list in order to assist a probe into Klan violence against black residents in a newly integrated housing project. The African American head of the Port Arthur branch of the NAACP subsequently fires Griffin from his position as the unpaid general counsel for that organization when Griffin refuses to withdraw from representing the Klan.[1]

2. Judith Nathanson, a well-known Massachusetts divorce lawyer, is approached by Joseph Stropnicky to review a draft settlement agreement between he and his wife. Nathanson is well known for winning large settlements on behalf of women who have sacrificed their own careers to put their husbands through school while taking care of childcare and household responsibilities. Stropnicky is in precisely this situation, having put his former wife through medical school and delayed his own education for seven years while he stayed home as the primary homemaker and caregiver for the couple's children. Despite these similarities, Nathanson categorically refuses to represent Stropnicky on the ground that "she does not represent men." The Massachusetts Commission Against Discrimination subsequently concludes that Nathanson's "women only" policy violates her obligations as a "public accommodation" by discriminating in her selection of clients on the basis of gender.[2]

3. Gill Garcetti assigns a black prosecutor, Christopher Darden, to be one of the lead prosecutors in the racially charged prosecution of O.J. Simpson. During the course of the trial, Darden seeks to bar the defense from questioning Mark Fuhrman, a white police officer who found a damaging piece of evidence on Simpson's prop-

erty, about whether Fuhrman used racial epitaphs in the past. Subsequently, Johnnie Cochran, the black lead defense lawyer, argues to the predominately black jury that they should acquit his client in part as a means of "sending a message" that police racism and misconduct will not be tolerated.[3]

4. Robert Johnson, the elected black district attorney representing the Bronx, announces that he will refuse to seek the state's newly enacted death penalty in part because he believes it will inevitably be applied in a racially discriminatory manner. Subsequently, Governor Pataki removes Johnson from considering whether to seek the death penalty in a highly publicized case involving three minority youths accused of shooting a white police officer. Pataki replaces Johnson with a white lawyer who is a committed death penalty hawk.[4]

5. While representing Monica Lewinsky in connection with her possible appearance before the grand jury investigating President Clinton, William Ginsburg makes the following statement to an Israeli newspaper, "We are fans of president Clinton and admire his positions and policies concerning Israel. Clinton is very positive toward Israel and the Jews. Monica and I are Jews. I'm torn because I fear for the fate of the presidency in our democracy, and I don't want the president to resign. Who knows who will come after Clinton and how he will deal with Israel." When subsequently questioned about the propriety of this statement, Mr. Ginsburg responds, "I made the statement, I meant the statement, and I'm sincere about the statement. But my personal opinion has nothing to do with the Lewinsky matter. That's the point. The point is that the case is not about me. It's about our democracy. And so that particular statement, while it happens to be my opinion, has nothing to do with this case. As a lawyer, I could represent either or any side of this case. And my contention is we have to play by the rules."[5]

Each of these high profile cases has become a part of America's great conversation—or more accurately "angry polemic"[6]—about the importance of group-based identity in public life. For many Americans, these cases are proof that our legal system has been corrupted by identity politics. On this view, Johnny Cochran "played the race card" in his closing argument in the Simpson case; Robert Johnson allowed his personal agreement with his primarily minority constituency's opposition to the death penalty to undermine his professional obligations as the people's lawyer; and Nathanson and Ginsburg both illegitimately allowed group-based loyalties to undermine their ethical obligation as officers of a system committed to "gender-blind" or "religion-blind" justice. Many of these same individuals believe that lawyers like Griffin and Darden, who are willing to represent interests that appear to be opposed to those of other members of their group, deserve special praise for upholding the highest standards of professionalism in a manner destined to move America closer to the ideal of equal justice under law.

Other observers, however, take a different view. These observers applaud lawyers like Cochran, Johnson, and Nathanson for shedding light on the manner in which the legal system is anything but blind to the ascriptive characteristics of litigants and lawyers. Proponents of this view argue that it is officials like Governor Pataki and the Massachusetts Commission Against Discrimination who are actually undermining the fairness of our system of justice by sanctioning attorneys for seeking to protect members of their group from state oppression. Not surprisingly, these proponents typically reserve their harshest criticism for the lawyers most praised by the first group; that is, lawyers like Anthony Griffin and Christopher Darden, who, according to this way of thinking, are prepared to "sell out" their people for their own personal gain.

In this essay, I seek to move beyond these standard tropes and to set some preliminary ground work for thinking about the relationship between a lawyer's group-based identity and her professional role. Part I begins by examining the account of lawyer professionalism that underlies the traditional claim, captured by the first set of tropes, that professionalism requires lawyers to check their identities at the door when performing their professional roles. In this account, becoming a lawyer means adopting a "professional self" that supercedes all other aspects of a lawyer's identity. This self becomes the sole legitimate ground for actions taken within the confines of a lawyer's professional role. Professor Sanford Levinson aptly labels this traditional view "bleached out professionalism."[7] By instructing lawyers, clients, and the public that a lawyer's nonprofessional identity is irrelevant to her professional role, bleached out professionalism provides real and important benefits to those who produce and consume legal services and to our system of justice as a whole. Nevertheless, in Part II, I argue that bleached out professionalism fails as a professional ideal for real lawyers. As the second set of tropes underscores, bleached out professionalism neither accurately describes the manner in which real lawyers engage with their work, nor provides adequate answers for some of the most important ethical problems concerning the relationship between a lawyer's nonprofessional identity and her professional role. When all is said and done, this standard account of the lawyer's role reinforces an overly rigid understanding of lawyering that both curtails opportunities for the profession's traditional outsiders and inhibits innovation in the profession as a whole.

Part III, therefore, attempts to lay a foundation for a new understanding of the lawyer's role that moves beyond the limitations of bleached out professionalism without ignoring the important values that this traditional philosophy was designed to protect. I begin by arguing that the legitimacy of group-based considerations in professional decision making depends upon two contextual factors, (1) the moral standing of the group-based claim being asserted, and (2) the effect that asserting this claim will have on the lawyer's ability to carry out the legitimate social purposes of the specific lawyering role in question. I conclude by examining how these two criteria can help lawyers like those in the celebrated cases described above navigate the complex intersection between identity and professional role.

I. Identity and the Professionalism Project

The triumph of [this] . . . standard version of the professional project would . . . be the creation . . . of purely fungible [lawyers]. Such apparent aspects of the self as one's race, gender, religion, or ethnic background would become irrelevant to defining one's capacities as a lawyer.[8]

Professionalism is traditionally a greedy ideology.[9] In the standard view, becoming a professional involves more than simply performing a specific job or assuming a certain social standing. Instead, it involves becoming a particular kind of person; a person who both sees the world and acts according to normative standards and conventions that are distinct from those that govern nonprofessionals.[10] Through a complex process involving self-selection, professional education, collegial socialization, and the threat of professional discipline, individuals who enter into professions are presumed to adopt a new professional identity based on the unique norms and practices of their craft. This "professional self," in turn, subsumes all other aspects of a professional's identity—gender, race, ethnicity, religion—and becomes the sole legitimate basis for actions undertaken within the confines of his or her professional role.

Bleached out professionalism, as I will refer to this standard account, is central to the dominant model of American legal ethics. The legal profession has long claimed the right to define and inculcate its own normative standards and to enforce those standards through professional discipline. The resulting rules of professional conduct are explicitly cast in universalist terms that purport to apply to all lawyers in all contexts.[11] Moreover, when we shift our attention to the myths, lore, and narratives that lawyers have traditionally told themselves and the public about the nature of the lawyer's role, the claim that a lawyer's nonprofessional identity is (or at least ought to be) irrelevant to her professional role becomes even more salient.[12]

Consider, for example, the public's reaction to the possibility that racial considerations might have influenced the lawyers' conduct in the Simpson case. In addressing the so-called Darden Dilemma involving the alleged difficulties that black prosecutors such as Christopher Darden face in prosecuting black defendants, Ken Hamblin writes that society has a legitimate right to demand that anyone who becomes a prosecutor should "leave their biases behind to serve as the people's counsel."[13] Hamblin concludes that any minorities who believe that they have a "special allegiance to people of color" should "stop polluting the legal profession."[14] William Safire's charge that "Simpson's black attorney . . . blatantly urg[ed] [the predominately black jury] to ignore the evidence of murder and to get even for society's past injustices" reflects a similar assumption that Cochran improperly allowed racial considerations to "pollute" his legitimate obligations as defense counsel.[15] Even Gil Garcetti was accused of "play[ing] the race card" by assigning Darden to the case and by prosecuting Simpson in Los Angeles County, where there would likely be many blacks on the jury, rather than in virtually all-white Santa Monica County.[16]

Indeed, most of the participants in the celebrated cases described above, including virtually all those who have been accused of violating the norms of bleached out professionalism, have been careful to pay allegiance to this core professional ideal. Thus, Anthony Griffin sometimes claimed that race had "nothing to do" with his decision to represent the Klan,[17] branding as "racist" both "those black folks who told me I should have let a white lawyer take th[e] case" and "Anglos, who regarded me as some kind of oddity because I was a black man who represented the Klan."[18] Similarly, Darden flatly states that "[I]f I thought I was being assigned to the case primarily because I was black, I would've rejected it."[19] Nevertheless, Darden believes that for many Americans, he "was a black prosecutor, nothing more."[20] Even William Ginsburg, in the excerpt quoted at the beginning of this essay, claimed that his statement about his religion and Clinton's policy toward Israel "has nothing to do with this case" and that he "could represent either or any side" of the Clinton/Lewinsky matter.[21]

It is not surprising that bleached out professionalism has become a core professional ideal. Norms such as neutrality, objectivity, and predictability are central to American legal culture. Lawyers are the gatekeepers through which citizens gain access to these important legal goods. If the law is to treat individuals equally, the argument goes, than lawyers must not allow their nonprofessional commitments to interfere with their professional obligation to give their clients unfettered access to all that the law has to offer. A professional ideology that treats a lawyer's nonprofessional identity as relevant to her professional conduct appears to threaten this important role.

In addition to the benefits that bleached out professionalism offers to the consumers of legal services, it also appears to safeguard the interests of the women and men who become lawyers. The universalizing claims made on behalf of the professional self suggest that differences among those who become lawyers that might matter outside the professional sphere are irrelevant when evaluating these individuals' professional practices. This "professional" status is particularly important for the profession's new entrants—Jews, women, blacks, and other racial and religious minorities—who, in their nonprofessional lives, have been subject to discrimination on the basis of certain aspects of their identities. These traditional outsiders have a powerful stake in being viewed as lawyers *simpliciter*, freed by their professional status from the pervasive weight of negative identity-specific stereotypes. A professional ideology that explicitly recognizes the importance of a lawyer's nonprofessional identity runs the risk of reinforcing stereotypes about group membership in a manner that threatens the goal of ensuring equal opportunity within the profession.

Finally, bleached out professionalism appears to uphold the legal system's core commitment to the fundamental equality of persons. Thus, the idea that a lawyer's gender, race, or religion is irrelevant to her professional role seems to flow directly from the broader claim that the legal rules and procedures that lawyers interpret and implement should also be unaffected by identity. The claim that "our constitution"—and, indeed, justice itself—"is colorblind" (or "gender blind") is a bedrock principle of our legal order, and indeed of our public morality.[22] Lawyers who either explicitly or implicitly call attention to issues involving race or gender—including their own racial or gender identity—seemingly undermine this ideal.

Each of these three justifications for bleached out professionalism, (1) clients' need to receive a uniform professional product, (2) lawyers' (particularly lawyers from traditionally disadvantaged or marginalized groups) need to inherit the full trappings of professional standing, and (3) the public's need to reaffirm the fundamental equality of everyone before the law, stand as a powerful check against any attempt to modify or replace bleached out professionalism as a normative ideal for the American legal profession. Nevertheless, I will argue that we must do just that. To see why, it is necessary to look more closely at the justifications for—and, equally important, the costs of—this widely held, but rarely analyzed, professional ideal.

II. Unmasking the Professional Self

The claim that lawyers who interject identity issues into professional practice "pollute the legal profession" implicitly rests on the assumption that in the absence of this kind of intervention, identity-related considerations would *in fact* be irrelevant. This implicit factual assumption, however, is at best misleading, and at worst counterproductive, to creating appropriate ways for lawyers to respond to America's continuing failure to make good on its promise of providing equal justice under law. Three aspects of our contemporary environment make it crucial that lawyers account for the manner in which identity—including their own identity—continues to structure the legal rights of citizens. First, contrary to the "bleaching" metaphor, current understandings of lawyer professionalism continue to reflect the identities of those who founded the modern American legal profession. This historical legacy both undermines the normative claim that identity is "irrelevant" and poses important challenges for the careers of certain lawyers who do not share these identity characteristics. Second, what is true for lawyers is even more true for litigants. Although the American legal system promises that justice will be "blind" to identity, the reality is that certain groups continue to encounter substantial impediments to gaining access to the public goods encoded in law as a result of their identity. By obscuring this fact, bleached out professionalism fails to help lawyers determine how to respond to this reality. Finally, bleached out professionalism ignores the extent to which a lawyer's own identity affects that lawyer's ability to perform his or her job. Once we understand that lawyers will often not be able to "check" their identities at the door, it is not at all clear that instructing them to act as though their identities do not matter is the appropriate ethical response. The next three sections briefly explore each of these problems with the fundamental assumptions underlying bleached out professionalism. Part IV argues that, partly as a result of these limitations, there are benefits to certain forms of identity-conscious lawyering, benefits that must be weighed against the real—as opposed to ideal—benefits of bleached out professionalism in determining the role that identity should play in professional life.

Historicizing Professionalism

Proponents of bleached out professionalism implicitly assume that the profession's current norms and practices exist independent of any particular identity. History, however, teaches otherwise. Like every normative system, the current understanding of professional role was created at a particular time and a particular place. As many scholars have documented, this period was dominated by a handful of relatively homogeneous elite New York lawyers who wielded considerable influence over the creation of the modern professional ideal.[23] Moreover, these founders acted in an era in which various forms of identity-based discrimination were an accepted part of the legal and moral landscape. These initial conditions cast a continuing shadow over current understandings of professionalism.

Many of today's professional ideals can be traced to particular aspects of the identities of the profession's founding fathers.[24] For example, in his pioneering study of the American bar, Jerold Auerbach describes how the elite lawyers who created the rules of professional conduct raised entry requirements and pushed for stringent restrictions on commercial practices such as advertising and solicitation as a means of distancing themselves from the new wave of immigrant lawyers who, out of necessity, relied on many of these practices.[25] This historical legacy has lead Thomas and Mary Shaffer to characterize the prevailing understanding of the lawyer's role as "Gentleman's Ethics."[26] Other scholars assert that the understandings underlying the bleached out view of professionalism are in fact gendered. Starting from Carol Gilligan's influential hypothesis about gender differences in the moral reasoning styles of men and women, some feminist scholars have argued that the rigid, detached, hierarchical, and adversarial character of traditional notions of lawyer professionalism reflect a distinctly "male" identity.[27] Although many feminist scholars criticize this framework, the dramatic differences that have attended women's introduction into most spheres of contemporary social and political life support the idea that the presence of women at the creation of the modern understandings of professionalism would have "expand[ed] and transform[ed] the way we produce and use law."[28]

Even those who are not convinced that the content of professional norms are gendered will be hard pressed to deny that the traditional lawyer's career path was created to fit a male biography. The typical career path in a large law firm, for example, calls for a recent law school graduate to spend six to ten years locked in a highly competitive "tournament" at the end of which only a select few will be elevated to partnership.[29] This structure has been in existence since the early days of this century when it was pioneered by Paul Cravath and a handful of other prominent New York and Boston lawyers. Both then and now, firm leaders have justified their use of the "Cravath System" in distinctly professional terms.[30] This system of professional development, created at a time when women were formally barred from most elite firms, disproportionately burdens women lawyers. The six- to ten-year period after law school coincides almost exactly with a woman's prime childbearing years. Women, therefore, are faced with the choice of either postponing—and possibly forgoing—childbearing or adding childcare demands to the already substantial pressure of their work at the firm. Male associates, particularly those with wives who do not work outside of the home (or who have careers less demanding than those of a corporate associate) are not put to this choice. It is this particular kind of male identity—men with wives who do not work—that underlies the bleached out understanding of professional career development in elite firms.

This last point, that bleached out professionalism masks the gendered dimension of the typical legal career path at a large law firm, underscores the second problem with this traditional professional ideal; its failure to account for the extent to which the legacy of historic discrimination against certain groups continues to affect their ability to participate equally in our system of justice. For even if it were possible to truly bleach out of contemporary notions of professionalism all of the tell-tale residue of the identities of the profession's founding fathers, lawyers would still be left with the problem of how to respond to continuing identity-based discrimination. Once again, bleached out professionalism leaves lawyers ill prepared for this important task.

Conscious Blinding

Equal Justice under Law may be a core legitimating ideal of the American legal system, but it is hardly a reality. Although most of the trappings of de jure segregation have been eliminated in the last quarter century, blacks, women, gays and lesbians, Jews, and a number of other Americans continue to face substantial obstacles to obtaining equal access to the benefits and protections of the law; obstacles that are complexly, but nevertheless directly, connected to their identities.[31]

Bleached out professionalism tends to obscure this reality. One can, of course, subscribe to colorblindness as a normative ideal without also believing that our legal institutions fully, or even largely, live up to this ideal in practice. Too often, however, proponents of the ideal of colorblindness conflate these two propositions. This conflation, in turn, strengthens the claim that lawyers must bleach their minds and their actions of any reference to identity.

Jeffrey Rosen's critique of Cochran's "send a message" argument demonstrates how bleached out professionalism implicitly rests on factual claims about colorblindness.[32] Rosen identifies Cochran's decision to interject race into the Simpson trial as an example of how blacks and other minorities "[a]scrib[e] sympathetic attributes of victimhood to a defendant because of his race" based on claims about the continuing existence of widespread racism.[33] Rosen asserts, however, that such claims are false—not on the basis of any empirical argument, but rather, as Frank

Michelman argues, because "the premise of institutional racism carries normative and prescriptive implications at odds with liberal ideals of colorblindness and individual responsibility, and *for that reason* cannot be entertained in legal argument."[34] This a priori linkage between bleached out professionalism and the presumed reality of colorblindness puts black lawyers who have either experienced or witnessed the gap between the ideal and the actual of colorblindness in American law in a particular bind: "[they] must deny the realities of racism in order to appear balanced and fair in advancing the case of the client."[35]

If America is to come closer to fulfilling its promise of equal justice under law in the twenty-first century than it did in the one that just closed, then lawyers must find ways to acknowledge and account for the ways in which legal norms and practices—including some of those at the core of contemporary understandings of legal professionalism—continue disproportionately to disadvantage the members of certain identifiable identity groups. Bleached out professionalism, by perpetuating the false claim that identity is irrelevant in both professional norms and everyday life, takes us away from this important task. It also deflects attention from the manner in which a lawyer's own race can affect the outcome of a legal proceeding.

The Persistence of Identity

Bleached out professionalism rests on some combination of factual and normative claims about whether others are likely to view a given lawyer as bleached. Factually, the model seems to assume that if lawyers ignore their nonprofessional identity, that others will do the same; that is, that lawyers and nonlawyers alike will treat individual lawyers as generic ones, without reference to the contingent features of a given lawyer's identity. Alternatively, the model rests on the normative claim that lawyers should act as though others do not notice their identity even if they in fact do. Neither the factual nor the normative aspects of this argument are persuasive.

Empirical and anecdotal research confirms that contingent features of a person's identity exert a strong influence over how that person perceives and is perceived by others. For example, in his pioneering work on careers and developmental relationships inside corporations, David Thomas reports that race and gender significantly influence conduct and perceptions within organizations.[36] This influence takes many forms. Chief among them is the preference that senior mentors have for protégés who remind them of themselves. White men, as Thomas's work repeatedly demonstrates, feel more comfortable in working relationships with other white men. My own research on law firms suggests that, notwithstanding their professional training, lawyers are not immune to this tendency.[37]

The fact that perceptions and judgments are likely to be filtered through the prism of identity has important implications for lawyers. Consider, for example, Anthony Griffin's decision to represent the Ku Klux Klan. Griffin repeatedly stated that his identity as a black man was irrelevant to his decision to represent the Klan. Nevertheless, it is perfectly clear that other relevant actors, including Griffin's client, viewed Griffin's race as highly relevant. After recovering from the initial shock of discovering that he had been assigned a black lawyer, the Grand Dragon of the Ku Klux Klan gleefully exclaimed, "[i]t couldn't get any better than this. . . . I need a minority in my corner."[38] Similarly, Griffin's race may also have made it easier for the Klan to vindicate its position in the courts and in the court of public opinion. As Griffin himself acknowledged, his presence in the case "dramatically underscores" the importance of the Klan's legal position.[39] At the same time, many Americans may take the fact that the Klan was able to secure the services of a black lawyer as a sign that the Klan is at worst a "fringe" organization of no real consequence instead of the viscous terrorist organization that it really is. For their part, the black residents in the housing project who were being subjected to Klan violence and intimidation are likely to feel a special sense of agrievement knowing that those who terrorize them are being defended by a black lawyer.

Proponents of bleached out professionalism might offer two responses to this reality. First, advocates of this view might contend that regardless of what others actually do or think, a lawyer should always act as though his or her identity were irrelevant. Second, they might assert that by urging lawyers and the public at large to ignore contingent features of a lawyer's identity, bleached out professionalism constitutes the best way of minimizing the use of race and other identity-related characteristics in professional action, even if such use cannot be eliminated entirely.

The first of these responses is unpersuasive. Even taken on the narrow terms bleached out professionalism suggests, a lawyer would be foolish to ignore information concerning how his or her actions are likely to be received by relevant decision makers. Consider, once again, the Simpson prosecution. Assuming for the moment that black jurors would have had a more difficult time believing the state's case if the entire prosecution team had been white, Garcetti, as the chief prosecutor, was obligated to consider this reality when deciding how to meet his professional responsibility to present the state's case in its most persuasive light. I return below to the question of whether adding Darden to the prosecution team was a reasonable way of meeting this obligation. For the moment, my point simply is that in order to answer the question of whether it was ethically permissible to add Darden, Garcetti and the other white lawyers on the team had to notice the fact that underlying racial attitudes in society threatened to make their own racial identity an impediment to their client's cause.

When we broaden our ethical focus beyond the narrow question of what is best for the client, it becomes even more clear that ignoring the actual role that one's identity is playing in a particular situation is not always the appropriate ethical response. Darden, Griffin, and Nathanson should all recognize that when they represent clients whose interests are, or appear to be, opposed to the interests of some substantial number of those who share their respective identities, that their presence at counsel table sends messages—perhaps unintended but nevertheless predictable—about the merits, or at least the respectability, of these causes. As independent moral agents, they have a responsibility to account for these consequences. To be sure, when a jury, for example, assumes that the Klan is less dangerous because it is represented by a black lawyer, it is engaging in the worst form of group stereotyping. The fact that it is the wrongful conduct of others that makes a lawyer's identity relevant to her professional actions, however, does not relieve the lawyer of the moral responsibility to respond appropriately to the situation in which she finds herself. What constitutes an appropriate response will depend on many factors, including whether the predicament the lawyer faces is due to the wrongful conduct of others. Thus, as I will argue below, Griffin did not have an obligation to refuse to represent the Klan simply because some whites might interpret his willingness to do so as evidence that the Klan is harmless. He did, however, have an obligation to respond to how his race was affecting the Klan's cause; an obligation that bleached out professionalism implicitly denies.

Given that there are both professional and moral costs to ignoring the extent to which identity effects a lawyer's professional role, the persuasiveness of the second defense offered by proponents of bleached out professionalism—that by preaching that identity ought to be irrelevant, bleached out professionalism is the best hope of making this ideal a reality—will depend upon which is the greater harm: the harm that moving away from bleached out professionalism might cause in terms of reinforcing identity consciousness, or the harm created by ignoring the identity consciousness of others that already exists. This calculus, however, is far more complex than bleached out professionalism's supporters typically acknowledge.

Recognizing the extent to which identity continues to structure the legal process may very well encourage lawyers and others to focus somewhat more on identity issues. One can see this effect in the press's reaction to the presentation by Cheryl Mills, a black woman, on behalf of President Clinton during the impeachment trial. Mills expressly called on her identity as a black woman in refuting the House managers' charge that acquitting the president would be "bad for civil rights."[40] Not surprisingly, the press and others picked up on this argument and emphasized Mills's identity as a black woman when reporting her argument.[41]

Even conceding this effect, however, it is far less clear that instructing lawyers to refrain from acknowledging the manner in which their identities affect their professional role will discourage others from drawing identity-related conclusions. To stick with the impeachment proceedings, Clinton was also represented by Nicole Seligman, a white woman partner at Williams & Connolly. Unlike Mills, Seligman never mentioned either her race or her gender during the course of her defense of the president. Nevertheless, many in the press and public speculated that, like Mills, one of the reasons Seligman was selected to present part of the president's defense—and, even more important, to question Monica Lewinsky at her deposition—was that White House strategists believed that her presence undermined the contention that the president is hostile to women.

Of course, both Mills and Seligman might contend that they do not view the fact that their respective identities had the effect of bolstering the credibility of their arguments on behalf of the president as a "cost" because they are each convinced that his arguments are meritorious and deserve to prevail. Alternatively, they might contend that whether or not the president's arguments have merit, that they as advocates ought to have the same right to deploy their identities—along with their intelligence, knowledge, and skill—for their client's cause as white men have to deploy theirs. After all, Mills and Seligman were not the only lawyers who lent the credibility that flowed from their nonprofessional identity to the president's cause. To the contrary, Clinton reserved his most egregious assault on the ideology of bleached out professionalism for last when he enlisted former Senator Dale Bumpers to sum up his case. Bumpers was clearly selected because of his identity as a former United States senator, an identity that given the historical make up of the Senate, is not unrelated to his identity as a white male.[42] All of this brings us to a subject completely overlooked by bleached out professionalism: the value of allowing lawyers to bring their identities to their roles.

The Value of Identity Consciousness

Proponents of bleached out professionalism assume that identity consciousness is simply an impediment to efficient and ethical professional service. This view, however, ignores the extent to which identity-related issues have played a positive role for each of the three constituencies bleached out professionalism is designed to serve: clients, lawyers, and the legal system.

From the consumers' perspective, bleached out professionalism tends to discourage innovation in the delivery of professional services. Many of the most powerful critiques of current professional norms have been launched in the name of particular identities. Consider, for example, the feminist critique of adversary ethics discussed above. Not surprisingly, feminist scholars who support this critique have been in the forefront of the alternative dispute resolution movement.[43] This movement has, in turn, had a profound impact on lawyers—both male and female—and on clients. Although many of the movement's tenants and proposals remain controversial, few would deny that many clients have benefited from having access to a broader range of dispute processing alternatives.

One can tell a similar story about the critique mounted by blacks and other minorities of traditional hiring and evaluation policies in large law firms. Many corporate clients increasingly see good reasons to value law firm diversity in circumstances where those who are resisting greater integration in the name of "professional" standards may not. Consider a company that is being sued for dumping a dangerous chemical into a largely minority community in New Orleans, or an investment bank seeking to sell financial services to the city of Detroit, or a large bank that is seeking to diversify both its own work force and (with the gentle prodding of the federal government through the Community Reinvestment Act) its customer base. In each of these scenarios, the client is likely to see it as in its self-interest to be represented by a law firm that has one or more minority partners. Traditional bleached out practices that get in the way of this result are therefore arguably not in the client's best interests.

Indeed, contrary to the standard assumption of those who argue that lawyers should never allow their nonprofessional identities to influence their professional roles, sometimes it is precisely these identity-related commitments that provide the impetus for a lawyer to fulfill his or her most difficult role-specific obligations. Griffin, Nathanson, Johnson, Darden, and Cochran directly called on aspects of their nonprofessional identities when taking actions within the confines of their professional roles. In each case, however, one important consequence of this integration of identity and role was to *reinforce*, at great personal cost, professional norms. Thus, Anthony Griffin's strong suspicion of state power is rooted in his experience as a black man growing up in the South.[44] This suspicion, in turn, underlies his personal commitment to the ACLU and its strong support of First Amendment rights—a commitment that leads Griffin to uphold bleached out professionalism's highest aspirational goal of making legal counsel available to clients with unpopular views. Nathanson's strong feminist commitments have led her to devote her professional life to "remedying continuing gender discrimination against women in the area of family law and eradicating gender bias in the courts."[45] Similarly, Robert Johnson's opposition to the death penalty, rooted in his experience in and commitment to the black community, was the motivating force behind his willingness to risk his career in an effort to prevent the state from pursuing a course of action that threatens the legal profession's central bleached out maxim: the promise of equal justice under law. Finally, both Darden and Cochran directly called on their experiences as African American men to support their mutual professional obligation to advocate zealously for their respective client's positions regarding the admission of Fuhrman's prior racist statements.[46] As Alan Dershowitz eloquently argues in a related context:

> I know I chose to become a criminal defense lawyer at least in part because I am Jewish. I was taught from the earliest age that Jews must always remember that they were persecuted, and that we must stand up for those who now face prosecution. "Thou shall not stand idly by the blood of thy neighbor" was more than a slogan. "Repair the world" was an imperative. . . . I always wanted to be a Jewish lawyer, and, though many Jews disapprove of some of my clients, I believe I am a lawyer in the Jewish tradition.[47]

Group-based moral commitments need not undermine traditional role obligations. Sometimes they provide the very motivation that makes these difficult professional obligations possible.

Acknowledging a greater role for identity-specific professional commitments can also help the legal profession fulfill its fundamental mandate of promoting social justice. Consider, for example, the evolving role that black lawyers have played in the struggle for racial justice in the United States. The legal campaign to end "separate but equal" was spearheaded by Charles Hamilton Houston, Thurgood Marshall, and an elite core of black lawyers.[48] These black "social engineers" took an expressly racialist approach to their work as lawyers. As vice dean of Howard Law School in the 1930s, Houston expressly taught his students that they had an obligation to use their legal talents to improve the status of the black community.[49] Although this stance did not prevent Houston and his protégé Thurgood Marshall from forming valuable and enduring relationships with white lawyers, it was a direct call on black attorneys to carry their racial identity into their professional role.

Today, many of the brightest and best-educated black lawyers spend some or all of their careers working in large corporate law firms, in corporate legal departments, or otherwise servicing the needs of large corporations.[50] At first blush, it appears that these lawyers will have little to do with helping African Americans achieve social justice. There is, however, another way to look at the connection between black corporate lawyers and the social justice concerns of the African American community. Although these women and men may never be as directly involved in the struggle for racial justice as their forebearers in the civil rights movement, they nevertheless have important opportunities to contribute to this cause. These contributions include challenging stereotypes about black intellectual inferiority; acting as "role models" for other African Americans; helping to open up additional opportunities for blacks in law and elsewhere; directing their own resources and the resources of their employers toward projects that will benefit the black community; using corporate practice as a springboard to gain political influence to assist black causes; and persuading their powerful clients to act in ways that are less harmful (and perhaps even beneficial) to the interests of the black community.

In order to achieve these benefits, however, black lawyers must reject bleached out professionalism. Even the most modest of the above proposals—breaking stereotypes—requires that black corporate lawyers be seen as black. If they are not, their success will be dismissed as exceptional or idiosyncratic and will not benefit other blacks. The same can be said for "role model" arguments, particularly those that assume that black lawyers will take active steps—for example, challenging traditional hiring criteria—to open doors for other blacks. The last three options—devoting resources (including firm resources) to black causes, mobilizing political power for the black community, and counseling clients to refrain from injuring (and perhaps even to help) the fight for racial justice—all assume that black lawyers will incorporate the interests of the black community into their actions as lawyers in particular cases, and more generally, in designing a morally acceptable professional career.

Indeed, black lawyers have good grounds for rejecting the claims of bleached out professionalism apart from the concerns of social justice. For many blacks, having a strong sense of connection to the black community is an important source of strength and well-being in an otherwise hostile world. Bleached out professionalism suggests that these feelings must be confined to the "private" realm. At a minimum, such an attitude, to paraphrase Robert Gordon in a related context, is likely to produce "schizoid" lawyers who can never truly embrace either their identities or their roles.[51]

The true costs of bleached out professionalism for the personal integrity of a lawyer whose nonprofessional identity is central to her sense of self, however, may be a good deal higher than even the schizoid analogy suggests. As Professor Richard Wasserstrom trenchantly argues, the greedy claims of the professional self often extend beyond the confines of the role itself:

> [T]o become and to be a professional, such as a lawyer, is to incorporate within oneself ways of behaving and ways of thinking that shape the whole person. . . . In important respects, one's professional role becomes and is one's dominant role, so that for many persons at least they become their professional being.[52]

Moreover, if recent history is any indication, the demands of the professional self—and, therefore, of bleached out professionalism—are likely to become even more capacious than they are today. Lawyers are working longer hours than ever before, leaving little time for "personal" activities or commitments.[53] At the same time, clients are demanding ever greater loyalty from their lawyers, seeking to block any professional activities that might conflict with the client's pursuit of its own interests,[54] and turning lawyers into all-purpose public relations firms. Black lawyers who subscribe to this latest version of bleached out professionalism will find little if any space to act on their commitments to other African Americans.

A diminished space for race-based commitments harms black lawyers who value solidarity and, surprisingly, even those who do not. For blacks who value their connection to the black community, the capacious demands of modern bleached out professionalism are likely to produce an unhealthy alienation since, to quote Stephen Carter, "the light of solidarity, like the light of love, will go out if not carefully tended."[55] Even for those who eschew feelings of racial solidarity, however, the inability to participate in collective struggles to advance the interests of the black community is likely to be self-destructive. As Martin Kilson argues, even "self-identifying" blacks should recognize that if they do not "aggregate themselves into organizations and coalitions to combat the massive vestiges of American racism, no amount of . . . [individual] development is either conceivable or attainable."[56] At a minimum, this danger must be balanced against the perceived benefits of bleached out professionalism to black lawyers.

This last point underscores that the cost–benefit assessment of bleached out professionalism is a good deal more complex than the proponents of this standard ideal typically suggest. As I indicated at the outset, clients, lawyers, and the public benefit from a uniform understanding of the lawyer's role. Once we expose the assumptions underlying this ideology, however, these benefits are likely to be a good deal less robust than they might at first appear. Bleached out professionalism discourages clients and the public from acknowledging the ways in which identity inevitably shapes lawyer conduct, examining which of these uses are normatively problematic and creating a coherent account of how the conflicting demands of identity and role might be balanced in particular cases. Moreover, for certain lawyers—those whose nonprofessional identities play a crucial role in their own lives and in the lives of other members of their group—bleached out professionalism runs the risk of alienating these lawyers from themselves and their communities.

III. Toward a Theory of Identity-Conscious Professionalism

We are left, therefore, with a quandary: How can we preserve the values underlying bleached out professionalism while at the same time recognizing that this ideology neither can nor should be as "greedy" as traditionally understood. A comprehensive answer to this complex and important question would require far more space than I have here.[57] Instead, I want to argue that any attempt to integrate identity and professional role must address two related issues: the *moral justification* for considering any specific identity-related issue and the *social purposes* of the specific lawyering role into which the identity-related consideration is to be incorporated. I conclude by briefly explaining these concepts and applying them to the cases presented at the beginning of this article.

The Differing Moral Justifications for Identity Consciousness

Any proposal to allow lawyers to consider aspects of their nonprofessional identities in performing their professional roles must answer one fundamental challenge: What is the *moral* justification for allowing identity to influence *any* decision? As bleached out professionalism emphasizes, ours is a political community predicated on the fundamental moral equality of all persons. How can a contingent feature of an individual's identity—her race, gender, religion, or sexual orientation—have any bearing on how she should act in the world or treat any other human being?

The universal respect and concern that we owe to each other as human beings does indeed stand as a constant check against excessive particularism in all of our relationships. But this does not mean that we are morally obligated not to consider contingent features of our own identities, and those of others, when acting in particular situations. To the contrary, sometimes we are morally required to do so.

Proponents of bleached out professionalism assume that "blindness"—color-blindness, gender blindness, religion blindness—is a fundamental principle of justice. Although intuitively appealing, this argument conflates ideal theory with the morality that should govern us in the real world. As Amy Gutmann argues, although "blindness" may be the just policy in an ideal society, it is not the correct moral stance in a nonideal society such as ours where benefits and burdens continue to be distributed on the basis of identity characteristics such as race and gender.[58] Identity-blind policies treat individuals fairly when racism, sexism, and other forms of disadvantage based on identity no longer effect the lives of citizens. But when identity continues to exert a major influence on the ability of citizens to participate equally in public and private life, as it surely does in the United States, identity-conscious policies may be the only way to accord individuals the fair treatment that is their moral due. Fairness, not colorblindness, is the fundamental principle of justice in a nonideal world such as our own.

Not all forms of identity consciousness, however, are likely to promote fairness. Quite the contrary. The most dominant and prevalent form of identity consciousness in the United States, the long and sorry history of many white Americans believing in the inherent inferiority of anyone who does not share their identity, has been and continues to be one of the major impediments to the fair treatment of millions of citizens. Nor are the evils of identity consciousness restricted to situations in which a dominant group seeks to oppress a subordinate group. To continue with the example of race, nothing in America's long history of racial oppression against African Americans justifies the view that blacks cannot be racist or engage in the racist oppression of others.

That calls for group solidarity and advancement have been a part of some of this country's worst atrocities, however, does not mean, as advocates of bleached out professionalism insist, that all forms of identity consciousness should be suppressed. To do so, as I argued in Part II, quite literally "blinds" us to both the continuing significance of identity and its real costs and benefits. Instead, what is needed is critical reflection on the morality of particular identity-related claims in specific circumstances. Bleached out professionalism, like other universalizing tendencies inherent in the traditional model of legal practice, reduce all identity-related questions to a single yes or no answer. Either identity consciousness is "good," in which case white pride is a morally praiseworthy goal, or it is "bad," in which case black racial pride is simply a form of racism.[59] This way of framing the issue ignores important differences in the moral standing of various forms of identity consciousness.

Identity consciousness can take many different forms and play many different roles. One can group the forms of identity consciousness most relevant to bleached out professionalism into three broad categories.[60] At the most basic level, identity consciousness can help individuals "notice" the extent to which identity—both their own and others—continues to effect their own lives and the life chances of other citizens. Second, identity consciousness can be an essential attribute of self-understanding and self-worth. Finally, identity consciousness gives individuals special reasons for caring about others who share their identity and to work together to advance the interests of their group.

At this level of generality, it should be clear that each of these effects of identity consciousness can both contribute to and undermine important moral values. Thus, "noticing" identity can promote a healthy understanding of the continuing effects of discrimination or it can produce a vision of the world in which everyone has to be classified in terms of their morphology, biology, or beliefs; a view that can quickly degenerate into a tendency to meld all of these disparate factors into one overarching categorical scheme about human nature.[61] Connecting one's self-worth to the "recognition" of one's identity as a black (or as a woman, or as a Jew, or as a gay man) can be an essential step toward being treated as a whole human being, but it can also produce "scripts" about the proper way to be black (or a woman, or Jewish, or gay) that deny our individual humanity.[62] And caring about the welfare and advancement of group members can either help to produce a more equitable society or contribute to the oppression of one group over another.

When we look more closely at our contemporary situation, however, it is apparent that certain kinds of identity consciousness, based on certain kinds of identity, are more likely than others to produce either positive or negative effects. Thus, the first kind of identity consciousness—noticing how identity affects you and the world—is, in our contemporary era, both the least problematic and the most applicable to all forms of identity. Given the extent to which race continues to shape the lives of millions of individuals in this country, for example, one can make a strong argument that all Americans would benefit from a heightened degree of consciousness about racial identity. With the exception of white supremacists and the most committed multiculturalists, white Americans rarely see themselves as having a "racial" identity separate and apart from their identity as "Americans." Although the continuing legacy of racial discrimination in the United States ensures that most black Americans have a strong sense of their own racial identity, as well as of the racial identity of whites, both blacks and whites frequently have only a limited understanding of racial identities other than "black" and "white."[63]

Collectively, this state of affairs makes it more difficult to achieve racial justice. The fact that whites do not see themselves as "raced" frequently blinds them to the extent to which they enjoy important privileges simply because of the color of their skin—whether they intend to or not.[64] As a result, blacks must continually bear the burden of pointing out racial injustice and of convincing whites that their claims are valid.[65] At the same time, the fact that both blacks and whites overlook America's other racial minorities tends to obscure discrimination (by both blacks and whites) against these other groups while at the same time forcing other minorities into seeing themselves as either "like" or "not like" blacks.[66] A greater degree of race consciousness on the part of all Americans would help all groups to gain a better appreciation of the full extent of our continuing race problem.

One can see the benefits of this first form of identity consciousness by comparing Gil Garcetti's actions in the Simpson case with Governor Pataki's in the Johnson case. Garcetti took concerted steps to ensure that Simpson would be prosecuted in a jurisdiction where there were likely to be black jurors, by a prosecution team that included at least one prominent black lawyer. In the next section, I will argue that these race-conscious actions supported, rather than undermined, the social purposes of Garcetti's role as district attorney. For present purposes, however, it is important to note that Garcetti would not have been able to take these important steps unless he had first "noticed" the manner in which race was likely to play an important role in the case. Although Garcetti, like virtually all of the other participants in the case, initially took the position that race was not an issue in the Simpson prosecution,[67] this standard bleached out view was clearly false. Long before Fuhrman's racism or the racial composition of the jury surfaced as issues in the case, the simple fact that a black man was accused of murdering his white ex-wife and her handsome white friend ensured that race was likely to play an important role in how many participants in the process viewed the case. By coming to terms with this reality, Garcetti helped to produce a proceeding that would protect Simpson from unfair inferences based on the color of his skin.

Pataki's decision to replace Robert Johnson with a white attorney who was a committed death penalty hawk had the opposite effect. Once again, in the next section I will argue that the social purposes underlying the role of district attorney support Pataki's decision to remove Johnson. But by not "noticing" how race affects capital punishment cases, Pataki's actions arguably further entrenched existing racial divisions about the administration of capital punishment. For reasons that have been well documented, black citizens have reason to believe that equal justice under law is often not achieved in practice. This is particularly true in cases involving the death penalty. There is substantial evidence that race does play an important role in whether prosecutors seek the death penalty and whether juries are likely to impose this punishment.[68] Replacing a black district attorney who has expressly attempted to take this reality into account with a white lawyer who is a known death penalty hawk sends a powerful message to the black constituents of this district that their concerns about the discriminatory nature of capital punishment will not be heard.

Evaluating the moral weight of the remaining two arguments in favor of identity consciousness requires paying greater attention to context. Consider the second argument, that identity consciousness is an essential part of recognizing the fundamental equality of persons. Although many aspects of an individual's identity may be *personally* meaningful, not all of these attributes are *socially* important. Intelligence, beauty, habits, and interests all undoubtedly play a significant role in constructing one's sense of one's self as a unique human being. These attributes, however, do not form the basis of social groupings in any meaningful sense. Thus the claim that someone should be "recognized" in a social, as opposed to an individual, way as being a member of "the beautiful people," or "bridge players," or "compulsive eaters" simply misses the point of why society (as opposed to individuals) ought to value group identity.[69]

Nor is it even the case that all social forms of identity are equal candidates for social recognition on the ground that doing so is essential to treating the bearers of these identities as social equals. Although everyone has a gender, a sexual orientation, a social class, and a race (even if with respect to each of these categories, particular individuals straddle existing definitions), it is not true that all of these admittedly "social" distinctions have the same meaning either for individuals or for society as a whole. As I argued above, white Americans typically do not have a strong sense of racial identity. Black Americans typically do. As a result, a white American's and a black American's claim to be recognized *as* white or *as* black stand on substantially different ethical footing. Although whites should not be discriminated against *because* of their race, given America's history of ignoring—or privileging—white racial identity, recognizing whites *as* whites is not an essential part of treating whites equally. For black Americans, on the other hand, not to recognize race is to deny a key aspect of the everyday reality of the black experience. Not surprisingly, this everyday reality has made race a central component of the self-understanding of many blacks. But even for those who would rather reject race consciousness, the fact that their lives continue to be structured (albeit, not defined) by race means that being socially recognized *as* black is an essential part of being treated as an equal human being—and not just a human being who is equal *despite* being black.

Other forms of social identity—gender, sexual orientation, religion—will have their own unique claims for recognition. In order to evaluate the merits of these claims for identity consciousness based on the need to recognize the moral equality of certain individuals, one must first examine the historical and contemporary connections between the identity in question and the moral worth of persons. My point simply is that the results of such an examination are unlikely to be the same for all identities.

Let me be clear here. Individuals undoubtedly find important meaning in many aspects of their own identity and in their connection to others. For these attributes to be socially recognized, however, they must be linked in some important way to society's fundamental commitment to honor the equal moral worth of all human beings. And it is this claim—the claim that society should reject bleached out professionalism because it fails to recognize the ways in which identity consciousness facilitates treating individuals as moral equals—that is at the core of this second argument for allowing lawyers to bring their identities to their social roles as lawyers.

A recent case involving an avowed white supremacist's attempt to gain admission to the Illinois Bar highlights this distinction. Matthew Hale is the head of the World Church of the Creator, a quasi-religious organization dedicated to producing a racial holy war to "cleanse" America of blacks, Jews, and other racial and religious minorities. Clearly for Hale, his racial and religious identities are central to his understanding of his own self-worth. Nevertheless, for the Illinois Bar (or any other public organization) to "recognize" this part of Hale's identity—by accepting him *as* a white supremacist or otherwise sanctioning his racist views—would violate the basic moral injunction to treat all individuals fairly as moral equals. Whether or not this moral commitment to equality is sufficient to keep Hale out of the bar altogether is a close question that turns on whether the mere fact that an applicant holds racist views sufficiently undermines the social purpose of the lawyer's role in a manner that justifies his exclusion. I will return to this subject below. What is clear, however, is that if Hale, once admitted to the bar, were to act on the basis of his racist views—in other words, if he were to bring this aspect of his identity to his role—the bar would be justified in expelling him in order to preserve its fundamental commitment to equal justice under law.

Recognizing the connection between a black lawyer's racial identity and his or her moral personality, however, will (at least in some cases) further the goal of fairness. Consider, for example, Anthony Griffin's decision to represent the Ku Klux Klan. Assume for the moment that Griffin did not want to represent the Klan because he did not want his racial identity to be used by an organization committed to exterminating blacks. In the next section, I will argue that a proper understanding of the social purposes underlying the rules about client selection support Griffin's right to make this decision. For the moment, however, I want to emphasize that, unlike Hale's case, Griffin's decision to bring this part of his identity to his role would have been morally justified. Although some theorists believe that lawyers surrender their moral autonomy simply by becoming lawyers, such a requirement would demand too much. Given our society's commitment to both individual autonomy and moral pluralism, it would be wrong for the state (or the profession) to require an individual to commit a moral wrong for the sake of the greater good. This is why, for example, we allow conscientious objection from military service. And, like soldiers, lawyers must *advocate* for their clients. As the Klan's lawyer, Griffin was obligated to present arguments zealously on the Klan's behalf; arguments that both Griffin and his client acknowledged were likely to be perceived as being more credible precisely because Griffin was black. To refuse to allow Griffin to conscientiously object to lending his moral authority to a cause that he finds morally repugnant would be to fail to treat him as a moral equal.

The moral justifications for the last argument in favor of identity consciousness—that it promotes political efforts for group advancement—also vary by context. In Part II, I argued that identity consciousness for black lawyers facilitates projects for the collective advancement of black Americans as a whole. In order for such projects to be morally justified on fairness grounds—as opposed simply to being in the self-interest of blacks—there must be a plausible link between the specific project for group advancement and the unjustified status of the black community. In today's America, this link will often be easy to draw. Black Americans continue to lag behind whites in virtually every category connected with material wealth or social and political power. Although the reasons for this continued inequality are multiple and complex, there can be no serious doubt that racial prejudice, both in the past and in the present, is a substantial contributing factor.

Nevertheless, not every project for group advancement proposed by black Americans satisfies the moral requirement that it promotes fairness. For example, critics of Johnnie Cochran's closing argument in the Simpson case contend that his plea for the jury to "send a message" that police misconduct would not be tolerated was a thinly disguised attempt to get black jurors to vote to acquit regardless of their belief in Simpson's guilt. For reasons that I outline in the next section, I do not believe that this characterization is correct. There are, however, some who contend that black jurors should routinely refuse to convict black defendants accused of nonviolent crimes.[70] This proposal cannot be justified on fairness grounds.

In order to justify blanket nullification (by which I mean nullification in the absence of specific evidence that a given defendant's prosecution has been tainted by racism) by black jurors in cases involving nonviolent black defendants one would have to demonstrate that the American justice system is so pervaded by racism that no black defendant is able to get a fair trial. Thus, given the racism and corruption in Nazi Germany or Apartheid South Africa, these legal systems were arguably unworthy of any moral respect—particularly by Jewish or black lawyers. But the sad fact that the United States is far from achieving the ideal of colorblind justice does not mean that our legal system is similarly illegitimate. Although our system of justice continues to produce systematic injustice on the basis of race, it is capable of responding to racial injustice as well. To treat the victims of crime fairly—including those victims who happen to be white—all participants in the system must respect this basic reality.

Indeed, proposals for blanket nullification fail even to treat their intended beneficiaries fairly. Such proposals are expressly designed to empower black jurors to strike a blow for racial justice. Sadly, any indication that black jurors are engaging in blanket nullification is likely to have precisely the opposite effect. African Americans already face substantial obstacles, including eligibility requirements and peremptory challenges, to serving on juries.[71] Proposals for blanket jury nullification are certain to exacerbate this state of affairs.

Similar arguments apply to certain group-enhancement claims pertaining to women. Judith Nathanson's women-only client policy is instructive. Nathanson's desire to promote women's rights by protecting the interests of women in divorce cases is, standing alone, fully justified. As numerous studies have documented, gender discrimination is still pervasive in American courts.[72] Moreover, women lawyers have played and continue to play a crucial role in working to uncover and ameliorate these inequalities.[73] Finally, as I argued in Part II, Nathanson has good grounds for worrying that when she represents men in divorce cases, she inevitably lends her gender identity to their cause.

Nevertheless, her claim that her commitment to promote women's rights justifies her decision not to represent any man in a divorce case goes too far. Over the years, advocates for women's rights have won important victories by bringing cases on behalf of men ensnared in legal traps that traditionally disadvantage women. In the 1970s, for example, no less an advocate for women's rights than Justice Ruth Bader Guinsberg made representing men a mainstay of her legal strategy for overcoming sex discrimination.[74] Although criticized by some feminists, this strategy proved "highly appealing to male judges, who had to be educated to see the unfairness of sex-distinctions that had long been accepted."[75]

The fact that some may differ about the wisdom of a particular strategy does not mean that it is not a proper avenue for group advancement. Given the complexity of the issues confronting women, blacks, and other oppressed groups, it is imperative that advocates for these communities recognize that there are many strategies for advancing, for example, women's rights. And it is the *right*—in Nathanson's case the spouse's right to a fair share of the jointly acquired career—and not simple solidarity that defines the acceptable bounds of identity-conscious lawyering.[76]

Ginsburg's intimation that he and Monica Lewinsky might be justified in failing to cooperate with the independent counsel because of their commitment to ensure American support for Israel states an even more tenuous claim for identity consciousness. Prior to the 1960s, overt and thinly veiled anti-Semitism was rampant in American society in general and in the American legal profession in particular. Under these circumstances, the claim that Jewish lawyers should vigilantly protect the interests of other Jews (whether in Israel or the United States) seems quite defensible. Given the dramatic increase in the social and economic position of the Jewish community, both in general and in law in particular, such preferential treatment is less justifiable, particularly if it also has the effect of closing off opportunities for individuals from other groups whose members face more severe disadvantages. Although a plausible claim might be made that ensuring fairness in America's foreign policy toward Israel represents a special case justifying the continuing vigilance of American Jews, the "fit" between this goal and Ginsburg's proposed course of conduct is far too loose. The United States has supported Israel for almost five decades, under both Democratic and Republican administrations. At a minimum, there is no credible evidence that Al Gore, Clinton's constitutional successor, would be significantly less sympathetic to Israel's legitimate interests. And even if there was some doubt about this, the proper response would be to bring pressure to bear on Gore to improve his policies. To put the point bluntly, sabotaging an on-going investigation is not a necessary element of any legitimate project to promote the collective interests of Jews in the United States or Israel.

Finally, it should go without saying that identity consciousness for whites cannot be justified on the ground that it is necessary to promote collective projects for white advancement. There are many individual whites who are poor, uneducated, and mistreated. Whites as a group are not. Therefore, efforts by white lawyers to help poor whites, for example, by urging the government to commit more funding to legal aid, need not incorporate an identity-based component.

By carefully examining the moral claims underlying various calls for identity consciousness, we can begin to separate those moves away from bleached out professionalism that are likely to promote fundamental fairness and those that are likely to detract from this goal. If lawyers were merely ordinary citizens seeking to act morally in the world, this analysis might be all that is needed. But lawyers are not simply citizens; they are professionals who have made an express commitment to uphold the rules of legal ethics and to safeguard the interests of both clients and citizens. The partial, but nevertheless important truth about bleached out professionalism outlined in Part I underscores that these commitments carry significant moral weight. Therefore, in addition to examining the moral justifications for particular claims of identity consciousness, we must also address how recognizing even a legitimate claim might undermine values central to the lawyer's role. This leads us to the concept of social purpose.

Professionalism in Context: The Social Purposes of Lawyering

Bleached out professionalism is premised on the profession's long-standing commitment to the idea that American lawyers constitute a single unified profession, governed by a common set of ethical norms.[77] Thus, the American Bar Association's Model Code of Professional Responsibility explicitly states that the same ethical rules should be applied to "all lawyers, regardless of the nature of their professional activity."[78] Other sources of professional norms and enforcement practices either ignore differences among the tasks lawyers perform, the clients they represent, or the institutions in which they work, or treat these differences as insignificant.[79] As most observers concede, however, this traditional image of a homogeneous profession united by a common normative culture is increasingly out of touch with the growing heterogeneity and specialization of the contemporary bar.

Diversity within the lawyer's role poses a challenge to bleached out professionalism. Simply demonstrating that identity-related considerations tend to undermine *some* aspects of what lawyers do does not prove that these same considerations cannot play a legitimate role in *any* professional practice. Instead, one must find a criteria that will help lawyers to distinguish between those instances in which even legitimate identity claims must be rejected and those where they should be allowed to play at least some role.

The concept of "social purpose" begins to provide a way out of this dilemma. By social purpose, I mean those aspects of a particular lawyering role or task that disinterested social actors would consider to be essential to the proper performance of the job in question. The prosecution's strategy in the Simpson case illustrates how we can apply the concept of social purpose to distinguish those morally justified uses of identity that are *professionally* acceptable from those that are not. As I argued in the last section, Garcetti's statements denying that race would play any role in the Simpson prosecution were simply false. Nevertheless, his statements captured an important aspirational norm fundamental to the social purpose of our justice system: that race *ought not* to affect the determination of the accused's guilt or innocence. To honor this norm, however, prosecutors are sometimes justified in engaging in race-conscious lawyering strategies. Viewed from this perspective, Garcetti's decision to prosecute Simpson in Los Angeles County rather than in Santa Monica County, and his addition of Darden to the prosecution team, both support, rather than undermine, the legitimate aspirations of the criminal justice system. Given the composition of the respective jury pools, a Los Angeles jury was likely to include several blacks. A Santa Monica jury was not. In light of the racially charged atmosphere in Los Angeles at the time of the Simpson trial, and the long history of the demonization of black male sexuality, trying the case before a jury that included at least some blacks arguably made it more likely that the legal system would honor—and, just as important, that it would be seen as honoring—its commitment to the norm that race should not affect the determination of Simpson's guilt. Similarly, Garcetti's race-conscious decision to add a black prosecutor to the team—particularly one with a demonstrated history of uncovering and prosecuting police misconduct—plausibly increased the chance that Simpson's allegations of official bias and corruption in the investigation of his case would receive (and, once again, be perceived as receiving) a fair hearing.

The argument that these race-conscious lawyering strategies support rather than undermine the legitimate social purposes of the criminal justice system presumes that the blacks who are brought into the process will honor their legitimate role obligations and will not simply become racial patriots. This does not require bleached out professionalism. Thus, black jurors in the Simpson case were entitled to bring their experience with and understanding of racism and official corruption into the jury room. At the end of the day, however, they were obligated to acquit or convict Simpson on the basis of the evidence and arguments presented during the trial. Even nullification should be based on the presence of injustice (either in the content or the application of the law) in the particular case. Thus, even if blanket nullification were a morally acceptable strategy (which, as I indicated, I do not believe that it is), black jurors should refrain from engaging in this strategy because it undermines the legitimate social purpose of their role as jurors.

Similar arguments constrained Darden and Cochran. As I have already indicated, Darden's argument in favor of suppressing Fuhrman's racist statements was expressly color-conscious. Given that he was one of the lead prosecutors on the case, however, Darden was obligated to deploy this color-conscious strategy for the purpose of keeping Fuhrman's statements away from the jury. As a black man, and a strong opponent of racism within the police department, Darden may well have believed that exposing Fuhrman's racism would advance the black community's interests by highlighting the problems African Americans encounter with the police on a daily basis. Nevertheless as a prosecutor, Darden had an ethical obligation to make all reasonable arguments in favor of Simpson's guilt.

One can apply the same analysis to Cochran's "send a message" statement during his closing argument. Once again, Cochran's argument was race-conscious to the extent that it directed the jury's attention to the defense's claim that police racism infected the investigatory process. Nevertheless, Cochran's argument did not exceed the bounds of legitimate advocacy in a criminal case. "Send a message" arguments are a part of the standard lexicon of both prosecutors and defense lawyers in criminal cases. Although controversial, this rhetorical device arguably is not simply a call for nullification.[80] Unlike calls for blanket nullification, Cochran's argument was based on the alleged existence of racism and corruption in the Simpson prosecution itself. Moreover, Cochran did not limit his appeal to black jurors, emphasizing instead that all Americans have a stake in ensuring that police racism does not taint the trial process. Regardless of whether one finds these arguments convincing, as Simpson's defense lawyer Cochran was ethically obligated to present all reasonable arguments in favor of his client.

Ginsburg's attempt to introduce identity into the Clinton investigation cannot be justified on these terms. Even assuming that Ginsburg was right about the effect on Israel of removing Clinton from office—as I have already suggested, a dubious proposition in itself—this result is irrelevant to the social purpose of his task as Lewinsky's defense lawyer. Ginsburg had two charges in this role. First and foremost, to protect Lewinsky's interests. To the extent that Lewinsky did not in fact share Ginsburg's concerns, his statement to the Israeli press both failed to serve any purpose that Lewinsky may have had for the representation and posed a great risk of substantially prejudicing her case, since many in the United States (including many Jews) do not look favorably on a person who appears to be willing to subvert her own duties as a citizen to assist a foreign power. But even assuming that Lewinsky shared Ginsburg's views, a witness is not permitted to shade or distort her testimony before a grand jury simply because she does not want the target of the investigation to be convicted. Facilitating her doing so, therefore, would have been a violation of Ginsburg's duties as an officer of the legal system.

Social purpose considerations also put important constraints on the use of racial or gender identity. Nathanson's case is again instructive. Even if we were to give credence to Nathanson's construction of what is in the best interest of women—once again, for the reasons stated above, a dubious position—it should still be impermissible for a *lawyer* to engage in this form of status-based discrimination. This conclusion is not mandated by the profession's current rules. These rules presently give lawyers broad discretion to turn down clients for virtually any reason. These rules, as I argued in the last section, serve the legitimate goal of protecting the moral integrity of lawyers who do not wish to advocate on behalf of causes they find morally reprehensible. Status discrimination, however, undermines the legitimate social purposes underlying the rules regarding client selection. While it is true, as many have noted, that the attorney-client relationship is inherently personal, this should not be taken as a license for individuals to indulge their personal taste for discrimination. Lawyers have been granted a monopoly by the state to perform an essential service. Whether lawyers technically constitute a "public accommodation," as the Massachusetts Commission Against Discrimination held, the profession's commitment to equal justice under law is undermined if attorneys are allowed to refuse to represent individuals on the basis of considerations that have nothing to do with either the potential client's moral worth as a human being or the substance of the individual's legal claims.

Nor can rules permitting wholesale status-based discrimination be justified on the ground that they are necessary to protect clients. Sometimes clients will rationally prefer to work with lawyers who are hostile to the client for reasons extending beyond the attorney-client relationship. Consider, for example, how the Grand Dragon of the Ku Klux Klan reacted when he discovered that the ACLU had assigned him a black lawyer: "The way I look at it, he has to do a good job for me. . . . If he doesn't win, people are going to say, 'Yup, that's what you get for taking an African-American lawyer.' Everybody will know I got sold down the river by the ACLU."[81] Clients who obtain lawyers who would rather not serve them are protected by malpractice and other related doctrines against incompetence or deceit on the part of their reluctant champions.

Finally, the concept of social purpose helps us determine what to do when lawyers feel that their identities preclude them from performing their professional roles. Robert Johnson's case nicely illustrates the point. Johnson was the elected district attorney for the Bronx. In that capacity, he had wide discretion to set the law enforcement priorities for his jurisdiction. Moreover, as an elected official, he was obligated to consider his constituents views about how those priorities should be set. His constituents overwhelmingly supported his decision not to seek the death penalty.

Despite this clear popular mandate, however, Johnson did not have the authority to adopt a policy of refusing to seek the death penalty in all cases. The argument that a locally elected district attorney lacks such authority flows directly from the social purposes underlying the role of public prosecutor. Although prosecutors are given substantial discretion to decide which cases to prosecute and what penalties to seek, our system depends upon these decisions being made in a manner that is consistent with the will of the people as expressed through their legislative representatives. To hold otherwise would effectively disaggregate the state into a loose collection of local fiefdoms. A black district attorney, therefore, has a binding professional obligation to seek the death penalty in cases where, in his professional judgment, the punishment is warranted under the statute. To the extent that the district attorney feels that his commitments to the black community will not allow him to carry out this obligation, the governor has a right to remove him and appoint someone who will.

The governor's actions, however, should also be constrained by a proper understanding of the social purposes of prosecution. In this case, the governor's decision to replace the black district attorney with a white death penalty hawk fails to meet this standard. This is true for two reasons. First, by turning the decision over to someone who is virtually certain to seek the death penalty, the governor is undermining the social purposes of prosecution in a manner that is exactly parallel to Johnson's blanket refusal to seek the death penalty. Death penalty statutes expressly give prosecutors discretion so that they can make a case-by-case determination of whether this most extreme punishment is warranted by all of the facts and circumstances surrounding a particular crime.[82] Appointing someone who believes that the death penalty should be sought in every case authorized by the statute undermines this important discretionary element. Second, under the circumstances of this case, the fact that the death penalty hawk is white further compounds the error. Just as in the Simpson case, it is vital to the social purposes of the criminal justice system that citizens believe that decisions in racially charged cases do not depend upon either the victim's or on the alleged perpetrator's race. Pataki's decision to replace Johnson with a white death penalty hawk gives black citizens further reason to doubt the system's fairness.

Finally, Johnson's case underscores the fact that when a black lawyer feels compelled to violate an express professional command, considerations of social purposes dictate that she do so in a manner that respects the moral force of existing norms. One can see the value of this requirement by contrasting Johnson's actions with those of Robert Morgantheau, the respected district attorney for the Borough of Manhattan. Johnson publicly announced his intention not to seek the death penalty and carefully explained his reasons for not doing so. By all accounts, Morgantheau shares Johnson's view that the death penalty is administratively inefficient and morally reprehensible.[83] Unlike Johnson, however, Morgantheau has consistently taken the position that "he would enforce the will of the people but privately has done as little as possible to actually prepare a death case."[84] Although Morgantheau has largely escaped criticism by covertly submerging his opposition to the death penalty into case-by-case decision making, it is Johnson, not Morgantheau, who has demonstrated the appropriate respect for the social purposes of his role as prosecutor.

Considerations of social purpose, like the moral analysis in the preceding section, will not answer every question about when and how it is appropriate for lawyers to take account of identity-based considerations in their professional actions. Careful attention to both moral and social purpose considerations, however, can help us move beyond bleached out professionalism without ignoring the legitimate interests of clients, lawyers, and the public. This may be the best we can hope for in a world in which we recognize, rather than ignore, the inevitable intersection of identity and role.

Notes

1. See Sam H. Verhovek, "A Klansman's Black Lawyer, and a Principle," *N.Y. Times*, September 10, 1993, B9. See also David B. Wilkins, "Race, Ethics, and the First Amendment: Should a Black Lawyer Represent the Ku Klux Klan?," 63 *Geo. Wash. U.L. Rev.* 1030 (1995).

2. See *Stropnicky v. Nathanson*, No. 91-BPA-0061 (Mass. Comm'n Against Discrim.) (Feb. 25, 1997) (Charles E. Walker, hearing commissioner).

3. See Margaret M. Russell, "Beyond 'Sellouts' and 'Race Cards': Black Attorneys and the Straitjacket of Legal Practice," 95 *Michigan L. Rev.* 766 (1997).

4. See John M. Goshko, "Police Killing Sparks Debate on Death Penalty in New York," *Wash. Post*, March 24, 1966, A24.

5. NBC News Transcripts, "William Ginsburg, Attorney for Monica Lewinsky, Discusses the Progress of the Investigation," Meet the Press, February 22, 1998 (available in LEXIS, NEXIS Library, Script File).

6. K. Anthony Appiah, Epilogue to K. Appiah and Amy Gutmann, *Color Consciousness: The Political Morality of Race* (Princeton: Princeton University Press, 1996) (noting that "[t]here is a great deal of angry polemic about race in this country today").

7. See Sanford Levinson, "Identifying the Jewish Lawyer: Reflections on the Construction of Professional Identity," 14 *Cardozo L. Rev.* 1577 (1993).

8. Ibid., 1578–79.

9. See generally, Lewis A. Coser, *Greedy Institutions: Patterns of Undivided Commitment* (New York: Free Press, 1974), 5 (defining greedy institutions as those "which make total claims of their members [and] seek exclusive and undivided loyalty and attempt to reduce the claims of competing roles and status positions on those they wish to encompass within their borders").

10. See Alan Goldman, *The Moral Foundations of Professional Ethics* (Totowa, N.J.: Rowman and Littlefield, 1980).

11. See David B. Wilkins, "Everyday Practice *Is* the Troubling Case: Confronting Context in Legal Ethics," in *Everyday Practice and Trouble Cases*, A. Sarat, ed. (Chicago: Northwestern University Press, 1998).

12. I discuss this point at some length in David B. Wilkins, "Two Paths to the Mountaintop: The Role of Legal Education in Shaping the Values of Black Corporate Lawyers," 45 *Stan. L. Rev.* 1981, 2014–16 (1993).

13. Ken Hamblin, "No Excuse for Color-Coded Justice," *Atlanta J. & Const.*, April 10, 1996, 15 (available in 1996 WL 8200403).

14. Ibid.

15. William Safire, "After the Aftermath: Damage Done," *Atlanta J. & Const.*, October 13, 1995, A19 (available in 1995 WL 6556856).

16. See Brent Staples, "Millions for Defense," *N.Y. Times*, April 28, 1996, Section 7 (Book Review), 15.

17. Kevin Moran, "Black Lawyer Giving His Best to the Klan: Galveston Man Calls His ACLU Work a Way to Safeguard First Amendment," *Hous. Chron.*, July 27, 1993, 1A (available in LEXIS, News Library, Hchron File).

18. Nat Hentoff, "A Free Speech Lawyer Fired by the NAACP," *Wash. Post*, June 25, 1994, A21.

19. Ellis Coase, *The Darden Dilemma: 12 Blacks Write on Justice, Race, and Conflicting Loyalties* (New York: HarperPerennial, 1997), vii (quoting Darden).

20. Ibid.

21. Meet the Press, *supra* n. 5.

22. The phase "our constitution is colorblind" was first made famous by Justice Harlan in his dissent in *Plessey v. Fergusson*. See *Plessy v. Fergusson*, 136 U.S. 537, 557 (Harlan, J., dissenting), overruled by *Brown v. Board of Education*, 347 U.S. 483 (1954). For a discussion of the central importance of the claim that "all men [and, obviously, all women] are created equal" to our public morality, see George P. Fletcher, "Loyalty: An Essay on the Morality of Relationships" (New York: Oxford University Press, 1993), 13.

23. See, e.g., Russell G. Pearce, "Rediscovering the Republican Origins of the Legal Ethics Codes," 6 *Georg. J. of Leg. Ethics* (1992), 241; and Robert W. Gordon, "The Ideal and the Actual in the Law: Fantasies and Practices of New York City Lawyers," in G. Gawal, ed., *The New High Priests: Lawyers in Post-Civil War America* (Westport, Conn.: Greenwood Press, 1984).

24. I use the term "fathers" advisedly here since virtually all of the lawyers I am referring to were men.

25. See Jerold S. Auerbach, *Unequal Justice: Lawyers and Social Change in Modern America* (New York: Oxford University Press, 1976).

26. See Thomas L. Shaffer and Mary Shaffer, *American Lawyers and Their Communities: Ethics in the Legal Profession* (Notre Dame, Ind.: Notre Dame University Press, 1991).

27. See Carol Gilligan, *In a Different Voice: Psychological Theory and Women's Development* (Cambridge, Mass.: Harvard University Press, 1992). See also Rand Jack and Paula Jack, *Moral Vision and Professional Decisions: The Changing Values of Women and Men Lawyers*

(New York: Cambridge University Press, 1989) (adopting Gilligan's critique); and Carrie Menkel-Meadow, "Portia in a Different Voice: Speculations on a Women's Lawyering Process," 1 *Berkeley Women's Law Journal* 39 (1985) (same).

28. Carrie Menkle-Meadow, "Portia Redux: Another Look at Gender, Feminism, and Legal Ethics," in S. Parker and C. Sampford, eds., *Legal Ethics and Legal Practice: Contemporary Issues* (New York: Oxford University Press, 1995), 54. For criticism of the Gilligan framework, see Deborah H. Rhode, "Missing Questions: Feminist Perspectives on Legal Education," 45 *Stan. L. Rev.* 1547 (1992); Cynthia Fuchs Epstein, "Faulty Framework: Consequences of the Difference Model for Women in the Law," 35 *N.Y. L. Sch. L. Rev.* 309 (1990).

29. See Marc Galanter and Thomas Palay, *Tournament of Lawyers: The Transformation of the Big Law Firm 100* (Chicago: University of Chicago Press, 1991). Although Galanter and Palay are correct that associates compete in a "tournament" for promotion to partnership, that tournament is substantially different in character than the authors suppose. See David B. Wilkins and G. Mitu Gulati, "Reconceiving the Tournament of Lawyers: Tracking, Seeding, and Information Control in the Internal Labor Markets of Large Law Firms," 84 *U.V.A. L. Rev.* 1581 (1998).

30. See Robert Nelson, *Partners with Power: Social Transformation of the Large Law Firm* (Berkeley: University of California Press, 1988), 214-20 (documenting how firm leaders link the typical associate career path to core professional values such as training, competence, and ethical service); Edwin Smigel, *Wall Street Lawyer: Professional Organizational Man* (Bloomington: Indiana University Press, 1969) (linking organizational structure to professional norms).

31. See, e.g., Deborah Rhode, *Speaking of Sex: The Denial of Gender Inequality* (Cambridge, Mass.: Harvard University Press, 1998) (describing the continuing problems that women encounter in the legal system; and Andrew Hacker, *Two Nations: Black and White, Separate, Hostile, Unequal* (New York: Scribner's, 1995) (documenting how race continues to disadvantage black Americans).

32. See Jeffrey Rosen, "The Bloods and the Critics: O. J. Simpson, Critical Race Theory, the Law, and the Triumph of Color in America," *New Republic*, December 9, 1996, 27.

33. Ibid., 42.

34. Frank Michaelman, "Racialism and Reason," 95 *Mich. L. Rev.* 723, 728 (1997).

35. Ibid., 788.

36. See, e.g., David A. Thomas, "The Impact of Race on Managers' Experiences in Developmental Relationships (Mentoring and Sponsorship): An Intra-organizational Study," 11 *Journal of Organizational Behavior* 479 (1990); David A. Thomas, "Racial Dynamics in Cross-Race Developmental Relationships," 38 *Administrative Science Quarterly* 169 (1993); David Thomas and Clayton P. Alderfer, *The Influence of Race on Career Dynamics: Theory and Research on Minority Career Experiences*, in M. B. Arthur et al., *Handbook of Career Theory* (New York: Cambridge University Press, 1989), 133.

37. See David Wilkins and G. Mito Gulati, "Why Are There So Few Black Lawyers in Corporate Law Firms?: An International Analysis," 84 *Cal. L. Rev.* 493(1996).

38. Elizabeth Gleick, "The Odd Couple: A Black Attorney Defends a Texas Klansman in a Racially Heated Case," *People*, September 20, 1993, 71.

39. Gary Taylor, "Klan, Texas Embroiled in Legal Tug of War," *Nat'l L. J.*, August 16, 1993, 10.

40. See Ann Scales, "A Clinton Counsel Makes Her Mark: Mills Adds a Tone of Diversity to the Defense's Team," *Boston Globe*, January 21, 1999, A1 (reporting that Mills opened her argument by stating that "as a lawyer, as an American, and as an African-American," she is a strong proponent of the rule of law, and she rebutted the House managers' charge that acquitting Clinton would undermine the cause of civil rights by stating, "I stand here before you

today because President Bill Clinton believed I could stand here for him" and "I'm not worried about civil rights, because this president's record . . . is unimpeachable").

41. See ibid., A20 (reporting that Mills's presence constituted a "jolt" of diversity and that she "puts a face on the president and his commitment to civil rights"). Tellingly, Scales's article is subtitled "Mills Adds Tone of Diversity to the Defense's Team." Ibid.

42. As Eleanor Holmes Norton stated when comparing Clinton's decision to use Mills and Bumpers, "I'm not sure if a black lawyer helps him before the Senate. I don't know that a former member helps him. He's a member of the club, she is not a member of the club." Ibid.

43. Professor Carrie Menkel-Meadow is the leading example. See, e.g., Carrie Menkel-Meadow, "Ethics in Alternative Dispute Resolution: New Issues, No Answers from the Adversary Conception of Lawyers' Responsibilities," 38 *S. Tex. L. Rev.* 407 (1997); Carrie Menkel-Meadow, "The Trouble with the Adversary System in a Postmodern, Multicultural World," 38 *William & Mary L. Rev.* 5 (1996); and Carrie Menkel-Meadow, "Exploring a Research Agenda of the Feminization of the Legal Profession: Theories of Gender and Social Change," *Law & Soc. Inquiry* 289 (1989).

44. See Sam H. Verhovek, "Klansman's Black Lawyer," *supra* n. 1 at B1 (quoting Griffin as stating: "We've come a long way in this country when a black man from the Midwest tells a black man from the South that he trusts the State of Texas. . . . I do not.").

45. Terri R. Day and Scott L. Rogers, "When Principled Representation Tests Antidiscrimination Law," 20 *West. N.E. L. Rev.* 23, 36 (1998).

46. See Russell, "Beyond 'Sellouts' and 'Race Cards,'" 787 (quoting Darden as arguing that: "when you mention that word to this jury, or any African American, it blinds people. . . . They won't be able to discern what's true and what's not."), and 787 n.58 (quoting Cochran as replying: "It's demeaning to our jury. . . . African Americans live with offensive words, offensive looks, offensive treatment every day of their lives. And yet they still believe in this country").

47. Alan M. Dershowitz, *The Vanishing American Jew, Cal. Law.* Sept. 1997, 39.

48. Richard Kluger, *Simple Justice: The History of* Brown v. Board of Education *and Black America's Struggle for Equality* (New York: Vintage Books, 1975).

49. See David B. Wilkins, "Social Engineers or Corporate Tools: Brown v. Board of Education *and the Conscious of the Black Corporate Bar," in A. Sarat, ed., *Race, Law, and Culture: Reflections on* Brown v. Board of Education (New York: Oxford University Press, 1997), 141–42.

50. See ibid., 138.

51. Robert Gordon, "The Independence of Lawyers," 68 *B.U.L. Rev.* 1 (1988).

52. Richard Wasserstrom, "Lawyers as Professionals: Some Moral Issues," 5 *Hum. Rts.* 1, 15 (1975).

53. Anthony T. Kronman, *The Lost Lawyer: Failing Ideals of the Legal Profession* (Cambridge, Mass.: Harvard University Press, 1993), 300–307.

54. See John Dzienkowski, "Positional Conflicts of Interest," 71 *Tex. L. Rev.* 457, 531–35 (1993).

55. Stephen L. Carter, "The Black Table, the Empty Seat, and the Tie," in *Lure and Loathing: Essays on Race, Identity, and the Ambivalence of Assimilation* (New York: Penguin Press, 1992), 66.

56. Martin R. Kilson, "Realism about the Black Experience: A Reply to Steele, *Dissent,* Fall 1990, 519, 520.

57. For a more complete account of these ideas, see David B. Wilkins, "Identities and Roles: Race, Recognition, and Professional Responsibility," 57 *Md. L. Rev.* 1502 (1998); David B. Wilkins, "Fragmenting Professionalism: Racial Identity and the Ideology of "Bleached Out" Lawyering," 5 *Int'l J. of the Legal Prof.* 141 (1998).

58. See Amy Gutmann, "Responding to Racial Injustice," in K. Anthony Appiah and Amy Gutmann, eds., *Color Conscious, supra* n. 6, 108, 110.

59. See Suzanne Carter, "Moses Presides over Ames Courtroom: Charlton Heston Condemns Political Correctness, Ice T," *Harv. Law Record,* February 19, 1999, A1 (quoting Charlton Heston as arguing that "white pride is just as valid as black pride or red pride").

60. In addition to the three justifications discussed in text, one can also make a cultural defense of identity consciousness. I discuss the strengths and weaknesses of this justification with respect to blacks in David B. Wilkins, "Introduction: Race in Context," in Appiah and Gutmann, *Color Consciousness, supra* n. 6.

61. For a brilliant exposition of how arguments about morphology, biology, and belief were melded together to produce modern understandings of race and racism, see K. Anthony Appiah, "Race, Culture, Identity: Misunderstood Connections," in Appiah and Gutmann, *Color Conscious, supra* n. 6.

62. I borrow the idea of "recognition" from Charles Taylor's important discussion of the politics of recognition. See Charles Taylor, *Multiculturalism and "the Politics of Recognition"* (Princeton, N.J.: Princeton University Press, 1994). I borrow the concept of "scripts" from Anthony Appiah's criticque of Taylor. Ibid.

63. See, e.g., Viet D. Dinh, "Races, Crimes, and the Law," reviewing Randall Kennedy's "Race, Crime, and the Law," 111 *Harv. L. Rev.* 1289, 1290–93 (1998) (arguing that most blacks and whites engage in a "biracial simplification" when discussing issues of race); Deborah Ramirez, "Multicultural Empowerment: It's Not Just Black and White Anymore," 47 *Stan. L. Rev.* 957 (1990) (same).

64. For a general discussion of the privileges whites enjoy simply by being white, see Ian F. Haney López, *White by Law: The Legal Construction of Race* (New York: New York University Press, 1996).

65. See, e.g., Ellis Case, *The Rage of the Privileged Class* (New York: Harper Collins, 1993), 14–26 (discussing the burdens on black professionals of constantly having to be responsible for exposing and coping with the continuing effects of racism); and Joe R. Feagin and Melvin P. Sikes, *Living with Racism: The Black Middle Class Experience* (Boston: Beacon Press, 1994), chap. 4 "Navigating the Middle-class Workplace," 135.

66. See Janet Halley, "Like Race Arguments" (unpublished manuscript on file with the author).

67. Margaret M. Russell, "Beyond 'Sellouts' and 'Race Cards': Black Attorneys and the Straightjacket of Legal Practice," 95 *Mich. L. Rev.* 766 (1997).

68. Randall Kennedy, *Race, Crime, and the Law* (New York: Basic Books, 1998).

69. See Appiah, "Race, Culture, and Identity," *supra* n. 6, 93 (noting that "[t]here is a logical category but no social category of the witty, or the clever, or the charming, or the greedy"); and Iris Marion Young, *Justice and the Politics of Difference,* 186–87 (distinguishing between "interest groups" and "social groups" such as race and gender).

70. See Paul Butler, "Racially Based Jury Nullification: Black Power in the Criminal Justice System," 95 *Yale L.J.* 677 (1995).

71. See Randall Kennedy, *supra* n. 68, 295–301.

72. See, e.g., "The Effects of Gender Bias in the Federal Courts: The Final Report of the Ninth Circuit Gender Bias Task Force," 67 *S. Cal. L. Rev.* 745 (1994); and Ann J. Gels, "Great Expectations: Women in the Legal Profession, A Commentary on State Studies," 66 *Ind. L.J.* 941 (1991).

73. See Deborah Rhode, "Perspectives on Professional Women," 40 *Stan. L. Rev.* 1163 (1988).

74. Discussing *Weinberger v. Wiesenfeld,* 420 US 636 (1975), a landmark Supreme Court

decision in which Ginsberg represented a young widower denied social security benefits under circumstances in which a young widow would have been entitled to compensation, Ginsberg recently stated that her strategy in that case epitomized for me all that we were doing in the 70s." Jeffrey Rose, "The New Look of Liberalism on the Court," *N.Y.T. Mag.*, October 5, 1997, 60, 64.

75. Ibid.

76. See Deborah Rhode, "Can a Lawyer Insist on Clients of One Gender?," *Nat'l L. J.*, December 1, 1997, A21.

77. See Charles W. Wolfram, *Modern Legal Ethics* (St. Paul, Minn.: West Publishing, 1986), 54 (identifying and criticizing this idea).

78. American Bar Association, Model Code of Professional Responsibility, Preamble (1983).

79. I have written extensively on this topic. See David B. Wilkins, "Everyday Practice Is the Troubling Case: Confronting Context in Legal Ethics in Everyday Practice and Trouble Cases," 68 (Evanston, Ill.: Northwestern University Press, 1998); David B. Wilkins, "Making Context Count: Regulating Lawyers After Kaye, Scholer," 66 *S. Cal. L. Rev.* 1145, 1151–53 (1993).

80. For further development of this argument, see David B. Wilkins, "Straightjacketing Professionalism: A Comment on Russell," 95 *Mich. L. Rev.* 795 (1997).

81. Sam Howe Verhovek, "A Klansman's Black Lawyer, and a Principle," *N.Y. Times,* September 10, 1993, B9.

82. Jan Hoffman, "Death Penalty Raises Issue of Obligation of Prosecutor," *N.Y. Times,* March 17, 1996, § 1, 33, col. 5.

83. J. Taub, "The DA's Dilemma," *New Yorker,* July 28, 1997, 26.

84. Ibid., in Gerald W. Gewalt, ed., *The New High Priests: Lawyers in Post-Civil War America* (Westport, Conn.: Greenwood Press, 1984).

12

Contested Identities

Task Forces on Gender, Race, and Ethnic
Bias and the Obligations of the Legal Profession

DEBORAH R. HENSLER AND JUDITH RESNIK

Conceptions of Identity

During the past few decades, questions of identity have become central in legal discourse. We use the word "identity" here in reference to two sets of issues. First, we are interested in the relevance of "identity politics" to lawyering. Animated by concerns that individuals who share certain characteristics ("women," "women of color," "people of color," "Latinos," "gays") are not sufficiently represented or do not fully participate in economic, social, and political processes, identity politics incorporate efforts to increase recognition, inclusion, status, and authority of members of such groups. Supporters of identity politics argue not only that a commitment to equality requires attention to such issues, but also that bringing individuals of diverse backgrounds into various private and public arenas enriches the lives of all members of society by gaining an array of perspectives on shared problems. Opponents argue, in contrast, that such efforts divide individuals in ways that are harmful to the polity and that, in any event, personal characteristics do not correlate with ideas, values, or experiences, including participation in economic, social, and political processes.

Identity politics have become more relevant to the legal profession as the demographic profiles of both the profession and the population in the United States have changed. Over the past several decades, the profession has evolved from one that was overwhelmingly male and Euro-American to one now including men and women of more diverse sociocultural backgrounds. Concurrently, the United States' population (the users of its justice system) has also become more diverse. What these changes ought to mean for the legal profession is highly contested.

Our second interest in identity shifts the focus to alternative (and again, contested) conceptions about the meaning of being a lawyer. *Lawyers' identities* are linked to different roles, such as officers of the court, agents of change, zealous advocates for client interests, business people, and "statesmen."[1] Contemporary debates among lawyers reflect fears of the consequences of increased competition, heightened entreprenerialism, and adversarialism for the public images of lawyers,[2] as well as for lawyers' own understanding of their roles in society. The literature about lawyers considers whether, for example, because the services lawyers sell involve the justice system, lawyers have moral imperatives that should be incorporated into ethical rules, such as mandates for pro bono work.[3]

These two conceptions of identity—identity politics and lawyers' professional identity—are both implicated when discussion turns to professional obligations regarding equality. Should lawyers and judges be concerned about whether men and women lawyers of all colors are appointed to authoritative positions, recognized as professional colleagues, and treated as equals? Do lawyers and judges, as professionals, have *special* obligations to inquire about the treatment of men and women of all colors in the legal system, within and outside of courts, and to work toward remediating unfair differences? Are perceived differences in the treatment of men and women and people of color evidence of excessive adversarialism—to which the appropriate responses are codes of civility and better inculcation of professional mores—or do they reflect deeper problems of social ordering—requiring a change in professional ethical standards?

Such questions *about* lawyers' identities as members of a profession and members of diverse social groups are reflected in the development of organizations *for* lawyers and in their agendas. The American Bar Association (ABA), the largest nationwide organization of lawyers, was founded in 1878; for decades, it has served as the leading national organization for lawyers.[4] Over the succeeding decades, a series of specially identified bar organizations formed, in response to the entrance of small numbers of women, blacks, Asian Americans, Native Americans, and Latinos into the legal profession.

In 1980, a group of judges and lawyers created another general professional organization, the American Inns of Court (AIC), modeled after its English counterpart. As explained by one of its founders, "a felt need to save our professional souls" prompted the organization to dedicate itself to improving professional standards.[5] The focus of AIC on mentoring and civility evidences the concern of some lawyers and judges about a decline in professionalism and the belief that improving communication about the profession's norms across generations and among participants is an appropriate remedy. In its programs, AIC aspires to be perceived as neither political nor entrepreneurial.

While attorneys' ethics, role, and status are central topics for the ABA as well,[6] that organization also addresses issues of public governance; the ABA identifies such work as essential to its function as a professional body of lawyers. Thus, the ABA has long provided commentary on the needs of the judiciary and on proposed nominees for federal judgeships. The ABA also superintends legal education, promulgates policy, and creates commissions on topics ranging from the independence of the judiciary to the death penalty.[7] Moreover, during the 1980s and 1990s, the ABA became increasingly concerned about exclusion of diverse groups of people from professional activities and responded in a variety of ways, including forming commissions focused on the roles of women and men of all colors in the profession.

Such projects have, in turn, sparked criticism of the ABA by yet another relatively new organization of lawyers, the Federalist Society. Distressed at the ABA for espousing "policy" positions outside what the Federalist Society claimed to be the proper charter for a "professional" organization of lawyers, the Society began in 1996 to publish a newsletter, called *ABA WATCH*, devoted to discussing decisions by the ABA. In its inaugural issue, the newsletter argued that "[o]ne of the most disturbing social trends in the last two decades has been the growing politicization of institutions that were once praised and respected for being impartial and 'above politics,' " and then asked "whether such politicization has permeated the American Bar Association."[8]

In this chapter, we examine the relationship between the evolution of professional organizations of the bar, the projects that they adopt, and the normative questions of the reach and purpose of ethical rules identified with the legal profession. We focus on the creation, in the 1980s and 1990s, of "bias task forces" about gender, race, and ethnicity, generated by legal organizations as a means of addressing inequality and exclusion within the justice system, and particularly within courts. Bias task forces implicate all of the dimensions of identity discourse: the import of identity politics, the meaning of professional identity for lawyers in a pluralist society, the function of legal professional organizations, and the relevance of reports by individuals of diverse backgrounds about their experiences and perceptions of legal processes.

Below, we first show how the goals and modes of these task forces reflect their deep connections to the legal profession, expressing both its commitments to equal access to justice and to fair process and the concerns raised upon finding less than fulfillment of these aspirations. Second, we use findings from task force reports to learn more about professional identity, including lawyers' experiences of inclusion and exclusion and about how professional norms of adversarial exchange are used to express recognition and marginalization. Third, we examine the debate that the creation of task forces has occasioned for the profession. Within the struggle about the legitimacy of task force projects reside diverse conceptions of professional obligations held by lawyers, judges, and the organizations of which they are a part. We conclude by arguing that, because lawyers are specially situated actors within the justice system, their norms of professionalism must internalize law's commitment to equal treatment.

Projects of the Profession

Beginning in the 1980s, court systems in dozens of state and federal jurisdictions launched remarkable projects of self-study, aimed at asking about the effects of gender, race, and ethnicity within their systems. By the late 1990s, some sixty reports, commissioned by state and federal judiciaries, had been published.[9] A brief review of the history of these efforts reveals how deep connections to conceptions of professional identity and obligations helped to shape their goals, methods, and the ways in which they reported their results.

The Task Force Movement

The task force movement began as a collaborative effort of the National Organization for Women (NOW) Legal Defense Fund and the National Association of Women Judges, both seeking to educate judges nationwide about the insidious effects of gender stereotyping on judicial decision making. The two organizations cosponsored a NOW project, the National Judicial Education Program to Promote Equality of Women and Men in the Courts (NJEP), which in turn pressed individual jurisdictions to undertake self-studies of the effect of gender on court processes and outcomes.[10] Robert Wilentz, then chief justice of the New Jersey Supreme Court, responded in 1982 by commissioning the first such project.[11] Within two years, New Jersey created a second project, focused on racial and ethnic bias. Several other states soon did the same.

In 1988, lawyers and judges formed another national organization, the *National Consortium of Task Forces and Commissions on Racial and Ethnic Bias in the Courts*, aimed at dealing with unfair treatment of racial and ethnic minorities. The consortium also sought to link together task forces that were ongoing in several jurisdictions.[12] In the same year, the chief justices of all fifty states called for the study of gender, racial and ethnic bias in their jurisdictions.[13] Such projects also received support from other national organizations, including the Commission on Women and the Commission on Minorities of the American Bar Association, local specialized bar organizations, and the National Center for State Courts.[14]

In the early 1990s, the federal courts began to undertake similar projects. In 1992, the Ninth Circuit issued the first report about the effects of gender in the federal context.[15] The Judicial Conference of the United States also adopted resolutions in support of studies and educational programs about fairness and the extent to which bias affects participants in the judicial process,[16] and, in 1994, Congress endorsed task force activities through a section of then-new legislation, the Violence Against Women Act.[17] By the decade's end, more than half the federal circuits had commissioned projects on gender and four circuits had task forces addressing race, ethnicity, and (in one instance) religion.[18]

Institutional support for these efforts took various forms. In addition to organizational endorsements, charters to specific task forces, and statements of affiliation, several national conferences were held. Sponsors also published manuals to provide guidance about how to undertake these projects, one directed at gender task forces, one at race/ethnic task forces, and one focused on the federal system,[19] and most recently a guide to implementation efforts.[20]

As this brief overview demonstrates, from their inception, task force projects were creatures of the legal profession, embraced both by court systems and by institutions of the profession including general, as well as special purpose, professional associations. Lawyers, judges, and legal academics spearheaded the efforts, organized and provided the intellectual resources for study groups, disseminated information about how to implement task force projects, and advocated the adoption of measures to address the problems that task forces uncovered.

Shaping the Inquiries

While based in law and concerned about fair and equal treatment, task forces did not seek (as lawyers might) to "prove" discrimination in the justice system; they were interested not in finding evidence of intentional acts of exclusion[21] but in understanding the experiences that diverse participants had of justice. Purposefully eschewing a litigation model, the task forces fashioned themselves as kinds of "blue ribbon" commissions, commonplace within the traditions of judicial and legal professional organizations.[22] Task forces focused on describing processes and (less frequently) outcomes in which gender or race or ethnicity (and their combinations) played a significant role. As Judge Patricia Wald explained:

> The purpose of [these task forces] is of course not to hunt down actual incidents of provable bias or discrimination but rather to evaluate whether unconscious but nonetheless real bias infects significant relationships in the court house. . . . [The hope is that] once such biases or just plain insensitivities are surfaced, everyone in the system will be more careful, more civil, more willing to try to obliterate any distinctive treatments based on such irrelevancies.[23]

In each of the sixty-some projects, chief judges appointed commissions, task forces, and committees of specially designated judges and lawyers, assisted by law professors and social scientists, who, in turn, enlisted volunteers to augment often scarce resources. Using both legal and social science research techniques, the task forces embarked on fact-finding inquiries to discover whether and how, in a particular jurisdiction, the treatment of lawyers, parties, witnesses, jurors, judges, and court employees differed by gender, and/or race, ethnicity, and religion. They examined the demographic composition of the bench, bar, and court employees; reviewed appointments and hiring practices of courts and, sometimes, of law firms; investigated interactions of lawyers and judges in formal and informal court processes such as discovery, settlement, and alternative dispute resolution; and studied the role of gender, race, and ethnicity in a variety of areas such as criminal justice decisions on bail and sentencing, examinations of women as witnesses in cases involving violence against them, employment discrimination law, and legal regimes governing divorce and custody.

Ambitiously (particularly given their resource constraints), the task forces sought to develop new data through sample surveys aimed at capturing the views of tens of thousands of participants in legal processes. Because the focus of much of the quantitative research was on the most easily surveyed (lawyers and judges) and less frequently on litigants, witnesses, and jurors, these reports provide a rich source of data about the demographic profile of the legal profession and about lawyers' and judges' behavioral expectations and professional mores.

Friends, Not Foes

In articulating their goals, shaping their inquiries, and presenting their results, task force members cast themselves as members and friends of the legal profession rather than as outsiders. Acting in part on the guidance of leaders of the task force movement, the individual task forces were self-consciously positive about their goals. For example, task forces often used affirming titles for their efforts, invoking concepts of "fairness" and "equality."[24] As the chief judge of one circuit who chartered a task force explained, the project was "for all segments of the . . . community, lawyers, litigants, court staff, and judges, . . . [an] attempt in a creative manner to ascertain whether there are barriers to full treatment and, if so, whether we can assure they will be eliminated."[25]

The efforts reflected a common mode of mainstream legal professionalism, assuming the underlying legitimacy and rightness of U.S. legal processes and commitments. Designed to fix, not to accuse, task force reports are generally friendly commentaries, less adversarial in tone than many documents associated with law. In sharp contrast, a Canadian commission, charted by the government to investigate differential treatment of people of color in the criminal justice system, labeled its effort as an investigation into "systemic racism."[26] Further, Canadian commentators have criticized U.S. task forces' reliance on the concept of "gender bias"—popularly used to describe the investigation of differential treatment of women—as a "sugar-coated concept"[27] that "disguises sexual oppression."[28]

Task forces generally reported their findings in careful, and occasionally upbeat, tones. Some task force reports make plain statements of systemic problems of injustice. "Women uniquely, disproportionately and with unacceptable frequency must endure a climate of condescension, indifference and hostility."[29] Or, "[t]here is evidence that bias does occur with disturbing frequency at every level of the legal profession and court system."[30] But others present a rosier picture, emphasizing progress. "[The] Circuit has made great strides in the last decade toward a litigation process unburdened by disparate treatments of its participants because of gender."[31] "Many practitioners . . . confirm that experiences in the courts are not as bad as they once were."[32]

Still other reports present a melange of contradictory findings that reflect ambivalence as to their import. For example, one state reported both "no widespread and overt gender bias," but also "evidence that gender bias does exist"[33] within its judicial system. And one federal circuit reported: "The overall findings are positive

. . . [yet] the percentages of attorneys and employees who report that in the last three years they have heard demeaning remarks based upon a person's race, ethnicity or religion in a courthouse or courtroom are unacceptably and surprisingly high."[34]

Taken together, the task forces and their reports reflect tensions within the legal profession about undertaking inquiries so close to core conceptions of U.S. legal processes. Lawyers and judges in this legal system are proud of their own commitment to equal treatment. The notion that task forces are needed, the nature of their investigation (asking about the presence of bias), and, often, their findings are therefore unsettling. Among task force efforts, one finds praiseworthy attempts at self-examination, coupled with a willingness to report less than happy self-descriptions, suggesting a conception of legal professionalism as specially obliged to address fairness and to deliver on the promise of equal justice to all actors within the legal system. But one also discerns, in the texts of the reports, the anxiety engendered when legal professionals describe failings of a system with which they are deeply affiliated.

Experiencing Identity Differences

The task force reports provide an empirical basis for examining lawyers' and judges' beliefs about the nature of the legal profession: the kinds of people it comprises, the ways in which those people can serve the courts and the profession, and the types of behavior that are appropriate when dealing with judges, lawyers, and parties of diverse heritages and identities. Task force reports paint a picture of a profession that has not yet caught up to the demographic changes in its profile and of members of the profession who are not universally ready to accept women of all colors and men of color as full-fledged professionals. Task force reports tell stories (in qualitative and quantitative form) of groups not fully represented in the upper strata of professional hierarchies, of adversary techniques that use identity characteristics to undermine individuals appearing in formal and informal proceedings, and—poignantly—of failures to recognize women and people of color as lawyers and judges rather than as defendants, witnesses, or administrative support personnel.[35]

Such data about inclusionary and exclusionary practices might be relevant to any inquiry into many contemporary institutions, be they schools, businesses, or professional organizations. But these issues have special purchase for lawyers. To be a lawyer—especially a litigator—is to participate in social exchanges, whether in the formal setting of a hearing or the more informal setting of the judge's chambers or lawyers' offices. To be a successful lawyer requires not only performing well in such interchanges but also obtaining recognition by others of one's abilities. While lawyers who are lobbyists officially market their access to decision makers, access is also relevant to lawyers who work in courts and agencies. Law firms and some clients make choices about which lawyers appear in court, who is given "first chair," and who is chosen to argue an appeal. When judges select lawyers to serve in certain positions (such as special masters or as committee members) or to speak at judicial conferences, those choices both confirm and create the authority of the lawyers thus chosen.

Further, law in the United States is specially connected to an ideology of inclusion and the impermissibility of relying on distinctions based on identity. The stated goal is "equal justice for all," and the stated means is to exclude "irrelevant" information when making decisions. Thus, the treatment of members of identifiable groups *by* law and *in* law has particular import *for* law.

Representation

As women of all colors and men of color have increased their numbers in law schools, the demographics of the profession have begun to change. Nationwide, by 1990, women accounted for about 24 percent of practicing attorneys. Men and women of color accounted for about 7 percent of all lawyers; women of color accounted for 12 percent of all female practitioners.[36]

Task forces found that women of all colors and men of color are represented in greater numbers at lower echelons of the profession than in higher echelons—as that hierarchy is currently understood. There are smaller fractions of women of all colors and men of color among lawyers who practice in federal courts than in the profession as a whole.[37] And there are smaller fractions of women of all colors and men of color on the bench than in the profession as a whole.[38] Women and men of color are more likely than white men to serve as public defenders or other government lawyers or in legal aid practices; they are less likely to hold more lucrative positions, such as in-house counsel.[39] Women of all colors and men of color are represented in very small numbers in special (sometimes fee-bearing) positions such as special masters and members of court-appointed committees.[40]

With only a small fraction of all attorneys serving in some of these positions, women of all colors and men of color are likely to find few people in positions of power who share their gender, race, and ethnicity. Even when a few of those persons hold such positions, people of color and white women may assume that the relative absence of women or persons of color is a sign of systemic exclusion. For example, the Special Committees of the District of Columbia's Circuit asked on surveys about participation on committees and also reviewed lists of those appointed. The Special Committee on Race and Ethnicity learned that in 1992, 16 of 91 attorneys on a committee were African Americans.[41] But 80 percent of African American attorneys surveyed by the Special Committee on Race and Ethnicity to the D.C. Circuit Task Force on Gender, Race, and Ethnic Bias said that African American attorneys had fewer opportunities to serve than nonminority attorneys. Only 7 percent of white attorneys agreed.[42]

While women of all colors and men of color are only sometimes statistically under represented in upper-echelon positions, the small numbers in such positions lead women and men of color to perceive their professional worlds as under-inclusive.[43] White men, however, continue to assume that race and gender play little role in professional assignments.[44] As the Ninth Circuit Gender Bias Task Force described: "Taken together [the findings] suggest that the women and men of the Ninth Circuit inhabit different worlds, one characterized by feelings of exclusion and the other by feelings of acceptance."[45]

The task forces found similar patterns of perceptions when they turned to law firms. Some women lawyers and attorneys of color told task forces that they were less likely than white men to be given important assignments, such as first chair, lead counsel, or the responsibility for examining a key witness. For example, in the Ninth Circuit, 14 percent of female civil litigators and 25 percent of female criminal practitioners said they had lost an assignment to a case as a result of gender bias.[46] The District of Columbia task force also found that gender and race were relevant to appointments; respondents reported both losing and gaining appointments based on race and/or gender. Markedly, fewer white and male attorneys reported such experiences.[47]

Exclusionary Practices

The task forces found that women of all colors and men of color are sometimes deliberately excluded from professional activities. Some such instances are overt, as when a female attorney in the Ninth Circuit was asked to leave a judge's chambers during a settlement conference so that he could tell a dirty joke.[48] Other task force reports describe less conscious actions, such as when judges and lawyers direct "their comments and attention to male counsel and seemingly ignor[e] opposing female counsel; asking male counsel to speak before female counsel in situations where the woman attorney was in a position in which she as counsel would normally have been asked to speak first; and cutting off female counsel during argument more abruptly than male counsel."[49] (Male attorneys who hear women relate such examples say that they themselves have never noticed such behavior.[50]) The task forces found that attorneys of color share the experience of exclusion: one-third of African American male attorneys surveyed by the Special Committee on Race and Ethnicity to the D.C. Circuit Task Force reported sometimes feeling that federal judges ignored or did not listen to them because of their race; 45 percent of African American female attorneys believed that both their race *and* their gender caused their nonrecognition. In contrast, 1 percent of white males and 28 percent of white female attorneys reported such encounters.[51]

Nonrecognition

Exclusionary practices take vivid form when they result in a failure to recognize a person as the professional that she or he is. A poignant example is provided by the task force on race and ethnicity from Massachusetts, which described (as an animating event for commencing its work) how an African American assistant attorney general, approaching a judge in a court, was barred by a staff member from coming close to the bench; the government lawyer was assumed to be the defendant rather than the lawyer for the state.[52] An Eighth Circuit attorney reported that, after 18 years of practice, she was still frequently mistaken for a court reporter. Another attorney in that circuit said that she was asked in open court if she was an attorney, and then asked to produce her license to practice to verify her assertion; on another occasion, a court employee called her law firm to verify that she was really an attorney.[53] A female attorney of color told the Second Circuit Task Force: "I have been an attorney for ten years and for some reason I'm still mistaken for someone off the street."[54] Nonrecognition of women of all colors and men of color as fellow professionals is a finding reported by many task forces.[55]

While patterns of "mistaking" women of all colors and men of color for someone other than who they are may be depressingly commonplace, these "mistakes" have special power when they occur in law. Not only are there many social cues to forestall such errors, but the misidentification may itself have an adversarial edge. Whether inadvertent or deployed strategically, attributing lower status to an opposing attorney who is a white woman, a woman of color, or a man of color signals to clients, jurors, or judges that the person should be assumed to be less credible and authoritative than is appropriate. The expectation of such behavior may, in turn, become an excuse for denying assignment of important cases or denying important positions in cases to women of all colors and to men of color.

Adversarial Posturing

When lawyers are outside circles of power, it becomes more difficult for them to be effective adversaries. It may also become easier for other lawyers—be they colleagues or opposing counsel—to undermine them. In deploying gender and racial or ethnic stereotypes in professional interactions, lawyers send subtle (and, sometimes, not-so-subtle) signals to other actors that the lawyer-target is not a full-fledged member of the profession.

Stereotypes may be used in formal proceedings, judges' chambers and courtroom corridors, in alternative dispute processes, and in lawyers' exchanges outside of court. While some deployment of gender or race-biased stereotypes stems from judges, task forces generally have found that lawyers are a more frequent source of such conduct than judges, and that cruder examples of stereotyping behavior are more likely to occur outside judges' presence than in formal court proceedings.[56] Targets include opposing counsel, parties, witnesses, and (less frequently) judges.

Lawyers introduce gender or racial and ethnic bias into lawyering in a variety of ways, ranging from addressing women of all colors and men of color in an unprofessional fashion, to commenting on appearance when such comments are not expected in a particular context (e.g., a formal court proceeding), to more directly attacking a fellow lawyer's (or party's or witness's) competence, seemingly because of the person's gender, race, ethnicity, or language. Some of this behavior may seem innocuous to some observers (although not to the targets), such as a judge addressing a female attorney in a familiar fashion ("dear").[57] Other behavior is more blatant, such as a judge calling a lawyer "little girl" or trying to undermine the credibility of a female witness by suggesting that she is "emotional, unstable, or irrational."[58] All these forms of stereotyping can be found in the bias task force reports.[59]

Identity stereotyping and exclusionary practices have special power in legal practice because they can be deployed to gain an "edge" for one's own client or to "score points" for one's own interests. Just where adversarialism leaves off and unacceptable disparate treatment begins is a subject of debate and disagreement, as reflected in this comment from the Eighth Circuit Gender Fairness Task Force: "Issues of incivility are often dismissed as 'legitimate advocacy' or just 'part of the game' and female attorneys admonished that they are 'overly sensitive' or 'too thin-skinned' for the practice of law."[60]

Stereotyping individuals based on their identity and feeling discomfort with fellow professionals who look different from oneself are sometimes described as holdovers from an earlier era that will be left behind as time passes. But task forces' analyses of survey data show that differences in experiences and perceptions persist through younger generations.[61] Rather than fading away, adversarial use of identity differences may be passed down from older to younger professional cohorts. In short, deciding what behavior is legitimate "lawyer-like" adversarialism and what behaviors should be pushed outside the boundaries of legal professional behavior is an issue not only for today but for the future.

Identity and Obligation

What to make of the results of their fact-finding was a challenge that all task forces faced. Many task force members believed that the data they had collected indicated a need for corrective action; they turned to judges and lawyers to take the lead in efforts at improvement. Others, however, focused on task forces' positive findings— the relatively few instances of "on the record" bias from judges and the perceived improvements in the treatment of women and people of color—and celebrated, proclaiming that since there were "no statistically significant incidents of bias (as normally defined) in our courts,"[62] no action was necessary. As the task forces' efforts garnered more attention from bench and bar, their work became a symbol for political conservatives of perceived dangers in focusing on identity in the United States. Nearly twenty years after their inception, whether task forces were projects *of*, *about*, and *for* the legal profession was again a subject of debate.

Proposals for Change

In the wake of the publication of task force reports, many jurisdictions authorized remedial responses, ranging from educational programs on diversity to handbooks on how to improve the conduct of court proceedings, and from informal efforts to expand the diversity of those appointed by courts to revising internal policies on employment practices and sexual harassment.[63] From task force projects grew thousands of conversations in courthouses, bar associations, and law firms about how women and men of all colors experience the legal system and about how the legal system treats all of its participants.

In some instances, task force efforts also engendered formal rulemaking, encompassing a host of issues from the administration of courts to the conduct of legal proceedings. Some jurisdictions adopted policies to increase the inclusion of women of all colors and of men of color in court appointments; the methods varied from heightened efforts to disseminate information about opportunities, to targeted outreach, to mandated affirmative action.

A vivid example of an effort to change exclusionary patterns of judicial selection comes from Florida, where regional panels recommended individuals for judgeships to the governor. In 1991, after its two task forces reported the small numbers of judges who were women of all colors or men of color,[64] the Florida legislature enacted a statute requiring that one of the three members of the nominating panels selecting judges must be "a member of a racial or ethnic minority *or* a woman."[65] The statute included features that prompt criticism of simplistic versions of "identity politics": it appears to pit racial and ethnic minorities against women in competition for positions; it does not distinguish among women, with regard to race or ethnicity, and it similarly lumps all racial and ethnic minorities into one undifferentiated "other."[66] But a review of data on those appointed as nominators for judges in Florida indicates that the percentage of women and of minorities sitting on panels rose significantly after the statute was passed.[67]

In rulemaking and through case law, courts also addressed the use of gender, race and ethnicity as adversarial tools. Two national codes, promulgated by the American Bar Association, provide models, one for judges and one for lawyers. In 1990, the American Bar Association's Model Code, Canon 3(B)(6), governing *judicial* authority to regulate attorney behavior was amended to provide that judges shall "require lawyers in proceedings before the judge to refrain from manifesting, by words or conduct, bias or prejudice based upon race, sex, religion, national origin, disability, age, sexual orientation or socioeconomic status, against parties, witnesses, counsel or others."[68] By 1998, twenty-two states and the District of Columbia had adopted such provisions, and a few other states had written their own.[69] Efforts to alter the model code for *lawyers* did not succeed at a national level until 1998,[70] but a few states modified their codes, for example, by defining "professional misconduct" to prohibit lawyers from engaging in "conduct involving discrimination . . . because of race, color, religion, age, sex, sexual orientation, national origin, marital status, socioeconomic status or handicap where the conduct is intended or likely to create harm."[71] A few federal district courts also promulgated "local" rules specifically addressing bias in courts and in varying ways attempting to curb it.[72]

As the language of these codes suggests, prohibiting gender-based and race- and ethnicity-based bias is not the same as specifying what constitutes misconduct. Moreover, these prohibitions are usually accompanied by the caveat that "legitimate advocacy" does not constitution a violation.[73] To date, a few opinions consider challenges to lawyers (or judges) based on bias. Some appellate courts have found examples of lawyers or judges engaging on the record in behavior that undermines lawyers' or witnesses' credibility based on gender, race, or ethnicity; these courts have imposed sanctions, including, on rare occasions, reversing the underlying judgments.[74]

Opposition

The new policies soon came under attack, both individually and in the aggregate. In 1995, a white male lawyer attacked the Florida statute on the composition of judicial nominating panels. A federal district judge struck it as an impermissible form of affirmative action, unsupported by a "compelling state interest" and not sufficiently narrowly tailored to meet remedial goals.[75] In the Ninth Circuit, a district judge sanctioned an attorney for inappropriately using gender in the adversarial process; an appellate court reversed, finding the sanction to be based on too vague a professional regulation, broadly prohibiting lawyers from engaging in offensive behavior.[76]

At the national level, opposition to the task forces and their proposals mounted. In the 1990s, individual judges in one federal circuit "disassociated" themselves from the circuit's work on gender, race, and ethnicity.[77] One of these judges attacked task forces in a speech entitled "Political Correctness Rebuffed," given at a Federalist Society meeting and subsequently published in its journal.[78] These judicial opponents enlisted the support of other institutions. A few members of Congress entered statements into the *Congressional Record* regarding their views on the disutility of task forces; one senator, who in 1997 served as a co-chairman of the Federalist Society, argued that such studies were "ill-conceived, deeply flawed, and divisive, . . . [and] threaten the independence of the Federal Judiciary."[79] At another senator's request, the General Accounting Office investigated the projects, and concluded that because they dealt with "perceptions," their findings did not constitute "evidence that gender and/or racial bias exists."[80]

Mounting opposition chilled the federal task force efforts. Some circuits paused; others narrowed their efforts. Individuals also suffered professional hardship. For example, one nominee for a federal judgeship found herself addressing objections based on her service—at the request of the Executive Committee of the Ninth Circuit—on a judicially commissioned task force on gender bias.[81]

Defining Legal Professionalism in a Pluralist Society

Underlying the debate over the legitimacy of task force efforts and the proposals for change that they have engendered are conflicting visions of professional behavior and obligations. We see this conflict in the different understandings of the adversarial interactions that the task forces described. For some, data about deploying identity stereotypes evidence behavior that breaches the promise of equal treatment under law. For others, the data reflect a more general problem of "incivility"—of lawyers' unfortunate tendency to engage in unduly aggressive conduct. For a third group, the behavior is simply an example of "zealous pursuit of client interests." Depending on which interpretation one adopts, one may favor specific judicial sanctions, generic codes of conduct, or silence.

At a deeper level, the conflict over task forces' legitimacy reflects division over the profession's obligation to promote full participation in the profession and in the wider society by men and women of all colors. On the one hand, the ABA has embraced the goal of equal treatment as its own. In 1991, the ABA adopted a revised mission statement that includes the goal of promoting "full and equal participation in the legal profession by minorities and women."[82] Similarly, other lawyers' organizations have also argued that such efforts are central for lawyers. For example, the Lawyers' Committee for Civil Rights under Law has requested that the president of the United States "call" on lawyers "to join in a common effort . . . to renew the advance for racial justice, a goal that can only be reached if the law and the legal profession support such a result."[83]

On the other hand, the Federalist Society has convened special meetings to consider whether task force efforts can be "reconciled with traditional conceptions of the rule of law and with our Founders' concerns about faction in a civil society."[84] Further, the Federalist Society reports with concern, "a rapidly-increasing focus by the ABA on gender and minority issues, many of which generate substantial controversy."[85]

Should lawyers and judges talk about diversity? Should they engage in efforts to reduce perceptions of unfair treatment in the legal system based on gender, race, and ethnicity? Should members of the legal profession take affirmative actions to ensure that the legal system makes good on its promise of equal treatment for all? What relationship do these questions have to problems of undue competition and unpleasant adversarialism? Our answers are that lawyers have a distinctive role in enacting law's commitment to equality and hence a special relationship to the problems represented contemporarily by the moniker "identity politics." Lawyers need to add a new element to their professional identity, that of advocate for equality, and to distinguish that role from the modes proposed to respond to the other problems of unduly aggressive, uncivil interactions and the reorganization of legal markets.

Our reasons are several. First, U.S. courts have long made a point of claiming that they treat individuals without regard to their race, ethnicity, and/or gender. In the later part of the twentieth century, the judicial system began to implement aspects of that claim through announcing that both de facto and de jure discrimination conflict with constitutional obligations of equality and fairness. The judiciary is not only concerned with rules of law. Judges also pride themselves on their keen appreciation of the importance of specific contexts, and on their willingness to engage in fact-finding to obtain detailed knowledge of local situations to enable case-by-case appraisals. Judges care about law in practice as well as law on the books. Thus, even were other institutions to move away from addressing the experiences of identity groups, the legal system would need to continue to ask whether law is working, in practice, to deliver in all contexts and cases on its promises.

Second, law once maintained and authorized systems of discrimination. That history requires that lawyers and judges take special notice of and engage in special efforts to diminish the residue of that which they helped to create and to enforce and which they now know causes so much harm.

Third, law needs popular support and appreciation; it relies for its legitimacy on beliefs that legal institutions are equally responsive to all its citizens' legitimate claims.[86] To do its work, law not only needs to be fair, it must be perceived as fair. Lawyers and judges cannot simply assert that the citizenry accepts its claims, especially in the face of substantial evidence to the contrary. (Indeed, as we write, newspapers report survey data that indicate 47 percent of Americans believe the legal system to be less fair to minorities than to nonminorities.[87])

Fourth, constitutional jurisprudence does not purport to preempt ethical obligations. No matter how narrowly (or broadly) discrimination may be understood as a matter of federal constitutional law, lawyers and judges do not hold themselves up to meeting only such standards. Lawyers and judges make policies about what good and wise lawyering is, and sometimes, in good times, their judgments lead the way to understanding both the strengths and the limits of legal rules. That some sixty reports about fairness have been published in the name of lawyering provides significant promise for the profession. Task forces on gender, race, and ethnicity not only are projects *of* the profession and projects *on* the profession, they also identify hopes *for* the profession.

Some have argued that the route to take to fulfill these hopes is to insist on standards of civility and to embrace less adversarial modes of conduct, that the problems uncovered by the task forces stem from a profession that has failed to communicate how properly trained lawyers should talk to or oppose each other. But such a response diminishes the import of the findings of task forces, which documented problems much deeper than modes and manners of lawyering. Task forces have taught us that within courts, not all actors (lawyers and judges included) believe themselves to be full participants. The 1999 public opinion poll on attitudes toward courts echoed these two decades of task force work; a large fraction of people in the United States do not believe that courts treat all equally, and perceptions of inequality are linked to gender and race. For judges and lawyers to respond to such empirical work with programs to improve lawyers' manners is both distracting and insufficient.

Rather than conflate problems of adversarialism and entrepreneurship with obligations for equal treatment and build programs of reform from that amalgam, we urge a different agenda. The task force movement that we have analyzed, while imbedded within the profession, also challenges lawyers to generate a distinctive and new dimension of their professional identity. The findings of the task forces demonstrate that the list of professional descriptors—officers of the courts, entrepreneurs, zealous advocates, agents of change, and "statesmen"—no longer suffices. Having taken on the question of the degree to which legal commitments to equal treatment translate into practice, lawyers and judges should not now turn away from the implications of what they have learned. Instead, they need to revisit their conception of professionalism and modify it by including, as a professional obligation, advocacy for and insistence on the practice of equality.

Notes

Deborah R. Hensler is the Judge John W. Ford Professor of Dispute Resolution at Stanford Law School and Senior Fellow at the RAND Institute for Civil Justice. She was a member of the Ninth Circuit's Gender Bias Task Force and of the Ninth Circuit's Task Force on Race, Ethnicity and Religious Fairness.

Judith Resnik is the Arthur Liman Professor of Law at Yale Law School. She was a member of the Ninth Circuit's Task Force on Gender Bias and has served as a consultant to task forces and related projects in other jurisdictions.

Our thanks to Denny Curtis, Kim DeMarchi, Janet Guggemos, Vicki Jackson, Deborah Rhode, Tanina Rostain, Tara Veazey, and Diane Zimmerman for help in thinking through the issues discussed here.

1. See, e.g., Anthony Kronman, *The Lost Lawyer: Failing Ideals of the Legal Profession* (Cambridge, Mass.: Harvard University Press, 1993); Sol Linowitz, *The Betrayed Profession: Lawyering at the End of the Twentieth Century* (New York: Charles Scribner's Sons, 1994); David Luban, *Lawyers and Justice: An Ethical Study* (Princeton, N.J.: Princeton University Press, 1988); Deborah Rhode, *Professional Responsibility: Ethics by the Pervasive Method*, 2d ed. (New York: Aspen Law & Business, 1998); and William Simon, *The Practice of Justice: A Theory of Lawyers' Ethics* (Cambridge, Mass.: Harvard University Press, 1998).

2. Critics outside the profession—in jokes, cartoons, opinion editorials, and other expository forms—characterize lawyers as untrustworthy, as self-serving entrepreneurs and disagreeable technocrats who engage alternately in "legal hair-splitting" and "Rambo-style" litigating. See generally Marc Galanter, "The Faces of Mistrust: The Image of Lawyers in Public Opinions, Jokes, and Political Discourse," 66 *U. Cin. L. R.* 805 (1998).

3. See Deborah L. Rhode, "Cultures of Commitment: Pro Bono for Lawyers and Law Students," 67 *Fordham L. Rev.* 2415 (1999).

4. See *ABA Policy and Procedures Handbook*, 2 1991–92 ed. (Chicago: ABA Press, 1991), 2.

5. Patrick E. Higginbotham, "The American Inns of Court," 25 *Colorado Lawyer* 41 (November 1996). See also Joryn Jenkins, "The American Inns of Court: Preparing Our Students for Ethical Practice," 27 *Akron L. Rev.* 175 (1993). For additional discussion about the need to address professional failings, see Linowitz. For survey data about lawyers' understandings of their own profession, see Deborah R. Hensler and Marisa E. Reddy, *California Lawyers View the Future: A Report to the Commission on the Future of the Legal Profession and the State Bar* (Santa Monica, Calif.: RAND, 1994).

6. The ABA has promulgated two codes of ethics, one for lawyers and one for judges. See Model Rules of Professional Conduct, 1998 ed. (Chicago: ABA, 1997); Model Code of Judicial Conduct, 1998 ed. (Chicago: ABA, 1997).

In addition, the divisions of the ABA have endorsed its members' participation in the American Inns of Court. See James A. George, "The American Inns of Court in Louisiana," 43 *Louisiana Bar Journal* 35, 36 (June 1995) (citing a resolution of the ABA's Judicial Administration Division that "[a]ll judges and senior lawyers are encouraged to become members of American Inns of Courts and . . . to assist in the creation of new . . . Inns").

7. See *ABA Policy and Procedures Handbook*, 133.

8. See, e.g., The Federalist Society for Law & Public Policy Studies, *The ABA in Law and Social Policy: What Role?* (1994); Federalist Society Project, *ABA WATCH*. The creation of the *ABA WATCH*, published twice a year, is described as "incit[ing] much-needed debate about the legal and political role of the American Bar Association." 1997 Annual Report of the Federalist Society for Law and Public Policy Studies, 9; "From the Editors," *ABA WATCH* 1 (August 1996).

9. See Judith Resnik, "Asking about Gender in Courts," 21 *Signs* 952 (1996), including an appendix listing reports as of that date. Note that such efforts are official projects of courts, as distinct from more general commentary on the effects of race, ethnicity, and gender on careers. See, e.g., Cynthia Fuchs Epstein, *Women in Law*, 2d ed. (Urbana: University of Illinois Press, 1993); and Linn Washington, *Black Judges on Justice: Perspectives from the Bench* (New York: New Press, 1994).

10. The founding and current directors of this program have described its inception and evolution. See Lynn Hecht Schafran, "Documenting Gender Bias in the Courts: The Task Force Approach," 70 *Judicature* 280 (1987); Lynn Hecht Schafran, "Gender Bias in the Courts: An Emerging Focus for Judicial Reform," 21 *Ariz. St. L. J.* 237 (1989); Norma Wikler, "On the Judicial Agenda for the 80s: Equal Treatment for Men and Women in the Courts," 64 *Judicature* 202 (1980); and Norma Wikler, "Water on Stone: A Perspective on the Movement to Eliminate Gender Bias in the Courts," 26 *Court Review* 6 (Fall 1989). See also Jennette F. Swent, "Gender Bias at the Heart of Justice: An Empirical Study of State Task Forces," 6 *So. Calif. Rev. Law & Women's Studies* (1996).

11. New Jersey Supreme Court Task Force on Women in the Courts, *The First Year Report of the New Jersey Supreme Court Task Force on Women in the Courts* (1986), reprinted in 9 *Women's Rts. L. Rep.* 129 (1986).

12. Arline Tyler and Steven Montano, "State Panels Document Racial, Ethnic Bias in the Courts," 78 *Judicature* 154 (Nov./Dec. 1994). See also H. Clifton Grandy, *A New Paradigm for Fairness: The First National Conference on Eliminating Racial and Ethnic Bias in the Courts: Conference Proceedings* (National Center for State Courts, 1995).

13. 26 *S. Ct. Rev.* 5 (1989). See also Conference of Chief Justices, Resolution Urging Further Efforts for Equal Treatment of All Persons (adopted Jan. 28, 1993) (calling for implementation of reforms), available from the National Center for State Courts.

14. See Judith Resnik, *Summary of Activities and Publications Related to Gender, Race, and Ethnicity in Courts* (1997); Lynn Hecht Schafran, Norma J. Wikler, and Jill Crawford, National Judicial Education Program, *The Gender Fairness Strategies Project: Implementation Resources Directory* (National Judicial Education Program to Promote Equality for Women and Men in the Courts, Dec. 1998) (published with a grant from the State Justice Institute to the National Association of Women Judges, on behalf of the National Association of Women Judges, the National Judicial College, the National Center for State Courts, the ABA Commission on Women in the Profession, and the National Judicial Education Program to Promote Equality of Women and Men in the Courts, a project of the NOW Legal Defense and Education Fund in cooperation with the National Association of Women Judges) [hereinafter *Implementation Directory*].

15. See Ninth Circuit Gender Bias Task Force, *Executive Summary of the Preliminary Re-*

port of the *Ninth Circuit Task Force on Gender Bias* (July 1992), reprinted in 45 *Stan. L. Rev.* 2153 (July 1993); Ninth Circuit Gender Bias Task Force, *The Effects of Gender in the Federal Courts: The Final Report of the Ninth Circuit Gender Bias Task Force* (July 1993), reprinted in 67 *So. Cal. L. Rev.* 745 (May 1994).

16. See *Long Range Plan of the Judicial Conference of the United States,* 166 *F.R.D.* 49, 172-173 (1995) (Recommendation 78, calling for leadership of federal judges "to eliminate unfairness and its perceptions in the federal courts" and citing conference endorsement of studies).

17. See Violent Crime Control and Law Enforcement Act of 1994, Pub. L. No. 103-332, 108 Stat. 1796, 1944 (codified at 42 U.S.C. §14001a) (1994) (encouraging circuit judicial councils to conduct studies of "instances, if any, of gender bias in their respective circuits and to implement recommended reforms").

18. See "Symposium: The Federal Courts, Commentaries on Bias in the Federal Courts," 32 *U. Rich. L. Rev.* 645-768 (May 1998) (compilation of essays by judges and circuit executives from eleven of the federal circuits); Judith Resnik, "Foreword: 'The Federal Courts': Constituting and Changing the Topic," 32 *U. Rich. L. Rev.* 603 (May 1998); and Lynn Hecht Schafran, "Will Inquiry Produce Action? Studying the Effects of Gender in the Federal Courts," 32 *U. Rich. L. Rev.* 615 (May 1998).

19. See Lynn Hecht Schafran and Norma Juliet Wikler, *Operating a Task Force on Gender Bias in the Courts: A Manual for Action* (Washington, D.C.: Foundation for Women Judges, 1986); Edna Wells Handy, Desiree B. Leigh, Yolande P. Marlow, and Lorraine H. Weber, *Establishing and Operating a Task Force on Racial and Ethnic Bias in the Courts* (Washington, D.C.: National Center for State Courts, 1993); and Molly Treadway Johnson, *Studying the Role of Gender in the Federal Courts: A Research Guide* (Washington, D.C.: Federal Judicial Center, Foundation for Women Judges, 1995).

20. See *Implementation Directory.*

21. See, e.g., *Adarand Constructors, Inc., v. Pena,* 515 U.S. 200 (1995). As we discuss infra, objections to task forces sometimes rested on the claim that they were poorly executed efforts to demonstrate discriminatory employment practices and to promote affirmative action. Addressing bias in hiring and promotion practices has, in actuality, been a minor theme of task forces' efforts. For such criticism, see Stephen Thernstrom, "Critical Observations on the Draft Final Report of the Special Committee on Race and Ethnicity to the D.C. Circuit Task Force on Gender, Race, and Ethnic Bias," in *The Gender, Race, and Ethnic Bias Task Force Project in the D.C. Circuit,* Vol. 1 (1995), V App. 1-1 [hereinafter *D.C. Circuit Task Force Project*], also reprinted in 1995 *Public Interest Law Review* 119 (1995).

The two reports of the D.C. Circuit Task Force Project were also published in law journals. To facilitate access, subsequent citations to each of the committee reports will be to their respective journal citations. References to the technical appendices and statements of disassociation, only published as a part of the volume provided by the courts, will be indicated by citing to the *D.C. Circuit Task Force Project.*

22. For discussion of the framing of the reports and their relationship to other forms of legal documentation, see Judith Resnik, "Singular and Aggregate Voices: Audiences and Authority in Law & Literature and Law & Feminism," in *Law & Literature,* Michael Freeman and A. D. Lewis, eds. (Oxford: Oxford University Press, 1999).

23. Remarks of Circuit Judge Patricia M. Wald, *Aspen Law & Business, Third Annual Institute, Woman Advocate* 13 (June 1995).

24. Of 62 gender and/or racial and ethnic task force reports reviewed, 22 use the word "bias" in their titles; 16 use the word "fairness;" 16 use the words "equality," "justice," or "equal justice;" and 8 use the words "women in the profession," "women in the courts," or "women in the bar." Other titles include phrases such as "gender issues," "racial and ethnic issues," "oppor-

tunities for women and minorities," "where the injured fly for justice," "let justice be done: equally fairly and impartially," and "a difference in perceptions."

25. Press release; see also Dolores K. Sloviter, "Personal Reflections on the Creation of the Third Circuit Task Force on Equal Treatment in the Courts," 42 *Vill. L. Rev.* 1347, 1351 (1997).

26. See Commission on Systemic Racism in the Ontario Criminal Justice System, *Report of the Commission on Systemic Racism in the Ontario Criminal Justice System* (Toronto: Queen's Printer for Ontario, 1995) (defining systemic racism broadly as "the social processes that produce racial inequality in decisions about people and in the treatment they receive"), ii. As noted, unlike the reports from the United States, the Canadian work was chartered by the government rather than by the court system specifically.

27. See Sheilah L. Martin, "Proving Gender Bias in the Law and the Legal System," in *Investigating Gender Bias,* Joan Brockman and Dorothy E. Chunn, eds. (Toronto, Ont.: Thompson Educational Publishing, Inc., 1993), 19-20 n. 3.

28. Federalist Society, Brochure on the Society's Program on Race and Gender Bias in the Legal System, Chicago, August 6, 1995. The society's program was held concurrently with the ABA's Annual Meeting.

29. New York Task Force on Women in the Courts, *Report of the New York Task Force on Women in the Courts* (1986), reprinted in 15 *Fordham Urb. L. J.* 11, 17–18 (1986–87).

30. Michigan Supreme Court Task Force on Racial/Ethnic Issues in the Courts, *Final Report of the Michigan Supreme Court Task Force on Racial/Ethnic Issues in the Courts* (Dec. 1989), 2.

31. *Report of the Special Committee on Gender to the D.C. Circuit Task Force on Gender, Race, and Ethnic Bias* (1995), reprinted in 84 *Geo. L. J.* 1657, 1706 (1996).

32. Kentucky Task Force on Gender Fairness in the Courts, *Equal Justice for Women and Men* (Jan. 1992), 6 (also noting the "continued existence" of gender bias).

33. Georgia Commission on Gender Bias in the Judicial System, *Gender and Justice in the Courts: A Report to the Supreme Court of Georgia by the Commission on Gender Bias in the Judicial System* (Aug. 1991), xi, reprinted in 8 *Ga. St. U. L. Rev.* 539 (1992).

34. Ninth Circuit Task Force on Racial, Religious & Ethnic Fairness, *Final Report* (Aug. 1997), 9.

35. See Laura Gatland, "Courts Behaving Badly," 83 *ABAJ* 30 (Nov. 1997).

36. U.S. Department of Commerce, Census Bureau, *1990 Census of Population, Supplementary Reports, Detailed Occupation and Other Characteristics from the EEO File for the United States,* 1990 CP-S-1-1, Table 1, at 3.

37. About 16 percent of Ninth Circuit federal court practitioners surveyed were women, compared to about 22 percent in the Ninth Circuit bar as a whole. Ninth Circuit Gender Bias Task Force, *Effects of Gender in the Federal Courts,* 777. See also *Final Report & Recommendations of the Eighth Circuit Gender Fairness Task Force* (1997), reprinted in 31 *Creighton L. Rev.* 9, 43 (1997) (16 percent); *Report of the Second Circuit Task Force on Gender, Racial, and Ethnic Fairness in the Courts* (1997), reprinted in 1-2 *Annual Survey of American Law* 1, 35 (1997) (22 percent); *Report of the Special Committee on Gender to the D.C. Circuit Task Force* 1685–86 nn. 34, 36 (21 percent).

About 91 percent of federal practitioners surveyed in the Ninth Circuit were white, non-Hispanic Americans. *Ninth Circuit Task Force on Racial, Religious & Ethnic Fairness,* 37. See also *Eighth Circuit Gender Fairness Task Force,* 44 (4 percent); *Report of the Working Committees to the Second Circuit Task Force on Gender, Racial, and Ethnic Fairness in the Courts,* reprinted in 1–2 *Annual Survey of American Law* 117, 160–61 (1997) (6.6 percent, and among minority attorneys, 65 percent were male). *D.C. Circuit Task Force Project,* Vol. 2, app. D.2 (response to Question 3) (9 percent, 44 percent of whom were male).

38. As of 1996, about 19 percent of federal appellate judges and 17 percent of federal district court judges nationwide were women. In the Eighth Circuit, six percent of appellate judges and 11 percent of district court judges were women in 1997. *Eighth Circuit Gender Fairness Task Force,* 36–37. As of August 1991, women held 12 percent of judicial positions in the Ninth Circuit. Women were better represented among non–Article III judges than among Article III judges. Ninth Circuit Gender Bias Task Force, *Effects of Gender in the Federal Courts,* 773. In 1996, about 11 percent of Third Circuit Article III judges were women; about 17 percent of magistrate judges and 28 percent of bankruptcy judges were women. *Report of the Third Circuit Task Force on Equal Treatment in the Courts* (1997), reprinted in 42 *Vill. L. Rev.* 1355, 1369–70 (1997). In the Second Circuit, in 1996, there was one woman on the appellate bench (the only woman ever to have served on the Second Circuit appellate court); 19 percent of district court judges were women. *Report of the Working Committees to the Second Circuit Task Force,* 148 (calculations based on Table 7). In the D.C. Circuit, in 1994, 3 of 11 active appellate judges and 2 of 10 active district judges were women. *Report of the Special Committee on Gender to the D.C. Circuit Task Force,* 1678–79.

About 12 percent of judges responding to the Ninth Circuit's Racial, Religious and Ethnic Fairness survey identified themselves as members of ethnic and racial minority groups. *Ninth Circuit Task Force on Racial, Religious & Ethnic Fairness,* 31. In the Third Circuit as of 1996, 11 of 107 Article III judges were members of minority groups; there was 1 minority group member among magistrate judges and none among bankruptcy judges. *Third Circuit Task Force,* 1369–70. In the Second Circuit, in 1996, about 10 percent of Article III judges and 9 percent of non–Article III judges were members of minority groups. *Report of the Working Committees to the Second Circuit Task Force,* 153 (calculations based on Table 13). In the D.C. Circuit, as of 1995, of 11 active appellate judges, 2 were African American and the rest were white; of 15 active district court judges, 3 were African American, 1 Hispanic, and the rest were white. *Report of the Special Committee on Race and Ethnicity to the D.C. Circuit Task Force on Gender, Race and Ethnic Bias* (1996), reprinted in 64 *Geo. Wash. L. Rev.* 189, 201–2 (1996).

39. In the Ninth Circuit, 36 percent of federal public defenders surveyed and 31 percent of assistant U.S. attorneys surveyed were women, compared to 16 percent in all practice settings combined. Ninth Circuit Gender Bias Task Force, *Effects of Gender in the Federal Courts,* 778 (Table 2.1). About 9 percent of private federal practitioners surveyed by the Ninth Circuit were people of color, compared to 15 percent of assistant U.S. attorneys and 21 percent of federal defenders. *Ninth Circuit Task Force on Racial, Religious & Ethnic Fairness,* 37. Ninety-one percent of male federal practitioners surveyed in the Eighth Circuit were in private practice settings, compared to 74 percent of female attorneys. *Eighth Circuit Gender Fairness Task Force,* 45. Women of all colors and men of color are overrepresented in the public sector of the bar in the Second Circuit. *Report of the Working Committees to the Second Circuit Task Force,* 164.

40. The Ninth Circuit Gender Bias Task Force found that while circuit-wide, women were represented on bench and bar committees in numbers that matched their presence in the federal bar, some local district committees contained no women or far fewer than chance would predict. Ninth Circuit Gender Bias Task Force, *Effects of Gender in the Federal Courts,* 789. The Third Circuit found fewer women serving on criminal justice (CJA) panels, and as arbitrators and mediators in district courts, than the numbers of women practicing in that circuit would lead one to expect. *Third Circuit Task Force,* 1443, 1452. The Second Circuit found that women of all colors received 16 percent of fee-bearing appointments and men and women of color received 3.5 percent of such appointments, although they comprise 22 percent and 7 percent of federal practitioners, respectively, in that circuit. Significantly, women received 25 percent of unrenumerated appointments, and attorneys of color received 17 percent of such appointments. *Report of the Working Committees to the Second Circuit Task Force,* 193–95.

41. *Report of the Special Committee on Race and Ethnicity to the D.C. Circuit Task Force,* 239.

42. *D.C. Circuit Task Force Project,* Vol. 2, app. G.2, 10. See also *Third Circuit Task Force,* 1611 (noting that "numerous minority attorneys indicated that minorities are not well represented in appointments made by judges within the Third Circuit. They interpreted this lack of representation as bias and suggested that it fostered a perception within minority communities that such bias exists"); *Ninth Circuit Task Force on Racial, Religious & Ethnic Fairness,* app. C, 2.56–2.58 (finding that all attorneys, regardless of color, reported serving on special committees and in fee-generating positions infrequently but noted that some attorneys believe that opportunities for attorneys of color to serve varies in some districts).

43. See, e.g., Ninth Circuit Gender Bias Task Force, *Effects of Gender in the Federal Courts,* 789 (the Federal Bar Association "is perceived to be the ultimate men's club in this district").

44. Ibid., 790–92.

45. Ibid., 787. See also *Eighth Circuit Gender Fairness Task Force,* 127 (finding that "professional exclusion" was a topic "of frequent comments by female attorneys, many of whom not only found it discomforting, but also feared that it results in, or is symptomatic of, actual gender bias in decision making").

46. Ninth Circuit Gender Bias Task Force, *Effects of Gender in the Federal Courts,* 802 (Table 3.9). In contrast, only 2 percent of male criminal practitioners and 1 percent of male civil practitioners reported losing a case because of gender bias. When asked for reasons that "important cases" were assigned to men, male practitioners were more likely to offer reasons based on level of expertise and qualifications of the attorney, while women were more likely to offer as reasons that such cases needed a "heavy hitter" or "aggressive counsel." Ibid., 804–5.

47. Sixteen percent of the female attorneys surveyed in the D.C. Circuit reported losing an assignment while 9 percent reported gaining an assignment for reasons "associated with gender." In contrast, less than 2 percent of male attorneys reported either losing or gaining an assignment because of gender. *Report of the Special Committee on Gender to the D.C. Circuit Task Force,* 1735. Eleven percent of African American attorneys reported losing an assignment while 9 percent reported gaining an assignment for reasons associated with race or ethnicity. Of white attorneys surveyed, less than 2 percent reported losing an assignment and 1 percent reported gaining an assignment because of their race or ethnicity. *D.C. Circuit Task Force Project,* Vol. 2, app. G.2, at 14-15 (responses to questions 15 and 16).

48. Ninth Circuit Gender Bias Task Force, *Effects of Gender in the Federal Courts,* 824.

49. Ibid., 816–17.

50. Deborah Hensler, "Studying Gender Bias in the Courts: Stories and Statistics," 45 *Stanford L. Rev.* 2187, 2191 (1993).

51. D.C. Circuit Task Force Project, Vol. 2, app. G.2, at 66.

52. Massachusetts Supreme Judicial Court Commission to Study Racial and Ethnic Bias in the Courts, *Final Report: Equal Justice: Eliminating the Barriers* (1994), 3.

53. *Eighth Circuit Gender Fairness Task Force,* 133.

54. *A Report of the Perceptions and Experiences of Lawyers, Judges, and Court Employees Concerning Gender, Racial and Ethnic Fairness in the Federal Courts of the Second Circuit* (*Baruch Report to the Second Circuit Task Force*) (1997), reprinted in 1–2 *Annual Survey of American Law* 415, 450 (1997).

55. See, e.g., *Third Circuit Task Force,* 1405; *Eighth Circuit Gender Fairness Task Force,* 133; *Baruch Report to the Second Circuit Task Force,* 466 (Table 15); *D.C. Circuit Task Force Project,* Vol. 2, app. G.2 at 34-36, app. D.2 (responses to question 28).

56. Ninth Circuit Gender Bias Task Force, *Effects of Gender in the Federal Courts,* 810;

Ninth Circuit Task Force on Racial, Religious & Ethnic Fairness, app. C, 2.9; *Eighth Circuit Gender Fairness Task Force,* 129; *Baruch Report to the Second Circuit Task Force,* 452.

57. Ninth Circuit Gender Task Force, *Effects of Gender in the Federal Courts,* 812.

58. *D.C. Circuit Task Force Project,* Vol. 2, app. D.2 (responses to question 43). More than twenty reports describe how women as witnesses sometimes face special hurdles of credibility, and how women as parties find their claims undervalued. Judith Resnik, " 'Naturally' Without Gender: Women, Jurisdiction, and the Federal Courts," 66 *N.Y.U. L. Rev.* 1682 (1991).

59. See. e.g., Ninth Circuit Gender Bias Task Force, *Effects of Gender in the Federal Courts,* 811–30; *Ninth Circuit Task Force on Racial, Religious & Ethnic Fairness,* app. C, 2.9-2.47; *Eighth Circuit Gender Fairness Task Force,* 126–36; *Third Circuit Task Force,* 1422–25, 1570–82; *Baruch Report to the Second Circuit Task Force,* 450–70.

60. *Eighth Circuit Gender Fairness Task Force,* 136.

61. Ninth Circuit Gender Bias Task Force, *Effects of Gender in the Federal Courts,* 830-31; *Baruch Report to the Second Circuit Task Force,* 442.

62. Hon. Laurence H. Silberman, "The D.C. Circuit Task Force on Gender, Race, and Ethnic Bias: Political Correctness Rebuffed," 19 *Harv. J. L. & Pub. Pol'y* 759, 765 (1996). The issue, of course, is not only what standards should be used to "define" bias in courts and hence what is "normal" for litigation but also whether such definitions should be relied upon when considering the experiences of litigants.

Judge Silberman's remark illustrates another difficulty task forces faced, that some judges are uncomfortable with quantitative data. His use of the phrase "statistically significant incidents of bias" is puzzling. Statisticians speak about statistically significant differences and statistically significant relationships to note those that occur more frequently than would be expected by chance; what is meant by "statistically significant incidents" is unclear.

63. See generally Vicki C. Jackson, "Gender Bias: What Judges Can Learn from Gender Bias Task Force Studies," 81 *Judicature* 15 (July-August 1997); *Implementation Directory,* 11–110 (including bench books, case law, codes of conduct, complaint procedures, handbooks, employment and court rules, jury instructions, newsletters, and videos); *Implementation Directory,* 111–42 (detailing changes in substantive law).

64. *Report of the Florida Supreme Court Gender Bias Study Commission* (1990); *Report and Recommendations of the Florida Supreme Court Racial and Ethnic Bias Study Commission, "Where the Injured Fly for Justice"* Vol. 1 (1990), Vol. 2 (1991).

65. Fla. Stat. Ann. § 43.29 (West Supp. 1993, emphasis added) (enacted in 1991).

66. See, e.g., Kimberle Crenshaw, "Mapping the Margins: Intersectionality, Identity Politics, and Violence Against Women of Color," 43 *Stan. L. Rev.* 1241 (1991).

67. Of 520 people, 1976–90, 20 percent were women, 11 percent minorities (8 black, 3 hispanic); 16 percent not identified but most likely white. Of 247 appointments, 1992–95, 36 percent women, 31 percent minorities (3 percent not identified); of 77 people of color, 30 women. (Review of records provided by the Florida system; on file with the authors.)

68. Model Code of Judicial Canon S 3 B(6) (Chicago: ABA, 1990).

69. *Implementation Directory,* 24.

70. The ABA added a new comment to its rule on misconduct that states:

A lawyer who in the course of representing a client, knowingly manifests by words or conduct, bias or prejudice based upon race, sex, religion, national origin, disability, age, sexual orientation, or socioeconomic status" violates its code when "such actions are prejudicial to the administration of justice."

Model Rules of Professional Conduct, Rule 8.4, Comment 2 (amended 1998), also reprinted in *Implementation Directory,* 32.

71. New Jersey, Rules of Professional Conduct, Rule 8.4 (1990). For provisions from Florida, Rhode Island, Colorado, and Massachusetts, see *Implementation Directory*, 29–30.

72. For example, U.S. Dist. Ct. Rules E.D. Wash., Local Rule LR 83.4. (promulgated March 18, 1993) ("Judges, attorneys and judicial employees shall fulfill their roles under the highest standards of professionalism. Unjustified treatment will be avoided in both language and action. All are aware of the need to act without regard to gender, race, or religion or other inappropriate bias."). See also Arizona (U.S. Dist. Ct. Rules D. Ariz., Rule 1.20), Idaho (U.S. Dist. & Bankr. Ct., D. Idaho, Order 112), and the Northern District of Washington (U.S. Dist. Ct. Rules S.D.W. Va., LR Gen. PO. 3.02). Many state courts have promulgated rules on these issues as well.

73. See, e.g., ABA Model Code of Judicial Conduct, Canon 3B(6); ABA Model Code of Professional Responsibility, Rule 8.4, Comment 2.

74. See, e.g., *State v. Pace*, 425 SE 2d 73 (S.C.App. 1992), rev'd 447 S.E. 2d 186 (S.C. 1994). *Catchpole v. Brannon*, 36 Cal. App. 4th 237 (Ct. App. 1995); *Powell v. Allstate Ins. Co.*, 652 So. 2d 354 (Fla. 1995). Cases invoking task force reports are listed at *Implementation Directory*, 12–21.

75. See, e.g., *Mallory v. Harkness*, 895 F. Supp. 1556, 1560 (D. Fla. 1995).

76. An assistant U.S. attorney in the Central District of California sought sanctions after receiving a letter from her male opposing counsel who had just been disqualified. His letter included an attachment, announcing in bold print that "MALE LAWYERS PLAY BY THE RULES, DISCOVER TRUTH AND RESTORE ORDER. FEMALE LAWYERS ARE OUTSIDE THE LAW, CLOUD TRUTH AND DESTROY ORDER."

Federal district court judge Alice Marie Stotler found that the letter, while not a part of formal court proceedings, was a part of the litigation process and hence subject to the court's jurisdiction; further, she found it to violate California's professional rules (applied within that district to lawyers appearing before the federal courts), which prohibited lawyers from demonstrating "offensive personality." On appeal, however, the offending lawyer, assisted by the American Civil Liberties Union, successfully argued that the California prohibitions were overly vague, and therefore, unconstitutional limitations on free speech; the sanctions were reversed. See Matter of Swan, 833 F. Supp. 794 (D.Cal. 1993); rev'd *U.S. v. Wunsch*, 84 F.3d 1110 (9th Cir. 1996).

77. "Statement of Disassociation by Circuit Judges Buckley, Ginsburg, and Randolph," in *D.C. Circuit Task Force Project*, Vol. 1, V-1.

78. See Silberman, "D.C. Task Force."

79. Statement by Orrin Hatch, *Cong. Rec* S.14691 (Sept. 29, 1995). The Grassley-Gramm-Hatch colloquy was followed by a counter-colloquy by nine democratic senators—Paul Simon, Edward Kennedy, Joseph Biden, John Kerrey, Bill Bradley, Dale Bumpers, Barbara Boxer, Frank Lautenberg, and John Glenn—and one member of the House (Constance Morella, of Maryland), expressing their support for federal task force work and reminding everyone of enacted legislation—The Violence Against Women Act—supporting these projects. 141 *Cong. Rec.* S18127-05 (Dec. 8, 1995); 141 *Cong. Rec.* E2302-02 (Dec. 6, 1995). The federal judiciary was nonetheless reluctant to distress members of Congress who opposed task force work. Bruce D. Brown, "Judiciary Won't Fight for Court Bias Studies," *Legal Times of Washington*, Nov. 13, 1995.

80. General Accounting Office, Letter to Hon. Charles E. Grassley, GAO/GGD-96-72R, *Circuit Bias Task Force Reports* (March 8, 1996). As indicated above, most task forces collected many forms of data, from self reports to analyses of demographic materials and sometimes case law. And most task forces took as a given that it is important for the nation's judicial systems to be perceived as fair by all citizens.

81. Robert T. Nelson, "Conservatives Make an Example of Seattle Lawyer: Past Liberal Activism Haunts Federal Appeals Nominee," *Seattle Times* March 24, 1997, B1.

82. See *ABA Policy and Procedures Handbook* 3.

83. Submission by the co-chairs of the Lawyers' Committee for Civil Rights under Law to Deputy Attorney General Eric Holder and proposing that a "Presidential Call to Action to the Legal Profession on Racial and Ethnic Justice," Jan. 15, 1999, 3. President Clinton responded by doing so the following July.

84. Federalist Society, Brochure on the Society's Program on Race and Gender Bias in the Legal System, Chicago, Aug. 6, 1995. The society's program was held concurrently with the ABA's Annual Meeting.

85. ABA Commission Issues Reports on State of Women in Law Schools, 1 *ABA WATCH* (Aug. 1996).

86. A persistent and distressing finding of recent surveys on public attitudes toward the judicial system is that large fractions of Americans believe that minorities and the less affluent receive less favorable treatment than do others. See Deborah R. Hensler, Do We Need a Research Agenda on Judicial Independence?," in "Symposium, Judicial Independence," 72 *So. Calif. L. Rev.* 707 (1999).

87. Linda Greenhouse, "47% in Poll View Legal System as Unfair to Poor and Minorities," *New York Times*, February 24, 1999 A2, discussing ABA, perceptions of U.S. Justice System (1999) (also describing confidence levels varying with gender, race, and ethnicity).

13

Cultures of Commitment

Pro Bono for Lawyers and Law Students

DEBORAH L. RHODE

Mark Twain once reminded us that "to do right is noble: to advise others to do right is also noble and much less trouble for yourself." For too many lawyers, the issue of pro bono service reflects too wide a gap between professional rhetoric and professional practice. Bar ethical codes have long advised attorneys that they have obligations to assist individuals who cannot afford counsel. Yet the percentage of lawyers who actually do so has remained dispiritingly small. Recent estimates suggest that most attorneys do not perform significant pro bono work, and that only between 10 and 20 percent of those who do are assisting low-income clients. The average for the profession as a whole is less that a half an hour per week. Few lawyers come close to satisfying the American Bar Association's Model Rules, which provide that "a lawyer should aspire to render at least 50 hours of pro bono public legal services per year," primarily to "persons of limited means or to organizations assisting such persons."[1]

The bar's failure to secure broader participation in pro bono work is all the more disappointing when measured against the extraordinary successes that such work has yielded. Many of the nation's landmark public interest cases have grown out of lawyers' voluntary contributions. And many low-income clients, including homeless or disabled children, victims of domestic violence, and elderly citizens without medical care, have found that pro bono programs are crucial in meeting basic human needs. For lawyers themselves, such work is similarly important in giving purpose and meaning to their professional lives. Our inability to enlist more attorneys in pro bono service represents a significant lost opportunity for them as well as for the public.[2]

How best to narrow the gap between professional ideals and professional practice has been a matter of considerable controversy. Proposals for mandatory pro bono requirements have come and gone, but mainly gone. The bar generally has resisted mandatory service, although a few jurisdictions require lawyers to accept judicial appointments for limited categories of cases.[3]

This resistance to required contributions, coupled with the limited success of voluntary efforts, has encouraged more pro bono initiatives in law schools. By enlisting students early in their legal careers, these initiatives attempt to inspire an enduring commitment to public service. The hope is that, over time, a greater sense of moral obligation will "trickle up" to practitioners. With that objective, an increasing number of schools have instituted pro bono requirements for students. So too, in 1996 the American Bar Association amended its accreditation standards to call on schools to "encourage students to participate in pro bono activities and to provide opportunities for them to do so." These revised ABA standards also encourage schools to address the obligations of faculty to the public, including participation in pro bono activities.[4]

Despite such initiatives, pro bono still occupies a relatively marginal place in legal education. Although most law schools support pro bono in principle, only about 10 percent require any service by students and only a handful impose specific requirements on faculty. At some of these schools, the amounts demanded are quite minimal: less than twenty hours by the time of graduation. While almost all institutions offer voluntary programs, their scope and quality varies considerably. About a third of schools have no law-related pro bono projects or projects involving fewer than 50 participants. In others, only a small minority of students participate. As the Association of American Law School's Commission on Pro Bono and Public Service Opportunities has noted, most students graduate without pro bono legal work as part of their educational experience.[5]

What the bar could or should do to expand public service commitments is subject to increasing debate. This essay attempts to place that debate in broader perspective. Although much has been written about the value of public service, too little attention has focused on the factors that encourage it or on the role of law school programs. The effort here is to increase our understanding of what can promote a culture of commitment to pro bono work.

To that end, discussion begins with the rationale for pro bono involvement by lawyers. Attention then turns to the characteristics and experiences that foster charitable work among Americans in general, and among lawyers and law students in particular. Subsequent analysis centers on legal education's efforts to encourage such work and the strategies most likely to increase their effectiveness.

The Rationale for Pro Bono Services

The primary rationale for pro bono contributions rests on two premises: first, that access to legal services is a fundamental need, and second, that lawyers have some responsibility to help make those services available. The first claim is widely acknowledged. As courts and commentators have long recognized, the right to sue and defend is a right that protects all other rights. Access to the justice system is particularly critical for the poor, who often depend on legal entitlements to meet basic needs such as food, housing, and medical care. Moreover, in a democratic social order, equality before the law is central to the rule of law and to the legitimacy of the state. Social science research confirms what political theorists have long argued: public confidence in legal processes depends heavily on opportunities for direct participation.[6]

In most circumstances, those opportunities are meaningless without access to legal assistance. Our justice system is designed by and for lawyers, and lay participants who attempt to navigate without counsel are generally at a disadvantage. Those disadvantages are particularly great among the poor, who typically lack the education and experience necessary for effective self-representation. For example, studies of eviction proceedings find that tenants with attorneys usually prevail; tenants without attorneys almost always lose. Inequalities in legal representation compound other social inequalities and undermine our commitments to procedural fairness and social justice.[7]

While most lawyers acknowledge that access to legal assistance is a fundamental interest, they are divided over whether the profession has some special responsibility to help provide that assistance and, if so, whether the responsibility should be mandatory. One contested issue is whether attorneys have obligations to meet fundamental needs that other occupations do not share. According to some lawyers, if equal justice under law is a societal value, society as a whole should bear its cost. The poor have fundamental needs for food and medical care, but we do not require grocers or physicians to donate their help in meeting those needs. Why should lawyers' responsibilities be greater?[8]

One answer is that the legal profession has a monopoly on the provision of essential services. Lawyers have special privileges that entail special obligations. In the United States, attorneys have a much more extensive and exclusive right to provide legal assistance than attorneys in other countries. The American bar has closely guarded those prerogatives and its success in restricting lay competition has helped to price services out of the reach of many consumers. Under these circumstances, it is not unreasonable to expect lawyers to make some pro bono contributions in return for their privileged status. Nor would it be inappropriate to expect comparable contributions from other professionals who have similar monopolies over provision of critical services.[9]

An alternative justification for imposing special obligations on lawyers stems from their special role in our governmental structure. As a New York report explained, lawyers provide "*justice,* [which is] . . . nearer to the heart of our way of life . . . than services provided by other professionals. The legal profession serves as indispensable guardians of our lives, liberties and governing principles. . . ." Because lawyers occupy such a central role in our governance system, there is also particular value in exposing them to how that system functions, or fails to function, for the have-nots. Pro bono work offers many attorneys their only direct contact with what passes for justice among the poor. To give broad segments of the bar some experience with poverty-related problems and public interest causes may lay critical foundations for change.[10]

A final justification for pro bono work involves its benefits to lawyers individually and collectively. Those benefits extend beyond the enormous personal satisfactions that can accompany such work. Particularly for young attorneys, public service also can provide valuable training, trial experience, and professional contacts. Through pro bono assistance, lawyers can develop capacities to communicate with diverse audiences and build problem-solving skills. Involvement in community groups, charitable organizations, and public-interest activities is a way for attorneys to expand their perspectives, enhance their reputations, and attract paying clients. It also is a way for the bar to improve the public standing of lawyers as a group. In one representative ABA poll, nearly half of nonlawyers believed that providing free legal assistance would improve the profession's image.[11]

For all these reasons, the vast majority of surveyed lawyers believe that the bar should provide pro bono services. However, as noted earlier, only a minority in fact provide significant assistance and few of their efforts aid low income clients. The reasons do not involve a lack of need. Studies of low-income groups find that over four-fifths of their legal problems remain unaddressed. Moreover, these legal needs studies do not include many collective problems where attorneys' services are often crucial, such as environmental risks or consumer product safety.[12]

The bar's response to inadequate access alternates between confession and avoidance. Some lawyers simply deny the data. Unburdened by factual support, they insist that "no worthy cause" goes unassisted, given voluntary pro bono efforts, legal aid programs, and contingent fee representation. A more common approach is to acknowledge the problem of unmet needs but to deny that mandatory pro bono service is the solution. Opponents raise both moral and practical objections. As a matter of principle, some lawyers insist that compulsory charity is a contradiction in terms. From their perspective, requiring service would undermine its moral significance and compromise altruistic commitments. And as a practical matter, opponents argue that mandatory contributions would be inefficient or unenforceable.[13]

There are several problems with these claims, beginning with the assumption that pro bono service is "charity." As the preceding discussion suggested, pro bono work is not simply a philanthropic exercise; it is also a professional responsibility. Moreover, in the small number of jurisdictions where courts now appoint lawyers to provide uncompensated representation, no evidence indicates that voluntary assistance has declined as a result. Nor is it self-evident that most lawyers who currently make public service contributions would cease to do so simply because others were required to join them. As to lawyers who do not volunteer but claim that required service would lack moral value, David Luban has it right. "You can't appeal to the moral significance of a gift you have no intention of giving."[14]

Opponents' other moral objection to mandatory pro bono contributions involves the infringement of lawyers' own rights. From critics' vantage, conscripting attorneys undermines constitutional rights of due process and just compensation; it is a form of "latent fascism" and "involuntary servitude."[15]

Neither the legal nor the moral basis for such objections is convincing. A well-established line of precedent holds that requirements of uncompensated service are permissible as long as the amounts are not unreasonable, and do not involve incarceration or physical force. From a moral perspective, demanding the equivalent of an hour a week of uncompensated assistance hardly seems like slavery. Michael Millemann puts the point directly: "It is surprising, surprising is a polite word, to hear some of the most wealthy, unregulated, and successful entrepreneurs in the modern economic world invoke the amendment that abolished slavery to justify their refusal to provide a little legal help to those, who in today's society, are most like the freed slaves."[16]

The stronger arguments against pro bono obligations involve pragmatic rather than moral concerns. Many opponents who support such obligations in principle worry that they would prove ineffective in practice. A threshold problem involves defining the services that would satisfy a pro bono requirement. If the definition is broad, and encompasses any charitable work for a nonprofit organization or needy individual, then experience suggests that poor people will not be the major beneficiaries. Most lawyers have targeted their pro bono efforts to friends, relatives, or matters designed to attract or accommodate paying clients. A loosely defined requirement is likely to assist predominately middle-class individuals and organizations such as hospitals, museums, and churches. By contrast, if a pro bono requirement is limited to the low-income clients given preferred status in the ABA's current rule, then that definition would exclude many crucial public-interest contributions, such as work for environmental, women's rights, or civil rights organizations. Any compromise effort to permit some but not all charitable groups to qualify for pro bono credit would bump up against charges of political bias.[17]

A related objection to mandatory pro bono requirements is that lawyers who lack expertise or motivation to serve underrepresented groups will not provide cost-effective assistance. In opponents' view, having corporate lawyers dabble in poverty cases is an unduly expensive way of providing what may be incompetent services. The performance of many attorneys required to accept uncompensated appointments in criminal cases does not inspire confidence that unwillingly conscripted practitioners would provide acceptable representation. Critics also worry that some lawyers' inexperience and insensitivity in dealing with low-income clients would compromise the objectives that pro bono requirements seek to advance.[18]

Requiring all attorneys to contribute minimal services of largely unverifiable quality cannot begin to satisfy this nation's unmet legal needs. Worse still, opponents argue, token responses to unequal access may deflect public attention from the fundamental problems that remain and from more productive ways of addressing them. Preferable strategies might include simplification of legal procedures, expanded governmental subsidies for poverty law programs, and elimination of the professional monopoly over routine legal services.

These arguments have considerable force, but they are not as conclusive as critics assume. It is certainly true that some practitioners lack skills and motivation to serve those most in need of assistance. But the current alternative is scarcely preferable. If a matter is too complex for a nonspecialist lawyer, then those who cannot afford any attorney are unlikely to do better on their own.

To be sure, providing additional government-subsidized legal aid by poverty law experts would be a more efficient way of increasing services than relying on reluctant inexperienced practitioners. But the budget increase that would be necessary to meet existing demands does not seem plausible in this political climate. Nor is it likely, as critics claim, that requiring pro bono assistance would divert attention from the problem of unmet needs. Whose attention? Conservatives who have succeeded in curtailing legal aid funds do not appear much interested in increasing representation for poor people through government-subsidized programs, whether or not pro bono services are available. And as earlier discussion suggested, exposing more lawyers to the needs of poverty communities might well increase support for crucial reform efforts.[19]

Moreover, mandatory pro bono programs could address concerns of cost-effectiveness through various strategies. One option is to allow lawyers to buy out of their required service by making a specified financial contribution to a legal aid program. Another possibility is to give credit for time spent in training. Many voluntary pro bono projects have effectively equipped participants to provide routine poverty-related services through relatively brief educational workshops and materials, coupled with accessible backup assistance.[20]

A final objection to pro bono requirements involves the costs of enforcing them. It would be difficult to verify the amount of time that practitioners reported for pro bono work or the quality of assistance that they provided. However, supporters of mandatory pro bono programs have responded with low-cost enforcement proposals that would rely heavily on the honor system. In the absence of experience with such proposals, their effectiveness is difficult to assess. But there is a strong argument for trying pro bono requirements, even if they cannot be fully enforced. At the very least, such requirements would support lawyers who want to participate in public interest projects but who work in organizations that have failed to provide adequate resources or credit for these efforts. Many of the nation's most profitable law firms and corporate employers fall into that category, and need to be nudged toward greater support. As to lawyers who have no interest in public interest work, a rule that allowed financial contributions to substitute for direct service could materially assist underfunded legal aid organizations.[21]

In any event, however the controversy over mandatory pro bono service is resolved, there is ample reason to encourage greater voluntary contributions. Lawyers who want to participate in public interest work are likely to do so more effectively than those who are fulfilling an irksome obligation. How best to encourage a voluntary commitment to pro bono service demands closer scrutiny.

The Roots of Pro Bono Commitments

Despite the substantial scholarly literature and bar resources focusing on pro bono contributions, surprisingly little attention centers on their origins. Few systematic attempts have been made to explore the roots of commitment among public-interest and poverty lawyers, and virtually none have addressed pro bono participants. Nor have there been significant efforts to draw on research concerning altruism and volunteer activity among the general public for insights relevant to the legal profession. The discussion that follows aims to fill some of those gaps. From the limited evidence available, attorneys' public service contributions seem motivated by the same range of internal and external factors that account for voluntary assistance by other individuals. Internal factors include the personal characteristics, values, and attitudes that influence decisions to help others. External factors involve the social rewards, reinforcement, costs, and other situational characteristics that affect voluntary assistance.[22]

Of the internal factors linked to volunteer activity, two personal characteristics appear most significant: a capacity for empathy and a sense of human or group solidarity. Volunteers generally seem able to identify with others and with the particular group giving or receiving aid. Lawyers who assist civil rights, women's rights, and community organizations often report a feeling of responsibility to give something back to others with whom they share common bonds. For many individuals, voluntary assistance also is a way to express deeply felt ethical and religious commitments. Socialization of children and young adults clearly plays an important role in encouraging such characteristics. Students who participate in volunteer activities and observe such participation by parents or other admired role models are much more likely to volunteer later in life than individuals who lack such experiences. By the same token, those who observe others' failure to assist people in need also tend to replicate such behavior. In this, as in other contexts, actions speak louder than words and example works better than exhortation.[23]

External factors also influence the likelihood of pro bono assistance. The rewards and costs of such conduct play the most obvious role. Volunteer work is more likely if it presents opportunities to gain knowledge, skills, and personal contacts. Individuals are more willing to contribute if they feel competent to help or if they receive specific requests for aid. The chances of involvement similarly increase when individuals are asked to focus on others' needs and their own ethical obligations, or when they are given some face-to-face contact with the misery of others. As Arthur Koestler put it: "Statistics don't bleed." Personalized appeals work better than abstract references to unmet needs. But no appeal will be successful if the costs appear excessive in relation to benefits because of the time and resources required or the controversial nature of the activity.[24]

The influence of these factors on voluntary assistance is not, however, quite as straightforward as simple cost-benefit analysis might suggest. Social science research finds that individuals who receive praise or money for their assistance are less likely to volunteer aid in other settings than individuals who believe that their actions reflect altruistic concerns. As one study concluded, "extrinsic incentives can . . . decrease intrinsic motivations to help. A person's kindness, it seems, cannot be bought." So, too, research on civil rights activists indicates that individuals motivated by internalized values are more likely to make substantial and sustained contributions than individuals responding to external rewards.[25]

Taken together, these research findings offer some useful insights about pro bono programs for lawyers and law students. As a threshold matter, the capacities of even the best designed programs should not be overstated. By the time individuals launch a legal career, it is too late to alter certain personal traits and experiences that affect public-service motivations. If positive formative influences are lacking, pro bono programs may have limited impact.

Yet while the potential effectiveness of such programs should not be overestimated, neither should it be undervalued. The preceding research suggests that well-designed strategies by law schools, bar associations, and law firms could significantly affect pro bono commitments. A request for involvement, coupled with an array of choices that match participants' interests with unmet needs, is likely to increase participation. Providing direct exposure to the human costs of social problems could prove similarly important. Pro bono commitments can be further reinforced by educational efforts that focus attention on the urgency of unmet needs and on the profession's obligation to respond. Enlisting well-respected practitioners and faculty as mentors and role models could promote those efforts. Adequate training can enable individuals to offer competent services; it can also reward participation by enhancing skills that are of value in other practice settings. Other incentives could include awards, publicity, recognition on academic transcripts, and credit toward billable-hour requirements. The point of all these efforts should be to help participants see pro bono service as a crucial part of their professional identity.

A more complicated question is whether a mandatory or voluntary program would better serve this goal. On this point, social science research yields no definitive answers, although it clarifies relevant tradeoffs. A pro bono requirement offers several advantages. Most obvious, such a requirement would make failure to contribute services morally illegitimate, and reinforce the message that such contributions are not only a philanthropic opportunity, but also a professional obligation. Institutionalizing that obligation could force organizations to provide greater support for pro bono projects. And at least some individuals who would participate only under a mandatory but not voluntary program are likely to become converts to the cause and to offer services beyond what a minimum requirement would demand.

The potential disadvantages of compelling service are equally clear. By diminishing participants' sense that they are acting for altruistic reasons, a pro bono requirement could erode commitment and discourage some individuals from contributing above the prescribed minimum. If adequate programs are not in place to train participants, accommodate their interests, and monitor their performance, the results could be unsatisfying for clients as well as participants.

Similar tradeoffs are likely under voluntary pro bono initiatives. Their advantages are readily apparent. By reinforcing participants' sense of altruism, such programs may foster deeper commitments than mandatory approaches. Those who volunteer also are likely to pick an area of practice where they are competent or wish to become so; those compelled to serve may lack adequate choices or motivation. On the other hand, if purely elective programs fail to attract widespread participation, they undermine the message that pro bono service is a professional responsibility. In the absence of a formal requirement, some law firms and law schools may remain unwilling to provide appropriate pro bono resources or credit. And individuals who might learn most from direct exposure to unmet needs may be least inclined to volunteer.

How these tradeoffs will balance out in particular contexts is difficult to predict. Any adequate assessment would require much more research on mandatory and voluntary programs than is currently available. However, experience with law school public service programs yields at least some basis for comparative evaluation.

Law School Pro Bono Programs

The primary justifications for pro bono service by law students parallel the justifications for pro bono service by lawyers. Most leaders in legal education agree that such service is a professional responsibility and that their institutions should prepare future practitioners to assume it. During the formative stages of their professional careers, future lawyers need to develop the skills and values that will sustain commitments to public service.[26]

So too, many law faculties share the enthusiasm for school-based public service programs that are gaining support among other educators. Such programs share a common premise: that students benefit in unique and valuable ways from community involvement, particularly if it is coordinated with their academic experience. On that assumption, a growing number of secondary schools are requiring community service, and many colleges and graduate schools are expanding support for such service as part of their curricular and extracurricular offerings. Supporters of these requirements believe that public-interest experiences encourage future public service, and that they have independent educational value.[27]

The limited evidence available supports these views, although more adequate research remains necessary. Law schools with pro bono requirements have found that between two-thirds and four-fifths of participants report that their experience has increased the likelihood that they will engage in similar work as practicing attorneys.

However, no systematic studies have attempted to corroborate such claims by comparing the amount of pro bono work done by graduates who were subject to law school requirements and graduates who were not. Nor have researchers tested the long-term impact of community service by non-law students, although the short term impacts are positive. From the evidence available on adult volunteer activity, the safest generalization seems to be that positive experience with pro bono work as a student will at least increase the likelihood of similar work later in life. Such experience can also break down the rigid distinctions that prevail in many law schools between students who are preparing for public interest careers and those who are not. These "on the boat or off the boat" dichotomies send the wrong message about integrating private practice and public service.[28]

Moreover, there are reasons to support pro bono programs in law school whatever their effects on later public service. Like other forms of clinical and experiential learning, participation in public service helps bridge the gap between theory and practice, and enriches understanding of how law relates to life. For students as well as beginning lawyers, pro bono work often provides valuable training in interviewing, negotiating, drafting, problem solving, and working with individuals from diverse backgrounds. Aid to clients of limited means exposes students to the urgency of unmet needs and to the law's capacity to cope with social problems. As former Tulane law school dean John Kramer notes, pro bono work can help "sensitize professionals to worlds they usually ignore." It also can increase their awareness of ethical issues and the human costs of professional inattention or incompetence.[29]

So too, pro bono programs can provide other practical benefits to law students and law schools. For many individuals, public service offers valuable career information and contacts. For their institutions, pro bono programs offer opportunities for cooperation with local bar organizations and for outreach to alumni who can serve as sources, sponsors, and supervisors for student projects. Successful projects can contribute to law school efforts in development, recruitment, and community public relations.[30]

Yet too many schools have failed to realize these benefits. As noted earlier, only about 10 percent of schools make pro bono service mandatory, and they differ widely in what counts as service and how much is required. Some schools impose minimal demands, such as 10 or 20 hours, which can include nonlegal as well as legal assistance. Administrators generally believe that meaningful experiences are most likely to come from more demanding programs such as those requiring 40 to 70 hours of law-related service. Voluntary pro bono programs also vary, and again some are quite limited. At about a third of schools, most student involvement appears confined to traditional charitable activities requiring minimal time commitments and no legal skills. Common examples include blood or food drives, tutoring programs, food kitchens, and fund-raising events. Although few schools appear to collect data on the amount of voluntary service, administrators estimate that only about a quarter to a third of the law students participate and that average time commitments are quite modest. Some individuals' involvement remains at token levels and seems intended primarily as resume padding.[31]

Not all faculty or administrators seem interested in setting a better example. Most law schools do not even have a policy requiring or encouraging professors to engage in such work. Nor does expanding pro bono participation appear to be a priority. About two thirds of law school deans report satisfaction with the level of pro bono participation at their schools. Given the absence of involvement among most students and the absence of data concerning faculty, that level of satisfaction is itself somewhat unsatisfying. But it is scarcely surprising. Why should deans see a problem if no one else does?[32]

And at most institutions, no one is complaining. Nor is the extent of any problem plainly visible. Neither ABA accreditors nor AALS membership review teams ask for specific information on pro bono contributions by students and faculty, and as noted earlier, there appears little interest in collecting it. The absence of data on non-participation makes it easy to draw unduly positive generalizations from examples of involvement that are easily visible and especially vivid. High-profile cases involving faculty or student clinics, or widespread participation in fund-raising events for public-interest activities are likely to skew perceptions in positive directions. That tendency is reinforced by natural cognitive biases. When an event is particularly vivid, individuals generally overestimate its frequency, especially if it reflects well on themselves. Particularly memorable experiences with pro bono work may similarly lead faculty and students to overestimate their own voluntary contributions, particularly if they are not asked to record the actual time spent.[33]

So too, although most alumni and university administrators undoubtedly support public service in principle, they have not translated rhetorical support into resource commitments. Public-service initiatives generally seem less pressing than other budget items more directly linked to daily needs and national reputations. National rankings, such as those by *U.S. News and World Report,* have become increasingly important. And not only are pro bono opportunities excluded from the factors that determine a school's rank, they compete for resources with programs that do affect its position.

Meeting these challenges is no small task, and appropriate responses will vary across institutions. Designing an appropriate strategy will require schools to assess their own priorities, capacities, and constraints. However, for most law schools, the primary objectives of pro bono programs are likely to involve encouraging future public service and providing an effective educational experience for students. The difficulties in designing programs arise from the absence of consensus on how to achieve the first of these objectives, and on the conflicts involved in trying to achieve both.

If the principal goal of law school pro bono programs is to maximize future contributions by lawyers, it makes sense to maximize current contributions by students. And the simplest way to accomplish that is to require service. Such a requirement sends the message that pro bono work is a professional obligation. A mandatory program generally increases resources for public service programs and reaches individuals who would not voluntarily participate. By their own accounts, some of these individuals become converts to the cause, and most students report a greater interest in future pro bono service as a result of required participation.[34]

Yet as noted earlier, we lack sufficient information to determine whether mandatory programs yield greater pro bono contributions than well-supported optional alternatives. Some law school administrators are concerned that requiring participation will undermine the voluntary commitment that is necessary to sustain involvement after graduation. Such concerns are consistent with research indicating that internal commitment is more likely to encourage public-service contributions than external rewards or sanctions. Students who see pro bono work simply as one more graduation requirement are missing the message that program supporters intend.[35]

When participants are unmotivated or end up in unsuitable placements, the results can be counterproductive for all concerned. Program administrators do not lack for examples of students who feel ignored, bored, and unchallenged by their assignments. For these reluctant participants, client contact often confirms adverse stereotypes of poverty communities. For example, one Pennsylvania student's work on welfare appeals left him with disgust for undeserving "able bodied" claimants who were abusing the system. Experience with such participants can, in turn, breed resentment among client communities and discourage overburdened supervising lawyers from accepting further placements or from spending the time necessary to structure and monitor assignments. They prefer working with more motivated volunteers or students doing externships or clinical coursework. These preferences compound the challenges of finding appropriate placements for mandatory service, particularly if a school has small networks of local service providers and restrictive definitions of pro bono work. Under such circumstances, administrators often report difficulties identifying sufficient positions to accommodate students' time constraints, academic schedules, and skill levels.[36]

A further difficulty with mandatory pro bono programs involves the definition of public service. Should it include only legal work or only assistance targeted to the poor? What kind of assistance should qualify? Expansive definitions pose fewest problems in securing student placements. Nonlegal community service also can provide many participants with broader perspectives on their law-related work. But inclusive definitions also offer fewest opportunities for training students to meet the legal needs of underserved groups. And programs that settle for minimal contributions of routine assistance may reinforce an inadequate understanding of poverty-law practice, which is insufficiently responsive to the broader needs of low-income communities. By contrast, more restrictive criteria for pro bono service bump up against shortages in supervised positions and claims of ideological bias. Organizations such as the Washington Legal Foundation have criticized law schools' public-interest placements for being skewed in favor of liberal causes.[37]

Related problems involve enforcing pro bono requirements and ensuring the quality of client service provided. The difficulties of monitoring students and their supervisors have led some experts to prefer voluntary programs or school-based clinics. Other educators worry about the hypocrisy of having a faculty impose a requirement on students that it is unwilling to impose on itself. Of course, pro bono requirements serve educational values apart from reinforcing a service ethic and these provide some basis for including only students. But if the primary goal of a mandatory program is to create a culture of commitment to public service, then exempting faculty role models is counterproductive. As research on giving behavior makes clear, individuals learn more by example than exhortation. Unless and until faculty are willing to include themselves in any mandatory program, a voluntary alternative has obvious advantages.[38]

In short, the single most important insight from law school pro bono efforts is that no single model is clearly preferable. Different approaches create different trade-offs, which vary at different institutions. Designing an appropriate program requires schools to assess their own resources, community networks, faculty support, and student culture. But certain strategies are critical no matter what kind of program is in place. The most obvious and essential initiatives must come from law school administrations. They need to provide adequate resources, recognition, and rewards for public service. At a minimum, as the Association of American Law Schools' Commission has recommended, law schools should seek to make available for every student at least one well-supervised pro bono opportunity and to insure that the great majority of students participate. Special awards and publications can honor outstanding pro bono service by students, faculty, and alumni. Law schools could also encourage faculty involvement by requiring professors to report their annual pro bono activities, and by valuing those activities in promotion and tenure decisions.[39]

Finally, and most important, pro bono strategies need to be part of a broader effort to deepen professional responsibility for public interests. As research on legal education has long noted, the "latent curriculum" at most law schools tends to erode these efforts. Issues of legal ethics and access to justice are not well integrated in core courses. Nor are such concerns reinforced by other aspects of law school culture. The low pay and tight market for public-interest work, coupled with high debt burdens, discourage many students from pursuing such careers and from focusing on problems of social justice during legal education.[40]

Traditional teaching methods can further erode professional ideals. Faced with a steady succession of hard cases and doctrinal ambiguities, students often conclude that there are no right answers: "there is always an argument the other way and the devil often has a very good case." The result is to leave many future lawyers "skeptical at best, cynical at worst." Legal work seems largely a matter of technical craft, divorced from the broader societal concerns that led many students to law school.[41]

Countering these forces is no modest enterprise; it is a central challenge of modern legal education. To create cultures of commitment, professional responsibility and access to justice must become higher priorities. Legal educators should focus more attention on the structural forces that undermine public interest values in legal practice. In short, pro bono efforts are only a modest part of the reform agenda facing legal education. And increases in lawyers' pro bono work are an equally modest part of the answer to the nation's unmet legal needs. Yet while we should not overstate the value of public-service initiatives, neither should we overlook their potential. Pro bono opportunities reinforce the profession's best instincts and highest aspirations. By making those opportunities a priority, lawyers and legal educators can translate rhetorical commitments into daily realities.

Notes

1. For an earlier discussion of the issues raised in this essay, see Deborah L. Rhode, "Cultures of Commitment: Pro Bono for Lawyers and Law Students," 67 *Fordham Law Review* 2415 (1999). See the sources cited in Tigran W. Eldred and Thomas Schoenherr, "The Lawyer's Duty of Public Service: More Than Charity?," 96 *West Virginia Law Review* 367, 384 (1994), and in Deborah L. Rhode, "The Professionalism Problem," 39 *William and Mary Law Review* 283, 291 (1998); ABA Model Rules of Professional Conduct, Rule 6.1 (1994).

2. Richard C. Reuben, "The Case of a Lifetime," *ABA Journal,* April 1994, 73. American Bar Association, *Promoting Professionalism* (Chicago: American Bar Association, 1998), 77–80.

3. The first draft of the ABA Model Rules of Professional Conduct required a minimum contribution of forty hours a year for no or reduced fees, or the financial equivalent. See *Legal Times of Washington,* Aug. 27, 1979, 45. For a history of unsuccessful state proposals, see Esther F. Lardent, "Mandatory Pro Bono in Civil Cases: The Wrong Answer to the Right Question," 49 *Maryland Law Review,* 78, 92–99 (1990); for local requirements, see Deborah L. Rhode and David Luban, *Legal Ethics* (Westbury, New York: Foundation Press, 1995), 792, 803–8.

4. John Kramer, "Law Schools and the Delivery of Legal Services—First, Do No Harm," in *Civil Justice: An Agenda for the 1990s,* (Esther F. Lardent, ed. Chicago: American Bar Association, 1989), 47, 57; American Bar Association, Recodification of Accreditation Standards 302 and 404 (1996).

5. William B. Powers, *Report on Law School Pro Bono Activities* (Chicago: American Bar Association, 1994), 2–5 (reporting pro bono requirements for faculty in 3 of 105 responding schools and noting the lowest minimum requirement for students as 8 hours); Association of American Law Schools, Commission on Pro Bono and Public Service Opportunities in Law Schools, *Learning to Serve: A Summary of the Findings and Recommendations of the AALS Commission on Pro Bono and Public Service Opportunities* (1994), 4; Association of American Law Schools, Commission on Pro Bono and Public Service Opportunities in Law Schools, Focus Group Interviews, June 1998.

6. See David Luban, *Lawyers and Justice: An Ethical Study,* (Princeton, N.J.: Princeton University Press, 1988) 252–55, 263–64; E. Allan Lind and Tom R. Tyler, *The Social Psychology of Procedural Justice* (New York: Plenum Press, 1998), 102–3.

7. Committee to Improve the Availability of Legal Services, "Final Report to the Chief Judge of the State of New York," reprinted in 19 *Hofstra Law Review* 755, 773, (1991) [hereinafter New York Report]; Access to Justice Working Group, State Bar of California, *And Justice for All: Fulfilling the Promise of Access to Civil Justice in California* (San Francisco: State Bar of California, 1996), 33–34.

8. Marvin E. Frankel, "Proposal: A National Legal Service," 45 *South Carolina Law Review* 887, 890 (1994); New York Report, 782.

9. David Luban, "Mandatory Pro Bono: A Workable (and Moral) Plan," 64 *Michigan Bar Journal* 280, 282 (1985). For example, nonlawyers in other countries can provide legal advice. See Deborah Rhode, "The Delivery of Services by Nonlawyers," 4 *Georgetown Journal of Legal Ethics* 209, 231 (1990).

10. New York Report, 782.

11. Donald W. Hoagland, "Community Service Makes Better Lawyers," in *The Law Firm and the Public Good,* (Robert A. Katzmann, ed., Washington, D.C.: Brookings Institution, 1995), 104, 109; Jack W. Londen, "The Impact of Pro Bono Work on Law Firm Economics," 9 *Georgetown Journal of Legal Ethics* 925, 926 (1996); Gary Hengstler, "Vox Populi," *ABA Journal,* September 1993, 61.

12. Eldred and Schoenherr, "The Lawyer's Duty," 390 and n. 94; see studies cited in Roy W. Reese and Carolyn A. Eldred, Institute for Survey Research, Temple University for Consortium on Legal Services and the Public, American Bar Association, *Legal Needs among Low-Income and Moderate-Income Households: Summary of Findings from the Comprehensive Legal Needs Study* 7–30 (1994); Rhode and Luban, *Legal Ethics,* 729.

13. See sources quoted in Deborah L. Rhode, "Ethical Perspectives on Legal Practice," 37 *Stanford Law Review* 589, 609 (1985); Vito J. Titone, "A Profession under Siege," *New York Law Journal,* May 20, 1992, 2; "Few Attorneys Willing to Help with 'Access' Problem," *California Bar Journal* November 1994, 16; Frankel, "National Legal Service," 890–91.

14. Esther F. Lardent, "Structuring Law Firm Pro Bono Programs: A Community Service Typology," in Katzmann, *The Law Firm and the Public Good,* 59, 83–84; see also Michael Millemann, "Mandatory Pro Bono in Civil Cases: A Partial Answer to the Right Question," 49 *Maryland Law Review* 18, 64 (1990) (noting experience with Maryland bar that casts doubt on the assumption that contributions would decline); and Luban, "Mandatory Pro Bono," 283.

15. See sources cited in Rhode, "Ethical Perspectives on Legal Practice," 610; Eldred and Schoenherr, "The Lawyer's Duty," 391 and n. 97; and Frankel, "National Legal Service," 890.

16. *Family Division of Trial Lawyers v. Moultrie,* 725 f.2d 695 (D.C. Cir. 1984); *Stephen v. Smith,* 747 p.2d 816, 846–47 (Kan. 1987); Amendments to Rules Regulating the Florida Bar, Rules 1–3.1(a) and Rules of Judicial Admin. –2.065, 573 So. 2d 800, 805 (Fla. 1990). According to *Powell v. Alabama,* 287 U.S. 45, 73 (1932), "[a]ttorneys are officers of the court, and are bound to render service when required by such an appointment." In *Sparks v. Parker,* the Alabama Supreme Court upheld an uncompensated assignment system for indigent criminal defense, and the Supreme Court summarily dismissed an appeal, *Sparks v. Parker,* 368 So. 2d 528 (Ala. 1979), appeal dismissed, 444 U.S. 803 (1979). Both *Powell* and *Sparks* involved criminal proceedings. In civil cases, because the courts have found no right to counsel except under narrow circumstances, the scope of judicial appointment powers is less clear. The Supreme Court reserved decision on the issue in one case involving interpretation of federal statutory authority. *Mallard v. United States District Court for the Southern District of Iowa,* 490 U.S. 296, 310 (1989). For the moral objections, see Millemann, "Mandatory Pro Bono," 70.

17. Philip R. Lochner Jr., "The No Fee and Low Fee Practice of Private Attorneys," 9 *Law and Society Review* 431, 442–46 (1975); Esther F. Lardent, "Pro Bono in the 1990s," in *Civil Justice: An Agenda for the 1990s* (Esther F. Lardent, ed., Chicago: American Bar Association, 1989), 423, 434; Carrol Seron, *The Business of Practicing Law* (Philadelphia: Temple University Press), 129–35.

18. Roger C. Cramton, "Mandatory Pro Bono," 19 *Hofstra Law Review* 1113, 1137 (1991); Frankel, "National Legal Service," 890; Report of the Committee to Review the Crimi-

nal Justice Act, January 29, 1993, reprinted in 52 *Criminal Law Reporter* 2265 (March 10, 1993).

19. For a representative overview of conservatives' position, see Jonathan R. Macey, "Not All Pro Bono Work Helps the Poor," *Wall Street Journal*, December 30, 1992, A7.

20. John Greenya, "Partners in Justice: Mentoring in the Pro Bono Program," *Washington Lawyer*, May–June 1997, 26–28; Eileen J. Williams, "PSAC in Action," *Washington Lawyer*, May–June 1996, 36–38.

21. For objections, see Ted R. Marcus, "Letter to the Editor," *California Lawyer*, August 1993, 12; and Cramton, "Mandatory Pro Bono," 1128. For proposals, see Luban. "Mandatory Pro Bono," 280; Marc Galanter and Thomas Palay, "Let Firms Buy and Sell Credit for Pro Bono," *National Law Journal*, September 6, 1993, 17. For inadequacies among firms and corporate law departments see David E. Rovella, "Can the Bar Fill the LSC's Shoes?" *National Law Journal*, August 5, 1996, A1.

22. For the most comprehensive research effort, and discussion of the absence of such work, see Carie Menkel-Meadow, "Causes of Cause Lawyering," in *Cause Lawyering* (Austin Sarat and Stuart Scheingold, eds., New York: Oxford University Press, 1998), 31, 38. For influential factors, see, e.g., Richard Bently and Luana G. Nissan, *Roots of Giving and Serving* (Indianapolis, Ind.: Center on Philanthropy, 1996), 9; Jane J. Mansbridge, "On the Relation of Altruism and Self-Interest," in *Beyond Self-Interest*, (Jane J. Mansbridge, ed., Chicago: University of Chicago Press, 1990), 133–34; Neera Kapur Badhwar, "Altruism Versus Self-Interest: Sometimes a False Dichotomy," in *Altruism* (Ellen Frankel Paul, Fred D. Miller Jr., and Jeffrey Paul, eds., New York: Cambridge University Press, 1993), 90, 93; Margaret S. Clark, "Introduction," in *Prosocial Behavior* (Margaret S. Clark, ed., Newbury Park, Calif.: Sage, 1991). For lawyers, see Reuban, "Case of a Lifetime;" Lochner, "No Fee and Low Fee Practice;" David Rosenhan, "The Natural Socialization of Altruistic Activity," in *Altruism and Helping Behavior* (Jacqueline R. Macaulay and Leonard Berkowitz, eds., New York: Academic Press, 1970), 251.

23. For empathy and group identification, see Samuel P. Oliner and Pearl M. Oliner, *The Altruistic Personality* (New York: Free Press, 1988), 165–67, 173–75; Menkel-Meadow, "Causes of Cause Lawyering," 39; David Horton Smith, "Determinants of Voluntary Association Participation and Volunteering: A Literature Review," 23 *Nonprofit and Voluntary Sector Quarterly* 243, 251–52 (1994); David B. Wilkins, "Two Paths to the Mountain Top? The Role of Legal Education in Shaping the Values of Black Corporate Lawyers," 45 *Stanford Law Review* 1981, 1996–2002 (1993). For ethical commitments and moral identity, see Robert Coles, *Call of Service: Witness to Idealism* (Boston: Houghton Mifflin Co., 1993), 91; E. Gil Clary and Mark Snyder, "A Functional Analysis of Altruisn and Prosocial Behavior: The Case of Volunteerism," in Clark, *Prosocial Behavior*, 119, 125; Jerzy Karylowski, "Two Types of Altruistic Behavior: Doing Good to Feel Good or to Make the Other Feel Good," in *Cooperation and Helping Behavior: Theories and Research* (Valerian J. Derlega and Janusz Grzelak, eds., New York: Academic Press, 1982), 397, 410. For socialization, see Joan E. Grusec, "Socialization of Altruism" in Clark, *ProSocial Behavior*, 9, 13; Virginia Hodgkinson et al., *Giving and Volunteering in the United States*, (Washington D.C.: Independent Sector, 1996), 12–13, 87–88; Rosenhan, "The Natural Socialization of Altruistic Activity,"; and Gil Clary and Jude Miller, "Socialization and Situational Influences on Sustained Altruism," 57 *Child Development* 1358, 1359, 1365–66 (1986). For observation of others' behavior, see Bibb Latane and John M. Darley, *The Unresponsive Bystander: Why Doesn't He Help* (New York: Appleton Center Crofts, 1970), 38, 41, 90; and Alfie Kohn, *The Brighter Side of Human Nature* (New York: Basic Books 1990), 68.

24. Clary and Snyder, "A Functional Analysis of Altruism," 125; Clark, *Prosocial Behavior*, 119, 125; Smith, "Determinants of Voluntary Association," 251–52; Coles, *The Call of Service*,

93–94; Menkel-Meadow, "The Causes of Cause Lawyering," 59 n. 57; Mansbridge, "On the Relation of Altruism and Self-Interest," 137; Bently and Nissan, *Roots of Giving and Serving,* 8, 109–10; Nancy Eisenberg, *Altruistic Emotion, Cognition, and Behavior,* (Hillsdale, N.J.: Laurence Erlbaum, 1986), 207; Oliner and Oliner, *The Altruistic Personality,* 135–36. For exposure to need, see Kohn, *The Brighter Side,* 71; Hoffman, "Empathy and Prosocial Activism," 82; Janusz Reykowski, "Motivation of Prosocial Behavior," in *Cooperation and Helping Behavior,* 358–63; Arthur Koestler, "On Disbelieving Atrocities," in *The Yogi and the Commissar* (New York: Macmillan, 1945), 92.

25. C. Daniel Batson, Jay Coke, M. L. Jasnoski, and Michael Hanson, "Buying Kindness: Effect of Extrinsic Incentive for Helping on Perceived Altruism," 4 *Personality and Social Psychology Bulletin* 86, 90 (1978). Kohn, *The Brighter Side of Human Nature,* 202–3; Clary and Miller, "Socialization," 1367. For civil rights activity, see Rosenhan, "The Natural Socialization of Altruistic Activity," 263–67.

26. Ninety-five percent of deans responding to the AALS survey agreed that "[I]t is an important goal of law schools to instill in students a sense of obligation to perform pro bono work during their later careers." AALS Commission, *Learning to Serve.* See Thomas J. Schoenherr, Thomas M. Quinn, and Roslyn Myers, "The Fordham Model: Student Initiated Projects for the Public Interest," unpublished, 1999, on file with *Fordhan Law Review,* 2.

27. Some commentators distinguish between "community service learning" and "community service volunteering." The former term refers to service that is directly integrated into students' coursework. The latter term refers to volunteer activity that is not part of the formal curriculum. See Daniel F. Perkins and Joyce Miller, "Why Community Service and Service-Learning? Providing Rationale and Research," *Democracy and Education,* Fall 1994, 11–12. See Dirk Johnson, "Volunteers: Now That's an Order," *New York Times,* Sept. 13, 1998, E2; Dennis D. Hirsh and Suzanne Goldsmith, "Community Service Builds Citizenship," *National Law Journal,* Feb. 5, 1996, A19; Jeremy Cohen, "Matching University Mission with Service Motivation: Do the Accomplishments of Community Service Match the Claims?" 1 *Michigan Journal of Community Service Learning* 98 (1994).

28. For surveys, see John Kramer, "Mandatory Pro Bono at Tulane Law School," National Association for Public Interest Law, *Connection Closeup,* Sept. 30, 1991, 1–2; Committee on Legal Assistance, "Mandatory Law School Pro Bono Programs: Preparing Students to Meet Their Ethical Obligations," 50 *The Record,* 170, 176 (1995); AALS Focus Group Interview, Chicago, June 24–25, 1998; AALS Commission, Focus Group Interviews, Chicago; Kimberly M. Allen, "The University of Pennsylvania Public Service Program, Alumni Survey" (unpublished paper, 1994); Gregory B. Markus, Geoffrey B. Hazard, and David C. King, "Integrating Community Service and Classroom Instruction Enhances Learning: Results from an Experiment," 15 *Educational Evaluation and Policy Analysis* 410, 413 1993); and Cohen, "Matching University Mission with Service Motivation," 98, 103.

29. Law School Affinity Group, *From the Classroom to the Community: Enhancing Legal Education through Public Service and Service Learning* 5 (Washington, D.C.: Corportation for National Service, n.d.); Kramer, "Mandatory Pro Bono," 1.

30. Committee on Legal Assistance, "Mandatory Law School Pro Bono Programs," 174–75, 177. In the AALS survey, over 90 percent of deans agreed that pro bono activities had provided valuable good will in the community, and two-thirds felt that such work had proven similarly valuable with alumni. AALS, *Learning to Serve.*

31. AALS Focus Group Interviews, Chicago and Los Angeles. The few published references do not quantify the amount of pro bono service contributions provided.

32. AALS, *Learning to Serve.*

33. Richard Nisbett and Lee Ross, *Human Inference: Strategies and Shortcomings of Social*

Judgment (Englewood Cliffs, N.J.: Prentice-Hall, 1980), 54; David O. Meyers, *The Pursuit of Happiness* (New York: W. Morrow, 1992), 110–12.

34. Kramer, "Mandatory Pro Bono;" Committee on Legal Assistance, "Mandatory Pro Bono," 176; AALS Focus Group Interviews, Chicago and San Francisco.

35. Pamela DeFanti Robinson, "Insurmountable Opportunities or Innovative Choices: The Pro Bono Experience at the University of South Carolina Law School, 42 *South Carolina Law Review,* 959–71 (1991); Kohn, *Brighter Side,* 202–3; Batson et al., "Buying Kindness," 90.

36. Allen, "University of Pennsylvania Public Service Program Alumni Survey," 3–4. Robinson, "Insurmountable Opportunities," 969.

37. Washinton Legal Foundation, *In Whose Interest? Public Interest Law Activism in the Law Schools* (Washington, D.C.: Washington Legal Foundation, 1990), 45; Alan M. Slobodin, "Forced Pro Bono for Law Students Is a Bad Idea," 1 *Boston University Public Interest Law Journal,* 199, 202–3 (1991).

38. For quality, see New York Report, 773; and Commission on the Future of the Legal Profession and the State Bar of California, *The Future of the California Bar* (San Francisco: State Bar of California, 1995), 67. For faculty, see Saundra Torry, "On Public Service Issue, Professors Urged to Teach by Example," *Washington Post,* January 7, 1991, F5. For social learning, see Kohn, *Brighter Side,* 91; and Grusec, "Socialization of Altruism," 20–22.

39. AALS, *Learning to Serve,* 4. The Appleseed Foundation, *Sowing the Seeds of Justice: Law Schools and the Public Interest* (Washington, D.C.: Appleseed Foundation, 1997), 17; Robinson, "Insurmountable Opportunities," 964; AALS Focus Group Interviews, San Francisco; Schoenherr, Quinn, and Myers, "The Fordham Model."

40. See Rhode and Luban, *Legal Ethics,* 906–8; Robert V. Stover, *Making It and Breaking It: The Fate of Public Interest Commitment during Law School* (Urbana: University of Illinois Press, 1989), 43–67; and Robert Granfield, *The Making of Elite Lawyers: Visions of Law School at Harvard and Beyond* (New York: Routledge, 1992), 178–83. For the absence of curricular integration, see Deborah L. Rhode, "Into the Valley of Ethics: Professional Responsibility and Educational Reform," 58 *Journal of Law and Contemporary Problems* 139 (1995).

41. Stewart Macaulay, "Law School and the World Outside the Doors" (working paper, 1982), 25; Jay Feinman and Marc Feldman, "Pedagogy and Politics," 73 *Georgetown Law Journal* 875, 878 (1985).

Index